The United Irishmen, Their Lives and Times

THE

UNITED IRISHMEN,

THEIR

LIVES AND TIMES.

BY

R. R. MADDEN, M.D.,

AUTHOR OF " TRAVELS IN THE EAST," &c. &c.

" The mind of a nation, when long-fettered and exasperated, will
struggle and bound, and when a chasm is opened, will escape
through it, like lava from the crater of a volcano."—J. K. L.

IN TWO VOLUMES.

VOL. I.

LONDON:

J. MADDEN & CO., LEADENHALL STREET.

MDCCCXLII.

DEDICATION.

PREFACE.

It has been justly observed, in reference to the times and movements I have attempted to illustrate, that the political convulsions which agitated Europe at the close of the last and the commencement of the present century, are removed from our days by a space longer than the average which Nature assigns to a generation; they have passed from the turmoil of cotemporary events, to take their place for ever in the sober records of history. The shadows, clouds, and darkness, which the heat of passions, the fury of parties, and the violence of selfish interest, threw around every event of this period, have been solved and dispelled since the passions have cooled—the parties disappeared, and the interests dwindled away which were then predominant. England can do justice to the reformers of 1794—can bear to have their merits shewn, and their errors displayed;—

Scotland has already enrolled the names of Muir and
Palmer in the list of those who have loved their
country "not wisely, but too well." It remains as
a task to do justice to the United Irishmen, to point
out the wrongs by which they were goaded to resistance, the nature of the political evils they desired to
remove from their suffering country, the good at
which they aimed, and the errors into which they
were betrayed.

However venal pamphleteers or party writers may
labour to distort events, FACTS will survive in their
original strength ; and it is well that men of the
present generation, should know how few are the
years which suffice to wither away the veil which
corruption and venality have woven over delin-
quencies, and how soon the sons may be compelled to
blush for their fathers' deeds, and to learn that the
moral retribution of providential justice, is not
delayed nor limited to the third and fourth generation, but begins earlier and extends further. Faction
is proverbially short-sighted ; but in Ireland it seems
to be stone-blind—neither enlightened by the past,
nor speculating on the future. It may—or rather,
it must—be of moral value to look at a period
attentively, when the triumph of faction was the
herald of its overthrow, and when party kindled its

own funeral pile by the excessive violence of its own fanaticism.

To elucidate this period of Irish, or rather British History, has been the great object of the writer of these volumes. Setting out with a determination "to extenuate nought, and to set down nought in malice," he has devoted time, labour, and expense, to collecting documents which in the ordinary course of events must soon have been lost irrecoverably, from whence any reasonable reader, unprejudiced by party, may be able to form a correct estimate of the motives and actions of men, who have hitherto been praised and blamed with little or no reference to the real circumstances of their conduct or their principles.

If the tendency of this work were to revive the remembrance of past evils, from party or from vindictive motives, and if it did not contribute to prevent the possibility of their recurrence, the task I have undertaken would be a culpable one indeed. The subject of these volumes, however, is not one to which reference is to be made only from motives of idle curiosity. The policy which availed itself of the agency of an intolerable and overbearing faction, for the accomplishment of its designs, has ceased to exist; but the spirit of the latter, the breath that made it has the power to revive.

It is not unprofitable, even now, to reflect on the use which its partizans made of their power in those bad times, when every man who became obnoxious to their body, by taking a prominent part in any political proceedings opposed to their views and interests, was accounted disaffected to the state; and even when loyal men, indignant at the treatment they received, were driven by unfounded accusations and dishonourable suspicions into criminal courses. It behoves the persons who take any leading part in liberal politics, to recur a little to past events, and to recall the first agitation of the question of Reform in Ireland, and the subsequent fate of a great number of the men who were its early advocates.

In Ireland the ascendancy party marked out its political opponents at that period, as covert traitors, who were to be legally *removed* at a convenient opportunity. It panted only for the exercise of "that vigour beyond the law," which was the privilege of its exclusive loyalty. Its victims were not the least influential, the least estimable, the most insignificant of the opposing party. The public service was made the pretext for the destruction of opponents, and with these they filled the prisons and provosts of Ireland.

Little do the people of England know of the class
of persons who were driven into rebellion. Englishmen may probably have heard that a number of obscure, ill-disposed and reckless men, had engaged in
an unnatural and unprovoked rebellion, and were
executed; that the leaders of it were poor, discontented, embarrassed wretches, persons of no standing in society, of no character in private life, con-
taminated by revolutionary doctrines and popish
principles. If such persons read this work, they
will find that a great portion of these unfortunate
persons, were gentlemen by birth, education, and
profession:—many of them celebrated for their
talents, respected for their private worth; several of
them scholars who had distinguished themselves in
the University of Dublin; the majority of them
members of the Established Church; some of them
Presbyterian ministers; few, if any, of them who
did not exert more or less influence over their countrymen. While Scotland preserves the memory of
those who fell in the Rebellion of 1745, while their
lives and actions are recorded by loyal Scotchmen,
and read by loyal Englishmen, there can be no reason why the reminiscences of the Irish Rebellion of
1798, and of those who unfortunately were engaged
in it, should not be faithfully recorded, without pre-

judice to the loyalty of the writer, or the reader of their history.

We have outlived the wrongs that made rebels of these men.

In our times their descendants are possessed of rights, for the enjoyment of which they have reason to be good and loyal subjects. It is now not only their duty, but their interest to be so.

Their fathers lived at a period when the great body of the people laboured under grievous wrongs. They thought, perhaps erroneously, that "Tyranny was not government, and that allegiance was due only to protection."

There is a degree of oppression, which we are told, by Divine authority, drives even "wise men mad." Whether the wrongs of the people, and their sufferings under the penal code, amounted to that degree, the reader must determine. Their leaders certainly acted on the belief, that their grievances had reached, and passed, the limits of human patience.

One who has seen the miserable effects of political commotions and revolutions in other countries, is not likely to regard engagement in similar struggles as the result, at all times, of the exercise of the highest courage or the purest patriotism,—or to consider the advantages obtained by force or violence, on many occasions, worth the perils, terrors, and penalties of the strife.

In the times of the United Irishmen, that dependence on the power of public opinion for the redress of political grievances, which has now happily superseded the employment of physical force, was unknown; and every political measure of great magnitude, was either carried by the menace of violence, or recourse to the demonstration of it.

No party seemed sensible of the awful responsibility of those, who "let loose the dogs of war" on the country; and the leading men of the society of United Irishmen, who first had recourse to violent means for effecting their objects, were themselves less aggrieved by the unjust and partial laws they sought to overturn, than the great mass of the people, who were oppressed and borne down by them.

But where there is tyranny that "grinds the faces of the poor," and galls the hearts of the people, it is not the wise or the reflecting who are first driven to revolt, but the multitude, whose passions are exasperated, whose labour is robbed, or privileges invaded; who are goaded to madness by a bad government—and, in the first outbreak of their fury, whose vengeance bursts forth in the form of a wild justice, bootless of results, badly directed, indefinite in its objects, and, at the onset, striking at all around, like a drunken man in a quarrel, dealing blows, no matter how or where they fall.

At the commencement of such struggles, the first movers never act in the way, which those who reflect on their movements might suppose best calculated to enable them to redress their wrongs. They proceed from one false step to another, till their cause is brought to the brink of ruin.

If that cause were just, it is at such a juncture that a wise man, who loved his country and compassionated the people, were he called upon to take a part in their struggle, would deem it his duty to put these questions to himself :—

Have the wrongs that are complained of, and the dangers that menace the community, reached that point, when, to leave the people without guidance, is to leave them to destruction?

Are they embarked in a good and righteous cause?

Are they likely to succeed?

Are they sure to be bettered by success?

Have they risen in defence, not only of civil rights, but of the highest interests of all?

Have their discontents arisen from the temporary, or the permanent, pressure of physical sufferings?

Have they overrated the value of the privileges they are seeking to obtain?

Have they been misled by ambitious and designing men, or been goaded into rebellion by ruthless tyrants?

Can their wrongs be redressed without resistance?

Who is to decide for the people when resistance is allowable, or likely to be successful?

At what period of oppression does the law of nature justify resistance to the laws of man?

In the Divine Law, what sanction is there to be found for resistance to constituted authority?

These are questions it would behove a conscientious man to put to himself, and to have answered satisfactorily before he stirred in the cause of a revolted people. These are questions that could not be seriously asked and truthfully replied to, without leading to the conclusion that the experience of the past, had seldom realized the expectation of future benefits from civil war, and without bringing the enquirer to Cicero's opinion on this subject, "Iniquissimam pacem, justissimo bello antifero."

The grand question, in which all the preceding queries are involved, is one, which, on political

grounds alone, can never be argued with advantage
to rulers or the ruled.

The appeal to heaven, as the appeal to the sword
in such extremities as those of 1798, has been impi-
ously termed—has been too often made without a
due consideration of the importance of the foregoing
enquiries, before those who had recourse to it had
decided on a question which involved the interests of
an entire people.   Sir James Macintosh has well observed, "though the solution of this tremendous problem requires the calmest exercise of reason, the circumstances which bring it forward commonly call
forth mightier agents, which disturb and overpower
the understanding.

" In conjunctures so awful, when men feel more
than they reason, their conduct is chiefly governed
by the boldness or the weakness of their nature, by
their love of liberty or their attachment to quiet, by
their proneness or slowness to fellow-feeling with
their countrymen."

He tells us " in such a conflict there is little quiet
left for moral deliberation.   Yet, by the immutable
principles of morality, and by them alone, must the
historian try the conduct of all men, before he allows
himself to consider all the circumstances of time,
place, opinion, principle, example, temptation, and

obstacle, which though they never authorize a removal of the everlasting landmarks of right and
wrong, ought to be well weighed in allotting a due
degree of commendation or censure to human actions." *

I am indebted to a gentleman well known in the
literary world, than whom, few persons are better
acquainted with Irish history, and none to my knowledge equally so, for the Historical Introduction
which precedes the First Chapter of this Work.

R. R. M.

London, 10th May, 1842.

* "Sir James Macintosh's History of the Revolution of 1688,"
Chap. X.

HISTORICAL INTRODUCTION.

UNITED IRISHMEN,

THEIR

LIVES AND TIMES.

HISTORICAL INTRODUCTION.

"THERE is no greater error," says Sismondi, "than to suppose that any great event, or epoch, can be profitably viewed apart from the causes by which it was produced and the consequences by which it was followed; the habit of viewing facts apart from the circumstances by which they are connected and explained, can have no other result than the fostering of prejudice, the strengthening of ignorance, and the propagation of delusion." To no portion of history is this truth more strikingly applicable than to the " Lives and Times of the United Irishmen:" it is impossible to appreciate their motives or form a right estimate of their conduct, without an accurate knowledge of the circumstances of their age and the condition of their country, and this knowledge can only be obtained by examining the causes that produced the very anomalous state of society in which they lived and acted. Ireland is a puzzle and perplexity to Englishmen and English statesmen, chiefly

because they are unacquainted with its history; or,
what is worse, that they have received as its history,
fictions so monstrous, that many of them amount to
physical impossibilities. A brief outline of the history
of the English connection with Ireland, is therefore
necessary to show how it happened that, at the close
of the last century, two distinct bodies were preparing to reject allegiance to England, what motives led
them to unite, and how their formidable union was
dissolved.

The four first centuries after Strongbow's invasion,
passed away without the conquest of Ireland being
completed; the wars with France and Scotland, the
insurrections of the Barons, and the murderous wars
of the Roses, prevented the English monarchs from
establishing even a nominal supremacy over the
entire island; instead of the Irish Princes becoming
feudal vassals, the Anglo-Norman barons who obtained fiefs in Ireland, adopted the usages of the
native chieftains. The attention of Henry VII. was
forcibly directed to this state of things, by the
adherence of the Anglo-Norman Barons and the
Irish Princes with whom they had formed an alliance or connection, to the cause of the Plantagenets.
They supported Lambert Simnel and Perkin War-
beck; when these adventurers were defeated, they
showed the greatest reluctance to swear allegiance to
the Tudors, and Henry could not but feel that his
crown was insecure, so long as the Irish Lords had
the power and will to support any adventurer who
would dispute his title. From that time forward it became the fixed policy of the Tudors to break down

the overgrown power of the Anglo-Irish aristocracy, and to destroy the independence of the native chieftains. In England, the Tudors were enabled to create a new nobility; the progress of the Reformation was accompanied by the elevation of several new families to the peerage, and the struggle between the Protestants and Catholics in that country, was for a considerable time, identical with the contest between the old and new aristocracy. In Ireland it was impossible to adopt the same course of policy; there was not a gentry from which a new aristocracy could be formed, and the Tudors were forced to supply their place by grants of land to colonists and adventurers. The Irish and the Anglo-Norman Barons looked upon these men as intruders, while the ruling powers regarded them with peculiar favour, as being the persons most likely to establish and promote an " English interest in Ireland." This political motive must not be confounded with the religious movement which took place about the same time; it was as much the object of Mary as it was of Elizabeth, to give Irish lands to English settlers, in order to obtain a hold over Ireland; it was under Mary that the lands of Leix and O'Fally were forfeited, and the lord deputy permitted to grant leases of them, at such rents as he might deem expedient.

In the midst of this political convulsion, an attempt was made to bring Ireland to adopt the principles of the Reformation, which had been just established in England. There was a vast difference between the situation of the two countries, which

deserves to be more attentively considered than it
usually has been.   It was on a papal grant that the
English monarchs, from the very beginning, had
rested their claims to the allegiance of Ireland, and
there was consequently something like an abandonment of these claims when they called upon the
Irish to renounce the supremacy of the Pope.   But
not only had the English kings described the
Pope as the source of their power, they had for
centuries made it a principle object of their policy,
to maintain the power of the episcopacy and priesthood in Ireland, against the ambition or avarice of
the Anglo-Norman Barons.   They had themselves
armed the Church with power and influence greater
than they could overthrow.

After the long night of the Middle Ages, an intellectual revival had filled Christendom with discussions which weakened the strength of ancient
institutions, and prepared men's minds for the reception of new opinions.   Ireland had not shared in
the general movement; whatever may have been the
condition of the Island before the English invasion,
the four centuries of political chaos and constant
war subsequent to that event, had rendered it one
of the most distracted countries in Christendom;
there had been no precursors to make way for a
religious change; the Irish had never heard of
Huss, or Wickliffe, or Luther, or Calvin.   The only
intelligible reason proposed to them for a change of
creed, was the royal authority; and they were already
engaged in a struggle against that authority, to
prevent their lands being parcelled out to strangers.

Add to this, that the reformed religion was preached by foreigners, ignorant of the very language of the country, and there will be little difficulty in perceiving that the attempt under such circumstances to establish Protestantism in Ireland, by the conversion of the Irish, was utterly impossible. In fact, the project of converting the natives was soon abandoned, for the more feasible plan of colonizing Ireland with Protestants from England.

The calamitous wars of Elizabeth's reign, were waged by the Irish and by the descendants of the Anglo-Normans settled in Ireland, equally in defence of their land and their creed; when the insurgents prevailed, they expelled the Protestant ministers and seized the goods of the English settlers; when the royalists triumphed, they established churches and confiscations. After ten years of almost incessant war, an expenditure of money that drained the English exchequer, and of life that nearly depopulated Ireland, the entire island was subdued by the arms of Elizabeth; but the animosity of the hostile parties was not abated, they had merely dropped their weapons from sheer exhaustion. Colonies had been planted in the south of Ireland, on the estates forfeited by the Earl of Desmond and his adherents, but the settlers were nothing more than garrisons in a hostile country, they continued " aliens in language, religion and blood" to the people by whom they were surrounded. Under such circumstances it was not to be expected that many of the higher ranks of the English clergy or laity would seek a settlement in Ireland; most of those who emigrated,

were more or less attached to the principles of Puritanism, which Elizabeth hated at least as much as
she did Popery, and this circumstance gave the
Protestant Church in Ireland a stronger tendency to
Calvinistic doctrine and discipline than would have
been allowed in England. Geneva was a greater
authority with the Irish Protestants than Lambeth,
as any one may see who consults the canons of the
Irish church; and this unfortunately widened the
difference between them and the natives of the
country they came to colonize.

A new difficulty about the tenure of land arose,
which afterwards produced very fatal consequences.
According to English law, the ultimate property of
all estates is in the crown, and land is held only by
virtue of a royal grant: according to the Irish law,
the property of land was vested in the sept, tribe or
community, who were co-partners with their chief,
rather than his tenants or vassals. Whenever a
change was made from Irish to English tenure, an
obvious injustice was done to the inferior occupants,
for they were reduced from the rank of proprietors
to that of tenants at will. This principle was never
thoroughly understood by the English Lords Justices,
and hence they unintentionally inflicted grievous
wrongs, when they tried to confer upon any portion
of the country the benefits of English law. In fact,
the change from Irish to English tenure involved a
complete revolution of landed property, which would
have required the most delicate and skilful management to be accomplished safely, but those to whom
the process was entrusted, were utterly destitute of

any qualifications for such a task. The Commission of Grace issued by James I. for the purpose of securing the titles of Irish land, was viewed with just suspicion by the great and the small proprietors, and its results were an uncertainty of tenure and possession, which kept every person in a state of alarm.

The real or supposed plot of Tyrone, Tyrconnel and O'Doherty, afforded a pretext for confiscating the six northern counties over which the sovereignty of these chieftains extended; but whatever was the amount of their guilt, it is obvious that they could only forfeit that which they themselves possessed. They were not the proprietors of these counties; the actual occupants of the soil were not accused, much less convicted, of any participation in the plot; and therefore the sweeping seizure of half a million of acres, without any regard to the rights of those who were in actual possession, was a monstrous injustice, to which few histories can furnish a parallel. It must however be confessed, that this violent and odious measure, was quite in accordance with the spirit of the age; confiscations and grants of land had become a regular part of the public administration under the Tudors, and was continued under the Stuarts; the old Norman aristocracy was thus broken down, and means provided for endowing a new nobility; the security of the reformed religion was ensured, because its interests were identified with the tenure of the new estates. The Ulster confiscation differed from the forfeitures in England and the South of Ireland, chiefly by its vast extent;

in order that the grants to new settlers should be efficient, it was necessary either to remove or exterminate an entire population.

Setting aside the consideration of justice, the plans which James formed for the Plantation of Ulster, were on the whole wise and prudent. It was resolved that the land should be divided into estates of moderate size; that the grantees should within a limited time erect *bawns*, that is, castles with fortified court-yards; that they should settle a number of English or Scotch tenants on the lands; that they should reside on their estates and never alienate any portion of them to the mere Irish. Had the King combined with this scheme a plan for doing justice to the native occupants, and had the local government executed the royal instructions as they were originally framed, the Plantation of Ulster might have produced all the good which is ascribed to it, without the attendant evils by which it was, at least for a considerable time, more than overbalanced. At first every thing seemed to promise a favourable result; the City of London took an active share in the scheme, and built on its grants the cities of Colerain and Londonderry; the new order of Baronets was created, and the sums paid by those who purchased this new dignity, were destined to the support of soldiers for the defence of the new Plantation.

The first difficulty which presented itself, arose from James's resolution to give a proportion of the forfeitures to his Scottish countrymen; a determination which gave great offence to the English, and

which eventually exercised a fatal influence over the
fortunes of the Stuarts, for the Scotch who settled
in Ireland were subsequently the staunchest of adherents to the Covenant. A more fatal error was the
choice of settlers: surrounded by a set of hungry
favourites and mendicant courtiers, James bestowed
grants of lands with a reckless profusion surpassing that of Henry VIII. at the suppression of
monasteries. Instead of a valuable body of settlers,
he created a hungry horde of land-jobbers; English
tenants were sparingly introduced, few *bawns* were
built; proprietors remained at court and entrusted
the management of their grants to agents, and the
fatal system of subletting was established under the
sanction of the City of London.

It is not necessary in the present day to dwell
upon the notorious profligacy, corruption and infamy
of the court of James I., or to show that no iniquity
was too monstrous, and no craft too mean, for the
royal idiot when he sought the means of gratifying
his rapacious favourites. Irish forfeitures had
proved a most valuable supply, but the extravagance
with which they were given away soon exhausted
the stock, and it became necessary to seek out
new sources of plunder. An inquisition into titles,
based on the principle of English law, that the right
of possession to estates must be ultimately derived
from the King, was the expedient which presented
itself; but as English law had not been introduced
into the whole of Ireland until the close of Elizabeth's reign, and as four hundred years of anarchy
had produced countless usurpations and uncertain-

ties, there was scarce a landed proprietor in Ireland,
whose estates were not placed at the mercy of the
crown.   A new host of harpies was let loose on the
devoted country; the lawyers and the judges were
incited to use every device of legal chicanery, by promises of a share in the spoil; and to the half-million
of acres confiscated as we have before described,
another half-million was added under pretence of
informality in the title.   Even this amount of forfeitures was insufficient to gratify the rapacity which
the King's lavish distribution had excited, but in the
midst of the proceedings James died, and the task of
completing his project devolved upon his unhappy
successor.

The pecuniary distresses of Charles inspired the
Irish proprietors with the hope of obtaining security;
they presented to the king certain regulations for
confirming the titles of estates, and establishing an
indulgence of religion, called " Graces," and offered
the King a very large subsidy provided he would
permit them to become the law of the land.   Charles
took the money, and eluded the performance of his
promise.   He had adopted his father's principle of
policy to create at all hazards an " English interest
in Ireland," and to effect this by pushing the principle of forfeiture to an extent which James himself
had not contemplated.   Wentworth, afterwards Earl
of Strafford, was the Lord Deputy chosen to execute
this iniquitous project, and he commenced his proceedings on the largest possible scale, by attempting
to obtain the forfeiture of the entire province of
Connaught, under the pretence of defective titles.

One jury in the county of Galway had the courage
to find a verdict against the crown; Wentworth
arrested the jurors, brought them before the court
of Star Chamber in Dublin, sentenced each to a fine
of four thousand pounds, and to imprisonment until
the said juror had confessed on his knees that he
was guilty of wilful and corrupt perjury. The sheriff
was thrown into prison, and Wentworth pressed
hard that he should be executed as a warning to
other functionaries, adding "my arrows are cruel
that wound so mortally, but it is necessary that the
King should establish his rights." The forfeiture of
the lands of Connaught, and perhaps of all Ireland,
would have been completed, had not the increasing
troubles in England and the open revolt of Scotland,
induced Charles to recal his Deputy to scenes
of more immediate interest and importance. It
became the King's interest to conciliate his Irish
subjects, and the Graces became the law of the
land.

The Graces it is true were passed, but the King
was no longer a sovereign; his power had been
transferred to the Puritan Parliament of England
and the Covenanters of Scotland; both of these
bodies formally declared that they would not consent
to the toleration of Popery in Ireland, which was in
fact to proclaim a war of extermination against the
Irish Catholics. A conspiracy was organized against
the supremacy of the British Parliament; the main
object of those who joined in it, being to obtain for
Catholicism in Ireland, the same freedom which the
swords of the Covenanters had won for Presbyterian-

ism in Scotland. An associate revealed the plot to
the Puritan Lords Justices at the moment it was
about to explode, and Dublin was saved from the
insurgents. But the first signal of revolt spread
desolation over the northern counties; the native
Irish, who had been driven from their lands at the
time of the Great Plantation, rose upon the settlers;
and in spite of the exertions of their more merciful
leaders drove them from their settlements, and when
they encountered any resistance, slaughtered them
without mercy. This massacre has been absurdly
exaggerated, and prejudice has often induced writers
to involve all the Catholics of Ireland in its guilt,
but in truth it was confined to the northern counties,
and was directed exclusively against the English
settlers on the confiscated lands. The Scotch Presbyterians were not only spared, but allowed to retain
possession of their property until they took up arms
to support the cause of the English Puritans: in fact,
the Ulster revolt was rather a *Jacquerie* than a rebellion, and it was of course accompanied by all the
outrages and cruelties which might be expected from
an infuriate and starving peasantry, brutalized by
long oppression and goaded by ostentatious insult.
About twelve thousand persons were probably murdered in the first outbreak of popular rage, before
the Catholic lords and gentry could interfere and
give the insurrection the dignity of a civil war. A
sanguinary proclamation issued by the Lords Justices, and a formal vote of the British Parliament
that Popery should be exterminated in Ireland,
rendered the civil war inevitable, and rendered it

impossible for any person to devise a means of compromise and conciliation.

This dreadful war, in which both sides manifested an equal degree of exterminating fury, is one of the most perplexing recorded in the annals of any country, from the great variety of the parties engaged, and from their rancorous hostility towards each other. The English were divided into the friends of the Parliament and the friends of the King; the latter again, were subdivided into a party disposed to grant reasonable terms to the Catholic Lords, and a party which agreed with the Puritans that Popery should not be tolerated; all were however united in a desire, that advantage should be taken of the commotions to reap a new harvest of confiscations and grants. On the other side were the Lords of the Pale, Catholics, indeed, by religion, but English by descent, inclination and prejudice, zealous Royalists, and the more so, as the King's enemies upbraided him with a secret inclination in favour of Popery;—the Irish of the north, whose chief anxiety was to recover their ancient lands and expel the intrusive settlers;—the men of Connaught and Leinster, whose great objects were to attain security for their property and toleration for their religion;—a large body, chiefly among the southern Irish, aiming at establishing the independence of their country under a Catholic Sovereign appointed by the Pope:—there were other subdivisions of party, each obstinately bent on its own object, without any regard for the general interest of the country, or any very fixed principle of action. Had it been possible for the

Catholic Royalists to trust the Protestant friends of
the King, and the native Irish to coalesce with the
Lords of the Pale, Ireland would have been tran-
quillized and secured for the King in a week, for the
Puritans were a miserable minority; but during the
whole duration of the civil war in England, the
several divisions of the royal party in Ireland spent
their time in despicable squabbles, which served no
purpose but to increase their mutual animosities.

In the midst of the almost incredible blunders and
follies of the Royalists and the Irish, Cromwell
landed, and by the massacres of Drogheda and Wexford, diffused terror over the land. But even these
fearful warnings failed to produce an union of parties;
the friends of the Papal Nuncio thwarted the plans
of the King's Lieutenant; the Protestant Royalists
openly expressed dislike of their allies; the native
Irish could not be brought to coalesce with men of
English descent. Whichever party prevailed in the
council, the minority took vengeance for defeat by
betraying the common cause to the common enemy;
and it seemed as if Cromwell had only to look on
tranquilly until his adversaries had torn each other
to pieces. But he was too hurried to wait; he
marched onward, marking his track by fire and desolation. Some places, particularly Clonmel, made a
resistance which would have afforded an opportunity
for changing the whole course of the war, but the
Commissioners of Trust, appointed by the council of
confederate parties, countermanded the orders of the
Lord Lieutenant, and he thwarted every one of their
projects; the garrisons were abandoned to their fate,

and a handful of Puritans became masters of Ireland. The confederates had nothing more to do than to dispute which party had the greatest share in producing such a calamity.

Cromwell's system of confiscation was on a still more magnificent scale than that of the Stuarts; he shared the lands of Leinster and Munster amongst his soldiers, and amongst the private individuals or public companies that had advanced money to defray the expenses of the war; he restored James's Plantation in the northern country, and extended it so as to include nearly the whole of Ulster. Finding it difficult to realize his first plan for the total extirpation of the Irish nation, he resolved to confine the Irish Catholics to the more remote of the Four Provinces into which the Island is divided, and he issued the order of removal with Spartan brevity, " To hell or Connaught." In Connaught itself, he ordered the Catholics to be expelled from all the walled towns, though they were of English descent, and scarcely less jealous than himself of the native Irish. The strictest orders were issued for the suppression of Popery, and priests found in the exercise of their religious duties were hanged without ceremony.

The soldiers who accompanied Cromwell to Ireland were the fiercest of the Republicans and the most bigoted of the Puritans; they had been selected on this very account, because they were the most likely to resist the usurpation which Cromwell meditated in England. But the possession of property has a very soothing influence on political and religious fury; the Cromwellians, as the new settlers in

Ireland were generally called, acquiesced in their general's assumption of royal power, and would not have opposed his taking the title of king. They soon foresaw that the death of Oliver would lead to the restoration of Charles II. and they made their bargain with Charles II. before Monk commenced his march from Scotland. They represented to him that the great object of the policy, both of the Tudors and Stuarts, was accomplished to his hand, "an English interest was established in Ireland," and the future dependence of the island on the British crown was ensured. Charles was a Catholic in his heart, but he readily consented to become the patron of "the Protestant interest" in Ireland, because that interest was wholly English.

There was, however, such monstrous injustice in confirming the forfeitures of persons whose only crime was loyalty to his father and himself, that Charles found it necessary to establish a Court of Claims, in which those who had only taken up arms to support the King's cause, might be permitted to prove that they had not shared in the insurrection against the supremacy of England. So many established their innocence, that their restoration would have involved a new and almost a complete revolution in the landed property of Ireland. The Cromwellians were alarmed and threatened an appeal to arms; their wiser leaders offered Charles a share in the confiscations; the Court of Claims was closed; a Parliament was assembled from which the Catholics were excluded; the Acts of Settlement and Explanation were passed, and were called, not without good reason, "The Magna Charta of the Protestants of Ireland," for they bestowed the property of nearly the entire country on "the Protestant and English interest."

No greater misfortune could fall upon any nation, than to be delivered into the hands of a body of proprietors who felt that their title was defective, and that the tenure of their estates was constantly exposed to the hazards of revolution. They believed, and they believed justly, that if ever the Catholics and native Irish recovered political ascendancy, they would immediately demand the restoration of the forfeited estates; they lived therefore in a state of continual alarm and excitement, and they were forced to place themselves completely under the control of England, in order to have British aid in protecting the property which they had acquired. But this servile dependence on the British Government and British Parliament, was a painful bondage to men who had not quite forgotten the stern republicanism of their ancestors; and, on more than one occasion, they evinced symptoms of parliamentary independence, which not a little annoyed their British protectors. But these struggles were rare; they felt that they were a garrison in a conquered country, and that if they were abandoned to their own resources they would soon be compelled to capitulate.

The accession of James II. was not at first very alarming to the Cromwellians; they knew that this imbecile and obstinate man, was blindly attached to his hereditary policy of maintaining an " English

interest in Ireland," and they had proof of his determination when the Irish gentlemen deputed to
remonstrate on the injustice of the act of settlement, were dismissed with ignominy by the King
and Council.

The Revolution was an event wholly unexpected in
Ireland; it took both parties by surprise, filling the
Protestants with alarm, but inspiring the Catholics
with little hope. At this time the destinies of Ireland
were entrusted to the Earl of Tyrconnel, who had undertaken the hopeless task of preserving the English
interest and at the same time destroying the Protestant ascendancy. His first impulse was to capitulate with the Prince of Orange, who was very willing
to give Ireland most favourable terms; unfortunately,
he was persuaded by Hamilton that James's party
had every chance of recovering England, and he
broke off the negociations. James came to Ireland,
distrusting his Irish subjects and distrusted by them.
One of his earliest measures was to disband several
regiments of the Irish army, which was actually
done at the very moment when he was preparing to
resist an invasion from England. He might with
ease have quelled the northern Protestants in Derry
and Enniskillen, but he feared that the unpopularity
of such an act would destroy his chances of restoration in England; for the same reason, he did all in
his power to prevent the Irish from gaining the
victory at the Boyne, and he secretly exerted every
art in his power to defeat the repeal of the act of
settlement.

The dread of the Cromwellians that they would

be compelled to restore the forfeited estates to the original owners, or their representatives, whenever the Catholics regained the ascendancy, was now proved to be well founded. An act for the repeal of the act of settlement was hurried through both Houses, and had this cruel injustice, that no provision was made to remunerate the Protestant occupants for the improvements and outlay they had made. This was accompanied by an act of attainder against the partisans of William, which was scarcely less iniquitous than any of the preceding confiscations. It had the effect of uniting all the Protestants of Ireland against James, and though they were not a numerous body, they were trained to the use of arms and full of all the vigour arising from continued ascendancy.

The flight of James, the battle of Aughrim and the siege of Limerick, are sufficiently known. Ireland was finally subjected to English dominion by the Treaty of Limerick, and the title of the Cromwellians to their estates formally recognized by the Irish themselves. A fresh act of attainder took away most of the land which had been left in the hands of the Catholics by the act of attainder, and the " English interest in Ireland," virtually possessed nine tenths of the property of the country.

The Anglo-Irish, or Cromwellian landlords, had been thoroughly frightened; there were moments in the contest when William's success had been very problematical, and at such times they must have felt that they stood on the brink of ruin. They resolved therefore to adopt a course which would prevent the Catholics from attaining such power, political, pecuniary or intellectual, as would ever enable them to renew the consequences. The system which they adopted was a collection of Penal Laws : " it was," says Edmund Burke, " a machine of wise and elaborate contrivance, as well fitted for the oppression, impoverishment and degradation of a people, and the debasement, in them, of human nature itself, as ever proceeded from the perverted ingenuity of man." These laws, in which fanaticism and intolerence seem to have been carried to their most savage excess, were not in fact derived from either passion. They were designed for the protection of property which had been unjustly acquired, the tenure of which was derived from an act of parliament passed by the possessors themselves, and which was therefore liable to be repealed when they ceased to command a majority in the legislature. The code, with terrible consistency, began its severities with infancy ;—Catholic children could only be educated by Protestant teachers at home, and it was highly penal to send them abroad ;—Catholics were excluded from every profession except the medical,—from all official stations, however trifling,—from trade and commerce in corporate towns,—from taking long leases of land,—from purchasing land for a longer tenure than thirty-one years,—from inheriting the lands of Protestant relatives, and from possessing horses of greater value than five pounds. On the other hand appropriate rewards were offered for conversion ; a child turning Protestant could sue his parent for sufficient maintenance, the amount of

which was determined by the Court of Chancery ;—
an eldest son conforming to the Established Church,
at once reduced his father to the condition of a
"tenant for life," reversion in fee being secured to
the convert, with a proviso that the amount allocated
for the maintenance and portions of the other children should not exceed one-third. There were rigorous laws against priests and the celebration of mass,
while a small annual stipend was proffered to any
priest who recanted.

We have said that these laws were dictated by
self-interest and not by religious passion ; the proof
is easy and irrefutable : it is notorious that the laws
prohibiting Catholic worship, were executed far less
strictly than those which excluded from public offices,
civil professions and lucrative industry ; the latter
were never relaxed until they were totally repealed,
and even after their repeal it was attempted to defeat
the efficacy of the concessions made to the Catholics
by various legislative devices. Fanaticism, like every
other passion which is real, has something respectable
in its character ; but spoliation and nothing else was
the object of the Penal Laws, they were designed
solely to maintain the monopoly of wealth and influence for a party. The sacred name of religion was a
convenient cry to secure the prejudices of the English
people in support of the system, a support which
would scarcely have been afforded if it had been
known that the true meaning of the cabalistic phrase
" Protestant Interest," was " pounds, shillings and
pence."

The original Cromwellians were Republicans and

Puritans; they abandoned a large portion of their political feelings, but they retained much of their ancient hostility to Prelacy, and would very gladly have got rid of the Established Church. Swift's works sufficiently prove that the Irish Whigs of his day, were eager to get rid of the Bishops and to establish the Presbyterian form of Church government. Though the sacramental test excluded conscientious Dissenters from the House of Commons, there were many who conquered their scruples to the form, and sat in Parliament ready to embrace every opportunity of weakening the episcopal establishment. They gave a remarkable proof of their feelings, and a very edifying example of their logic, by unanimously voting that "whoever levied tithe of agistment was an enemy to the Protestant interest!"—it was an improvement on Lord Clarendon's witty proposal, "that the importation of Irish cattle into England should be deemed adultery." It was this dislike of prelacy which made the great body of the Irish Protestants hostile to a union with England. When such a measure was proposed at the beginning of the last century, a Protestant mob broke into the Irish House of Lords, placed an old woman on the throne, got up a mock debate on the introduction of pipes and tobacco, and compelled the Lord Chief Justice to swear the Attorney-general, that he would oppose the measure. The hostility of these men to the supremacy of the English Church, rendered them jealous of the supremacy claimed by the English Parliament, and of the restrictions imposed upon their trade by the English people. It is impossible

to read the pamphlets published by the party just
before the accession of George III., without perceiving that their aspirations for legislative and trading
independence, logically carried out, would have gone
to the full length of making Ireland a Protestant
republic. Dread of the Irish Catholics, however,
kept them quiet, and it might almost be said that
the Catholics at the time were really the "English
interest in Ireland."

There was a marked difference between the Protestants of the north and those in the rest of the
country. The Plantation of Ulster had been completed, the Protestants there were able of themselves
to protect their lives and properties, and they were
conscious of their own strength. In the rest of Ireland, the Protestants, thinly scattered over a wide
surface, were obliged to rest their hopes of defence
on the British Government, and were therefore led
to cling to the Established Church as a bond of connection with England, and to make concessions
which were odious to the sturdy northerns. This
difference between the Episcopalians and the Presbyterians, which was at once geographical, religious
and political, fostered the developement of republican principles among the latter; "the spawn of the
Old Covenant," of which the governing powers frequently complained, was not, as some have represented, an unmeaning danger; up to the close of the
last century, it was an actual and increasing element
of organized resistance to the existing system of
government. Many, now alive, can remember to

have heard from their fathers that the custom of eating a calf's head on the 20th of January was observed in most Presbyterian families, and the favourite toast " The pious, glorious and immortal memory of William III.", was clearly as strong a pledge to revolutionary principles as to religious supremacy. It was for this reason that Lord Plunket called the insurrection of 1798 " a Protestant rebellion," because, so far as the revolt had aim or object, it derived both from the Protestants by whom it was originally devised.

It is necessary to bear in mind the nature of the republican party which had been formed in Ireland previous to the American and French revolutions, in order to understand how it was influenced by both events. The party was exclusively Protestant, and more bitterly hostile to Popery than the adherents of episcopacy and monarchy; its views, at least its ultimate views, were speculative rather than practical, for it stood opposed, at the same time, to the population of Ireland and the power of England; its efforts for legislative and commercial independence were illogical, for they were made to assert rights abroad, which rights the asserters ostentatiously denied at home.

" The south of Ireland," says a writer of the last century, " offers an almost unvarying picture of Protestant oppression and Popish insurgency;" and in his view, as well as in the view of many others, the oppression was excusable because it was " Protestant," and the insurgency criminal because it was

" Popish." · The truth is, that the Whiteboy disturbances to which he refers, had no more connection with religious controversy than with the disputes between the Scotists and Thomists. Whiteboyism was an association against high rents and
tithes; a barbarous *Jacquerie*, and its causes were
obvious to all who were not wilfully blind; in the
words of Lord Charlemont, they were "misery!
oppression! famine!" It was a war of the peasantry
against the proprietors and occupiers of the land,
undertaken and still occasionally revived to wring
from them means of subsistence. The barbarities
inflicted by these rural revolters, were such as have
ever marked the career of similar insurrections in·
various ages and nations; the landlords employed
executioners, and the serfs hired assassins, the
gallows and the pike were military implements, the
legal rights and power of property were set in opposition to the natural rights and physical power of
existence. In all these contests the might of England
enabled the landlords of the south to obtain temporary triumph, but they purchased it at an enormous
cost, and every new pressure of distress produced a
fresh explosion of resistance. There was no connection whatever between the republican spirit of the
north and the insurrectionary spirit of the south, the
Whiteboys contended for no specific form of government; they contended for a more substantial
and intelligible object, food. If they were permitted to cultivate their lands and live peacefully
on the fruits of their industry, they would not

have cared, indeed they would scarcely have known, whether they were governed by a king or by a directory.

The disturbances in the American colonies threatening to make large demands on the resources of England, it was deemed prudent to conciliate the Irish Catholics by some relaxation of the Penal Laws. Such wisdom had its reward: during the whole of that arduous contest the Catholic body remained faithful to the English government, and evinced little or no sympathy for the revolted colonies. It was far different with the northern Presbyterians; on the alarm of an invasion Ireland was destitute of troops; the Volunteers suddenly sprung into existence and took the defence of the country into their own hands. Self-officered, self-armed and self-directed, an armed association stood in the presence of a feeble government, dictated what terms it pleased, and established at once the legislative and commercial independence of their country. The Catholics had contributed a little to this successful result, and they were rewarded by an abolition of the laws which restricted their possession of property.

The Volunteers next demanded a reform of parliament, which was an utter absurdity when disconnected from Catholic emancipation, while to this they were most vehemently opposed. The two questions were so intimately connected that they could not be dissevered, for it is impossible to conceive "a full, fair and free representation of the people," when three-fourths of the nation were excluded from the class of electors and representatives. The Volunteers could not combine reform and Protestant ascendancy, but yet would abandon neither; as a necessary result their powerful confederacy was broken to pieces.

Ireland had hitherto been ruled by the supremacy of the English parliament, it was now to be governed by the corruption of its own. The experiment was very expensive, but it so far succeeded that the annals of the world could not furnish a more servile, mercenary and degraded legislative body than the independent parliament of Ireland. Votes were openly bought and sold, "infamous pensions were bestowed on infamous men," the minister in direct terms threatened the country with the cost of " breaking down an opposition," and the legislature was viewed with contempt wherever it was not regarded with hatred. Parliamentary reform began again to excite attention; it was supported by a very able though not numerous body in the legislature, and in the interval between 1782 and 1789, it made a very rapid progress among the Protestant gentry and freeholders. Already measures had been proposed for organizing a new association to extend the franchise, when the French Revolution, which astounded all Europe, produced its most powerful effects on the miseries and passions of Ireland.

Previous to the year 1789, the idea of slavery was associated or rather identified with the names of Catholics and Frenchmen; the Revolution was toast-

ed because it had delivered the country from "popery,
slavery, brass money and wooden shoes," and it was
part of the British popular creed "to hate the French,
because they are all slaves and wear wooden shoes;"
the assertion of freedom by Catholics and Frenchmen at once put to flight a whole host of honest prejudices, and removed the objections which many of
the northern reformers entertained against the admission of Catholics within the pale of the constitution.   The determined supporters of the Protestant
ascendancy were therefore finally separated from
the ranks of the reformers, and the latter professed their determination to extend the blessings
of constitutional freedom " to all classes of men
whatever."

It is now necessary to cast a glance at the social
changes in the south, which were nearly cotempora-
neous with the alteration in the state of the political
parties of the north.   We have already seen that
every civil war, rebellion, insurrection and disturb-
ance in Ireland, from the reign of Elizabeth down-
wards, had arisen, more or less directly, from questions connected with the possession of land.   The
abolition of the tithe of agistment rendered pasture-
age so much more profitable than tillage, that the
landlords throughout Ireland began to consolidate
their farms and expel their tenantry, most of whom
were Protestants, for few of the Catholics had risen
above the rank of agricultural labourers.   Gold-
smith's Deserted Village, which was written about
the time that the clearing system commenced, is by

no means an exaggerated picture of the recklessness
with which landlords removed whole villages of Protestants, the descendants of those who had been
induced to settle in Ireland by the exclusive privileges
conceded to them by the policy of the government.
Vast numbers of Protestant tenants emigrated from
Ireland, and chiefly from Ulster, to America, just
before the commencement of the revolutionary war;
they supplied the United States with a body of brave
determined soldiers, animated by the bitterness of
exiles, and a thorough detestation of the supremacy
of England. Their place was chiefly supplied by
Catholics, who appeared ready to work as labourers
for lower wages, and to pay higher rents as tenants.
The Protestants of Ulster felt themselves injured by
these new competitors in the labour and land-market,
and they resolved to drive the Catholics back to Connaught. Armed bodies, under the name of "Peep-
of-day boys," attacked the houses of the Catholics,
ill-treated their persons, burned their houses, and
wrecked their property. On the other hand the
Catholics formed an association for self-protection,
under the name of "Defenders," and the two parties
engaged in a desultory and murderous warfare, in
which it is obvious that the name of religion was a
mere pretext, by which the parties disguised their
real objects from others and even from themselves.
This social war excited a rancorous animosity between
the lower ranks of Protestants and Catholics, and
stimulated their mutual bigotry, at the moment when
liberality of sentiment was beginning to become

fashionable among the higher and better educated
ranks of both communities.

A further relaxation of the Penal Laws aggravated
these evils; so calamitous had been the results of the
perverse system so long pursued, that even the bene-
ficence of government could not be displayed without
injury.   The trafficking in seats for parliament was
so profitable, that every landholder became anxious
to increase his interest in the counties by the manu-
facture of votes ; but as the elective franchise was
restricted to Protestants, who were limited in numbers, the demand for Protestant tenants was greater
than the supply, and of course they were able to
make their own terms in taking land.   But in 1794,
the elective franchise was conceded to the Catholics,
without admissibility to parliament; there was no
longer a reason for shewing a preference to Protestant tenantry, and the question of religion was absorbed in that of rent.   The Protestants of the
middle and lower ranks throughout Ireland, felt that
this new competition was a direct injury to their
interests, and most of them vented their rage in renewed hatred of the Catholics, while an enlightened
few more justly blamed the selfishness of their own
landed aristocracy.

The republicans and the reformers had been united
under the common name of Volunteers, without
very distinctly perceiving that there was any difference in their designs and objects, until the progress
of the French Revolution began to fill the Irish
whigs with alarm ; they seceded from the Volunteers,

many of them began to oppose the projects of reform which they had previously advocated, and once more the party to which the country had looked for redress of legislative grievances was broken into hostile fragments.

The republican party in Ulster felt that it must either be annihilated, or that it should lay aside the spirit of sect and the pride of race to form a frank conciliation with the Catholics of the south, on equal terms for obtaining equal rights. The remnant of the once powerful Volunteers was a feeble inefficient body, it could only regain numerical strength by transforming itself into the new association of United Irishmen.

Theobald Wolfe Tone was the most active agent in effecting this apparent union; apparent, we say, for Tone's own memoirs show that at no time was there a perfect harmony between the Presbyterians of the north and the Catholics of the south; even had they united in a successful rebellion, the exasperating passions called into action by civil war, would have prevented them from uniting in forming a settled government.

This was the capital error of the United Irishmen; they did not see that no principle of union really existed. The peasantry of Munster and Connaught cared not a jot for their plans of an ideal republic; they might be induced to take arms, for they were almost constantly on the verge of insurrection against their landlords, but their revolt was sure to be nothing better than a *Jacquerie*, accompanied by all its

horrors and all its blunders. Their Presbyterian adherents would indeed have given to their insurrection more of the dignity of civil war, but the feuds
between the "Peep-of-day Boys" and the "Defenders" still rankled in Ulster, and, if they once learned
to look on the southern insurrection as "a popish
rebellion," and such a character, at least in appearance, it must necessarily have assumed, it was all
but certain that they would aid the government in
its suppression. The United Irishmen, or rather
the leaders who acted for them, believed that all
these difficulties would have been overcome by the
presence of an auxiliary army from France, and they
therefore adopted the perilous measure of inviting a
foreign invasion.

The Parisian massacres of September 1792, had
an immense effect in Ireland; men who were moderate republicans, feared to accept freedom accompanied by such horrors; the Catholic aristocracy,
always a timid and selfish body, offered to support
government in withholding their own privileges;
the Catholic clergy separated in a body from the
Reformers, and denounced the atheism of France
from their altars; if the Government had only
united conciliation with coercion, the tranquillity of
Ireland would have been ensured. Such was the
policy which the English minister first resolved to
adopt. Earl Fitzwilliam was sent to Ireland; measures were introduced, which at that crisis would
have been received with enthusiastic gratitude; but
unfortunately the intrigues of party interfered, and

to all the causes of discord which had been accumulating for centuries, were added unexpected triumph in the party of the few, and unexpected disappointment in the party of the many.

There was never a body of men placed in so strange a position at this crisis as the Catholic priests; in their hatred of French infidelity and atheistic republicanism, they had become zealous royalists, and had the mortification to hear themselves universally represented by the dominant party, as the apostles of sedition. For more than two centuries, it had been the fashion to represent every Irish rebellion as " Popish," and it would have been strange, if so convenient an excuse as " Popery" for refusing justice and continuing oppression, should have been neglected, at the moment when the perpetuation of wrong was the avowed policy of government.

In order to compensate for the abandonment of measures of conciliation, the ministry urged forward their coercion laws with railway speed; the Volunteers were disarmed, the towns garrisoned, public discussions prohibited, the sale of arms and ammunition forbidden, and all conventions of delegates subjected to legal penalties. These energetic measures were promptly enforced; they encountered a momentary resistance in Belfast alone, and then all opposition was speedily quelled at the point of the bayonet.

The United Irishmen were now changed into a secret society: on the one hand, its members being removed from popular control, were less trammelled in forming their plans for the regeneration of their country; on the other hand, they were secluded from gaining any knowledge of the state of public opinion, they had no means of discovering how far the nation was prepared to adopt and support their schemes. Under these circumstances nothing but aid from France would have afforded the slightest chance of success; the failure of Hoche's expedition rendered their cause hopeless. In their increased danger of detection and dread of consequences, they fixed and adjourned the day for taking up arms, until the boldest became timid and the prudent withdrew altogether. In one of these intervals, the northern insurrection had been nearly precipitated by a daring exploit, which if attempted would probably have succeeded. At a splendid ball, given in Belfast, the magistrates of the county and the military officers had met to enjoy the festivities, without the remotest suspicion of danger; the principal leaders of the United Irishmen, stood in the crowd looking at the gay assembly; one of them proposed to seize so favourable an opportunity, to anticipate the day appointed for the signal of revolt, at once assemble their men, arrest and detain the magistrates and officers as hostages, and establish a provisional government in Ulster. The bold counsel was rejected by the majority, but the wiser minority saw that the timidity which rejected such an opportunity was unworthy of reliance, and either made their peace with the government, or quitted the country.

France, at the close of the eighteenth century, adopted the same selfish and erroneous policy towards Irish insurrection, which the courts of Rome and Madrid had pursued in the end of the sixteenth. Its rulers encouraged civil war in Ireland, chiefly as a means of distracting the attention of the British government, and preventing its interference in the political changes which French ambition meditated on the Continent. Holland and the Netherlands were the real objects at which the French Directory aimed, when they promised to assist the republicans of Ulster; and, singular enough, these countries were the prize for which the kings of Spain contended, when they tendered their aid to John O'Neil and the earl of Tyrone, two centuries before. A reasonable suspicion of the French alliance began to extend itself among the wisest of the United Irishmen. Tone himself, in his Memoirs, reveals to us that there were moments when his enthusiasm was not able to conquer the lurking fear, that France might either take the opportunity of making Ireland a province tributary to herself, or restoring it to England in exchange for the frontier of the Rhine, or the supremacy of Italy. Every delay in sending the promised auxiliary force increased the fears and suspicions of the United Irishmen; their best leaders were hopeless of success without foreign aid, and were, at the same time, alarmed at the prospect of foreign influence in their councils. Hence arose fresh sources of dismay and disunion, which soon afforded plausible excuses—for treachery

to the base, and for desertion to the timid.   The informer was amongst them, with the price of their
blood in his pocket; their plans were made known to
the government as soon as they were formed; the
snares of death compassed them around; the hand
that clasped them in simulated friendship had written
their doom; the lips professing the warmest zeal in
their cause had sworn to their destruction. They had,
in fact, become mere tools in the hands of the very
government which they had intended to overthrow;
they were mere puppets, to be worked until they had
produced so much of alarm as their rulers deemed
necessary for ulterior objects—and then to be delivered over to the executioner, with the double odium
upon their memory, of having been at once dupes
and conspirators.

When all their secrets were betrayed, all their
measures known, and all their leaders seized, the
United Irishmen allowed the Rebellion to begin.   It
had been too long languishing and uncertain to
inspire the people with confidence, or enthusiasm;
it was ill concerted, worse directed, received with
coldness by some and terror by others; there was
division between its leaders, there was disunion
amongst its followers, it had neither guidance nor
support.   In fact, it might have been said to have
been dead before its birth, had not the government
forced it into premature existence, by the stimulants
of whipping and free quarters.

The terrible convulsion which ensued, exhibited all
the passions of the past history, exploding in one

burst of irrepressible violence. "Woe to the van-
quished" was never so fearfully exhibited as the rule
of war. But the history of this sickening period
enters not into the purpose of this Introduction;
our duty has been simply to show the circumstances
which produced that state of Ireland, in which the
United Irishmen moved and acted, and thus to
explain how far the circumstances by which they
were surrounded, influenced their motives and their
conduct.

CHAPTER I.

THE period between the successful issue of the struggle for the independence of the Irish Parliament, and the outbreak of the Rebellion in 1798, was one of the most stirring and memorable epochs in the history of Ireland. The momentous events which were then taking place in other countries, exerted a powerful influence on the political sentiments of the Upper and Middle Classes of our people.

This period abounded with events of greater importance than any that preceded it for many centuries. The evil genius of George the Third, which strongly disposed him to take the side most adverse to the people on any popular question, and invariably opposed his inclinations to the extension of freedom, civil or religious, succumbed eventually to the spirit of liberty in another hemisphere, and *the Independence of a New World was the consequence.*

In France, the royal adherence to despotic principles, rather than the King's abuse of despotic power, prepared the way for the accomplishment of the ends of those political philosophers who, in the words of

Condorcet, " without foreseeing all that they have
done—have yet done all that we have lived to see
accomplished." The arrogance of a nobility ener-
vated by luxury, and emboldened in its vices by the
servility which had been long regarded as the allegiance of the vulgar to its pomp, had brought the
court into contempt and militated at last against
the monarchy itself. In Ireland, the two great examples I have quoted, of the power of the people and
the success of its united efforts for the attainment of
objects nationally desired, were not overlooked ; on
the contrary, they were regarded with feelings of
wonder and admiration. No country in the world,
at that period, stood in a position more likely to
be affected by such examples; every thing was
anomalous in her condition. She belonged to England and was said to be an independent nation ;
she had a Parliament, and, it might be presumed,
therefore, legislative power; she owned allegiance
to a king who owed his crown to a revolution which
was risked in defence of civil and religious liberty.
It might, therefore, be expected that the creed of
his Irish subjects could not prejudice their civil
rights; nevertheless, Ireland, at this period, was regarded by England, not as a sister, but as a rival
whose clashing interests were constantly to be re-
pressed. Her Parliament was a theatre of automaton
performers, with an English minister behind the
scenes ; he pulled the wires, and, as he willed, the
puppets moved; and while the spectators wondered
at the nimble members that were set in motion, and
listened to the words that seemed to issue from their

mouths, they almost forgot the British mechanist who stirred or stayed the "fantoccini" of the Irish Parliament. Her judges were dependent on the crown. Her military establishment was independent of her Parliament. Her trade was impeded by prohibitory statutes which utterly sacrificed her interests to the aggrandisement of England. The result of three general confiscations of the property of the natives of the country in the course of two hundred years, had left five-sixths of the landed property of the nation in the hands of the Protestant inhabitants, who hardly amounted to one tenth of the whole population. It unfortunately was considered, at the time of King William's settlement, that the Reformation was not sufficiently cemented to bear the weight of toleration on the same pedestal on which religion was placed by Henry the Eighth. The old plea for spoliation—the civilization of the subdued by means of compulsory conversion—had never been abandoned; but the effort was not successful, and the Church gained only a few indifferent members, whilst the sovereign lost the affections of some millions of subjects, by the attempt.

In the early part of the reign of George the Third, Roman Catholics were debarred from holding any office in the state, civil or military, above that of constable, parish overseer, or any like inferior appointment. They could not endow any school or college; they could not contract marriage with Protestants, without subjecting the priest who solemnized such marriage to the penalty of death, if unfortunately discovered; any justice of the peace, even without information, might enter their houses by day or night to search for arms ; they could obtain no degrees in the University of Dublin ; they, with all the inhabitants of this realm, were charged to attend divine service, according to the established religion, upon Sundays and holidays, on pain of ecclesiastical censure, and forfeiture of 12*d.* for every time of absence; their clergy dared not officiate at any funeral, or any other public ceremony, outside their own place of worship.   A child of a Catholic (by the 8th of Queen Anne), at any age, on conforming to the Protestant faith, might file a bill against his father, and compel him on oath to give an account of his property: whereupon the chancellor was empowered to allot, for the child's immediate maintenance, one-third of the father's goods and personal chattels, and, on the death of the father, the statute assigned no limits to the power of the chancellor over the property, in favour of the Protestant child.   Neither the concessions of 1778, nor those of 1782, secured the Catholics in property acquired in that interval, against the provisions of the 8th of Anne.   Every Catholic (male or female), of every grade, was compellable, on pain, not only of fine and imprisonment, but of the *pillory and whipping*, to appear, when summoned before any justice of the peace, to give information against any Papist he or she might know to keep arms in his house; and not the least offensive of these disabilities was, their exclusion from the exercise of the elective franchise, a right enjoyed by the Catholics from the first adoption of the English constitution, secured to them by the treaty of Limerick, in 1691, guaranteed by King

William and Queen Mary, and even ratified by Parliament, and which was taken from them in the first year of the reign of George the Second. Even by the Act of concession of 1778, " no Popish university or college" could "be erected or endowed." The chief concessions of the Act of 1778 were the following :—Papists were empowered to take leases for any term, not exceeding nine hundred and ninety-nine years, or any number of lives, not exceeding five; to purchase or take by grant, descent, or devise, any species of property; to educate youths of their own persuasion; to be guardians of their own children; to intermarry with Protestants, provided the marriage was solemnized by a Protestant clergyman ; and a popish clergyman duly licensed to officiate in any church or chapel, without a bell, or any symbol of ecclesiastical dignity or authority ; and, by subscribing the oaths of allegiance, Papists might qualify to be called to the bar, to become attorneys. Such was the state of Ireland, when "a voice from the New World shouted to liberty," in the words of Flood, and the example of America found a plea, in the apprehension of invasion, for calling forth the Volunteers of Ireland. Their first demands were made somewhat in the spirit of the Spanish beggar's supplication. Their artillery corps appeared on parade in Dublin with labels on the mouths of their cannon, bearing the words—" Free trade or speedy revolution." Their importunity increased with their strength, and at length they demanded from England *the independence of their country*—and England was not then in a condition to refuse it.

This extraordinary association of armed citizens

owed its origin to a letter of Sir Richard Heron, in
reply to an application from the inhabitants of the
town of Belfast to government, for the protection of
a military force, on the alleged ground of the danger
of invasion, the apprehension of which was then
loudly talked of over the country.   To this demand,
the answer of the Secretary, Sir Richard Heron, was,
that Government could afford none.

   In fact, in 1777 the Government had no means of
national defence, and "the people," says Hardy,
"were left to take care of themselves."   An English
army at that time was captive in America—the war
had drained both countries of their forces.   Previously
to the Secretary's admission of the weakness of the
Government, or the negligence that had left the country without defence, a few straggling corps of armed
citizens were formed for the protection of the coasts;
but the volunteer institution soon spread over the
country, and in one year its numbers amounted, we
are told by Hardy, to 42,000 men.

   Here was an army self-raised, self-supported, self-
commissioned, in a country hitherto treated as a conquered one, which was only to be governed by the
weakness of a divided people ; whereas, the essential
strength of the volunteer association was the union
of Catholic, Protestant, and Presbyterian—" of Irishmen," in short, " of every denomination."   The reader
need not look further for the origin of the " United
Irishmen :" the association of the latter naturally
sprung out of the former institution, when it departed
from its original principles; but it is the fashion to
assert, there was nothing but loyalty and the fear of

French invasion amongst the Volunteers, and only
treason, and the influence of French politics, in the
principles of the United Irishmen." This is an important consideration, and one which the supporters
of the Volunteers do apparent injustice to that illustrious band of patriot soldiers, in attempting to take
up on these exclusive grounds. It may be asserted,
without fear of contradiction, it was something less
than loyalty alone, and something more than the
fear of invasion at all, that animated Ireland, and ar-
rayed its spirit in the volunteer associations, when
the voice from America was shouting " Liberty !"
across the Atlantic; and a little later, when the first
dawn of the revolution in France was beginning to
dazzle the eyes of our long benighted country. It
was the wrongs of Ireland which armed " its fears of
French invasion :" it was the robbery of its legislative
rights, that caused its people to demonstrate *their
loyalty* at the head of an army, over which His Majesty's Government had no control; and it was to
make a signal demonstration of the strength of their
effective force, and the martial vigour of their collective wisdom, that they called together a national
convention, first in Dungannon, and afterwards in
Dublin. In the former place, two hundred delegates of
the Volunteers, in their military uniform and accoutre-
ments, marched two by two to the Protestant church
of Dungannon, and there, after many days' deliberation, they agreed upon that celebrated declaration
of their rights, which procured for Ireland the tran-
sitory, the illusory independence of her Parliament.
The views of the British minister, in reference to that

measure, were rightly appreciated and characterized by Flood, when the declaration was made in Parliament, purporting to be a message from the King through the secretary, " that mistrusts and jealousies had arisen in Ireland, and that it was highly necessary to take the same into immediate consideration, in order to a *final* adjustment." On that occasion, to put the Duke of Portland's sincerity beyond a doubt, his friend Mr. Ponsonby took upon him to answer for his Grace, that " he would use his utmost influence in obtaining the *rights of Ireland*, an object *on which he had fixed his heart.*"

It appears there was one man at least in that House who doubted the sincerity of the Minister—and that man was Flood, to whose public character Lord Charlemont's biographer has done great injustice, and to whose views as a statesman, those of his great rival, Grattan, can bear no comparison, whatever superiority the fidelity of his attachment to his country may give him over his rival.

That Flood was right in his scepticism, and Grattan wrong in his credulity, the event fully proved. In 1799, the same Duke of Portland openly avowed, that " he never considered the independence of the Irish Parliament a *final* adjustment."

It is perfectly evident that Pitt, from the moment he came into power, never ceased to regard that independence as a measure which had been unconstitutionally extorted—and at any hazard, cost, or sacrifice, was " to be re-captured." The course of the Irish Parliament on the Regency question, still more strongly fixed his determination. The incaution of that great and noble Irishman, our illustrious Grattan, enabled Pitt to place his finger on a flaw in the title to our Parliamentary independence, while an oversight in the Place Bill—the favorite bantling, as it has been called, of Grattan's patriotism—enabled the minister to pack that suicidal Parliament.

From the period of the Duke of Portland's unexpected announcement, of the intention of the British Government to concede the demand of parliamentary independence to Ireland, the great intellect of Grattan appeared to sink under the obligation, and, to use his own words on another occasion, he "had given back in sheepish gratitude the whole advantage." After the speech of the viceroy was read on that occasion, Mr. Grattan, in seconding the Address observed, "I should desert every principle upon which I moved the former Address, did I not bear testimony to the candid and unqualified manner in which the Address has been answered by the Lord Lieutenant's speech of this day. I understand that *Great Britain gives up*, in toto, *every claim to authority over Ireland. I have not the least idea in repealing the Sixth of George the First, that Great Britain should be bound to make any declaration, that she had formerly usurped a power. No, this would be a foolish caution*—a dishonourable condition : the nation that insists upon the humiliation of another, is a foolish nation. Another part of great magnanimity in the conduct of Great Britain is, that every thing is given up unconditionally; this must for ever remove suspicion."—*Commons' Debates*, vol. 20. This fatal security at the termination of a struggle like this, at

the most critical moment of its history, in its fatuity,
reminds one of the mournful fate of the wife of La-
valette; straining every mortal energy for the preservation of a life dearer to her than her own, and
when all her efforts are crowned with success,—when
the object of her love is restored by her to life and
liberty,—the wonderful energy that braced up every
faculty of her soul and enabled her to make this
great effort, fails her only when the accomplishment
of her hopes appears complete, and the noble mind
that wrought the victory sinks under its success.

So far from giving up " *in toto*" every claim to
authority over Ireland, the British Minister distinctly stated, that " *internal* interference with the
Irish Parliament would no longer be attempted,
but the right of external legislation remained un-
changed." If the independence of the Irish Parliament was intended to be permanent, the repeal
alone of the 6th of George the Third, which made
it legal to bind Ireland by English acts of Parliament, was inadequate to the final settlement of the
question; the renunciation of the right for legislating
for Ireland was requisite, and that right not being
renounced, the simple repeal of an act in violation of
it, so far " for ever from removing suspicion," left
very great reason to fear a repetition of it whenever
the suppression of the Volunteers deprived the country of the strength that had rendered her claims
irresistible.

In the debate on this question, Flood ably pointed
out the insufficiency of the repeal of the 6th of
George the First. " Notwithstanding the laudable ac-

quiescence which appeared in the renunciation of
English Claims, who could engage," he said, "that the
present administration might not at some future
time change its mind? The English House of
Commons asserted a right to external legislation,
and he who seconded the motion on the Irish question, did not give up that right, but as a matter of
convenience and compact." A very able exposure
of the illusory independence of the Irish Parliament
was made in the debate on that measure, by Mr.
Walsh, a barrister; he said, "With regard to the repeal of the 6th George the First, I rely on it as a lawyer,
that it is inadequate to the emancipation of Ireland.
This act is merely a declaratory law, it declares that
England has a power to make laws to bind Ireland.
What then does the repeal of this law do with
respect to Ireland?—simply this, and not a jot more:
it expunges the declaration of the power from the
English statute book, but it does not deny the power
to make laws hereafter to bind Ireland, whenever
England shall think herself in sufficient force for
the purpose. I call upon the King's new attorney-
general, to rise in his place and declare whether the
assumed and usurped power of England to bind
Ireland, will not remain untouched and unrelin-
quished, though the 6th of George the First should
be repealed?"—" With respect to the fine-spun distinction of the English Minister, Mr. Fox, between
external and internal legislation, it seems to me the
most absurd position that could possibly be laid
down, when applied to an independent people. See
how pregnant this doctrine of Mr. Fox is with every

mischief, nay with absolute destruction to this country; the Parliament of Ireland can make laws for
their internal regulation, that is, he gives us leave to
tax ourselves, he permits us to take the money out
of our purses for the convenience of England. But
as to external legislation, there great Britain pre-
sides; in anything that relates to commerce, to the
exportation of our produce, there Great Britain can
make laws to bind Ireland." " Ireland," continued
Mr. Walsh, " is independent, or she is not; if she is
independent, no power on earth can make laws to
bind her externally, or internally, save the King,
Lords and Commons of Ireland."—" I therefore
again repeat it, that until England unequivocally
declares, by an act of her own legislature, that she
has no power to make laws to bind Ireland, the
assumed and usurped power of English legislation
over this country, is not relinquished."

The Recorder, Sir Samuel Bradstreet, forcibly
pointed out the absurdity of that part of Mr. Grattan's address, " that there will no longer exist any
constitutional question between the two nations that
can disturb their mutual tranquillity," he instanced
the recent embargo, the possibility of another; the
fact of the oaths taken that day by the Irish Secretary being under an English law, and the Speaker
himself sitting in the chair under an English law;
" were not these matters," he asked, " subjects for
constitutional enquiry, and could any man say that
the consideration of them might not interrupt the
harmony between the two kingdoms?" To all these
arguments Mr. Grattan replied, " an honourable

gentleman supposes that England will again as-
sume this power when she can find herself able, but
that supposition must lose all weight from the
solemn surrender England has made of this assumed
power."

Thus did this great man allow his reason to become the dupe of a generous credulity, and by the
power of his unrivalled eloquence he was enabled to
carry away the sober judgment of the House, with
the honourable exception of four dissentient votes.
The division on the address determined the fate of
Irish independence; there were 211 ayes for Mr.
Grattan's motion, and 4 votes against it.

This illusory phantom of national independence
pointed out the way to Parliamentary Reform and
Catholic Emancipation, and these objects haunted
the minds of the Irish people long after the expiring
efforts of the Volunteers had ceased to be a mockery
to the pride or hopes of Ireland. All the energy of
the nation concentrated in that volunteer association,
had been expended in obtaining this nominal independence, and had precluded its successful employment in the struggle for reform. The people, on the
disbanding of the Volunteers, discovered that they
had been deceived, that the nominal independence
of an unreformed parliament was worse than illusory,
that the evils which sprung from it had become irre-
mediable by ordinary means. Grattan himself found
out, but when it was too late, that all his labours
for the independence of Ireland, had only served to
make the influence of the Irish Parliament a monopoly for an unprincipled faction, and its power and

patronage, the private property of a family hostile to
the interests of the nation.

There can be no doubt that the inadequate measures taken by Grattan, for the security of the independence of the parliament, was the cause of the
rebellion of 1798; and little did he imagine when he
reviled the actors in it, in his place in parliament,
that all the blood that was shed in that struggle, was
spilt either in defence of the principles on which he
advocated national independence, or in the re-con-
quest of that independence on the part of England,
which he had imperfectly achieved.

In the first stage of the proceedings of the convention at Dungannon, the constitutional legality of the
proceedings of deliberating soldiers, was defended on
the principle of the English revolution, namely, "on
the people's right of preparatory resistance to unconstitutional oppression." Its members asserted,
by their first resolution, "that a citizen by learning
the use of arms does not abandon any of his civil
rights." Their other resolutions were expressive of
their wrongs, and resolutely indicative of their disposition to redress them. The patriotism that dictated
them was evident enough, but the manifestation of
loyalty was by no means conspicuous. The invasion-
panic had afforded a pretext for putting arms into
the hands of the advocates, first of national independence and then of parliamentary reform; the Dungannon convention effected the former by its declaration of the 15th February, 1782. The national
convention which assembled in Dublin, the 10th
November, 1783, consisted of 300 delegates, who re-

presented 150,000 Volunteers. The volunteer grena-
diers attended as a guard on the convention during
its sittings, the delegates were escorted into town by
troops of armed citizens, the firing of twenty-one
cannon announced the commencement of their proceedings. The various battalions proceeded from the
Exchange to the Rotunda, the seat of the convention, in grand military array, displaying amongst
their banners the national standard of Ireland, and
devices and mottoes on their flags, which were not to
be mistaken. Broad green ribbons were worn across
the shoulders of the delegates, and according to Barrington, the lawyers even acknowledged the supreme
power of the will of the people—the motto on their
buttons was " Vox populi, suprema lex est."

This national convention of armed citizens was
assembled within sight of the Irish House of Parliament, and both these parliaments were sitting at
the same time, and the leading popular gentlemen
who were members of both, went from one assembly
to the other, as the affairs under deliberation required their presence in either house. Lord Charlemont, the chairman of the convention, we are told
by Hardy, spoke of the majority of the members as
" men of rank and fortune, and many of them
members of Parliament, lords and commoners;" no
sooner had the chairman taken his seat, than innu-
merable plans of reform were presented, which to
Lord Charlemont and his biographer appeared all
utterly impracticable; " so rugged and so wild in
their attire" were they, " as to look" not like the
" inhabitants of the earth and yet were on it:" and yet

" this motley band of incongruous fancies (as the latter terms them), of misshapen theories, valuable only if efficient, or execrable if efficacious," contained a vast number of proposals for parliamentary reformation, which in the course of half a century, have been found not only plausible but practicable suggestions, and have been of late years carried into execution. Mr. Flood's plan of reform was at length adopted by the convention. The Bishop of Derry then brought forward his resolution in favour of the immediate and complete emancipation of the Roman Catholics, and the good and virtuous Lord Charlemont strenuously and successfully resisted the resolution! To this same bishop, the noble earl replied, in defending himself from the charge of being a lukewarm reformer, "that in the struggle for an independent parliament, he had been willing to risk his life, and, what was far more important—the peace of his country, but for reform he was willing to do everything not inconsistent with the public peace." There were many in that assembly who did not participate in the sentiment of Lord Charlemont, and his lordship well knew it, for he trembled for the result of their determinations, and at last had recourse to a subterfuge for obtaining a final adjournment of the convention. The House of Commons, during the sitting of the convention, had refused Flood's motion for leave to bring in a bill for a reform of parliament, on the ground of its emanating from a body illegally constituted. Mr. Fitzgibbon openly and violently denounced the Volunteers, and his denunciations were compared by

Curran " to the ravings of a maniac and an incen-
diary." The language of Fitzgibbon was of a
very different description, when, carried away by the
stream of patriotism at the close of the struggle for
parliamentary independence, he addressed the House
of Commons to the astonishment of its members, in
terms that might have been expected from a Lucas
or a Molyneaux: "No man," said he, " can say that
the Duke of Portland has power to grant us that
redress which the nation unanimously demands,
but as Ireland is committed, no man I trust will
shrink from her support, but go through hand and
heart in the establishment of our liberties: and as
I was cautious in committing myself, so am I now
firm in asserting the rights of my country—my
declaration therefore is, that as the nation has determined to obtain the restoration of her liberty, it
behoves every man in Ireland to stand firm ! ! !"—
*The language of abuse a few years later was new to
the Volunteers, hitherto they had been accustomed
to constant commendation : every year they received
the unanimous thanks of parliament, the king
applauded their loyalty, the whole country rang
with their praises ; but the government looked on
their proceedings with the most serious apprehensions; as they had regarded their origin as an evil,
that was only to be tolerated, because it could not

---

* A singular commentary on these opinions, is to be found in the
speech of this gentleman on the Union, in which he declares, that
he had never ceased urging the necessity on the British Minister,
of the impracticability of the measure of Irish Parliamentary
independence, " for the last Seven years."—Vide Earl of Clare's
Speech on the Union. By Authority, 1800.

for the time being, be conveniently resisted or violently opposed. It was determined to make their own leaders their executioners, and for this purpose they contrived, in the first instance, to disarm the opposition of Lord Charlemont to their designs, by artful representations of apprehensions from the intemperance of his rival brethren in the convention, especially of the Bishop of Derry and Flood, and by insiduous assurances of confidence in his loyalty and enlightened patriotism. Lord Charlemont was the best and most honest of men, but in public matters he carried the refinement of a man of elegant manners to the extreme verge of plastic courtesy: as a man of honour, no earthly bribe could have caused him to swerve from his principles; as a courtier, the smiles of a viceroy or the blandishments of a minister might have caused him to listen too attentively to the suggestions of those in power. The proceedings in the House of Commons on the rejection of the Reform Bill, brought the question of the loyalty of the volunteer convention to an issue. It was now a crisis, which left no alternative but resistance or dissolution. The chairman dared not propose a dissolution, he proposed an adjournment till the Monday following, when they were to meet at the usual hour. On the Monday, accordingly, he repaired to the Rotunda at an earlier hour than usual; after passing some resolutions, he and a few of the partizans who accompanied him dissolved the convention. On the arrival of the great body of the delegates, they found the doors closed, they learned with astonishment that the convention was

dissolved, and when it was too late, they discovered
they had been deceived by their general. From
this time the power of the Volunteers was broken.
The government resolved to let the institution die a
natural death—at least to aim no blow at it in public;
but when it is known that the Honourable Colonel
Robert Stewart, afterwards Lord Castlereagh, was
not only a member of the convention (a delegate
for the county Down) but a chairman of the sub-
committee, and that he was the intimate friend of
Lord Charlemont, the nature of the hostility that
government put in practice against the institution
will be easily understood. While the Volunteers were
parading before Lord Charlemont, or manifesting
their patriotism in declarations of resistance to the
parliament, perfidy was stalking in their camp, and
it rested not till it trampled on the ashes of the
institution.

Of the esteem in which Lord Charlemont held
Col. Robert Stewart, we may judge by his letters: in
one he says—" I have seen Robert, and have given him
but little comfort with regard to his friend's administration. I cannot but love him; yet why is he so
be-Pitted."

The Catholics, who had flocked to the standard of
the Volunteers on the first cry of French invasion,
were groaning under the tyranny of the penal laws,
and, at the prospect of a deliverance, one cannot
wonder at "their patriotism catching fire at the presbyterian altar of parliamentary reform." But, when
they discovered the bigoted opposition of the leader
to their claims—when the Earl of Charlemont pub-

licly resisted the restoration of the elective franchise
to the Catholics, and the national convention had
the folly to let their prejudices defeat their interests,
by withholding from the Catholics (the great bulk of
the people) their just rights, the hopes of the latter
were destroyed; their attachment to the cause of the
Volunteers declined, and when the last blow was
struck at the existence of this force, the Catholic population of Ireland looked on with unconcern; and
never did an institution, so big with the highest political importance, dwindle away into such insignificance, and fall so little regretted by the majority of
the people.

The services of the Volunteers are, on the whole,
greatly exaggerated by our historians; the great wonder is, how little substantial good to Ireland was effected by a body which was capable of effecting so
much. As a military national spectacle, the exhibition was, indeed, imposing, of a noble army of united
citizens roused by the menace of danger to the state,
and, once mustered, standing forth in defence of the
independence of their country. But it is not merely
the spectacle of their array, but the admirable order,
conduct, and discipline of their various corps—not for
a short season of political excitement, but for a period
of nearly ten years—that, even at this distance of time,
are with many a subject of admiration. Their admirers certainly did not exaggerate their utility as
preservers of the public peace, when they asserted, at
one of the last resolutions passed at the dissolution of
the convention, that, through " their means, the laws
and police of this kingdom had been better executed

and maintained, than at any former period within
the memory of man." But what use did the friends
and advocates of popular rights make of this powerful
association ·of armed citizens, which paralyzed the
Irish government, and brought the British ministry
to a frame of mind, very different to that which it hitherto exhibited towards Ireland? Why, they wielded
this great weapon of a nation's collected strength to
obtain an illusory independence, which never could
rescue the Irish Parliament from the influence of the
British minister without reform, and which left the
Parliament as completely in the power of the minister, through the medium' of his hirelings in that
House, as it had been before that shadow of parliamentary independence had been gained : the only
change was in the mode of using that influence in the
Parliament; the material difference was but between
an open and a secret interference in its concerns. The
other adjuncts to this acquisition were, a Place Bill
and a Pension Bill, which had been the stock in trade
of the reforming principle of the opposition for many
years. No great measure of Parliamentary Reform,
or Catholic Emancipation, was seriously entertained,
or wrung from a reluctant, but then feeble government. The error of the leaders was, in imagining
that they could retain the confidence of the Catholics,
or the co-operation of that body, which constituted
the great bulk of the population, while their convention publicly decided against their admission to the
exercise of the elective franchise. At the great Leinster meeting of the Volunteer delegates, in October,
1783, the first serious attempt to force the claims of

the Catholics on the delegates was made by Mr. Burrowes. He said : " He was instructed to move the
extension of the elective franchise to the Roman Catholics, whose behaviour had manifested their attachment to the constitution. He was surprized to find
some gentlemen averse to entering upon the subject;
he was afraid an idea would go abroad, that they were
not to receive the power of voting for representatives
in Parliament. It would be an idea of the most fatal
nature, and gentlemen should consider, that their
resolution on this important question would, in all
probability, affect that assembly more even than it
would the Roman Catholics themselves."

Another delegate, Mr. Fitzgerald, asked—" Did
the Convention, when seeking freedom, mean to
make freemen of one million of subjects, and to keep
two millions slaves?" Mr. Burrowes was compelled to
withdraw his resolution ; another was substituted, of
a more general nature, by Major M'Cartney, namely :
" That the extension of the elective franchise to the
Catholics is a measure of the highest importance, and
worthy the atention of the national convention."
But even this resolution had also to be withdrawn.

In the grand national convention that sat in Dublin, the claims of the Catholics to the exercise of the
elective franchise were refused to be entertained. An
honourable delegate undertook, on the part of the Catholics, to object to that boon for them—that " they
were so grateful for the great concessions already
made to their body, that they could not think of asking for the elective franchise." This assertion was solemnly made by Mr. George Ogle, as he stated, on

the part of Lord Kenmare, and others of his particular friends of the Catholic persuasion; and it was
gravely listened to by the enlightened legislating Volunteers : its moderation was highly commended, and
it was in vain that a delegate, who appeared to have
some common sense and some liberality, which was
by no means common in that assembly, replied, that
he could not think " the Roman Catholics were like
the Cappadocians, who prayed for slavery." The Bishop of Derry, on the part of the recognized agents
of the Catholic body, submitted to the convention
the following document, in disavowal of the sentiments imputed to them :

" At a Meeting of the General Committee of the
Roman Catholics of Ireland, Sir P. Bellew, Bart., in
the Chair, it was unanimously resolved, that the message relating to us, delivered this morning to the National Convention, was totally unknown to and unau-
thorized by us.

" That we do not so widely differ from the rest
of mankind, as, by our own act, to prevent the removal of our shackles.

" That we will receive with gratitude every indulgence that may be extended to us by the Legislature, and are thankful to our benevolent countrymen for their efforts on our behalf."

This was tolerably explicit; but the medium of communication between Lord Kenmare and Mr. Ogle—
Sir Boyle Roche—was one which must have reminded
the convention of the mental fallibility of that great
bottle-conjuror, who contended that every quart bottle
should be made to hold a quart. The delegates

said they did not know which of the declarations
of the Catholics to believe; and, as the Catholics dis-
agreed among themselves on the subject, they deemed
it best not to decide upon it. Accordingly, in the plan
of reform drawn up by their sub-committee, the chairman of which was Colonel Robert Stewart, good care
was taken to exclude the Catholics from the elective
franchise, by the heading of the different resolutions,
viz. : " That it is the opinion of this Committee, that
every Protestant possessed of," &c. &c. The sentiments of Lord Charlemont, no doubt, had considerable influence over the assembly ; his character gave
a factitious importance to his bigotry. His hostility
to the claims of the Catholics had all the consistency of
Lord Clare's, without the savageness of its spirit. Even
ten years subsequent to this period, his lordship voted
in Parliament against the extension of the elective
franchise to the Catholics, thus contradicting, most
absurdly, his own principles and those of the national
convention, which prompted their appeal for " a full
and adequate representation of the people in Parliament," while, by excluding the Catholics, they virtually deprived the great majority of the people of
that privilege.

Lord Charlemont probably was influenced by the
opinions, or rather prejudices, of the celebrated Doctor Lucas, whose political views he adopted, and did
not presume to deviate from them in the smallest
degree. Lucas, like all his brother patriots of that
time, was an uncompromising bigot. At a period
when the unfortunate Catholics were crushed by oppression, this popular brawler about the independence

of Parliament, was reviling his Catholic countrymen with the bitterest invective in his "Barber's Letters," and assisting, by his illiberal abuse, to forge new chains for the great body of the Irish people. All the patriotism of Lucas and his followers was expended on the Parliament—they had none to devote to men who were not Protestants.

I am not writing a history of the Volunteers, or of the rebellion which succeeded the disbanding of that body; but it is necessary for me, in attempting to trace the motives of those who took a part in that rebellion, to enquire into the causes of the failure and ultimate fall of the volunteer association, of the errors which deprived them of the confidence of the people; and, lastly, to discover the origin of that rebellion; to find what objects it had in view at its commencement, and how far such objects differed from those of the Volunteers.

Without these enquiries, to consider the Rebellion of 1798 as a mere isolated movement of the people at that period; as simply one of those periodical outbreaks of sedition, which marks an era of famine or oppression every forty or fifty years in the annals of Irish history; as a secret conspiracy suddenly concocted, on the spurt of the pressure of some particular grievance, unconnected with preceding events, and uninfluenced by them,—would be to form a very erroneous opinion of the nature and causes of that rebellion, and, consequently, a very erroneous opinion of those engaged in it.

CHAPTER II.

THE principles advocated by the leading members
of the volunteer associations, the doctrines boldly
promulgated by the political clubs in Ireland, and the
language of the early champions of reform in Parliament, from the period of 1782 to the dissolution of
the volunteer association, had roused the minds of
the Irish people to the highest pitch of political excitement. It was only when the Volunteers had been
disbanded, and the real worthlessness of the nominal
independence of the Irish Parliament began to be
known; when the principal members of the Whig
Club had seceded, and the patriotism of other similar
societies had ceased to inspire confidence; when the
avowed reformers of 1782 had become the declared
opponents of reform, and when those who still lingered
on the opposition benches of both Parliaments, frightened at their own principles, and deterred from the
maintenance of them by the excesses of the French
revolution, made but a feeble show of adherence to
them, or waited in silence for happier times for their
support—that people began to despair of obtaining or

defending their rights by constitutional means : it was then only, that the deserted principles of the Volunteers—the unsupported doctrines of the Whig Club —the relinquished or discomfited plans of the political societies, and the abandoned cause of Parliamentary Reform, were taken up by a new political society, and that the United Irishmen acted on the speeches, writings, and the stirring sentiments of the early reformers of both countries—of Pitt, Stewart, the Duke of Richmond, Colonel Sharman, Flood, Grattan, and their liberal cotemporaries.

The society of United Irishmen was called into existence to adopt the principles of parliamentary reform, which had been abandoned at this period—by some in disgust, by others in despair, and by many who had been prominent, but never honest, in the cause. Those principles did not originate with the United Irishmen, but were advocated, to the extreme of democratic doctrines, by Pitt himself, and even by the moderate and good Lord Charlemont, whose loyalty has never been impugned—and by Flood and Grattan, whose prudence, at least, would have preserved themselves from the consequences of actual sedition. A few extracts, a little farther on, from the speeches and writings of the first reformers, will bear out the remark.

The origin of the Irish Volunteers, which, as an organized national military association, may be dated from 1777, ceased to exist, as such, in 1793. Its last effort was in Belfast, in defending the town from the earliest revival, at least in that century, of the dra-

...arman, Colonel Rowley
...oyal army to assemble
...patriots and firm...
...the memorable 15th
...on *the said* conside...
...*equal representation*
...*of Ireland*. And not
...in this requisition to
...sword in hand, on
...of obtaining parlia...
...advocating the ne...
...requisition, that " it
...consummate statesman,
...by the heir to his
...William P..."
...United Irishmen—of
...is accounts reason-
...confound with the...—
...Irishmen of an...
...very principle...

gooning system, by four troops of the 17th regiment, on the 15th of March, 1793.*

It is not inconsistent with truth, though it may be with the military glory of this institution of the Volunteers, to say that it combined, in one great national phalanx, the talent, the intolerance, the chivalry, the extravagance, the prodigality, the embarrassment, the republicanism and patriotism, for one brief epoch, of all ranks and classes. Here we find the ill-assorted names of the Earl of Charlemont and the Right Hon. Robert Stewart—of John Claudius Beresford and Henry Grattan—of Toler and Ponsonby—of Saurin and Flood—of Col. Rowley and Major Sandys—of Ireland's only Duke and Sir Capel Molyneux—of the rabid zealot, Dr. Patrick Duigenan, and the Right Rev. ultra-liberal, the Bishop of Derry—of Archibald Hamilton Rowan, and Jack Giffard—of the red-hot patriot, James Napper Tandy, and the facetious knight and slippery politician, Sir Jonah Barrington—and last, not least in celebrity, of George Robert Fitzgerald, of fighting notoriety, and Mr. Joseph Pollock, the great advocate of peace and order. These incongruous names are found jumbled together in the pages of the history of the volunteer association. The world never saw an army of such heterogeneous materials collected, from all conflicting parties, for a patriotic purpose.

On the 1st of July, 1783, at the Ulster meeting of the volunteer delegates at Lisburn, an address to the army, on the subject of Parliamentary Reform, was

* Pieces of Irish History, 55.

issued, signed by Lieut.-Col. Sharman, Colonel Rowley
and others, calling on that loyal army to assemble
with the same spirit of loyalty, patriotism and firmness, which actuated them on the memorable 15th
February, 1782, "*to deliberate on the most constitutional means of procuring a more equal representation
of the people, in the Parliament of Ireland.*" And not
the least singular circumstance in this requisition to
the Irish soldiery, to deliberate, sword in hand, on
the most constitutional means of obtaining parliamentary reform, is to find that, in advocating the necessity for it, it is stated in the requisition, that " it
was warmly supported by that consummate statesman,
the Earl of Chatham, and revived by the heir to his
abilities and name, the present William Pitt."

The first grand object of the United Irishmen—of
that body, whose principles it is accounted treasonable to the loyal volunteers to confound with theirs—
was " to promote union amongst Irishmen, of all religious denominations ;" and the very principle, and
even the words in which it is couched, the United
Irishmen borrowed from the Volunteers. At the
meeting of the celebrated Dungannon convention,
8th September, 1783 (Colonel Robert Stewart having
been called to the chair, vacated by Colonel J. Stewart), a communication was read from the 1st regiment
of the Irish Brigade, dated 15th February, 1782, which
concluded in these terms :—" At this great crisis,
when the western world, while laying the foundation
of a rising empire, temptingly holds out a system of
equal liberty to mankind, and waits with open arms
to receive the emigrants from surrounding nations,

we think it a duty we owe to our country, *to promote, as far as our example can reach, an affectionate coalition of the inhabitants of Ireland.* Animated by this sentiment, and convinced that national unanimity is the basis of national strength, this regiment affords a striking instance how far the divine spirit of toleration can *unite men of all religious descriptions* in one great object, the support of a free constitution."*

This idea of general union is said to have originated with the rebel, Theobald Wolfe Tone; but the merit or the demerit of its origin evidently belonged to the Volunteers, whom the King himself, and Parliament, session after session, thanked for their devoted loyalty. When this meeting took place in Dungannon, in which the Irish people were told the western world was temptingly holding out a system of equal liberty to mankind, to profit by which these Volunteers declared it was necessary to unite men in Ireland, of all religious persuasions, for one common object,—when this meeting took place, Tone was a loyal subject, and Colonel Robert Stewart was the chairman of a meeting at which sedition was pretty plainly inculcated, in the example held forth of the successful struggle for American independence.

But, in the course of the extraordinary events of this world, Tone was sentenced to be hanged, for attempting to carry into effect the project implied in the example so temptingly held forth, by "uniting men of all religious descriptions," and Colonel Robert Stewart (subsequently Lord Castlereagh), who sanc-

* History of the Proceedings and Debates of the Volunteer Delegates, p. 13.

tioned with his presence the sedition of the sword-in-
hand deliberators on reform, became a foremost man
in those councils which consigned the United Irishmen to the gallows. The meeting I speak of was not
an obscure country meeting—it was not what could
be well called " a farce :" the aggregate number of
Volunteers represented at the meeting was not less
than 18,000.*

The next remarkable meeting of the delegates of
the Volunteers, was that of the delegates from the
" Volunteer Army of Leinster," which sat on the 9th
October, 1783, at the Royal Exchange, Dublin, Lord
Charlemont in the chair. It is a striking feature in
the proceedings of the Volunteers, that, almost invariably, the first resolution at every meeting was, " that
the present state of the representatives of the people
of this kingdom requires to be reformed." On this
occasion Col. Hatton opposed the resolution, and
moved one to the effect: " That it is only through
the medium of the legislature that we do hope for
constitutional redress."† " This brought on (says the
History I have already quoted) a debate, in the course
of which it was urged, ' that the sacred majesty of the
people was, in all times, fully competent to correct
the abuses which might arise in the constitution, *and
to control and direct that branch of the legislature to
which they had only delegated a power*', but which interposition on the part of the people, it was allowed
to be impolitic to exercise, save only on the most im-

* History of the Proceedings and Debates of the Volunteer Delegates, p. 9.
† Idem, p 17.

portant occasions;'" and, in support of this doctrine, the secretary urged the authority of the celebrated Dr. Jebb, &c. The resolution, however, of Colonel Hatton, materially amended by Counsellor Michael Smith, was eventually carried.

On the 10th November, 1783, the grand national convention met at the Royal Exchange, Dublin, and subsequently adjourned to the Rotunda, Lord Charlemont in the chair, and continued to meet till the 2nd of December, 1783. The sub-committee of the convention, consisting of one delegate for each city and county, by whom the business of the convention was regulated, chose Colonel the Right Hon. Robert Stewart for their chairman.

On the 21st of November, the chairman of the sub-committee reported to the convention a series of resolutions of that committee, on the subject of reform, to the following effect:

" That it was the unanimous opinion of the committee, that no non-resident elector should be permitted to vote for any representative in Parliament, unless his right of voting arose from landed property of £20 per annum.

" That no elector be deemed a resident, who had not resided for six months in the year previous to the day of issuing the writ for the election, and unless that borough, town, or city, had been his usual place of residence during the period of his registry.

" That the sheriff of each county do appoint a deputy, to take the poll in each barony on the same day.

" That all depopulated places, or decayed boroughs,

which had hitherto returned representatives, by an extension of the franchise to the neighbouring barony be enabled to return representatives to Parliament.

" That every borough, town, or city, which hitherto had returned representatives, be deemed decayed, which did not contain 200 electors, over and above potwallopers, according to the plan for the province of Leinster; and should cease to return representatives till the aforesaid number of electors be supplied.

" That every *Protestant*, possessed of a freehold, shall have a right to vote for members to serve in Parliament for such city, town, or borough.

" That any bye-law made by a corporation to contract the franchise, shall be declared illegal.

" That every Protestant possessed of a leasehold, of the yearly value of £10, in any city, town, or borough, not decayed for thirty-one years or upwards, and of which ten years are unexpired, be entitled to vote; and every Protestant in any decayed city, town, or borough, having a leasehold of £5 yearly value, for thirty-one years, ten of which are unexpired, be permitted to vote.

" That every freeholder of 40s. per annum, in any decayed city, town, or borough, be entitled to vote.

" That the duration of Parliament ought not to exceed the term of three years.

" That all suffrages be given vivâ voce, and not by ballot.

" That any person holding a pension, except for life, or under the term of twenty-one years, be incapable of sitting in Parliament; and if for life or twenty-one years, should vacate his seat, but be capable of re-election.

" That any member accepting office under the crown do vacate his seat, but be capable of re-election.

" That every member, before he took his seat, should take an oath that he has not, nor any other person for him, with his knowledge or consent, given meat, drink, money, place or employment, or any consideration, for any expenses whatsoever voters may have been at for procuring votes at his election ; and do further swear, that he will not suffer any person to hold any place or pension in trust for him, while he serves in Parliament.

" And, lastly, that any person convicted of perjury by a jury, relative to the above oath, be incapable of ever sitting in Parliament."*

Such was the plan of reform submitted to the convention by the chairman of its sub-committee, the Right Hon. Robt. Stewart ; and, though not "the first whig," one might suppose there was something prophetic in the definition of the term that had reference to Irish politics, when it turns out, that Lord Castlereagh was the first reformer in 1783. This plan of reform, with the exception of two sittings, in which the claims of the Catholics to the elective franchise were discussed and scouted by the assembly, occupied the attention of the Convention during the whole time it sat, till the 2nd of December, the day of its dissolution—and it may be added, the date of the downfall of the volunteer association. The fears of Lord Charlemont,

* History of the Volunteer Convention, p 49.

and the mistaken views of Grattan, in holding himself aloof from the proceedings of the convention, and
depriving the question of reform of his powerful support, mainly contributed to accomplish this event.
In thus declining to advance the cause of reform, the
only chance was abandoned of maintaining the advantages which had already been acquired. It would
seem, at this period, as if his great mind reposed under the shadow of the laurels that had been planted
around a partial victory, and had become unconscious
of the danger of leaving the security of the independence of Ireland to an unreformed Parliament, under
the secret supremacy of British influence. The volunteer association, in fact, became a gorgeous pa-
geant of national chivalry, to be remembered in after
times, with wonder at the power and the pomp it
exhibited, and surprize at the insignificance of its
results.

But Grattan, from the time he imagined he had
gained his great object, turned away his face from the
ladder by which " he upward climbed," and bid the
Volunteers farewell—" the plumed troop, and the
big wars, that made ambition virtue;" " his occupation was gone." The wooden horse of national independence was received into Ireland, and the hands
of the opposition were held forth for the " dona fe-
rentes" of the British ministry. On the 5th of March,
1782, Grattan stated in the House of Commons—
" he was far from saying that, under the present administration, independent gentlemen might not accept of places. He thought that places were now honourable, and in taking one, he should be the friend

of the people and of His Majesty's government. He had no personal knowledge of the Lord Lieutenant; he was not acquainted with those about him—*nay, if he had sent for him, he was persuaded he should have declined the honour of seeing him.* But, as he believed him to be virtuous, so far he should have his free support."*

In 1785, Grattan discovered that the independence of the Irish parliament was but in name,—that he had been deceived. The acknowledgement is made in plain and affecting terms, in his speech, on the 12th of August, 1785, on the question of the final adjustment of the commercial intercourse between the two countries. To effect this adjustment, commissioners had been appointed in Ireland to arrange the basis with the British government : eleven resolutions were proposed and agreed upon. But when these propositions were brought forward by Mr. Pitt, ten new ones were found appended to them—nominally supplemental, but virtually striking at the very root of the independence of the Irish parliament. These were thrown into the heads of the bill introduced into the Irish House of Commons by Mr. Orde. In presenting that bill, Mr. Secretary Orde deprecated the idea of there being any thing derogatory in its provisions to the constitution of the country, " which had been," he said, " repeatedly and recently recognized on the other side, and which, after so many full, open and decided declarations made by Great Britain, there does not remain the least shadow of a reason for supposing she would be *so wild, so ab-*

* Parliamentary Debates; Dublin, 1782.

surd (I want words to express my abhorrence at the idea), so ungenerous as to attack." Such was the language of the Irish secretary of that day—and yet, even then, the Union was meditated, and, on the secretary's shewing, the conduct of the British minister towards Ireland, was wild, absurd, abhorrent, and ungenerous; and yet there are people who wonder at the events which followed. The wonder is, that any one should be affected by the remembrance of their causes, except with feelings of shame or sorrow.

Mr. Grattan endeavoured to stimulate the House to one great effort, to retrieve the error which left the independence of his country at the mercy of an administration adverse to its existence. There is a thrilling eloquence in the alternate appeals, on this occasion, to the pride and fears of his auditory, and he can have little sympathy with the sufferings of a noble mind, struggling ineffectually against predominant injustice, who can read this speech unmoved: one can trace the workings of the mind of the deceived patriot, in the stirring outbreaks of his indignation, and the mournful presentiment of impending evils breaking through the hopes he affects to feel, in order (vain effort!) to infuse a new spirit of liberty into the breasts of his auditors. One is reminded, even by the change of circumstances which had taken place, of the triumph of the father of his country in 1782,—the idol of a nation's gratitude, the object of a senate's homage: proud of his success, yet ashamed of a suspicion of a jealous nation's sincerity in her acquiescence in it: ardent in his

expectations, strong in his security, and, with generous confidence, disdaining to render that measure
" humiliating to England," by calling for the renunciation of a power which had been usurped. And,
within the short period of three years, we find his
parliamentary influence gone, his popularity diminished; conscious, at last, of having been over-
reached—deceived—by one party, and well aware
that he is soon to be deserted, with a few honourable
exceptions, by his own. It is impossible, without
sentiments of mournful interest in the feelings of
Grattan on that occasion, and of more than public
sympathy for the adversity of public life, to read the
following passages from the speech in question :—
" Sir,—I can excuse the Right Hon. Member who
moves you for leave to bring in the bill. He is an
Englishman, and contends for the power of his own
country, while I am contending for the liberty of
mine. His comment on the bill is of little moment;
a lord lieutenant's secretary is an unsafe commen-
tator on an Irish constitution. The Irish parliament
is now called on to determine, that it is most expedient for Ireland to have no trade at all in these
parts. This is not a surrender of the political rights
of the constitution, but of the natural rights of man ;
not of the privileges of parliament, but of the rights
of nations. Not to sail beyond the Cape of Good
Hope and the Straits of Magellan; an extensive
interdict ! Not only neutral countries excluded,
and God's providence shut out in the most opulent
boundaries of creation ! Other interdicts go to a
determinate period of time, but here is an eternity

of restraint. This resembles rather an act of God than an act of the legislature, whether you measure it by immensity of space or infinity of duration, and has nothing human about it but its presumption. To proposals, therefore, so little warranted by the great body of the people of England, so little expected by the people of Ireland, so heedlessly suggested by the minister, and so dangerous to whatever is dear to your interest, honour, and freedom, I answer, No !—I plead past settlements, and I insist on the faith of nations. If, three years after the recovery of your freedom, you bend, your children, corrupted by your example, will surrender; but if you stand firm and inexorable, you make a seasonable impression on the people of England, you give a wholesome example to your children, you afford instruction to his Majesty's ministers, and make (as the old English did, in the case of their charter) the attempt on Irish liberty its confirmation and establishment. This bill goes to the extinction of the most invaluable part of your parliamentary capacity: *it is an union, an incipient and a creeping union; a virtual union, establishing one will in the general concerns of commerce and navigation, and reposing that will in the parliament of Great Britain; an union, where our parliament preserves its existence after it has lost its authority, and our people are to pay for a parliamentary establishment, without any proportion of parliamentary representation.* If any body of men can still think that the Irish constitution is incompatible with the British empire—a doctrine which I abjure, as sedition against the

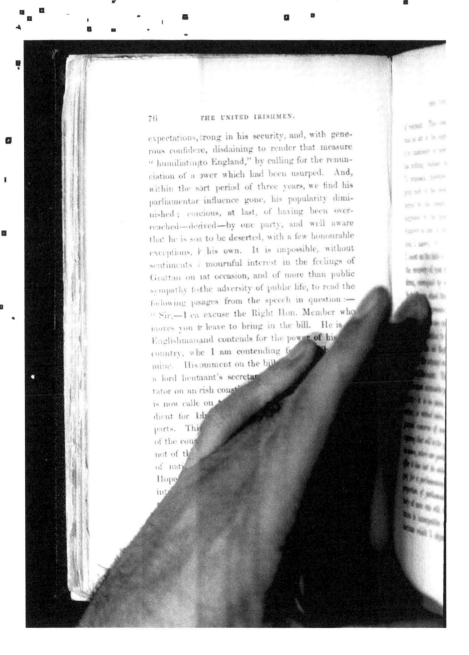

expectations, strong in his security, and, with generous confidere, disdaining to render that measure
" humiliating to England," by calling for the renunciation of a power which had been usurped. And,
within the sort period of three years, we find his
parliamentar influence gone, his popularity diminished; concious, at last, of having been over-
reached—deceived—by one party, and well aware
that he is soon to be deserted, with a few honourable
exceptions, by his own. It is impossible, without
sentiments of mournful interest in the feelings of
Grattan on that occasion, and of more than public
sympathy to the adversity of public life, to read the
following passages from the speech in question :—
" Sir,—I can excuse the Right Hon. Member who
moves you for leave to bring in the bill. He is
Englishman and contends for the power of his
country, whe I am contending for
mine. His comment on the bill
a lord lieutnant's secretar
tator on an irish const
is now called on
dient for Irl
parts. Thi
of the com
net of th
of nati
Hope
int

of restraint. This resembles rather an act of God than an act of the legislature, whether you measure it by immensity of space or infinity f duration, and has nothing human about it but s presumption. To proposals, therefore, so little warranted by the great body of the people of Englad, so little expected by the people of Irelanc so heedlessly suggested by the minister, and s dangerous to whatever is dear to your interest, honour, and freedom, I answer, No!—I plead past ettlements, and I insist on the faith of nations. If, hree years after the recovery of your freedom, you nd, your children, corrupted by your example, vill surrender; but if stand fir nexorale, you make a sea ressio eople f England, you g me o you children, you on esty' ministers, and ld in th case of their em berty s confirmation ent oes to the extinction ah our pr liamentary ca an ripient nd a creeping d ishing ne will in the n and avigation, and ci ment of Great Britain; re t preses its existence lo , and ou people are to ablishme, without any represent ion. If any k that th Irish consti- the Brish empire—a as sediti against the

connexion—but, if any body of men are justified in thinking *that the Irish constitution is incompatible with the British empire, perish the Empire! live the Constitution.* Reduced by this false dilemma to take a stand, my second wish is the British empire; my first wish and bounden duty is the liberty of Ireland. Whence the American war? whence the Irish restrictions? whence the misconstruction, of suffering one country to regulate the trade and navigation of another, and of instituting, under the name of general protectress, a proud domination, which sacrifices the interests of the whole to the ambition of a part, and arms the little passions of the monopolist with the sovereign potency of an imperial parliament? for great nations, when cursed with unnatural sway, follow but their nature when they invade, and human wisdom has not better provided for human safety, than by limiting the principles of human power. We, the limited trustees of the delegated power, born for a particular purpose, limited to a particular time, and bearing an inviolable relationship to the people who sent us to parliament, cannot break that relationship, counteract that purpose, surrender, diminish, or derogate from those privileges we breathe but to preserve. I rest on authority as well as principle; the authority on which the revolution rests. Mr. Locke, in his chapter on the abolition of government, says, that the transfer of legislative power is the abolition of the state, not a transfer. If I am asked how we shall use the powers of the constitution?—I say, for Ireland, with due regard to the British nation: let us be governed by

the spirit of concord, and with fidelity to the connexion. But when the mover of this bill asks me to
surrender those powers, I am astonished at him; I
have neither ears, nor eyes, nor functions to make
such a sacrifice. What! that free trade for which
we strained every nerve in 1779! that free constitution for which we pledged life and fortune in
1782! Our lives at the service of the empire; but
our liberties! No: we received *them* from our "Father which is in Heaven," and we will hand them
down to our children. In the mean time, we will
guard our free trade and free constitution as our
only real resources; they were the struggles of great
virtue, the result of much perseverance, and our
broad base of public action."*

It is pretty evident that the Union, "the incipient,
creeping Union," was, in Grattan's opinion, a project
to be resisted to the last extremity: that the British
government, in 1785, was inimical to the independence of Ireland, and that the Irish parliament
was not to be relied on for its defence.

The Volunteers were no longer able or inclined to
maintain what they had gained. They found they
had wasted their strength on an object valueless
without reform, and England was now in a condition
to resist that measure.

They lingered on in military array, occasionally ·
exhibiting, on a parade day, their diminished strength
to their enemies—all that was left of their martial
character, the trappings of their corps, at an annual
review. In 1793, an order from government to

* Parliamentary Debates, Dublin, 1785.

disperse every assemblage of that body by military
force, gave the death-blow to the Volunteers : they
made one faint effort in Antrim for their last review;
the army was marched out of Belfast to prevent its
taking place, and, in prudently giving up the review,
the great body of the citizen-soldiers of Ireland gave
up the ghost.   But their principles were not then
doomed to perish ; they rose from the ashes of the
Volunteers, and the course of reproduction was but
a short transition from langour and hopelessness to
activity and enthusiasm, and, with a perilous excess
of energy in both, their principles became those of
the United Irishmen in 1791.   In noticing the error
which led to the insecurity of the settlement of 1782,
the object is not to depreciate the merits of a man,
whose glory Ireland cannot afford to see disparaged.
The highest political wisdom is not always combined
with the most exalted genius ; a patriot may be pure
in his principles, gifted with the finest fancy, the
most varied powers of wit and eloquence, yet he may
not be a man on whose judgment alone a people
would do well to rest the adjustment of a great
national question, at a momentous crisis.   To no
one patriot who ever existed,—not even to Washington himself,—would it be prudent for a nation,
in political warfare, to confide alone, a question on
which its destinies depended.

In the field, weakness prevails in the multiplicity
of council ; but the strife of war and the struggles of
party, demand very different combinations of mental
faculties : in the former, the acutest perception, the
promptest determination, united with the coolest

judgment, constitute the able general—in the other, the qualities that are essential to great statesmen, are those which enable them warily and watchfully to approach the waves of public opinion, and to penetrate the depths of political cunning—to discern the distant dangers that beset advantages reluctantly conceded or fortunately obtained, and to look well to the intrenchments of the law which are thrown up around them. The single patriot throughout the turmoil of a protracted session, is no match for an entire administration; and at a game of diplomacy, Grattan, it must be admitted, had but a poor chance of success with such skilful dealers and accomplished shufflers as his opponents.

The dissolution of the Volunteers was supposed to be atoned for by the appointment of a liberal lord lieutenant. Lord Fitzwilliam came over, but neither reform nor Catholic emancipation followed. In 1795, the Irish opposition began to retrieve some of its errors, and to regain a little of its former popularity; its hostility, however, to " the incipient creeping Union," had determined Mr. Pitt to direct its attention to other objects, and he accordingly amused the nation's hopes with a popular viceroy.

The coalition with the Duke of Portland made it necessary to concede to that nobleman the management of Irish affairs. His Grace knew Ireland, and was an enemy to her wrongs: he obtained Pitt's consent to the appointment of Lord Fitzwilliam, and, what was more difficult, he obtained that noble lord's. During these arrangements, the duke was in communication with the leading members of the

Irish opposition; many of them were his private friends. " Mr. Grattan, Mr. William Ponsonby, Mr. Denis Bowes Daly, and other members of that party, were therefore invited to London; they held frequent consultations with the Duke of Portland and Lord Fitzwilliam, at which Mr. Edmund Burke also occasionally assisted."*

" The terms of the Irish members were, support of ministers, approbation of the war, and assent to the strong measures of government,—in consideration of Catholic emancipation, the dismissal of the Beresford faction (and for all reform), the prevention of embezzlement, and improvement in the mode of collecting and administering the revenues of the country. Burke alone had the boldness to demand, not only emancipation, but the immediate promotion of Catholics, in some ascertained proportion, to places of trust in the state. This, however, was asked from the liberality of government, not demanded from its justice; and the preceding arrangements were communicated to the British government, as the terms on which they were willing to take a share in the Irish government."†

Office was not the object of the patriotism of a Grattan, but it became the consequence of it; and ministerial patriots in Ireland seldom have long preserved or deserved the people's confidence. The breath of administration is not the atmosphere for their sturdy principles. That ominous annunciation, in 1782, at the close of the battle for parliamentary independence: " I think that places are

---

* Pieces of Irish History, 79.   † Ibid., 79.

now honourable, and, in taking one, I should be the
friend of the people and of His Majesty's government,"—was now acted on, under an administration
whose leader had become hostile to reform.

A man in the secrets of the opposition party of
that time—the head-piece of that system which grew
out of the insecurity of Irish independence, and the
failure of the measures which terminated in the
recall of Lord Fitzwilliam, a man whose word was
never doubted by friend or foe—Thomas Addis
Emmet—thus speaks of the proposals of the Irish
leaders, made to the Duke of Portland and acquiesced in by Mr. Pitt: " Mr. Pitt wished, and indeed
tried, to obtain that some of these measures should
be at least delayed in the execution for the season;
but Mr. Grattan and his friends insisted that they
should be brought forward in the very first session, in order to give eclât to their administration.
In the propriety of this demand, the Duke of Portland uniformly concurred; and even Mr. Pitt himself,
who had previously kept in the back ground, and
avoided personal communication with Lord Fitzwilliam's friends, was present at some of the latter
interviews, and certainly did not prevent its being
believed that he acquiesced in those demands, with'
which it was impossible to doubt his being unacquainted. The members of opposition had no great
experience of cabinets; they conceived that they
were entering into honourable engagements, on which
every thing that was allowed to be understood, was
equally binding with whatever was absolutely expressed. They rested satisfied that their stipulations

were known and acceded to; they neglected to get them formally signed and ratified, or reduced to the shape of instructions from the British cabinet to the viceroy; they put them unsuspectingly in their pockets, and set off to become ministers in Ireland."

The power of Lord Fitzwilliam was first tried, on the dismissal of the Beresford faction from the various offices which that grasping family had so long contrived to monopolize.

Pitt expostulated with the viceroy on the dismissal of the Beresfords, notwithstanding the institution of a parliamentary inquiry, at this period, respecting a public fraud, in which a subordinate clerk of the revenue was put forward as a sort of vicarious victim for the great national jobbers; and in this single instance, the public had been defrauded of £60,000. " Circumstances (on the same authority) raised a suspicion, that the transaction was the result of fraud and collusion, accomplished through the influence of one of this faction, who was generally believed to be a partner in the profits."* The family of the person referred to, overran every department in the state; but in the revenue, they monopolized the custom-house itself. That splendid palace for the collection of customs, in a city without trade, remains a lasting monument of the venality of parliament, and of the power of a faction, which a British minister dared not to oppose, and a representative of royalty was not permitted to offend. " To aggrandize this faction, a commissioner of excise was protected by parliament with all the jealous care of royalty itself; nay, so

---

* Pieces of Irish History, 107.

sacred was the person of the meanest officer under
this family department, that a bill was introduced
into the house by Mr. Secretary Orde, 12th August,
1785, which declared it felony to strike an excise-
man: but, even before that bill, the Chief Baron
Burgh had asked the house, " were they prepared to
give to the dipping-rule what they should refuse to
the sceptre ?"

Such was the power of a faction which Mr. Pitt
thought fit to uphold in Ireland. It is impossible
to give any explanation of his conduct, creditable to
his character as a statesman. The faction was not
essential to his policy with regard to the union, for
the best of reasons—some of its leaders were hostile
to it; they knew their reign must terminate with
the existence of an Irish parliament.

The following extracts from the two celebrated
letters of Lord Fitzwilliam to the Earl of Carlisle,
published in 1795, set the conduct of Mr. Pitt on
this question in the plainest light :—" I made proposals (he says) to the British minister, for the
removal of the attorney and solicitor-generals (Messrs.
Wolfe and Toler); Mr. Pitt and the Duke of
Portland knew perfectly well, that the men whom
I found possessed of these ministerial offices, were
not the men in whom I meant to confide in the
arduous measures I had to undertake. Was I, then,
to have two sets of men — one possessing confidence, without office; the other, office without confidence?

" And now for the grand question about Mr.
Beresford :—In a letter of mine to Mr. Pitt on this

subject, I reminded him of a conversation, in which I had expressed to him (in answer to the question put to him by me,) my apprehension that it would be necessary to remove that gentleman, and that he did not offer the slightest objection, or say a single word in favour of Mr. Beresford. This alone would have made me suppose that I should be exempt from every imputation of breach of agreement, if I determined to remove him; but when, on my arrival here, I found all those apprehensions of *his dangerous power*, which Mr. Pitt admits I had often represented to him, were fully justified, when *he was filling a situation greater than that of Lord Lieutenant*, and when I clearly saw, that if I had connected myself with him, it would have been connecting myself with a person *under universal heavy suspicions*, and subjecting my government to all the opprobium and unpopularity attendant upon his mal-administration, I determined, while I meant to curtail him of his power, and to shew to the nation, that he did not belong to my administration, to let him remain, in point of income, as well to the full as he had ever been. I did not touch, and he knew I had determined not to touch, a hair of the head of any of his family, or friends, and they are still left in the enjoyment of *more emolument than was ever accumulated in any country upon any one family.*

" You will recollect that the measure of emancipation to the Catholics, was originally the measure of Mr. Pitt and the Westmoreland administration. The (previous) declarations, both of Mr. Pitt and Mr. Dundas, on this subject, are well known in this country and often quoted: ' they would not risk a rebellion in Ireland on such a question.' But what they would not risk under Lord Westmoreland's administration, they are not afraid to risk under mine.

" But after all, why did not Mr. Pitt warn me of those horrid consequences (of emancipation) previous to my departure for Ireland, if he really felt them? why was the subject left open for my judgment and discretion? I trust that the evil genius of England, will not so far infatuate its ministers, as to induce them to wait for more decisive corroboration of the faithfulness and honesty with which I have warned them of the danger of persisting in their fatal change of opinion on this momentous question.

" The measure of arranging the treasury bench, the bare outline, or rather the principle of which, has been stated in the house preparatory to its introduction, was fully agreed on between Sir John Parnell and Mr. Pitt.

" Are those the measures on which I am to be accused—when the House of Commons of Ireland, had unanimously granted me the largest supplies that have ever been demanded, when I laid a foundation for encreasing the established force of the country, and procured a vote of £200,000 towards the general defence of the empire.

" The Catholic question entered for nothing into the cause of my recall. From the very beginning, as well as in the whole proceedings of that fatal business, for such I fear I must call it, I acted in perfect conformity with the original outline, settled between me and his Majesty's ministers, previous to my departure from London. From a full consideration of the real merits of the case, as well as from every information I had been able to collect of the state and temper of Ireland, from the year 1793, I was decidedly of opinion that not only sound policy, but justice, required on the part of Great Britain, that the work which was left imperfect at that period ought to be completed, and the Catholics relieved from every remaining disqualification. In this opinion, the Duke of Portland uniformly concurred with me, and when the question came under discussion, previous to my departure from Ireland, I found the cabinet, with Mr. Pitt at their head, strongly impressed with the same opinion. Had I found it otherwise, I never would have undertaken the government.

" As early as the 8th January last, I wrote the Secretary of State on this subject, *I told him that I trembled about the Catholics.*

" On the 9th February that gentleman (Mr. Pitt,) wrote to me to expostulate on the dismissal of Mr. Beresford, and on the negociations with Mr. Wolfe and Mr. Toler; by the same mail, and in a letter dated the 8th instant, the very day before Mr. Pitt had written to me, came a letter from the secretary of state, touching at length on the important subject (Catholic emancipation), and bringing it for the first time into play, as a question of any doubt or difficulty with the British Cabinet.

" Then for the first time, it appears to have been

discovered that the deferring it (the question of emancipation,) would not be merely an act of expediency, or ' a thing to be desired for the present,' but ' *the means of doing a greater service to the British Empire, than it has been capable of receiving since the Revolution, or at least since the Union*' (with Scotland.)

" In my answer to Mr. Pitt, a copy of which I send you, and which I wrote the very night I received his letter, I entered fully into the subject of my dismissals; I stated, as you will see, my reasons for having determined on them, as well as for adhering to them, when once resolved on. I then put it to himself to determine for me, and the efficacy of my government; *I left him to make choice between Mr. Beresford and me.*

" The same night I wrote to the Duke of Portland, I testified my surprise, after such an interval of time, and after the various details which I had transmitted to him, advising him of the hourly increasing necessity of bringing forward the Catholic question, and the impolicy and danger of even hesitating about it, I should now be pressed for the first time to defer the question till some future occasion. *I refused to be the person to run the risk of such a determination. I refused to be the person to raise a flame in the country, that nothing short of arms would be able to keep down.*

" Had Mr. Beresford never been dismissed, we should never have heard of them (Mr. Pitt's objections to emancipation at that time), and I should have remained. But it will be said, in proving this

point so strongly, I still leave myself open to other
accusations which affect my character, when I avow
the earnestness with which I had determined to pull
down the Beresfords. Charged with the government
of a distracted and discontented country, am I alone
to be fettered and restrained in the choice of the
persons by whom I am to be assisted?—and rather
than indulge me in that single point,—even considering it in the light of indulgence,—*must the people
of England boldly face, I had almost said, the certainty
of driving this kingdom into a rebellion, and open
another breach for ruin and destruction to break in
upon us?"* *

Volumes have been written on the events that
grew out of the recall of Lord Fitzwilliam, but here
is the germ of them all. Few of those who are now
aware of the existence of these letters, have leisure
to consult them; and those who are desirous to
know the true cause of the rebellion of 1798, will
not find fault with the length of these quotations.
These facts are to be gathered from them :—that the
union had been determined on at this period ; that
the peace of Ireland was to be sacrificed for its
attainment, and that attainment promoted by the
loss of influence on the part of the Irish opposition,
and the confirmed power of the Beresford oligarchy,
in order to exasperate the country—in one word, to
goad the people into a rebellion.

Whether that attainment was cheaply purchased,

* " Letters of a Venerated Nobleman, recently retired from this
country, to the Earl of Carlisle, explaining the cause of that event."
Dublin, 1795.

or whether the beneficial effects expected from it have compensated for the terrible consequences of a civil war, the progress of events has not yet proved in the affirmative.

But all the experience the world can afford, of subsequent advantages arising from civil commotion, will hardly justify subscription to the doctrine—that political foresight can ever so far determine the aspect of future circumstances, dependant as they are on the mutability of all human governance, and influenced by every tide in the affairs of empire, as to render distant good, and probable advantages, benefits to be sought after or secured by a wise statesman, at the cost of present evil, and a certain prospect of civil war.

Out of evil, good may no doubt come. The good effects of the legislative union may yet predominate over the evils that attended its attainment. The calamities of that period may be only remembered as curious historical facts; but the author of those evils can find no justification in those results. In putting a people to the sword, every drop of blood that was shed in that rebellion must be laid to his account. And in Ireland, at all events, his barbarous policy can be remembered only to be abhorred.*

* On the motion for public honours to the remains of William Pitt, on the grounds of his excellence as a statesman, Mr. Windham said : "With the fullest acknowledgement, both of the virtues and the talents of the eminent man in question, I do not think, from whatever cause it has proceeded, that his life has been beneficial to his country." Fox, on the same question, said . " I cannot consent to confer public honours, on the ground of his being an excellent statesman, on the man who, in my opinion, was the sole—certainly

the chief—supporter of a system, which I had been early taught to consider as a bad one " In 1785, Doctor Jebb declared that, politically speaking, Pitt was the worst man living, and would go greater lengths to destroy liberty than any minister ever did before him."

There is some exaggeration in this assertion. There were two men then living, the sphere of whose action was beyond the range of Jebb's observation, and there were no lengths they would not have gone, not only to destroy liberty, but to bring its advocates to destruction.

CHAPTER III.

THE preceding pages were intended to shew the vast influence over the mind of the nation, and its rulers, which the volunteer association at one period exerted; the failure of the only measure effected by it, namely, the independence of the Irish parliament; and the necessity for reform, more than ever felt at the time of its suppression. The society of the United Irishmen was formed with a view of accomplishing those objects which it had failed to carry into effect. The written and spoken sentiments of the leaders of the opposition of that period, and the proceedings of the various popular clubs from 1778 to 1795, had a powerful influence on the public mind. To this influence, fanned by the breath of Pitt, and kindled into flame by the eloquence of the reformers of that day, the leaders of the United Irishmen owed the early impressions they received of the rotten state of the representation, and the hopelessness of every attempt in Parliament for its restoration.

Independently of the example of France, which, at revolutionary periods, has always exerted a great influence over the popular mind in Great Britain, the question of reform began deeply to engage public attention in that country; and the hostility of Mr. Pitt, who now hated that question and its advocates with all the rancour of an apostate, tended to exasperate the public, and call forth the various clubs, which gave vent to the public discontent. In Ireland, the importance of the question of reform was enhanced, by the great dangers apprehended for the national independence, and the slow and stealthy, but steady progress of "the creeping and incipient Union," in every measure of the British minister in reference to Ireland.

The question that especially disclosed the views of the British minister with respect to the final nature of the settlement of the subject of Irish independence, was that which goes under the name of the Irish Propositions, and which, only three years after the period of the supposed settlement of that question, left no doubt on the minds of the people of Ireland, that the British government meant not to maintain the compact into which they had entered.

The eleven propositions were introduced into the Irish parliament by Mr. Orde, on the 7th February, 1785, and on the 22nd February, by Mr. Pitt in England. He concluded his speech with bringing forward a general resolution declaring " that it was highly important to the general interests of the empire, that the commercial intercourse between Great Britain and Ireland should be finally adjusted, and engaging that Ireland should be admitted to a permanent and irrevocable participation of the com-

mercial advantages of this country, when her Parliament should permanently and irrevocably secure
an aid out of the surplus of the hereditary revenue
of that kingdom towards defraying the expense of
protecting the empire in time of peace."

In a subsequent debate, Mr. Pitt declared " that
among all the objects of his political life, this was,
in his opinion, the most important in which he had
ever engaged, nor did he imagine he should ever
meet another that could call forth all his public
feelings, and rouse every exertion of his heart, in
so forcible a manner as the present had done. In
the progress of this measure the house was astonished
with an addition of sixteen new propositions to the
original eleven: they were pretended by Mr. Pitt to
be explanatory, but were wholly distinct, irrelevant
and contradictory to the first. It was evident to the
whole of the house, that the measure was an insiduous plan to regain the dependence of the Irish parliament. Mr. Sheridan said, that "Ireland, newly
escaped from harsh trammels and severe discipline,
was treated like a high mettled-horse, hard to catch;
and the Irish secretary was sent back to the field to
soothe and coax him, with a sieve of provender in
one hand and a bridle in the other." Fox was so
astonished at the conduct of Mr. Pitt on this occasion, that he declared " in the personal and political
character of the Chancellor of the Exchequer, there
were many qualities and habits which had often surprised him, and which he believed confounded the
speculation of every man who had much considered
or analyzed his disposition. But his conduct on that

night had reduced all that was unaccountable, incoherent and contradictory in his character, in times past, to a mere nothing. He shone out in a new light, surpassing even himself, and leaving his hearers wrapt in amazement, uncertain whether most to wonder at the extraordinary speech they had heard, or the frontless confidence with which that speech had been delivered."

He accused him, from the first moment the system had been proposed, of one continued course of "tricks, subterfuges and tergiversations, uniform alone in contradiction and inconsistencies." "That he had played a double game with England and a double game with Ireland, and sought to juggle both nations, by a train of unparalleled subtlety." He concluded by saying, " *he would not barter English commerce for Irish slavery.*"

The propositions were sent up to the House of Lords, here it was curious to see the question treated, not as a question of commerce, but as a proposal for a future Union. The Lords saw through the insidious project, and it was openly canvassed. Lord Lansdowne treated "the idea of an Union as a thing that was impracticable. High-minded and jealous as were the people of Ireland, we must first learn whether they will consent to give up their distinct empire, their parliament, and all the honours which belonged to them." In the Irish parliament the measures were no less freely canvassed, and the debate terminated in the rejection of the propositions, an offence which Pitt never forgot or forgave to Ireland.

The conduct of the Irish parliament in reference to the regency question, tended a good deal to precipitate events, and to render the course on which the English minister had already determined, one to be pursued more speedily and recklessly than it might otherwise have been attempted. On this subject two motions were made in the Irish Commons—one by Grattan, the other by Mr. Conolly. By the first, the royal incapacity was declared, and by the second, it was proposed to present an address to the Prince of Wales, requesting him to take upon himself the government, with its various powers, jurisdictions, and prerogatives. This motion was opposed by Mr. Fitzgibbon : he said—" The fact was, that the government of Ireland, under its present constitution, could never go on, unless they followed Great Britain implicitly in all regulations of imperial policy."—" And he would predict, that such unadvised rashness must ultimately lead to a legislative union with England, a measure which he deprecated, but which was more surely prepared by such violence, than if all the sluices of corruption were opened together, and poured in one overwhelming torrent upon the country's representatives." Both motions, however, were carried in the Commons, and likewise in the House of Lords. The viceroy refused to transmit their address. Lord Clare must have forgotten his deprecation of the Union, when, five years subsequently, he declared in his speech in favour of the Union, that for the last six or seven years, he had been pressing this measure on the attention of the British minister.

There can be no question that Pitt's defeat in
Ireland, on the great questions of the commercial
propositions, and the opposition to his views on the
Regency question, had exasperated the British minister against Ireland : in the words of the editor
of the Annual Register for 1790—" The defeat of
his commercial propositions, in the year 1785, had
left an impression of resentment against the nation
upon the mind of the minister." In 1787, De
Lolme, the author of the work " on the Constitution
of England," published " an essay," containing a
few strictures on the union of Scotland with England,
and on the situation of Ireland. The object of the
work is to recommend an incorporating Union be-
between Great Britain and Ireland.

In the same year, a Mr. Williams published a
pamphlet, entitled " An Union of England and Ireland proved to be practicable, and equally beneficial
to both Kingdoms."

The question of the Union was cautiously mooted
in 1793, as will be seen by the debate on the bill
for " prevention of traitorous correspondence with
the enemy." Mr. Fox said that this bill necessarily
included the people of Ireland, who were certainly
the subjects of the King; and consequently, it went
to legislate for Ireland, by making that treason in
an Irishman, by an English act of Parliament, which
was not treason by an Irish act." Mr. Pitt said
—" He felt this subject to be delicate, but he thought
he might venture to go so far as to say, that if England made an act, treason in all His Majesty's subjects, which act was not such by any law of Ireland;
if such act was done in Ireland by an Irishman, who

should afterwards come into England, he might be tried and executed for it;" and *vice versâ* with an Englishman in Ireland.

Mr. Fox called this the most extravagant doctrine he had ever heard.

Several members spoke upon the case, when applied to Ireland, and lamented that so delicate a subject should have been discussed.

The Annual Register, in 1790, plainly stated the views entertained in England of the independence of the Irish parliament:—" To whatever independence," says the editor, " Ireland may advance her claim, she is, in reality, nothing more than the province and servant of England. She is not the ally of the British government, but, on the contrary, acknowledges our king for her sovereign; that is, if we take into account the nature of the English constitution, acknowledges her dignities, her trusts, and her revenues, to be in the gift of an administration that depends on the parliament of Great Britain: she may, in a few cases, or in some emphatical and singular instance, assert her prerogative, and pursue her own interests in preference to ours; but the daily routine of her affairs, and the ordinary course of her administration, will be modelled in conformity to the interests, the prejudices, and the jealousies, of the country that is the seat of empire. She will not afford a theatre that will appear wide enough for the ardour of patriotism, or the excursiveness of ambition."—*An. Register*, 1790, *p.* 33.

In England, the democratic clubs began to be formed in 1780, and the greater number of them were suffered to subside without any prosecution. They again revived in 1794, and it was determined to put down democracy and the advocacy of parliamentary reform, by bringing the reformers to trial as traitors. In 1792, Pitt pledged himself that a traitorous " conspiracy did actually exist;" and a most insidious attempt to involve the opposition members in it was made, but quashed by the spirited conduct of some of them on that occasion.

In 1794, Pitt took up his pledge of the conspiracy of 1792. One of the reports on those societies states that the number of conspirators amounted to 20,000 persons. The arms found for them consisted of eighteen muskets, ten battle-axes, and twenty rough blades, and the general fund for the insurrection amounted to £9 sterling. Mr. Pitt, on bringing the conduct of these clubs before Parliament, depicted this horrible conspiracy in the most alarming colours—" that arms had not only been actually procured, but distributed by these societies," as the report states; and " that a conspiracy so formidable had never yet existed." The twelve honest men on their oaths, at the trials of these conspirators a short time subsequently, virtually decided that no such conspiracy existed. In the beginning of 1793, the ministerial prints, and even ministers themselves, made allusions, on various occasions, to plots and conspiracies, " the obvious intent of which was, indirectly to implicate the Whig members in the obnoxious charge," (see *Annual Register*, 1793). Under the auspices of government, a society had been formed, generally known under the name of Mr.

Reeve's Association, to procure information against seditious societies, and secret intelligence, which might serve to bring persons of suspected loyalty before the proper tribunal. In Plowden's " History of the Last Twenty Months" (p. 225) he remarks: " the spirit of espionage and information first engendered by the proclamation, and since openly fostered by Mr. Reeve's association, and certainly not discountenanced by government, had now grown into such strength, as to produce consequences of the most alarming nature. The agitated minds of the public were daily more and more inflamed, by the most terrifying accounts of domestic insurrections, and deep-laid plans to destroy the constitution. The dwindled phalanx of opposition was so openly, so grossly, and so confidently abused and calumniated, that, to many, their very names were synonimous with the term of traitor and enemy, even in the very houses of parliament; prejudices, alarms, and fears, had operated upon many, a conviction that to disapprove of the war against France, was treason to England; that to enquire into the grounds of public measures, had almost ceased to be the duty of a senator; and to divide with opposition, was little short of rallying under the standard of rebellion."

If the people pushed their efforts for reform to the length of resistance to authority, they were told by the Duke of Norfolk, in 1776, that " the doctrine of resistance was a principle of the constitution." Lord Lauderdale said, that " times and circumstances might be such as to make resistance become a duty." Lord Erskine, on the same occasion, in his place in parliament, declared—" He would say again and again, it was the right of the people to resist that government which exercised tyranny." Mr. Pitt, in 1782, asserted, that " we lost America by the corruption of an unreformed parliament, and we should never have a wise and honourable administration, be freed from the evils of unnecessary wars, nor the fatal effects of the funding system, till a radical reform was obtained." The Duke of Richmond's plan of reform embraced universal suffrage and annual parliaments; this plan he proposed to Colonel Sharman, at the head of an army in military array, namely, the Volunteers of Ireland. His Grace distinctly declared, that " he had no hopes of reform from the House of Commons—that reform must come from the people themselves." Burke said, that " no remedy for the distemper of parliament could be expected to be begun in parliament;" that " the value, spirit, and essence of the House of Commons, consists in its being the express image of the feelings of the nation:" and elsewhere—" by this want of sympathy with the people, they would cease to be a House of Commons." Mr. Pitt again, in 1785, in one of his last speeches in favour of reform, when he declared that, " without a parliamentary reform, the liberty of the nation could not be preserved." Fitzgibbon (afterwards Lord Clare), in 1782, said, in his place in parliament, that " as the nation was then committed to obtain a restoration of their rights, it behoved every man to stand firm." It would be tedious to adduce further instances of the mode in which the people's passions were inflamed, their hopes in the efficacy of legitimate means for the reformation of abuses dispelled, and their apprehensions of resistance removed, by constantly pointing it out as the only remedy for the evils of the nation.

"William Pitt of 1782," said Mr. Grey, "the reformer of that day, was William Pitt the prosecutor and persecutor of reformers in 1794. He, who thought fit to inflame the passions of the people, and to instigate them to contempt for the House of Commons, at that time,—now would not suffer the people to judge of their own dearest rights and interests, and persecuted, with the real bitterness of an apostate, his own partner in the question of parliamentary reform."

The 7th of May, 1782, Pitt made his first motion in furtherance of reform, for a committee of enquiry which was lost by twenty votes. He renewed the motion in 1783, and it was lost by forty-four votes. In 1785, he brought forward a specific plan of reform for adoption, and it was lost by thirty-four votes. A part of his first plan was, the application of a million of money to the purchase of the rotten boroughs. In 1794 he had thrown off the domino of a reformer; he declared on oath, at the trial of John Horne Tooke, that he recollected no particulars of the proceedings, at a meeting of the reformers of signal interest, which he attended the 16th May, 1782. He could not tell if Tooke was present; he could not say if delegates from cities and counties attended, but he believed not; but, on cross-examination, he admitted some of them might be deputies. One of the charges, be it remembered, against Tooke, was that of attending meetings where the members were delegated by other bodies. Major Cartwright, in his " Constitutional Defence of England," speaking of Pitt's speech on the 7th of May, 1782, says: " These very words were made the subject of a well-known resolution of the leading friends to a reform, assembled at the Thatched House very soon after the speech was delivered ; the original draft of that resolution, in 1791 or 1792, was in the possession of the author of this book, and shewn by him to the gentlemen present at a meeting of 'the Friends of the People,' with corrections in Mr. Pitt's own handwriting."

At the sale of the library of the late Mr. Hamilton Rowan, I happened to purchase, among other books, a volume of political tracts for the year 1793, in which I find the identical proceedings alluded to by Cartwright, at the meeting of reformers on the 16th of May, 1782, and a copy of the resolutions ordered to be printed and circulated by the society. It is in the following terms :—

" *Thatched House Tavern*, 16*th May*, 1782.

" At a numerous and respectable meeting of members of parliament, friendly to a constitutional reformation, *and the members of several committees of counties and cities :*

" Present,—The Duke of Richmond, Lord Surrey, Lord Mahon, the Lord Mayor, Sir Watkin Lewes, Mr. Duncombe, Sir C. Wray, Mr. B. Holles, Mr.

Withers, the Hon. William Pitt, Rev. Mr. Wyvill, Major Cartwright, Mr. John Horne Tooke, Alderman Wilkes, Doctor Jebb, Mr. Churchill, Mr. Frost, &c. &c. &c.

" Resolved unanimously,—That the motion of the Hon. William Pitt, for the appointment of a committee of the House of Commons, to enquire into the state of the representation of the people of Great Britain, and to report the same to the House, and also what steps it might be necessary to take, having been deferred by a motion for the order of the day, it has become indispensably necessary that application should be made to parliament, by petitions from the collective body of the people, in all their respective districts, requesting a substantial reformation of the Commons' House of Parliament.

" Resolved unanimously,—That the meeting, considering that a general application to the collective body of the House of Commons cannot be made before the close of the present session, is of opinion, that the sense of the people *should be taken at such times as may be convenient during the summer, in order to lay their several petitions before Parliament early in the next session, when these proposals for a parliamentary reformation (without which, neither the liberty of the nation can be preserved, nor the permanence of any virtuous administration be secure) may receive that ample and mature discussion which so momentous a question demands."*

Now the document, corrected by Pitt himself, collated with the evidence given by him at the trial of John Horne Tooke, on the matters referred to in it, shews the most extraordinary forgetfulness of important facts it is possible to conceive. On his examination by Tooke, he stated he was present at the meeting, in May, 1782, at the Thatched House Tavern. *"He could not recollect with certainty, but rather thought the prisoner was present.* That it was recommended to obtain the sense of the people on the question of parliamentary reform."

Quest.—" Was it recommended to obtain that sense by parishes and districts?"

Ans.—" I have no particular recollection as to that point : I remember it was agreed by the meeting, to recommend to the people during the summer to petition parliament."

Quest. by the Attorney-General.—" Was it, or was it not, a convention of delegates from different bodies?"

Ans.—" I do not, at this distance of time, remember how it was composed. *I did not conceive that the members were authorized to act for any particular body, but that each was acting for himself, and in his own individual capacity."*

On cross-examination by Mr. Erskine. Ans.—" I always understood that the members who composed that meeting were acting for themselves; *I don't know, however, but that some of them might be deputed.* I must again repeat that, at this distance of time, I cannot exactly ascertain how the meeting was composed."

Mr. Pitt's memory seldom failed him as it did on this occasion, when he could not remember how that meeting was constituted, described in the very resolution corrected by himself, as " consisting of members of parliament, and of members of several committees of counties and cities;" and could not recollect John Horne Tooke having been present at that meeting, and having taken a part in its proceedings.

Mr. Pitt, in 1794, May 11th, brought forward his motion for leave to bring in a bill, "to empower His Majesty to secure and detain such persons as His Majesty shall suspect are conspiring against his person and government,"—chiefly levelled against the London Corresponding Society and the Constitutional Society.

Fox, in opposition to this bill, said—" if he were asked without-doors what was to be done ?—he would say, this was not now a question of morality or of duty, but of prudence. Acquiesce in the bill only as long as you are compelled to do so. It was a bill to destroy the constitution, and part of the system of an administration aiming at that end. No attempt of the Stuarts called for more opposition than the present bills, and extraordinary times demanded extraordinary declarations."—*Annual Register*, 1806.

The number of political clubs which sprung up at the end of Mr. Pitt's abandonment of the cause of reform, was considerable. The origin and object of some of the most important of these are deserving of notice.

The objects of these societies were similar to those of the " Society for Constitutional Information," whose origin was of an earlier date, and is attributed to a proposal of Major Cartwright, in 1778, to establish a "Society of Political Enquiry." This object was not accomplished; but its proposal laid the foundation of the "Society of Constitutional Information," which was formed in 1780.* Dr. Jebb, Major Cartwright, and Capel Lofft, were the founders of it. Among its distinguished members, we find the Earl of Derby; the late Duke of Norfolk, then Lord Surrey; the Duke of Richmond; Duke of Roxburgh; Earl of Selkirk; Lord Dacre; Lord Sempill; Lord Kinnaird; Sir John Sinclair; R. B. Sheridan; the Earl of Effingham; Dr. Price; Dr. Towers; Granville Sharp, &c.† Its well-known "Declaration of Rights" was drawn up by Major Cartwright; Sir William Jones said this document "ought to be written in letters of gold."

This society thanked Tom Paine for his first and second parts of the "Rights of Man;" they sent addresses of congratulation, on the French revolution, to the Jacobin Club and the Convention of France. In these they assert, that "revolutions will now become easy." Horne Tooke, as a member of the committee, addressed a letter to Petion, then mayor of Paris, stating that 4,000 *livres* were sent with it, to assist the French in defraying the expenses of the war against all tyrants, who might oppose the liberty of the French, without excepting any of them, even if it should be his own country.

On Tooke's trial, Major Cartwright deposed he had the honour to be called the father of "the

* Vide Life and Correspondence of Major Cartwright, vol. i. p 120.

† Ibid. vol. i. p. 135.

Society for Constitutional Information;" that the original declaration of the Society for Constitutional Information was signed by Mr. Pitt, Mr. Fox, Mr. Sheridan, &c. The chief justice asked Mr. Tooke if his signature was to the declaration?—to which Mr. Tooke answered, "God forbid! my lord, that I should ever have signed any thing so criminal."

The society called the "Friends of the People," was established in 1792. The principal members were Charles Grey, the Earl of Lauderdale, Philip Francis, James Macintosh, Lord Kinnaird, the Hon. Thomas Erskine, G. Tierney, Esq., R. B. Sheridan, W. H. Lambton, John Cartwright, S. Whitbread, jun., Lord J. Russell, *Lord Edward Fitzgerald*, &c: &c. At the first meeting, W. H. Lambton, in the chair, 26th April, 1792, it was resolved unanimously,—

" That a motion be made in the House of Commons, at an early period in the next session of parliament, introducing a parliamentary reform.

" Resolved unanimously,—That Charles Grey, Esq. be requested to make, and the Hon. Thomas Erskine, to second the above motion.

"Signed, W. H. Lambton, *Chairman.*"

The next meeting was held, May 12, 1792, and the chairman of it was the Right Hon. Lord John Russell.

In 1795, this society suspended all proceedings on the subject of parliamentary reform, by public advertisement. Its grand object, however, was not lost sight of by "Charles Grey." For forty years his life was devoted to its accomplishment; and the forty years war with corruption, he lived to bring to a successful issue.

The Revolution Society of London, in commemoration of the Revolution of 1688, sprung up in 1789, Dr. Price and Earl Stanhope being its leading members. They conducted a correspondence with the National Assembly of France. Towers and Cooper were the president and secretary. Cooper was a man of great abilities, bold, upright and energetic; he fled to America, to avoid the fate of Muir and Palmer; he rose to distinction there, and died universally honoured and beloved in the 70th year of his age, the 22nd of October, 1829. Cooper and Watt were likewise members of the Manchester Constitutional Society, and in its name having presented an address in France, to the Jacobin Society, were attacked for so doing by Burke, in the House of Commons; and Cooper defended himself and his brother delegate, in one of the best written pamphlets of that time " A reply to Mr. Burke's invective." Watt was subsequently executed in Scotland, on a charge of treason.

The other societies of this period, of minor importance were, the " Friends of Universal Peace and the Rights of Man," originally established at Stockport. Of the " Westminster Committee of Reform," the first meeting took place in 1780 : its resolutions in favour of annual parliaments were signed by Fox. The society called the " Friends of the Liberty of the Press," was established in 1792: the declaration of this society was drawn up by Erskine. In this admirable paper, the system of espionage which had been recently adopted by Pitt, was denounced.

The language and writings of the members of these different clubs, were sufficiently strong to be taken, or mistaken, by many for sedition.

The "Society of United Englishmen," according to the account given of its ramifications in the "secret report" of 23rd January, 1799, had forty divisions formed in London, extended to Wales, Lancashire, and communicated with Ireland; had made great progress in Manchester, till checked by the arrest of its members in 1798; had eighty divisions there, and each consisted of not less than fifteen members. In the report it is stated to have been very active in its attempts to seduce the soldiery; and that it had tests, signs, and symbolic devices. The whole of the divisions were governed by a Committee, styled the National Committee of England, whose members were unknown to the rest of the Society, and was said to have corresponded with the executive of the United Irishmen.

" The London Corresponding Society" originated about 1792, its grand object, parliamentary reform, on the Duke of Richmond's plan. Chief Justice Eyre, in his charge on the trial of Tooke, said, " It is so composed, as by dividing and subdividing each division, as soon as it amounted to a certain number, sending off a new division so as to spread over the country, every other society, no matter how remote, it incorporates or affiliates, till it embraces an extent incalculable. It is undoubtedly a political monster," &c.

John Edwards, on Hardy's trial, deposed that this society was reading the address of Mr. Pitt and the

Duke of Richmond, when it was assailed by the police.

" A National Convention" was first suggested in a letter from Stockport, 7th December, 1792.

The Convention in Scotland was set on foot in 1793. Watt's plan for seizing the castle of Edinburgh was formed at this period. He had previously been employed as a secret informer by government, and dismissed; had subsequently joined Cooper in Paris, and presented an address to the Jacobins from the Manchester Society. In laying traps for treason, in the Scotch conspiracy, he got entangled in his own snares and was executed.

Mr. Muir, one of the faculty of advocates of Edinburgh, and the Rev. Fyshe Palmer, a dissenting clergyman of Dundee, a member of the University of Cambridge, were the two first reformers brought before the tribunal of justice on charges of sedition, trumped up on evidence of taking a part in the public proceedings of the associations at that time formed, for the purpose of obtaining a reform. Both these gentlemen, men eminent for their talents, highly respected in their several professions, and amiable in private life, were convicted and sentenced to transportation, sent· to the hulks chained; and worked in chains, previous to their departure for Botany Bay, with the common gang of convicts.

The formation of Trades' Unions appears to be pointed out in 1782, by Sir William Jones: in writing to Major Cartwright, in a postscript, he states, " It is my deliberate (though private) opinion, that the people of England will never be a people, in the

majestic sense of the word, unless 200,000 of the
civil state be ready before the 1st of November, to
take the field without rashness or disorder, at twenty-
four hours' notice."* This is a pretty plan manifestation of the power ascribed to the demonstration
of physical force in contradistinction to the employment of it, for I am persuaded the latter was never
contemplated by Sir William Jones. Fox said, " all
the proceedings of these societies went on the Duke
of Richmond's plan of reform."

But it is impossible not to perceive in the acts
and words of these bodies the spirit of republicanism pervading their proceedings, whether infused
by spies and informers or fanatics and " exaltados"
of their own party, it is hard to say : in all probability, by both.

The Manchester Constitutional Society was addressed by the Members of the Jacobin Club in
Paris, as " Generous Republicans."

One of the leading members of the Corresponding
Society was J. Frost. In 1793 he was convicted of
uttering seditious expressions, " I am for equality,
and no king," &c. Another member, Mr. John
Cook, for the words, " D—n the monarchy, I want
none," &c.

The sentiments of reformers of the upper classes
of society, a few years later were couched in language
better adapted for " ears polite," but certainly not
less indicative of the strong spirit of democracy.
The Duke of Norfolk, in 1798, presiding at a dinner

---

* See Life and Correspondence of Major Cartwright, p. 150.

at the Crown and Anchor, gave for a toast, " The sovereign majesty of the people," and for this act he was dismissed from the office of lord-lieutenant of the west riding of Yorkshire. Fox followed it up at the Whig Club, shortly after, by another sentiment of a similar character, " I will give you" (said he) " a toast, than which I think there cannot be a better according to the principles of this club—I mean, ' the Sovereignty of the People of Great Britain,' " and for this act he was dismissed from the Privy Council.

In Ireland, Lord Castlereagh imitated the example of Mr. Pitt. He entered on political life in the domino of a reformer, and aped the character, if not with all the tact, at least, with all the effrontery of his master. Of his early ardour for reform we have an account in Sampson's Memoirs: at page 43, he informs us " Robert Stewart (afterwards Lord Castlereagh) at the general election in 1790, set himself up for representative of the county of Down, against what was called the lordly interest; and in order to ingratiate himself with the popular party, took the following oath or test upon the hustings, as a solemn compact between him and his constituents—namely: " That he would, in and out of the House, with all his ability and influence, promote the success of a bill for amending the representation of the people; a bill for preventing pensioners from sitting in Parliament, or such place-men as cannot sit in the British House of Commons; a bill for limiting the number of placemen and pensioners, and the amount of pension; a bill for preventing revenue officers from voting at elections; a bill for rendering the servants of the Crown of Ireland, responsible for the expenditure of the public money; a bill to protect the personal safety of the subject against arbitrary and excessive bail, and against the power of attachment beyond the limits of the constitution."

In Ireland, at the same period, the formation of political clubs and societies kept pace with those in England. "The Northern Whig Club, at a meeting held in Belfast, the 16th April, 1790, Gowan Hamilton in the chair, passed a series of resolutions, the first of which was to the following effect : ' Resolved unanimously, That when an unmasked and shameless system of ministerial corruption, manifests an intention to sap the spirit, virtue, and independence of parliament, it is time for the people to look to themselves."

Among the original members of this society were Lords Charlemont, De Clifford, Moira, O'Neill, the Hon. Robert Stewart, Archibald H. Rowan, William Todd Jones, Colonel Sharman, Hon. E. Ward, Hon. H. Rowley, &c. &c. The toasts of the honourable members at their festive meetings comprised, " Our Sovereign Lord the People," &c. Vide " Teeling's Narrative."

" The Whig Club," was established in 1790, in Ireland, in imitation of that in England. " The frequent theme," says Plowden, " of panegyric to Mr. Grattan, and of invective to Mr. Fitzgibbon, the heads of most of the great families were members of it, and it contributed, not lightly, to give popularity to the leading objects of their institution, which it was the universal object of Mr. Pitt's system to counteract." Vide Plowden, vol. i. page 293.

Against Fitzgibbon's abuse of this club, Theobald Wolfe Tone was the first to publish a defence, which recommended him strongly to the Whigs, but they found him too warm an advocate, and he appears to have found them too little to his mind for their acquaintance to be of long duration.

The most memorable act of this club, was its petition to the King, adopted at a meeting of the society, 5th April, 1798, Mr. Grattan in the chair; in order to lay before his majesty the state of the country, and " a vindication of his people against the traduction of his ministers." The Catholic question was not permitted to be discussed in the club. Plowden, vol. i. page 324.

It may be here permitted for me to state, that Grattan entered parliament, and set out in public life, an opponent of the Catholic claims. He told the late Dr. Hussey, his most intimate friend, that he owed his change of opinion to the accidental perusal of Currie's " Civil Wars."

The Club, called the " Friends of the Constitution, Liberty and Peace," is described by Pollock in 1793, as a moderate Club, and its members as " most respectable and independent gentlemen."

The " Friends of Parliamentary Reform" in Belfast, in 1793, made a declaration of their principles, stating " that the enemies of reform would be answerable to God and their country for the consequences that would ensue, for all the crimes and calamities that would follow."

The "Volunteers" in 1793, intimated plainly the objects they had in view would be accomplished by force, if necessary. The lawyers' corps adopted the motto, ' Inter arma leges;' another corps took the name of National Guards, and placed on their banners the significant device of a harp without a crown. The Maghera corps, in 1792, made a declaration of their political sentiments, in which they stated that " they would not be deterred from their duty, until their country should taste the sweets of freedom, and they plucked the fruit from the tree of liberty." One of the last memorable acts of the Irish Whig Club, was the presentation to the crown, of a petition (known to be drawn up by Mr. Grattan,) to the King, setting forth the various acts of oppression and injustice on the part of several administrations in Ireland, from 1792 to 1798. In this admirable document, the recent rebellion is clearly and irrefragably shown to be the result of their measures: the dishonour brought on both Houses so early as 1792, by the scandalously open, and shamefully avowed sale of the Peerage, to procure seats in the Commons: the people's confidence in parliament destroyed: the unconstitutional nature of the act 33 George the Third, to prevent what was called, unlawful assemblies of the people, under pretence of preparing petitions, or other addresses to the crown or the parliament. the rigour of the gunpowder and convention bills in 1793: the persecutions of the people, on the part of the Orangemen in the north, sanctioned and protected in 1790, by a Bill of Indemnity: the partiality exhibited in the resolutions brought forward in the House of Commons by the attorney-general in that year, as a kind of supplement to his insurrection act, wherein all the disturbances of the four preceding years are ascribed to the Defenders, and not one syllable is mentioned of the atrocities of the Peep-of-day Boys, committed on the people, who having no protection to look to from the law, were compelled in self-defence, to resist their exterminators. The suspension of the Habeas Corpus Bill in 1797, the extreme severity of military government, Lord Carhampton's wholesale transportation of the people without trial or legal proof of guilt, General Lake's death-denouncing proclamation, the free quarters in the country, the proscription of the Catholics, the burning of their dwellings and their chapels; and lastly, in a country where female chastity was held in in the highest respect, the licentiousness of a military rabble, who, in the words of their commander-in-chief, at a later period, were "terrible to all except the enemy," are likewise referred to.

These are the topics which are treated in this able document, and it is impossible to bestow our attention on them, without coming to the conclusion that the parliament was corrupted, and the people were dragooned, for the especial purpose of promoting a rebellion, which was to prove so destructive to the energies of the country as to enable the British minister to accomplish his long-projected measure of the Union:

There was nothing in the project too wicked for

the old proverbial wisdom, of an inveterate hostility of opinion to the people of Ireland, which had represented them for ages as "Irascible and quellable, devoted to superstition, deaf to law, and hostile to property."

CHAPTER IV.

THE Peep-of-day Boys sprung up in the year 1784, in the county of Armagh. The members of this secret association were also known by the name of " Protestant Boys," and " Wreckers," and, finally, by that of " Orangemen." The character of their proceedings must have been particularly atrocious, when Sir Richard Musgrave felt the impossibility of palliating the exuberancy of their zeal in the cause of ascendancy. He says : " They visited the houses of their antagonists (victims, he ought to have said) at a very early hour in the morning, to search for arms; and it is most certain that, in doing so, they often committed the most wanton outrages—insulting their persons and breaking their furniture."

The ardour of the religious zeal of this privileged association, could be appeased by nothing short of the popish lands and tenements of the Roman Catholic peasantry, in all the neighbouring districts. In the fervour of their assumed enthusiasm for the diffusion of pure religion, they posted the following

* Vide Sir R. Musgrave's History, p. 54.

pithy controversial notice on the door of the benighted
Romanists—" To hell or Connaught :" now as they
were held to be going to the former region their own
way, in turning them out of their houses and homes,
it would seem that it was their lands and tenements,
and not the cause of true religion, about which these
champions of the church were interested. Lord Ches-
terfield speaks of Lady Palmer, a young Irish lady
of the old religion, who frequented the Castle in his
time, as " a very dangerous Papist." The possession
of beauty, like the occupation of land, on the part of
the Romanists, was no doubt of a very dangerous
tendency.

In the beginning of 1796, " it was generally believed (says Plowden) that 7,000 Catholics had been
forced or burned out of the county of Armagh ; and
that the ferocious banditti who had expelled them,
had been encouraged, connived at, and protected by
the government."* In the analysis of the report of
the committee on Orange Institutions, in the Edinburgh Review of January, 1836, the following account
is given of the proceedings of " the Peep-of-Day
Boys ;" and of their more systematic atrocities in
1795, under the newly-adopted name of Orangemen.

" The first Orange lodge was formed on the 21st
September, 1795, at the house of a man named
Sloan, in the obscure village of Loughgall. The
immediate cause of those disturbances in the north
that gave birth to Orangeism, was an attempt to
plant colonies of Protestants on the farms or tene-

* Plowden's History, v. ii. p. 377.

G

ments of Catholics, who had been forcibly ejected.
Numbers of them were seen wandering about the
country, hungry, half-naked, and infuriated. Mr.
Christie, a member of the society of Friends, who
appears to have passed sixty or seventy years on his
property as quietly as a man may, in the neighbourhood of such violent neighbours, gives a painful
account of the outrages then committed. He says
(5573), 'he heard sometimes of twelve or fourteen
catholic houses wrecked in a night, and some destroyed:' (5570) ' That this commenced in the
neighbourhood of Churchill, between Portadown and
Dungannon, and then it extended over nearly all the
northern counties. In the course of time, after the
Catholics were many of them driven from the county,
and had taken refuge in different parts of Ireland, I
understood they went to Connaught. Some years
after, when peace and quietness was in a measure
restored, some returned again, probably five or six
years afterwards. The property which they left was
transferred, in most instances, to Protestants : where
they had houses and gardens, and small farms of
land; it was generally handed over by the landlords
to Protestant tenants. That occurred within my
knowledge.' He further says: ' It continued for
two or three years, but was not quite so bad in 1796
and 1797 as it was earlier. After this wrecking, and
the Catholics were driven out, what was called ' The
Break of Day' party merged into Orangeism ; they
passed from the one to the other, and the gentlemen
in the county procured what they termed their
Orange warrants, to enable them to assemble legally,

as they termed it. The name dropped, and Orange-ism succeeded to Break-of-Day Men.' (5575).

" At first, the association was entirely confined to the lower orders; but it soon worked its way up-wards, and, so early as November, 1798, there appears a corrected report of the rules and regula-tions officially drawn up, and submitted to the Grand Lodge of Ireland, under the presidency of Thomas Verner, Esq. Grand Master; J. C. Beresford, Esq., Grand Secretary, and others. The state of the country, soon after the formation of these societies, is faithfully described in an address, which the late Lord Gosford, as governor of Armagh, submitted to all the leading magistrates of the county. His Lordship stated, that he had called them together to submit a plan to their consideration, for checking the enormities which disgraced the county. He then proceeds: ' It is no secret that a persecution, accompanied with all the circumstances of ferocious cruelty which have, in all ages, distinguished that dreadful calamity, is now raging in this country. Neither age, nor even acknowledged innocence, as to the late disturbances, is sufficient to excite mercy —much less afford protection. The only crime which the wretched objects of this merciless perse-cution are charged with, is a crime of easy proof—it is simply a profession of the Roman Catholic faith. A lawless banditti have constituted themselves judges of this species of delinquency, and the sentence they pronounce is equally concise and terrible: it is no-thing less than a confiscation of all property, and

painful, and surely unnecessary, to detail the horrors
that attended the execution of so wide and tremendous a proscription, which certainly exceeds, in the
comparative number of those it consigns to ruin and
misery, every example that ancient and modern
history can afford: for where have we heard, or
in what history of human cruelties have we read,
of more than half the inhabitants of a populous
country deprived, at one blow, of the means, as well
as the fruits of their industry, and driven, in the
midst of an inclement winter, to seek a shelter for
themselves and their hapless families where chance
may guide them? This is no exaggerated picture of
the horrid scenes now acting in this country; yet
surely it is sufficient to awaken sentiments of indignation and compassion in the coldest heart. Those
horrors are now acting, and acting with impunity.
The spirit of impartial justice (without which, law is
nothing better than tyranny) has for a time disappeared in this country; and the supineness of the
magistracy is a topic of conversation in every corner
of this kingdom.'—*Evidence*, 3251.

" The resolutions moved by his Lordship were
adopted, and signed by all the leading magistrates,
who thus bore undeniable testimony to the persecution the Catholics were then suffering in that
county, which was the cradle, and has ever been the
hot-bed, of Orangeism.

" We have carefully examined the documents
submitted by the Orange society to the committee,
respecting the objects of their institution, the motives
of its members, and the qualifications necessary for

candidates, and nothing apparently can be more humane, tolerant, moral, and praiseworthy. Certain doubtful features occasionally, however, do peep through this coating of amiable professions. For instance, this society enforced on its members an oath of qualified allegiance :—' I, A. B. do solemnly swear,' &c. 'that I will, to the utmost of my power, support and defend' the King and his heirs, ' so long as he or they support the Protestant Ascendancy.' Another suspicious article (No. 5) declares—" We are not to carry away money, goods, or any thing, from any person whatever, except arms and ammunition, and those only from an enemy'—enemy no doubt meaning Catholic."

So much for the report, with regard to the objects of this society, and the obligations of its oaths, &c.

Now the oath above referred to is sufficiently objectionable, on the score of the conditional allegiance it embodies; but the original oath or purple test of this society, was not produced by the officers of this society, on the enquiry entered into by the committee in 1835,—but the existence of this diabolical test was given in evidence before the secret committee of 1798, by Mr. Arthur O'Connor, and the knowledge of it admitted by the committee on that occasion, when O'Connor's statement was answered by one of the members belonging to the administration, in these words : " Government had nothing to do with the Orange society, nor with their oath of extermination."

In the memoir of the examination of Messrs.

themselves, O'Connor's answer is given to this observation :—" You, my Lord Castlereagh, from the
station you fill, must be sensible that the executive
of any country has it in its power to collect a vast
mass of information, and you must know, from the
secret nature of the Union, that the executive must
have the most minute information of every act of
the Irish government. As one of the executive (of
the United Irishmen), it came to my knowledge
that considerable sums of money were expended,
throughout the country, in endeavouring to extend
the Orange system, and that the Orange oath of
extermination was administered ; when these facts
are coupled, not only with the general impunity
which has been uniformly extended to all the acts of
this diabolical association, but the marked encouragement its members have received from government, I find it impossible to exculpate the government from being the parent and protector of these
societies."*

The fact of the protection of " the Peep-of-Day
Boys," or the Orangemen, on the part of the government, admits of no doubt. When the insurrection act and the convention bill were introduced,
the excesses of the peasantry, whom they had goaded
into resistance, were denounced by the viceroy and
the legal officers of the government, but not the
slightest allusion was made to the outrages of the
exterminators of Armagh ; nay, bills of indemnity
were passed, to protect their leaders and magisterial

* Vide Memoir of the Examination of Messrs. O'Connor, Emmett, M'Nevin, &c.—(Published by the State Prisoners.)

accomplices from all legal proceedings on the part
of their victims. As to the effect of these societies
in promoting the views of the United Irishmen, it is
clearly admitted by the members of the executive of
the society of the United Irishmen, that the persecution of the people in Armagh, the protection of
the exterminators, and the enactment of sanguinary
laws, and especially of the insurrection and indemnity acts, had not only filled the ranks of their
society, but led the executive to the conclusion, that
the government had forfeited all claims to obedience,
and was to be resisted. " No alliance whatever was
previously formed," says O'Connor, " between the
Union and France"—namely, before the middle of
1796. The same answer is given by Emmett. So
much for the power given to the United Irishmen, by
the persecution of the people on the part of the Orangemen permitted by the government; and as for the immediate causes of the outbreak of the subsequent
and consequent rebellion, we can only refer to the
question put by the Lord Chancellor—" Pray, Mr.
Emmett, what caused the late rebellion?" and to
the reply to it of Emmett—" The free quarters, the
house-burnings, the tortures and the military executions, in the counties of Kildare, Carlow, and
Wicklow."* In fact, persecution and disaffection
followed in the order of cause and effect; the
turbulence of the Defenders can only be looked on
as the consequence of the Orange depredations, and
the excesses of both parties the plea for the attempt

* Vide " Memoir of Examination," &c.

of uniting the people, of all religious denominations, in one great national society.

Sir Jonah Barrington considers the idea of Orange societies arose from the association of the aldermen of Skinners' Alley; the latter owed its origin to the restoration of the old corporate body to their former power and privileges, at the departure of James the Second. Their meetings were chiefly for the indulgence of that kind of Cherokee festivity, which is indicative of sanguinary struggles or successful onslaughts, past or expected. Their grand festival was on the 1st of July, the anniversary of the Battle of the Boyne, on which occasion the charter-toast was drunk by every member on his bare knees. At the time of Sir Jonah's initiation, "his friend Dr. Patrick Duigenan was the Grand Master." The *standing* dish, at the Skinners'-alley dinners, was sheep's trotters, in delicate allusion to King James's last use of his lower extremities in Ireland; and the cloth being removed, the charter-toast, the antiquity of which was of so ancient a date as the year 1689, was pronounced by the Grand Master on his bare joints to the kneeling assemblage, in the following words: " The glorious, pious, and immortal memory of the great and good King William, not forgetting Oliver Cromwell, who assisted in redeeming us from popery, slavery, arbitrary power, brass money, and wooden shoes; &c. &c. &c." The concluding part of this loyal toast is a tissue of vulgar indecencies, and impious imprecations on " priests, bishops, deacons," or any other of the fraternity of the clergy who refuse this toast, consigning their members to the operation of red-hot harrows, and their mangled carcases to the lower regions. In detailing the particulars of these brutal and bacchanalian proceedings, Sir Jonah says, "it may be amusing to describe them"—and then he denominates the association as "a very curious, but most loyal society;" and that their favourite toast was afterwards adopted by the Orange societies, and was still considered the charter-toast of them all."* Sir Jonah's notions of mirth and loyalty were, no doubt, in accordance with those of the circle in which he moved. Indeed, he prefaces this account of the exuberance of zeal of the Skinners'-alley aldermen, with a declaration of his own political sentiments; as being, though not an ultra, one in whom loyalty absorbed almost every other consideration.

Few of the Orangemen in the north were probably actuated by the motives to which their proceedings are commonly attributed. It is generally supposed that they were animated by a blind, indiscriminate fury against the people, solely on account of their religion. This is not a fair statement, and whoever enquires into the history of these times will find it is not true. These men were impelled, as their descendants are, by a simple desire to get possession of property belonging to people who had not the power to protect it, and to give their rapacity the colour of a zeal for the interests of their own religion.

It is doing the Ascendency party a great injustice

to suppose that their animosity to their Roman Catholic countrymen arose from a spirit of fanaticism,
or of mistaken enthusiasm in their religious sentiments.   The plan of converting souls by converting
the soil of the old inhabitants of a country to the use
of the new settler, is of an ancient date.   With this
party the matter is one of money and of property
in land, which wears the outward garb of a religious
question.

The Puritans who sought a refuge in America,
when they found the most fertile portion of Massa-
chusetts in the possession of the Indians, did not
think of dispossessing the rightful owners of the
broad lands they coveted, without giving the sancti-
monious air of a religious proceeding to their contemplated spoliation.

They convened a meeting, which was opened with
all due solemnity, and the following resolutions are
said to have been passed unanimously :—

Resolved,—That the earth is the Lord's, and the
fullness thereof.

Resolved,—That the Lord hath given the earth as
an inheritance unto his Saints.

Resolved,—That we are the Saints.

How far the ludicrous may be found herein to
mingle with the historical data, it is hard to say, but
the spirit in which similar conclusions are arrived
at in "the Island—proverbially—of Saints," it is
impossible not to recognize in the above-mentioned
theological and political resolutions.   The zeal of
Orangeism in behalf of religion cannot impose on a
close observer.   The penal code was framed for the

protection of confiscated property ; and the assumed hostility to the religion of the people who were dispossessed, was only a practice in accordance with the purport and pretence of the iniquitous statutes, which had already legalized three general confiscations within a period of 200 years. This legalized system of rapine and proscription has been productive of evils which still are felt, and those who, along with the lands of the proscribed people, obtained all the political privileges that were thought essential to the security of their new possessions, would have been more just than the generality of mankind, if, having power to protect the spoils they had obtained, or were encouraged to expect, they had not abused their privileges, and did not see in every extension of the people's liberties, another encroachment on the limits, now daily narrowing, of their power, property, and political pre-eminence.

The Defenders had their origin in the year 1785, but they were hardly known as a distinct and formidable body till the year 1792 ; their first object, as their name imports, was self-protection, when the exterminating system was carried into effect by the Ascendency party in the north. But as their strength increased, their views became more political, and resistance to aggression led them to offensive measures against their enemies, and the government which protected the latter.

After the battle of " the Diamond" terminated in their defeat, the success of their conquerors was followed up by the rigorous measures of the military and magisterial authorities ; the jails were filled with these unfortunate people, and about 1300 of them were taken from the prisons by Lord Carhampton, without any legal process or form of trial, and sent on board the ships of war or transport vessels.

This was the first display of "the vigour beyond the law" which had been openly announced in parliament, and when carried into effect was protected there by an act of indemnity.

Analagous bills to the "Treacherous Correspondence Bill," passed in Ireland in 1793, but one was of a nature which would not have been tolerated in England, namely, to prevent persons meeting *under pretence* of preparing or presenting petitions, &c. This act was reprobated in England no less than in Ireland.

A system of agrarian outrage had been dragging on a protracted existence in Munster from the period of the suppression of the "White Boy" disturbances, and had even spread into the northern counties, under the name of "Oak Boys," and "Hearts of Steel Boys," but they had been subdued by the military long before the exterminating proceedings of the "Peep-of-day Boys" had come into operation. Their system however had been revived in Munster by a new set of disturbers called "Right Boys," after the supposed leader, Captain Right.

Mr. Fitzgibbon's bill for preventing these tumultuous assemblages, contained a clause directing the magistrates to demolish the Roman Catholic chapels in which any of these associations should have been formed or countenanced, which Mr. Grattan stigmatized as a legal sanction to sacrilege, and Mr. Secretary Orde declined to concur in such an enactment, and prevailed on his friend to withdraw it. Fitz-gibbon was only desirous, whether in the exter-mination of the people or the demolition of their chapels, of carrying into effect the doctrine which had been laid down by the judicial authorities in 1759, on the trial of Mr. Saul, a Catholic merchant in Dublin, namely, "that the laws did not presume a papist to exist in the kingdom, nor could they exist in it without the connivance of government."*

The Right Boys, however, had been likewise put down before the wrecking system began in Armagh. The former society was a feeble remnant of the White Boy Association, which had its origin in 1759, in the south of Ireland. The White Boys took their name from the frocks or shirts they were in the habit of wearing when they assembled; and armed with scythes, clubs, and swords, they sallied forth at night and committed many acts of agrarian outrage. The wrongs they professed to redress, were those con-nected with the holding of lands on exorbitant terms, the inclosing of waste lands, the extortion of tythe-proctors, &c. Various laws were enacted to repress their excesses, all of which were of an agrarian character, wild, daring, ill-concerted, sometimes cruel, seldom premeditated, and, eventually, easily put down. The cause of these excesses is justly ascribed, by Plowden, to the agricultural distress which pre-vailed in the whole of the South of Ireland, conse-quent upon the practice generally adopted at this time, of converting the large farms into grazing

* See Plowden's History, vol. ii. p. 270.

lands, which were set to wealthy monopolists, who turned the wretched peasantry adrift. At the close of 1762, Lord Halifax congratulated parliament on the suppression of the insurrection of the White Boys.

In all these confederacies of the people, arising from agricultural distress—no matter how grinding the oppression of the authorities, how cruel the exactions of their landlords, how galling the exorbitant demands and proceedings of the tythe proctors—there was no available sympathy for them either amongst the aristocracy or the squirearchy of the land.

The association of the Defenders, about 1782, had changed its character, from that of a society engaged in religious feuds, to one actuated by political motives, and the change was effected by the endeavours of the United Irishmen to reconcile the ultra Protestants and Catholics. Their views, however, continued so indistinct, that Messrs. Emmett and M'Nevin could form no other opinion of their objects, except that a general notion prevailed amongst them that " something ought to be done for Ireland." They had no persons in their body of the upper or even middling class in life. The only man known among them above the condition of a labourer, was a schoolmaster in Naas, of the name of Laurence O'Connor, who was executed in 1796. This man met his fate with a fortitude which has endeared his memory to the lower orders of his countrymen; his defence of the people, rather than his own, from the slanderous charges of his prosecutors, proves him to have been a person of no less intrepidity than superior talents.

In the same year, Napper Tandy, on the part of the United Irishmen at Dublin, had an interview with the Defenders at Castlebellingham, in the county of Louth, when the oath of secrecy was administered to him. The object of Tandy was to ascertain their real objects, and (though the fact has not been avowed, it cannot be concealed from any persons inquiring into the matter) to turn the strength of the association into the channels of the " Union." One of the Defenders who was present when Tandy was sworn, lodged informations against him, and he was fortunate enough to effect his escape out of the kingdom. The Defenders gradually merged into the United Irishmen, and in a short time there was no distinction between them.

The Society of the United Irishmen was formed in Belfast in the month of October, 1791, by Theobald Wolfe Tone, a young barrister of much promise, then in his 28th year. A political club, composed of the liberal volunteers of that city, under the guidance of a secret committee, had been previously in existence, the leading members of which club were Neilson, Russell, Simms, Sinclair, M'Tier, M'Cabe, Digges, Bryson, Jordan, &c. Tone, in his Diary, says, he went down to Belfast on the 11th of October, 1791, by invitation of the members of this club, and " on the 12th did business *with the secret committee,* who are not known or suspected of co-operating, but who, in fact, direct the movements of Belfast." He at once set about remodelling certain resolutions of the United Irish. On the 18th of October, Tone speaks of the first regular meeting of the United

Irishmen which he attended in Belfast; twenty members present; the club consisting of thirty-six original members.

The declarations and resolutions of the Society of United Irishmen, drawn up, or modified, by Tone, and read at the first general meeting in October, 1791, in Belfast, stated, " the great measure essential to the prosperity and freedom of Ireland was *an equal representation of all the people of Ireland.*

To effect this object, the declaration states, " *The Society of United Irishmen has been formed,*" and the following resolutions were carried :—

" 1st. That the weight of English influence in the government of this country, is so great as to require a cordial union among all the people of Ireland, to maintain that balance which is essential to the preservation of our liberties and the extension of our commerce.

" 2nd. That the sole constitutional mode by which this influence can be opposed, is by a complete and radical reform of the representation of the people in parliament.

" 3rd. That no reform is just which does not include Irishmen of every religious persuasion."*

In the month of November, 1791, Tone, having returned to Dublin, consulted with Napper Tandy about the formation of another society like that of Belfast, in Dublin; and, in a few weeks, the Society of United Irishmen was established in the capital.

The first chairman of the meetings in Dublin was the Hon. Simon Butler, and the first secretary, James

* Vide Life of T. W. Tone. Washington edition, vol. 1.

Napper Tandy. It is worthy of attention that both Tone and Tandy at this period were republicans, and yet the society they founded was formed expressly to obtain a reform in parliament and the abolition of the penal code. In fact, whatever their own views were with respect to republicanism, or separation, the great body of the original members looked to the achievement of reform alone ; and even Tone himself says, "at this time the establishment of a republic was not the immediate object of my speculations, my object was to secure the independence of my country under any form of government," &c. Tone states, "the club was scarcely formed before he lost all pretensions to anything like influence in their measures." That he "sunk into obscurity in the club, which, however, he had the satisfaction to see daily increasing in numbers and importance."

The first meeting of the Dublin Society of United Irishmen, took place at the Eagle Tavern, in Eustace Street, the 9th of November, 1791, the Hon. Simon Butler in the chair, James Napper Tandy, secretary. The declaration and resolutions of the Belfast society were adopted at that meeting, and a test was adopted, to be taken by every member on admission, to the following effect :—

" I, A. B., in the presence of God, do pledge myself to my country that I will use all my abilities and influence in the attainment of an impartial and adequate representation of the Irish nation in parliament; and as a means of absolute and immediate necessity in the establishment of this chief good of Ireland, I will endeavour, as much as lies in my ability, to forward a brotherhood of affection, an identity of interests, a communion of rights, and an union of power among Irishmen of all religious persuasions, without which every reform in parliament must be partial, not national, inadequate to the wants, delusive to the wishes, and insufficient for the freedom and happiness of this country."*

At the different meetings of the society in 1791 and 1792, the language used was bold, and sometimes imprudent, but at the close of the latter year, at a meeting of which William Drennan was chairman, and Archibald Hamilton Rowan, secretary; an address was prepared, in which a convention was proposed, and the object of the society was declared to be, " a national legislature, and its means an union of the people. The government is called on, if it has a sincere regard for the safety of the constitution, to coincide with the people in the speedy reform of its abuses, and not by an obstinate adherence to them to *drive the people into republicanism.*"

At a meeting of the society in February, 1793, the Hon. Simon Butler in the chair, Oliver Bond, secretary, a declaration was proposed and adopted by the meeting, pronouncing the proceedings of the Secret Committee of the House of Lords appointed to enquire into the recent disturbances, in compelling witnesses to answer interrogatories on oath, compromising themselves, and directed principally to the discovery of evidence in support of prosecutions already commenced, to be illegal. For this offence Messrs. Butler and Bond were brought to the Bar of

* Vide Tone's Life, vol. i. p 55.

the House of Lords; and on admitting the declaration to have been put from the chair and carried at the meeting in question, the judgment of the House was pronounced by the Lord Chancellor, each of the prisoners to be imprisoned for six months, and to pay a fine of £500 to the King.*

In December, 1792, at a meeting of the society, William Drennan in the chair, and A. H. Rowan, secretary, an address was determined on to the Volunteers of Ireland, intimating to them, as they "first took up arms to protect their country from foreign enemies, and from domestic enemies, for the same purposes it now becomes necessary that they should resume them." The following expressions, "Citizen soldiers, to arms! Take up the shield of freedom," were meant to induce the disbanded Volunteers to rally once more, and re-assemble in their different districts, and the nature of their views was plainly exhibited in the subsequent part of their declaration: "By liberty we never understood unlimited freedom, nor by equality, the levelling of property or the destruction of subordination." They state that they have nothing to depend on but on public opinion—"no power to terrify, no artifice to cajole, no funds to seduce:—in four words lies all our power—Universal Emancipation and Representative Legislature."

For distributing this address A. H. Rowan, in 1794, was prosecuted for a seditious libel, sentenced to two years imprisonment and a fine of £500.

It was at this celebrated trial that Curran made a speech never to be forgotten in Ireland, and parts of

* Vide Appendix, vol. ii.

which furnish specimens of oratory more widely diffused in England and America, and more frequently
cited, than any passages in the appeals of orators
dead or living.   One passage in that speech is better
remembered, and more generally admired, than any
separate portion of an address ever delivered at the
bar in either country; that wherein he refers to the
words included in the libel—" Universal Emancipation."—" I speak in the spirit of British law, which
makes liberty commensurate with and inseparable
from British soil ; which proclaims even to the
stranger and the sojourner, the moment he sets his
foot upon British earth, that the ground on which
he treads is holy, and consecrated by the genius of
Universal Emancipation.   No matter in what language his doom may have been pronounced, no
matter what complexion incompatible with freedom,
an Indian or an African sun may have burnt upon
him—no matter in what disastrous battle his liberty
may have been cloven down—no matter with what
solemnities he may have been devoted upon the altar
of Slavery—the first moment he touches the sacred soil of Britain, the altar and the god sink
together in the dust, his soul walks abroad in her
own majesty, his body swells beyond the measure of
his chains that burst from around him—and he stands
redeemed, regenerated, and disenthralled by the irresistible genius of *Universal Emancipation.*"

It is to be noted, that the seditious libel was uttered in the year 1792, and the prosecution did not
take place till the year 1794.   The postponement of
t he trial was attributed, not without justice, by Mr.

Rowan and his friends, to the new plan that had been devised of securing a conviction, in cases similar to the present, through the medium of packed juries, by the intervention of the hirelings of government, placed in the office of sheriffs. This matter it was found impossible to accomplish before the year 1794, when one Jenkins, and that Cimmerian zealot John Gifford, were thrust into the shrievalty, the latter having been sworn into his office the 1st of October, 1793. But this trial not only exhibited the adoption of the new jury-packing system—a darker feature was also presented, in the employment of wretches without character or credit, to act as witnesses.

On Rowan's trial, a disreputable and a worthless man, of the name of Lyster, was the principal witness against Rowan. His evidence of Rowan's having distributed the libellous paper was false; it was declared to be so by Rowan himself at the trial, and the able and enlightened editor of his autobiography, the Rev. Dr. Drummond, states, on unquestionable authority, that Rowan was not the man who distributed the libel on the occasion sworn to, but a person of the name of Willis, a skinner, formerly a member of the volunteer association.

It would be now useless to refer to this fact, but that it shews the influence which the recourse to packed juries, and the employment of perjured witnesses, had on the minds of the people, and especially of their leaders, at this period. So long as the fountains of justice were believed to be even moderately pure—so long as it was unknown that they were poisoned at their very source, there were some bounds to the popular discontent. The language of the liberals of that day, might be bold, violent, and intemperate—not more so, nay, not so much so, as the language used with impunity at political societies in the present day—but they still had privileges and advantages to lose by sedition, and the most valuable of all was the trial by jury, which had now, in public opinion, ceased to be a safeguard or a security to the people.

The Society of United Irishmen, on the 7th February, 1794, presented an address to Mr. Rowan, then undergoing the sentence of imprisonment in Newgate, in which, after expressing the obligations the country was under to him, for his bold assertion of its rights, and its sympathy with his sufferings in its cause, the society observed: " Although corruption has been leagued with falsehood, to misrepresent and vilify this society, we have reposed in honest confidence on the consoling reflection, that we should at all times find an impregnable barrier in ' the trial by jury,' wherein character and intention should be regarded as unerring guides to justice. But while we have been earnestly endeavouring to establish the constitutional rights of our country, we suddenly find ourselves at a loss for *this first and last stake of a free people;* for the trial by jury loses its whole value when the sheriff or the panel is under the influence of interest, prejudice, or delusion, and that battery which liberty and wisdom united to construct for the security of the people, is turned against them. However, in defiance of that system of proscription, which is no longer confined to a particular persuasion, but which visits with vengeance every effort in the cause of freedom, we trust you are assured of our inflexible determination to pursue the great object of our association—*an equal and impartial representation of the people in parliament,* an object from which no chance or change, no slander, no persecution, no oppression, shall deter us."

In 1794, the violence of the language, and the publicity with which the daring proceedings of the United Irishmen were carried on, brought the vengeance óf government on their society. On the 4th of May, their ordinary place of meeting, the Tailors' Hall in Back Lane, was attacked by the police, their meeting dispersed, and their papers seized.* The leaders had been successively prosecuted and imprisoned; many of the timid and more prudent part of the members seceded from the society; the more determined and indignant, and especially the republican portion of the body, remained, and, in 1795, gave a new character to the association, still called

* The Tailors' Hall in Back Lane had become the arena of liberal and democratic politics, and also of the agitation of the Roman Catholic question, as the old Tholsel had previously been of national and corporate struggles. The Tholsel, a part of the façade of which now only remains, was erected in 1683 ; it derived its name from the toll-stall, where the impost on goods received into the city was taken. It was situate in Nicholas-street, near Christchurch. In 1703, the city of Dublin gave a grand entertainment in the Tholsel to the Duke and Duchess of Ormond, when " the corporations marched through the city to the banquet, with their several pageants." Here the lord mayor, áldermen and commons, transacted their business, and the merchants met on 'change in a spacious hall in the upper part of the building. In 1779, a meeting was held in the

the " Society of United Irishmen." The original
test of the society was changed into an oath of secrecy and fidelity; its original objects—reform and
emancipation—were now merged in aims amounting
to revolution, and the establishment of a republican
government. These designs, however, were not
ostensibly set forth; for a great number of the
members, and even of the leaders, were not prepared
to travel beyond the Hounslow of reformation.
The proceedings of the society, however, ceased to
be of a public nature; the wording of its declaration
was so altered, as to embrace the views both of reformers and republicans, and the original explanation
of its grand aim and end—*the equal representation
of the people in parliament* — was now changed into
the phrase, " a full representation of all the people
of Ireland;" thus adding the word "all," and omit-
ting the word "parliament."

The civil organization of the society was likewise
modified; the arrangement was perfected of committees, called baronial, county, and provincial.

Tholsel, at which resolutions were passed " against the use of English
manufactures, till the grievances were redressed." James Napper
Tandy took the foremost part in the proceedings of this meeting "

The Tholsel, as the corporation vaxed more loyal, ceased to be
the Crown and Anchor of the popular party. The Tailors' Hall
was the first public place of rendezvous of the Roman Catholic
committee, and it became the theatre of the earliest performances
of the United Irishmen. From the meetings of both bodies it acquired the name of the Back-lane Parliament James Napper
Tandy, as " a patriot" and an alderman, figured for a time at both
places, but when " the aldermen of Skinners'-alley" quarrelled
with their democratic brother, the Back-lane Parliament became the
sole arena of Tandy's ground and lofty " patriotic tumblings "

The inferior societies originally were composed of thirty-six members: in the new organization, each association was limited to twelve, including a secretary and treasurer. The secretaries of five of these societies formed a lower baronial committee, and had the immediate direction of the five societies from which they had been taken. From each lower baronial committee, one member was delegated to an upper baronial committee, which had the superintendence and direction of all the lower baronial ones in the several counties.

In each of the four provinces there was a subordinate directory, composed of two or three members of the society delegated to a provincial committee, which had the general superintendence of the several committees of that province.

In the capital, the executive directory was composed of five persons, balloted for and elected by the provincial directories. The knowledge of the persons elected for the executive directory was confined to the secretaries of the provincial committees, and not reported to the electors; and the executive directory, thus composed, exercised the supreme and uncontrolled command of the whole body of the Union.

The orders of the executive were communicated to one member only of each provincial committee— and so on in succession to the secretary of each upper and lower baronial committee of the subordinate societies, by whom they eventually were given to the general body of the society. The plan was considered by the executive to be admirably

calculated to baffle detection. The key-note of the
new overture of their declaration and re-organization,
was evidently representation. The attraction of
such an extensive mechanism of election and delegation, for a people vainly struggling for the acquisition or extension of the elective franchise, no doubt
was the great inducement with the directory, for the
adoption of this complicated and widely-extending
system of organization.

But, in my humble judgment, this organization,
instead of being calculated to baffle detection, tended
directly to excite attention, to awaken suspicion, to
induce a false security, to keep treachery concealed
—in short, to lead to discovery. There was too
much of political economy—too little of knowledge
of human nature, and the foresight which is the
creature of it—manifested in the formation and
extension of these societies, and the means taken
to induce the masses to become members of them.
There was too much organizing in the directory—
too much marshalling of men on paper—too much
vapouring in the columns of the press, and the
Northern Star—too much barking, where and when
there was no power to do more—to lead to any
other result than that of exasperating opponents,
and of nurturing agents for the destruction of the
confiding party in the bosom of their own society.
Emmett was lamentably mistaken in his view of the
matchless fidelity of the members of the Union to
their cause. One man's infamous celebrity in the
society, as an informer, at this time was only known
to Emmett; but, in the lapse of years, the facts

which have transpired in relation to the question of
the continuance or discontinuance of pensions, and
the nature of the services for which they had been
granted, have brought the names of individuals connected with the society, whose fidelity to it was
considered by its leaders as beyond all suspicion,
into juxtaposition with those of Messrs. Reynolds
and Armstrong; and in this catalogue of treachery,
the names of persons are to be found, who were at
the same time the prominent partizans—nay, the
professional advocates—of the party committed in
this unfortunate struggle, and the secret agents and
paid servants of the government, employed as spies
on their own accomplices and companions. The
treason of these men to their comrades, no doubt
was serviceable to government—nay more, beneficial
to the country itself; but the traitors were despicable, even then, in the sight of their employers,
and cannot be otherwise now, in the eyes of their
successors. Every important proceeding of the
United Irishmen was known to government. Lord
Clare acknowledged, in a debate in the English
House of Lords in 1801, that "the United Irishmen
who negotiated with the Irish government, in 1798,
had disclosed nothing which the King's ministers were
not acquainted with before." Then why did they
suffer the conspiracy to go on? To promote rebellion, for the purpose of breaking down the strength
of the country, in order to effect the unpopular measure of the Union. Carnot the director, in August,
1797, told Doctor M'Nevin, that the policy of Mr.
Pitt was known to the directory; "that a Union

was Mr. Pitt's object, in his vexatious treatment of Ireland." *

In Emmett's examination before the secret committee of the House of Lords, he was asked by Lord Clare—" Did you not think the government very foolish to let you proceed so long as you did?" To which Emmett replied, " No, my lord, whatever I imputed to government, I did not accuse them of folly; I knew we were very attentively watched."†

But Emmett did not know that however cautious they had been, the most secret proceedings of the directors had been disclosed to government, even prior to the application to France for assistance; and the knowledge of their negotiation with foreign states, we are told by M'Nevin, was in the full possession of government, and that " knowledge was obtained by some person in the pay of England and the confidence of France."

The memoir which the Irish directory had addressed to the French government, demanding military assistance, in 1797, with which Dr. M'Nevin was charged, the same gentleman was astonished to find an authentic copy of, in the hands of Mr. Cooke, the Irish secretary in 1798.

The betrayers of their society were not the poor or inferior members of it; some of them were high in the confidence of the directory; others not sworn in, but trusted in its concerns, learned in the law, social in their habits, liberal in their politics, prodigal in their expenses, needy in their circumstances, and

* Vide " Memoir of the Examination of the State Prisoners," &c.
† Ibid.

therefore covetous of money; loose in their public and private principles, therefore open to temptation.

The want of good faith, however, was not alone on the side of the disaffected; in the closets of the most influential friends and agents of government, there existed channels of communication with the leaders of the United Irishmen, by means of which the most important measures of the administration were made known to the directory, and to others in the confidence of its members, which frequently baffled the designs of government, and disconcerted the plans of the law-officers of the crown, in the course of the proceedings instituted against the members of this society.

Arthur O'Connor, on his examination before the secret committee of the House of Lords, stated— that "minute information of every act of the Irish government" was obtained by the executive directory."*

A person in the employment of government, necessarily entrusted with all important matters, was habitually visited. by two members of the society, and when measures of moment to it were under consideration, the knowledge of them was obtained from this source.

On one occasion when this person was waited on by these members of the society, (persons of unquestionable veracity, from one of whom I have this statement,) they were warned to be silent on certain subjects, that a dangerous man was in the adjoining room, and that person was Mr. Walter Cox. With

* Vide Memoirs of the Examination, &c.

which party he was then appearing to play fast and loose, it would be difficult to say, but Cox, at that period, was the editor of an infamous journal called "The Union Star;" it advocated the assassination of the persons supposed to be most obnoxious to the United Irishmen : and that journal, which professed to be established for the especial advocacy of their cause, had been repeatedly repudiated by the society, and its principles denounced in "The Press," the organ of the United Irishmen.

The fact seems to have escaped the notice both of the government and of the United Irishmen :—that on whatever side there is a deviation from humane, moderate, and justifiable proceedings, there is no confidence to be reposed in the fidelity of the agency employed in promoting its violent or unlawful measures. The administration of that day had not the slightest suspicion, that many of the most important measures on which it meditated, and some of its most secret designs, up to the period of the arrests at Bond's, were known to the directory of the United Irishmen ; but that such was the fact there is unquestionable evidence—the evidence of members of that directory —of two of them especially, on whose veracity even Lord Clare had a perfect reliance.

There were channels of communication, the existence of which would now hardly be believed, between the agents of government and the emissaries of the United Irishmen. On Dr. M'Nevin's authority (unpublished) it may be stated, that amongst those who were privately known to be favourable to their views, was a member of the privy council and a general officer then serving in the army. The time has not yet come when more may be said on this subject; the general statement of the fact, however, ought to be made—and the lesson may be useful, whether it works upon the fears of tyranny or treason.

In the course of the enquiries connected with this work, it has come to the author's knowledge that the expenses of the defence of the United Irishmen have been borne by officers of distinction at that period. In one case, I was informed by Bernard Duggan, a person deeply implicated in the rebellion, some of whose exploits are mentioned in Sir Richard Musgrave's History—that his life would have been forfeited, had it not been for the ample and timely pecuniary assistance sent to him by an officer serving in that part of the country where he was then imprisoned, to whom he was utterly unknown. That assistance which enabled him to procure legal assistance on his trial, was sent to him by a Colonel L——.

While Lord Edward Fitzgerald was concealed in the house of Murphy, we are informed by Mr. Moore, that he was in the habit of " receiving the visits of two or three persons, among whom were, if he was rightly informed, Major Plunkett and another military gentleman of the rank of colonel, named Lumm."*

Teeling, in his " Personal Narrative of the Irish Rebellion," speaking of the persons who, in the relative situations in which they stood with the govern-

* Vide Lord E. Fitzgerald's Life and Death. By Moore. Vol. ii. p. 50. American edition.

ment, must have made great sacrifices, and incurred considerable risk in communicating with the leaders of the United Irishmen, says : " I was one evening in conversation with Lord Edward, when Colonel L—— entered his apartment, accompanied by two gentlemen with whose persons I was unacquainted, but who, I have reason to believe, were members of the Irish legislature. The colonel, after embracing Lord Edward with the warmest affection, laid on his table a large canvas purse filled with gold, and smiling at his lordship, while he tapped him on the shoulder, "There," said he ; " there, my Lord, is provision for ———." " A few hours more would have placed Lord Edward at the head of the troops of Kildare."* In the month of May, 1798, Colonel Lumm was arrested in England, and brought to Dublin, in custody of a king's messenger.

* Vide Teeling's Personal Narrative, &c. p. 147.

CHAPTER V.

THE new organization of the society of United Irishmen was completed on the 10th of May, 1795; separation and a republican government became the fixed objects of its principal leaders, but not the avowed ones till a little later, when, at the conclusion of every meeting, the chairman was obliged to inform the members of each society, " They had undertaken no light matter," and he was directed to ask every delegate present what were his views, and his understanding of those of his society, and each individual was expected to reply, " A republican government, and a separation from England."*

Early in 1794, the question had been mooted of soliciting the co-operation of France, and a person was appointed to go on that mission, but various circumstances conspired to prevent his departure, till the trial of Jackson, an emissary of the French government, brought to general notice the intentions of the French with respect to invasion; and at this period, Tone, who was implicated more or less in Jackson's guilt, and permitted to go to America, was solicited by certain persons openly to set forth to the French government, through its agents in America on his arrival there, " the state of Ireland and its dispositions." These dispositions are to be gathered from a communication addressed to Tone in America, and published in the Life of Tone by his Son, styled " A Letter from one of the Chief Catholic Leaders in Dublin, September 3rd, 1795," wherein Tone is told " to remember and to execute his garden conversation."

Reference is made to a conversation by Tone, which had taken place a day or two previously to his departure from Dublin, at Emmett's country residence at Rathfarnham. The persons present were Emmett, Tone, and Russell. Tone's account of this interview is told in simple and expressive language. " A short time before my departure," he says, " my friend Russell being in town, he and I walked out together to see Emmett, who has a charming villa there. He showed us a little study, of an elliptical form, which he was building at the bottom of the lawn, and which he said he would consecrate to our meetings if ever we lived to see our country emancipated.

" I begged of him, if he intended Russell to be of the party, in addition to the books and maps it would naturally contain, to fit up a small cellaret, capable of holding a few dozens of his best claret. He showed me that he had not omitted that circumstance, which he acknowledged to be essential, and we both rallied Russell with considerable success. As we walked together towards town, I opened my plan to them both. I told them I considered my compromise with

government to extend L' further than the banks of
the Delaware, and the moment I landed I was to
follow any plan that might suggest itself for the
emancipation of my country. I then proceeded to
tell them, that my intention was, immediately on my
arrival in Philadelphia, to wait on the French minister, to detail to him fully the situation of affairs in
Ireland, and endeavour to obtain a recommendation
to the French government, and having succeeded so
far, to leave my family in America, set off immediately for Paris, and apply, in the name of my
country, for the assistance of France to enable us to
assert our independence. It is unnecessary, I believe, to say that this plan met with the warmest
approbation and support, both from Russell and Emmett; we shook hands, and having repeated our professions of unalterable regard and esteem for each
other, we parted; and this was the last interview
which I was so happy as to have with these two invaluable friends together. I remember it was in a
little triangular field that this conversation took
place, and Emmett remarked, that it was in one
like it in Switzerland, where William Tell and his
associates planned the downfall of the tyranny of
Austria."*

· Tone took his departure from Dublin on the 20th
of May, 1795, and the conversation alluded to having
taken place immediately after Jackson's trial at the
latter end of April, this first suggestion of the employment of force, with the concurrence of Emmett
and Russell, must have been made in the month of

* Tone's Life, vol. 1. p. 125. Washington edition.

May, 1795. O'Connor, on his examination before the secret committee in 1798, stated that the executive had sent to seek an alliance with France in May, 1796, which was formed in the August following— "the first entered into between the Irish Union and the French Government." *

The opinion, however, of the necessity and advantage of independence and separation, had been declared so early as the year 1790, in a private letter addressed by Tone to his friend Russell, which subsequently fell into the hands of government. "In forming this theory, (Tone says, in reference to his political sentiments in 1790,) I was exceedingly assisted by an old friend of mine, Sir Laurence Parsons, (the late Lord Rosse,) and it was he who first turned my attention to this great question, but I very soon ran far ahead of my master. It is, in fact, to him I am indebted for the first comprehensive view of the actual situation of Ireland; what his conduct might be in a crisis I know not, but I can answer for the truth and justice of his theory." †

The congenial sentiments of Sir Laurence Parsons at this period, with Mr. Tone's, on the subjects alluded to, are found expressed strongly enough in a poem on the state of Ireland, by Sir Laurence Parsons, the following lines of which may be taken as a sample of its political tendency :— ‡

" What, though with haughty arrogance and pride,
England shall o'er this long-duped country stride,

* Memoir of the examination of O'Connor, Emmett, and M‘Nevin, p. 48.
† Tone's Life, vol. i. p. 32.   ‡ Tone's Life, vol. i. p. 564.

And lay on stripe on stripe, and shame on shame,
And brand to all eternity its name:
'Tis right well done. Bear all, and more, I say,
Nay, ten times more, and then for more still pray.
What state in something would not foremost be?
She strives for shame, thou for servility.
The other nations of the earth, now fired
To noblest deeds, by noblest minds inspired,
High in the realms of glory, write a name,
Wreath'd round with Liberty's immortal flame:
'Tis thine to creep a path obscure, unknown,
The palm of ev'ry meanness all thy own.

  *   *   *   *   *

Search your own breast, in abject letters, there
Read why you still the tinsell'd slav'ry wear:
Though Britain, with a trembling hand, untied
The fetters fashion'd in her power and pride,
Still are you slaves, in baser chains entwin'd,
For though your limbs are free, you're slaves in mind."

Poor Tone unfortunately acted on his opinion, and was doomed to an ignominious death; Sir Laurence Parsons was fortunate enough to outlive his early principles, succeeded to a title, forgot the wrongs that had been the subject of his poetry, frequented the fashionable circles of London, and died a loyal subject—the whole amount of praise his lordship's public career had any claim to. The men who perished in these disastrous times on the scaffold, might have become as loyal subjects as Sir Laurence Parsons, if mercy had more influence in the councils of the rulers of the land in those days.

After the indemnity and insurrection acts had been moved by the attorney-general, and the system

of coercion and extermination in the north had received the sanction of those laws, the important
meeting of the executive took place in May, 1796,
and it was determined that no constitutional means of
opposing oppression were available, and that assistance must be sought from a foreign power. An
agent was accordingly appointed to communicate
with the French government, and Lord Edward
Fitzgerald proceeded on that mission, accompanied
by Mr. Arthur O'Connor, to Switzerland, and had an
interview near the French frontier with General
Hoche, where arrangements were entered into between the parties with a view to a descent.

In November, 1796, an agent, a native of France,
from the French republic, arrived in Ireland, and
communicated to the directory the intention of the
French government to send the assistance required,
and a large quantity of arms and ammunition; and
in the month of December following, the attempt at
invasion was made at Bantry Bay. One of the principal causes of its signal miscarriage, was attributed
by the directory of the United Irishmen, to the circumstance of being left by the French government
in total ignorance of the part of the coast where the
descent was to be made. Arthur O'Connor states
there are only two persons now living who have a
knowledge of the place where the disembarkation
was originally intended to have been effected.

In March, 1797, another agent, Mr. Lewins, an
attorney of Dublin, had been sent by the directory
to France, to press on the government the fulfilment
of its promise of another expedition, and to effect a

loan of half-a-million. The difficulties, however, of the French government at this period, stood in the way of the success of the application, and another agent, Dr. M'Nevin, was dispatched in the month of June, to impress on the French government the immediate necessity of granting the succour that had been applied for. Dr. M'Nevin was unable to proceed beyond Hamburg, where he communicated —most imprudently, it must be admitted—*in writing* to the French minister the object of his mission. The force required was 10,000 men at the most, and 5,000 at the least, and about 40,000 stand of arms. Dr. M'Nevin, after some time, was allowed to proceed to Paris, and there renewed with the government the solicitations of the directory for immediate assistance. Dr. M'Nevin returned to Ireland in October, 1797, when he reported to the directory the result of his mission—that they might rely with confidence on the promised succours from France. Lewins remained in Paris, the accredited agent of the directory. In July or August, 1797, the directory received a communication from him, announcing the Dutch armament in the Texel, intended for Ireland, being about to be dispatched. That expedition, however, was totally discomfited by the British fleet under Lord Duncan. The last application for French succour was attempted to be made in January, 1798, but that attempt failed; and the last communication from Lewins to the directory, with the new promise of assistance, was in the latter part of 1797, stating that an invasion of

Ireland would take place in the month of April, 1798.

The following observations of Mr. Shiel, in reference to the three expeditions undertaken in France, with a view to the invasion of this country, place that subject in a clearer light than any thing that has been hitherto written.

Mr. Shiel, in a speech delivered in Dublin, in 1826, said : " I hold a book in my hand which has recently arrived here from America, and in which there is a remarkable passage, illustrative of the necessity of opposition to secret societies, and to all ill-organized associations among the peasantry, of which spoliation is the object, and of which their own destruction must be the result. The book to which I refer, is the life of the unfortunate and deluded Theobald Wolfe Tone. Of his character, upon this occasion, it is not necessary to say any thing, except that he was loved and prized by all who knew him. He was chivalrous, aspiring and enthusiastic, and possessed not only of great talents, but, what is in politics of still more importance, of dauntless determination. In the diary which he kept in Paris, when engaged in a guilty enterprize for the invasion of Ireland, he states that the late General Clarke, who was afterwards Duke of Feltre, conceived that a system which, during the French revolution, was called *chouannerie*, and which corresponds with the Captain-Rockism of this country, would be of use in Ireland, and that, through its means, the government might be embarrassed, and the people might be prepared for a general junction with an invading force. Tone objected utterly to this proposition. He said, in the first place, that it would lead to unavailing atrocities, in the promotion of which no good man could assist; and that, in the second place, it would produce a barbarous and irregular warfare, which it would be extremely easy to suppress, and which would give the government the opportunity of passing coercive laws, of introducing a military police, and crushing the spirit of the people. That Wolfe Tone was right, events have abundantly proved. The supporters of ascendency ought to look pale, in turning over the memoirs of Tone. I would fain commend them to the nocturnal vigils of the cabinet; and if there be any man who, in reading what I say, shall be disposed to smile, I would bid him to recollect that a fleet, composed of seventeen sail of the line, with 15,000 Frenchmen on-board, an immense park of artillery, and 50,000 stand of arms, to support an insurgent population, ought to awaken reflections, of which scorn should not constitute a part:—I allude to the expedition from Brest in the year 1796, which Tone projected; and which was commanded by Hoche. It is necessary to be in possession of the exact circumstances in which Tone was placed, in order to judge how much was accomplished by a single man in the midst of difficulties, which it is almost wonderful that he should have surmounted. In the year 1795, Tone retired to America with his wife (an incomparable woman) and two children. He had £800 in the world. At first, he formed an intention of re-

maining in the United States; but Tone was one
of those restless spirits who feel that they are born
for great undertakings, if not for great achieve-
ments, and who, though they may not be able to
wed themselves to Fortune, woo her at all hazards.
He set sail in an American vessel for France, with
no more than one hundred guineas in his pocket.
He arrived at Havre on the 1st of February, 1796,
and proceeded at once to Paris. When he was
placed in the midst of that city, and stood upon the
Pont-Neuf, he looked upon the vast array of palaces,
turned into the domiciles of democracy—he saw the
metropolis of France in all its vastness, and he felt
what Seneca has so well expressed—'urbs magna,
magna solitudo;' still, although without a friend or
an acquaintance, poor, desolate as it were, and ship-
wrecked upon France, his great and vast design did
not leave him. He was sufficiently daring to present himself to the minister of war, Charles Lecroix.
What were his chief credentials? Two votes of
thanks from the Catholic committee. He scarcely
knew a word of the French language, yet he succeeded in communicating his views to Lecroix. The
latter referred him to General Clarke, the son of an
Irishman, and who had been in Ireland himself. It
is not improper to observe, in this place, the extraordinary ignorance of General Clarke respecting his
father's country. Clarke asked Tone two of the
most extraordinary questions that ever were proposed :—first, Whether Lord Clare would join in an
insurrection? And, secondly, Whether the Irish,
who he heard were addicted to regal government,

would be disposed to put the Duke of York on the throne? The French have become better acquainted with the state of Ireland, and therefore how much more imperatively necessary is it to conciliate the Irish people. It was with the utmost difficulty, that Tone could break through the crust of prejudices with which Clarke's mind was covered. He took at last a wise determination, and went directly to Carnot, the president of the directory of France. Carnot, was justly called the ' Organizer of Victory,' and he was induced to extend his genius for organization to Ireland. Theobald Wolfe Tone, succeeded so far, as to induce the French government to determine upon an invasion of this country. At first the project was lamely and imperfectly got up, but to prevail to any extent was to do much. It is really matter for surprise, that such a man as Tone, without rank, fortune, or a single friend, could accomplish so much. Yet it remains to be seen, that Tone did much more than has hitherto appeared. The French at first proposed to send only 2,000 men : Tone saw at once that such a measure would be utterly absurd. By much ado, he persuaded them to increase the army to 8,000, with 50,000 stand of arms. At length Hoche, a general of great fame, was induced to put himself at the head of the expedition, and as he felt that great objects must be attained by great means, he required 15,000 men, an artillery force, a large supply of cannon, and arms for the insurgent population : such was the force that sailed from Brest. There were seventeen ships of the line, in attendance upon the army. It was Wolfe Tone who accomplished all this; but that navigation, fortunately for Ireland, was not happy for Tone. A storm separated the fleet. The ships had to pass through a Strait, called, 'The Raz,' which caused them to part; Hoche was driven back with seven ships of the line; but ten sail of the line with 6,000 troops and an abundance of arms, commanded by Grouchy, reached the Irish coast. Tone says that he was so near the land, that he could have thrown a biscuit on shore; a landing might have been most easily effected. But the instructions of the directory were that they should proceed to Bantry Bay. there they did proceed, and for five days—mark it! five days—ten French sail of the line lay in one of our harbours, having a body of troops on board, who, with the aid of the people, (and they had muskets for them) might have marched to Dublin. It may be here remarked, that Grouchy was the commander. Tone says, 'All now rests upon Grouchy, I hope he may turn out well.' Grouchy did not turn out well. Twice had this man the destinies of nations in his hands, and twice he abused his trust. The expedition failed. Pious men attributed the failure to Providence, and navigators to the wind. I put this plain question, if steam vessels were then in use, would not the event have been different? I answer :—had steam vessels been at that time in use, the expedition would not have failed; or, in other words, 15,000 Frenchmen would have landed with arms sufficient for the array of an immense population. The failure of this enterprize did not break the spirit

of Wolfe Tone. In the year 1797, another expedition was prepared in the Texel, which consisted of fifteen sail of the line, eleven frigates and
several sloops. There were 14,000 men on board.
A second time the winds, 'the only unsubsidized
allies of England,' conspired in her favour; the foul
weather prevented them from sailing. A third expedition was undertaken—and had it been executed
with the sagacity with which it was planned, the
result might have been different. But Humbert,
who had no reputation as a general, and did not
deserve any, precipitated events, and, by his absurdity, frustrated the whole project. Yet the 1,200
men commanded by Humbert arrived at Castlebar,
and struck terror through Ireland. Lord Cornwallis
advanced with the whole British army to meet him.
Tone fell into the hands of his enemies, and antici-
pated the executioner. Men risk their lives for a
shilling a day—mount the breach for a commission
—perish for a word; it is not to be wondered,
then, that such a man as Tone should, for the accomplishment of such great ends as he proposed to
himself, 'have set his life upon a cast;' and as it is
to be feared that, so long as human nature continues
as it is, individuals will be always readily found with
a passion for political adventure, and who will
'stand the hazard of the die,' it would be wise on
the part of government to snatch the dice from the
hands of such men, and, if I may so say, to leave
them no table for their desperate game. I have not
introduced the name of Wolfe Tone for the purpose
of panegyric—nay, I will go further, and hope to

of Wolfe Tone. In the ... ed in February,
pedition was prepared in ... of co-operation
sisted of fifteen sail of the ... and, or of insur-
several sloops. There ... to it before the
A second time the winds ... ectory was deter-
allies of England,' ... memoir delivered
weather prevented them ... Emmett, O'Con-
pedition was undertaken ... none of them
with the sagacity with ... em until Septem-
result might have been ... Emmett became
who had no reputation ... month of January,
deserve any, precipitated ... till the month of
dity, frustrated the wise ... in the month of
men commanded by ... to it till the 12th
and struck terror through ... took place. Dr.
advanced with the whole ... new organization
Tone fell into the hands ... having previously
pated the executions ... dectory, he become
shilling a day—meant for ... 797, and continued
—perish for a want, it ... Athur O'Connor be-
then, that said a man as ... mber of the direc-
... connued to belong to
... Ireland, and his
... up. Oliver
... m executive,
... directory-
... ntinuing
... onsulted
... ormick,
... secre-
... m-

content his old friend and companion, the present
attorney-general, when I say, that I regard his
projects with strong and unaffected condemnation.
In any convulsion which may take place in Ireland,
it is likely that the individuals who are most active
in Catholic affairs would be amongst the first victims. The humblest man amongst us is substan-
tially interested in arresting those disasters, of which
we have had already some sort of experience: he
who lives on the ground-floor, ought not to wish
the roof to fall in. But, while my ardent wishes
are offered up for the peace and tranquillity of my
country, I own that my apprehensions are differ-
ently directed. If I refer to the past, it is because
I consider it an image of the future. In incidents
gone by, it is easy to discover the archetypes of
events that yet may come. Let me, then, put this
question,—If a single man, without fame, rank,
influence, or authority, unknown and unrecognized,
was, by dint of his unaided talents and his spirit of
enterprise, able, in the space of two years, to effect
three expeditions against Ireland, what might not
be dreaded in other circumstances? When Tone
embarked in his enterprise, there were but three
millions of Catholics; now there are at least six :—
secondly, the French are at present infinitely better
acquainted with the state of Ireland :—thirdly, the
Irish clergy were, in 1796, opposed to the deists of
the republic; Wolfe Tone says they cannot 'be relied on.' Dr. Troy was persuaded to fulminate
anathemas against the United Irishmen, and fling
the innocuous lightning of excommunication against

the abettors of the French. Now I hold excommunication to be of exceeding good and proper efficacy, in all matters of private and personal immorality—but in politics, excommunication is of no avail."

Such are the dangers with which the empire was menaced by these expeditions. Who can reflect on the magnitude of such dangers, without wondering at the folly of governing a people for the benefit of a faction, whose ascendancy could not be maintained without involving the government which could tolerate its oppression, and affect to be imposed on by the vain assumption of its exclusive loyalty, in the hostility which its intolerance and arrogance called forth?

CHAPTER VI.

THE military organization was engrafted on the civil, and originated in Ulster about the latter end of 1796, and in Leinster at the beginning of 1797. On the 19th of February, 1798, the provincial committee of the latter passed a resolution, "that they would not be diverted from their purpose by anything which could be done in parliament," and this resolution was communicated to the directory. By the new organization, the civil officers received military titles, the secretary of each society of twelve was called the petty officer, each delegate of five societies a captain, having sixty men under his command; and the delegate of ten lower baronial societies was usually the colonel: each batallion being composed of six hundred men. The colonels of each county sent in the names of three persons to the directory, one of whom was appointed by it adjutant-general of the county, who communicated directly with the executive. The total number of members of the Union who had taken the test amounted to 500,000; the total number capable of bearing arms, and counted on by the directory as an available force, was 300,000.

A military committee was appointed in February, 1798; its duty was to prepare a plan of co-operation with the French when they should land, or of insurrection, in case they should be forced to it before the arrival of the French, which the directory was determined if possible to avoid. In the memoir delivered to the Irish government by Messrs. Emmett, O'Connor and M'Nevin, it is stated that none of them "were members of the united system until September or October of the year 1796." Emmett became a member of the directory in the month of January, 1797, and continued to act in it till the month of May; he was again appointed to it in the month of December, and continued to belong to it till the 12th of March, 1798, when the arrests took place. Dr. M'Nevin became a member of the new organization in September, or October, 1796; having previously been secretary to the executive directory, he become a member of it about November, 1797, and continued to be one till March, 1798. Arthur O'Connor became a United Irishman, and a member of the directory in November, 1796, and continued to belong to it till January, 1798, when he left Ireland, and his place in the directory was then filled up. Oliver Bond became a member of the northern executive, and in 1797 was elected a member of the directory-general, but declined to act officially, continuing however to be in its confidence, and to be consulted with on all affairs of moment. Richard M'Cormick, a stuff manufacturer of Mark's-alley, formerly secretary of the Catholic committee, was the other member of the directory, though not ostensibly or by specific appointment belonging to it.

I

Though a national committee was a part of the plan of the original organization, the election of national delegates did not take place till the beginning of December, 1798, and then only partially.

There was no detailed plan of insurrection formed by the Dublin directory previously to March, 1798. There was one drawn up in April or May, 1797, for the north, but the plan was given up and the writing destroyed.

With respect to the entire force armed throughout the country, as estimated by Lord Edward Fitzgerald, when a rising was eventually determined on in the month of March, 1798, the particulars are specified in a document presented by Lord Edward to that man, whose name and notoriety are never likely to be forgotten, in his own country at least—to Mr. Thomas Reynolds, the informer. The document referred to is dated 26th February, 1798.

	Armed men	Finances in hand.		
Ulster . . .	110,990	£436	2	4
Munster . . .	100,634	147	17	2
Kildare . . .	10,863	110	17	7
Wicklow . . .	12,895	93	6	4
Dublin . . .	3,010	37	2	6
Dublin City . .	2,177	321	17	11
Queen's County	11,689	91	2	1
King's County .	3,600	21	11	3
Carlow . . .	9,414	49	2	10
Kilkenny . .	624	10	2	3
Meath . . .	1,400	171	2	1
Total . .	279,896	£1,485	4	9

By this document it would appear that the total number of armed men throughout the country, was estimated by Lord Edward at 279,896.

But from another source, and one whose authenticity is unquestionable, the writer has reason to know that Lord Edward imagined that when once he had raised the standard of revolt, 100,000 effective men might be immediately expected to rally round it.

Lord Edward's precise views on the subject of the rising of the people, have never been given to the public; they are now laid before it, in the following memorandum of a conversation with one who possessed his entire confidence, who communicated with him on the subject of the contemplated rising immediately before its intended outbreak, and who fruitlessly endeavoured to dissuade him from it. On the accuracy of the information given respecting this matter the most implicit confidence may be reposed. The person in question met Lord Fitzgerald by appointment at the Shakespeare Gallery, Exchequer-street, about one month before the arrests in March, to confer with the delegates from the different counties respecting the projected rising. After Lord Edward had received the different reports of the number of men ready for the field in the different counties, he called on the gentleman above referred to for his opinion. Lord Edward said, " he deeply regretted his friend should have withdrawn himself so long from any active interference in the business of the Union, and that one in whose judgment he so much confided, should stand aloof at such a moment: if he unfortunately persisted in so doing, the friends of

the Union might be led to imagine he had deserted
them in the hour of need; that he, Lord Fitzgerald
had determined on an immediate and general rising
of the people, their impatience for which was no
longer to be restrained, nor, with advantage to the
cause, to be resisted." He then appealed to the
delegates for the truth of this assertion, and his opinion was confirmed by them.   His friend, it is well
to state, had withdrawn himself from the Union,
about the beginning of the year, when the system
was changed from a civil to a military organization.
He could only regard this change as one likely to
direct the attention of their opponents to their proceedings.   In fact, the people had not been sworn in
at this time, and no danger was apprehended from
them.   But when the system was changed, and secretaries, and chairmen, and delegates, were called
captains, and colonels, and adjutant-generals, a military aspect was given to the business of the Union,
the government became necessarily alarmed, and
recourse was had to spies and informers.   The danger of this course was obvious to those who felt that
any premature display of military preparation must
prove fatal to their cause.   In any similar combination,
they thought the people should be left alone, and that
the system only needed to be previously well organized among the leaders, and in due time the people
would rise, if they felt themselves oppressed.   Such
persons likewise deprecated the want of caution
in the leaders, in confiding in strangers, and
speaking and writing rashly and intemperately on
the subject of the Union.   On the Sunday pre-

vious to the arrests, the gentleman I allude to had
declined an introduction to Reynolds, at Jackson's in Church-street, notwithstanding M'Cann's
recommendation of him, as "one of the best and
honestest men in the Union." He had avoided Reynolds, because he did not like his character. He
informed Lord Edward, though he had taken no
part for some time in the affairs of the Union, he
did not cease to give his opinion when consulted,
and especially by Lord Edward—though he was well
aware, when once his lordship had made up his mind
on a point, he was little influenced by the counsel of
any man : when Lord Edward had spoken of his
deserting the cause, the latter felt hurt by the observation, and replied in strong terms that he had
not deserted the people, nor betrayed their cause,
but those people had done so, who had precipitated
measures prematurely taken, which did not afford
the least promise of success. " My Lord," said he,
" I am not a person to desert a cause in which I have
embarked. I knew the dangers of it when I joined
it: were those dangers only for myself, or the friends
about me, I am not the man to be deterred by
the consideration of what may happen to myself or
them—we might fall, but the cause might not fail;
and, so long as the country was served, it would
matter little : but when I know the step that you
are taking will involve that cause in the greatest
difficulties, my fears are great—I tremble for the
result. My Lord, all the services that you or your
noble house have ever rendered to the country, or
ever can render to it, will never make amends to

the people for the misery and wretchedness the failure of your present plans will cause them." " I tell you," replied Lord Edward impetuously, " the chances of success are greatly in favour of our attempt: examine these returns—here are returns which shew, that one hundred thousand armed men may be counted on to take the field." " My Lord," replied his friend, " it is one thing to have a hundred thousand men on paper, and another in the field. A hundred thousand men on paper, will not furnish fifty thousand in array. I, for one, am enrolled amongst the number; but I candidly tell you, you will not find me in your ranks. You know for what objects we joined this Union, and what means we reckoned on for carrying them into effect. Fifteen thousand Frenchmen were considered essential to our undertaking. If they were so at that time, still more so are they now, when our warlike aspect has caused the government to pour troops into the country." " What !" said Lord Edward, " would you attempt nothing without these fifteen thousand men—would you not be satisfied with ten thousand?" " I would, my Lord," replied his friend, " if the aid of the fifteen could not be procured."

" But," continued Lord Edward, " if even the ten could not be got, what would you do then?"

" I would then accept of five, my Lord," was the reply.

" But," said Lord Edward, fixing his eyes with great earnestness on him, " we cannot get five thousand, and with respect to the larger force we originally

wished for, had we succeeded, with so large a body
of French troops we might have found it difficult
enough to get rid of our allies." To this it was
replied, " My Lord, if we found it possible to get
rid of our enemies, ten times as numerous as our
allies, we could have little difficulty in getting rid of
the latter when necessity required it."

" But, I tell you we cannot," said Lord Edward,
" get even the five thousand you speak of, and when
you know that we cannot, will you desert our cause ?"
The eyes of the delegates were turned on the person
thus addressed. He felt that Lord Edward had put
the matter in such a light before those present, that
he would have been branded as a traitor if he abandoned the cause, while there was a ray of hope for
its success.

" My Lord," said he, " if five thousand men could
not be obtained, I would seek the assistance of a
sufficient number of French officers to head our
people, and with three hundred of these, perhaps we
might be justified in making an effort for independence, but not without them. What military men
have we of our own, to lead our unfortunate people
into action against a disciplined army ?"

Lord Edward ridiculed the idea of there being
anything like discipline at that time in the English
army. " Besides, the numbers," he said " of the
United Irishmen, would more than counterbalance
any superiority in the discipline of their enemies."

" My Lord," said his friend, " we must not be
deceived; they are disciplined, and our people are

not: if the latter are repulsed and broken, who is to reform their lines? Once thrown into disorder, the greater their numbers the greater will be the havoc made amongst them."

Lord Edward said "without risking a general engagement, he would be able to get possession of Dublin."

"Suppose you did, my Lord," was the reply, "the possession of the capital would not insure success; and even when you had taken the city, if the citizens asked to see the army of their brave deliverers, which might be encamped in the Phœnix Park, the citizens would naturally expect to see some military evolutions performed, some sort of military array, exhibited on such an occasion. Who would there be, my Lord, to put the people through these evolutions? What officers have you, to teach them one military manœuvre; and if they were suddenly attacked by an army in the rear, what leader accustomed to the field have you to bring them with any advantage to the attack? You, my Lord, are the only military man amongst us, but you cannot be everywhere you are required; and the misfortune is, you delegate your authority to those whom you think are like yourself: but they are not like you, we have no such persons amongst us."

The delegates here assented to the justice of these remarks, declaring that the proposal for the aid of the French officers was a reasonable one, and they were proceeding to remonstrate, when Lord Edward impatiently reminded them that they had no assistance to expect from France, and that consequently the determination had been come to, to prepare the country for an immediate rising.

Lord Edward and his friend, nevertheless, parted with the same cordiality and confidence in each other that had always subsisted between them.

"Lord Edward," says that individual, who knew him perhaps better than any other of his associates, "was the noblest-minded of human beings. He had no deceit, no selfishness, no meanness, no duplicity in his nature; he was all frankness, openness, and generosity; but he was not the man to conduct a revolution to a successful issue:"—that man was Thomas Addis Emmett. Perhaps, if he had said the men to effect this object were Arthur O'Connor and Thomas Addis Emmett, provided they could have acted through such a struggle—and to its end, in concert, and with singleness of purpose and forgetfulness of self—his opinion might have been better founded.

CHAPTER VII.

THE revolution in France had a great influence on the public mind in Ireland; but, in all probability, the rebellion of 1798 would have taken place, had that revolution never been effected.

The necessity of reform for the security of parliamentary independence, was strongly felt by the popular party so early as 1790, and that opinion was first acted upon by the northern presbyterians. Various political clubs, emanating from the volunteer associations, had been formed in Belfast, advocating reform and Catholic emancipation, before either of these questions had gained any ground in the metropolis. The Belfast leaders were so far in advance of those of Dublin on both subjects, that, long before the change in the organization of the United Irish Societies, ulterior views to those they set out with advocating, were entertained by a great many of the former.

The Dublin leaders were chiefly of the Protestant religion, and, till the year 1794, reform was not only the ostensible, but the real object they had in view. The Belfast politicians were presbyterians, and the old leaven of republicanism unquestionably worked more or less in all their hostile feelings to parliamentary corruption. Both parties founded their hopes of success for the struggle they had engaged in, on the discontent of the people, who groaned under the burden of the penal laws.

Belfast stood foremost in the early struggle with intolerance and corruption, in the bold discussion of political subjects, and in the dissemination of reform principles. The latter were embodied, in 1793, in a series of papers written by several persons, called " Thoughts on the British Constitution." This collection of pieces is one of the earliest and the ablest expositions of arguments in detail, in favour of reform, that is to be met with. Another admirable series of letters on the same subject, under the signature of Orellana, were written at this time by Dr. Drennan. The subversion of the government was disclaimed by the leaders of the people, and there can be little doubt on the mind of any one who reads the discussions of the Belfast politicians, that, although many of them entertained views that went much farther than reform, it was long before they acted on them, or extended their projects beyond the attempt to strengthen the democratic principle, and to combine the monarchical form of government with republican institutions. They were content to see the constitution restored and perpetuated, though, in the abstract, the predilections of such men as Tone, Neilson, Russell, Emerson, Kelburn, Joy, Simms, M'Cracken, &c. might be in favour of republicanism; but they could not overlook diffi-

culties that lay in the way of any efforts for obtaining that object, and the probability of so far assimi-
lating existing institutions to the latter, by means
of reform, as to prevent the evils which had arisen
from the monarchical form of government having
become (in Ireland at least) an oligarchical one.

To have taken the government out of the more
than regal power of Clare and the Beresfords, and
restored its usurped authority to the constitutional
sovereign of these realms, with the guarantees for
protection against the future inroads of this detested
oligarchy, which they looked for in reform, would,
at any period previous to 1794, have satisfied the
expectations of the popular leaders in the north, and
cut the ground for ulterior agitation from under the
feet of the more violent and uncompromising adherents to republicanism.   In Dublin, the popular
leaders, at any period previous to 1797, would have
gladly accepted that boon, and relinquished the idea
of separation.   Few of their leading men were, in
ordinary circumstances, more than strenuous advocates of constitutional liberty, while those of the
north had certainly a considerable portion of their
old attachment for republican principles remaining
in their politics.   But even the most uncompromising of them (and, amongst others, the Rev.
Sinclair Kelburne), at a very critical period of their
struggle, declared that rather than have recourse to
violence, though they might esteem another form of
government more perfect, their views went not beyond
a government of King, Lords and Commons, were
that government to be the true and real representative

of the people. The precise nature of their views, and the extent of them, can only be rightly appreciated by examining their proceedings in 1792 and 1793, and referring to their discussions and avowed writings. The following extracts, with the exception of the comments on them, are taken from a highly interesting, and now rare, collection of these documents published in Belfast by their body, and edited by one of them (Henry Joy) in 1794.

The first important movement in Belfast in the cause of reform, was the presentation of a petition to the House of Commons, praying for the immediate and unconditional emancipation of Roman Catholics. And this petition is worthy of notice, as being the first that ever emanated in Ireland from a Protestant body in favour of emancipation. The avowed object of its advocates, was the promotion of the cause of reform, arising from the conviction that every effort in that cause which did not embrace the interests and enlist the support of the Roman Catholics on its side, must prove abortive. Acting on this opinion, the society of United Irishmen in Belfast, set out with the following declaration of their principles :—
" We have agreed to form an association, to be called ' The Society of United Irishmen :' and we do pledge ourselves to our country, and mutually to each other, that we will steadily support, and endeavour by all due means to carry into effect, the following resolutions :—

" I. Resolved, That the weight of English influence in the government of this country is so great, as to require a cordial union among *all the people of*

Ireland, to maintain that balance which is essential to the preservation of our liberties and the extension of our commerce.

" II. That the sole constitutional mode by which this influence can be opposed, is by a complete and radical reform of the representation of the people in parliament.

" III. That no reform is practicable, efficacious, or just, which shall not include Irishmen of every religious persuasion."

In the beginning of January, 1792, the following requisition was addressed to the inhabitants of Belfast :

" GENTLEMEN,—As *men,* and as *Irishmen,* we have long lamented the degrading state of slavery and oppression in which the great majority of our countrymen, the *Roman Catholics,* are held—nor have we lamented it in silence. We wish to see all distinctions on account of religion abolished—all narrow, partial maxims of policy done away. We anxiously wish to see the day when every *Irishman* shall be a citizen—when Catholics and Protestants, equally interested in their country's welfare, possessing equal freedom and equal privileges, shall be cordially *united,* and shall learn to look upon each other as brethren, the children of the same God, the natives of the same land—and when the only strife amongst them shall be, who shall serve their country best. These, gentlemen, are our sentiments, and these we are convinced are yours.

" We, therefore, request a general meeting of the principal inhabitants at the town-house, on Saturday next, at noon, to consider of the propriety of a petition to parliament, in favour of our Roman Catholic brethren.

" We are, Gentlemen,

" Your most obedient Servants,

Robert Thompson,	Hu. Johnson,
Thomas Sinclaire,	Christ. Strong,
Robert Simms,	George Wells,
Gil. M'Ilveen, Jun.	James Stephenson,
Thomas Milliken,	Sam. M'Clean,
Samuel Neilson,	John Graham,
Samuel M'Tier,	Wm. Bryson,
Hu. M'Ilwain,	John Tisdall,
Wm. M'Cleery,	Hugh Crawford,
Wm. Tennent,	Robert Getty,
Wm. Magee,	James Hyndman,
Wm. Simms,	Robert Major,
Robert Callwell,	Walter Crawford,
Hu. Montgomery,	Sam. M'Murray,
John M'Donnell,	Thos. Brown,
Henry Haslett,	John Bankhead,
David Bigger,	Isaac Patton,
John Haslett,	J. Campbell White,
Thos. Neilson,	J. S. Ferguson,
Thos. M'Donnell,	John Todd,
Robert Hunter,	Richard M'Clelland,
Thos. M'Cabe,	John M'Connell,
Wm. Martin,	John M'Clean,
James M'Cormick,	And. M'Clean,
James Luke,	Thos. Ash,
James M'Kain,	John Caldwell.
Ham. Thompson,	

Names will be found in the above list, which may afford ample food for reflection to the descendants of some of those who bore them, and show abundant reason for being tolerant to others whose opinions may differ from those they now profess. Some names in that list, can suggest no other feeling than one of deep concern, that the bearers of them—men of high intelligence, and then, at least, of pure and noble principles—should have fallen, or been driven, into desperate courses, and have been reserved for all their evil consequences; and not a few of these gentlemen have been forced to quit their country, and their friends and homes, for ever.

In the year 1816, when Lord Castlereagh came on a pilgrimage (of repentance for his early opinions, perhaps,) to the scene of his first exertions in the cause of reform, and honoured with his presence the town of Belfast—the cradle, and then the grave of public spirit—his lordship was publicly entertained by the " ci-devant" patriots and ultra-liberals of our Irish Athens. At that dinner the waters of Lethe must have been largely mingled with the wine of the masters of the feast.

The following names recall associations not quite in union with his lordship's repute " in those days of governmental abandonment," which it was not the fashion then in Belfast to mark with a white stone.

GILBERT M'ILVAINE,	A. CRAWFORD,
REV. DR. BRUCE,	CUNNINGHAM GREGG,
NARCISSUS BATT,	HUGH WILSON,
ALEXANDER STEWART,	JOHN SINCLAIR,
HENRY JOY,	DR. THOMPSON,
SIR JAMES ISAAC BRISTOW,	JOHN VANCE,
JOHN M'CRACKEN,	&c. &c. &c.

14th July, 1792.—Belfast Review, and celebration of the French Revolution.

" On Friday evening, the several country corps marched into town, and were billeted on the inhabitants; who were happy in renewing expressions of affection for their neighbours and friends in the fourteenth year since the commencement of reviews, and in the *sixteenth* of the volunteer æra. The number of corps having been considerably reduced, it was not thought proper to call on the venerable General of the Volunteer Army of Ulster, the Earl of Charlemont, to attend on this occasion. The gentleman appointed in his place was Colonel Sharman, of Moira Castle, who presided with such dignity last year in the civil assembly of the inhabitants of Belfast and its neighbourhood, at the celebration of the French Revolution. An unexpected illness having prevented that justly admired character from filling an office for which he was so eminently qualified, Major Crawford, of Crawford's-burn, was unanimously nominated to act as Reviewing-general, in testimony of the respect due to decided virtue in public and private life.

" On Saturday morning a brigade was formed in High Street, extending from the Bank to the Quay; and the whole were marched off to the old review-ground in the *Falls*, at about eleven o'clock, by the Exercising Officer, Major M'Manus.

" On their return to town, at three o'clock, there was a *grand procession*, the order of which is mentioned underneath, and feu-de-joyes were fired in

Linenhall Street, by the whole body, in honour of that day, which presented the sublime spectacle of near one *sixth* of the whole inhabitants of *Europe* bursting their chains, and throwing off, almost in an instant, the degrading yoke of slavery."

" *Order of the Military and Civil Procession.*

MAJOR CRAWFORD, GENERAL AND PRESIDENT FOR THE DAY.

Belfast Troop of Light Dragoons, Captain Thomas Brown.—17.

MAJOR M'MANUS, *Exercising Officer,*
and his Aides-de-Camps.

Artillery of the Belfast First Company,
(their number included in that of the corps under-mentioned.)

The Colours of Five Free Nations, viz. :—

Flag of IRELAND—motto, *Unite and be free.*

Flag of AMERICA—motto, *The Asylum of Liberty.*

Flag of FRANCE—motto, *The Nation, the Law,
and the King.*

Flag of POLAND—motto, *We will support it.*

Flag of GREAT BRITAIN—motto, *Wisdom, Spirit,
and Liberality to the People.*

A flag was prepared for the Dutch, (but no one could be found to bear it,) who were to be represented by a piece of *common* woollen stuff, half hoisted on a pole, and to be hooted by the populace; on account of the States having joined the *wicked conspiracy of tyrants* against the LIBERTIES of MAN :

Motto, *Heav'ns! how unlike their Belgian Sires of old!*

Portrait of Dr. FRANKLIN—motto, *Where Liberty is,* THERE *is my Country.*

First Brigade of Volunteers—532 men.

Artillery of Belfast Blues.

THE GREAT STANDARD.

Elevated on a triumphal car, drawn by four horses, with two Volunteers as supporters, containing on one side of the canvas a representation of

The Releasement of the Prisoners from the Bastile.

Motto, *Sacred to Liberty.*

The reverse contained a figure of Hibernia, one hand and foot in shackles; a Volunteer presenting to her a figure of Liberty.

Motto, *For a People to be* FREE, *it is sufficient that they* WILL IT.

Second Brigade of Volunteers—258 men.

Portrait of Mons. MIRABEAU.

Can the African Slave Trade be morally wrong, and politically right?

Motto, *Our Gallic Brother was born in* 1789, *alas! we are still in embryo.*"

————

" *Rejoicings for the recent Victories of the French.*

" The town of Belfast was almost universally illuminated. Every thing demonstrated sincere pleasure in the disgrace of two tyrannical courts, that attempted to dragoon an united nation into that deplorable state of spiritual as well as political bondage, from which it was just recovering; and that dared to tell twenty-five millions of men—YE SHALL NOT BE FREE.

" In the windows of six or seven houses, a number of transparencies presented themselves:—A few of the mottoes are subjoined, as trifling circumstances sometimes mark the disposition of the times.

" Perfect union and equal liberty to the men of Ireland.—Vive la Republique : Vive la Nation.— Church and State divorced.—Liberty triumphant.— The Rights of Men established.—Despotism prostrate.—The Tyrants are fled ; let the People rejoice. ·—Heaven beheld their glorious efforts, and crowned their deeds with success.—France is free ; so may we : let us will it.—Awake, O ye that sleep.—A gallows suspending an inverted Crown, with these words : ' May the fate of every Tyrant be that of Capet.'—A check to Despots.—The cause of Mankind triumphant.—Irishmen rejoice.—Union among Irishmen. — Rights of Man. — Irishmen ! look at France.—Liberty and Equality.

IRELAND.

8th Sept. 1783.—Armed Citizens spoke.

2nd Dec. 1783.—Their Delegates ran away.

30th Oct. 1792.—We are taxed, tithed, and enslaved, but we have only to
unite and be free.

FRANCE.

·14th July, 1789.—Sacred to Liberty.

10th August, 1792.—The People triumphant.

22nd October, 1792.—Exit of Tyranny.

" The night closed in the most orderly manner, without either bonfire, or any kind of irregularity whatever.

" The festival concluded with an entertainment at the Donegall Arms, where 104 persons sat down at dinner, when the General, who was also President of the day, announced the toasts prepared by a committee, of which the following is a copy.

" *The First Toast*—'THE FOURTEENTH OF JULY, 1789.'

" The King of Ireland.—The Constitution of France; may it be permanent.—The constitutional Assembly of France.—The National Assembly of France; may wisdom, spirit and decision, direct its counsels.—The French army; may an ardent love of their country be held paramount to every other duty in the character of a soldier.—Confusion to the enemies of French liberty.—May the Glorious Revolution of France teach the Governments of the earth wisdom.—May the example of one Revolution prevent the necessity of others.—Lasting freedom and prosperity to the United States of America.—The people of Poland, and success to their arms.—The Rights of Man; may all Nations have wisdom to understand, and spirit to assert them.—The Union of Irishmen, without which we can never be free.—The Sovereignty of the People, acting by a just and equal Representation.—The Liberty of the Press.—The Volunteers of Ireland, and their revered General, Earl of Charlemont.—The Constitutional Societies of Great Britain and Ireland.—The Society for the abolition of the Slave Trade.—President Washington.—Stanislaus Augustus, may his example be imitated.—Mr. Paine ; may perverted eloquence ever find so able an opposer.—Mr. Fox and the rights of Juries, in substance as well as form.— Mr. Grattan, and the minority of the Irish House of Commons.—The Literary Characters, who have vindicated the Rights of Man, and may genius ever be employed in them.—May all Governments be those of the Laws, and all Laws those of the People.— May the free nations of the world vie with each other in promoting liberty, peace, virtue and happiness, among men.—The increased, increasing, and sacred flame of Liberty.—Ireland.—The cause of freedom.—The memory of John Locke.—The memory of William Molyneaux.—The memory of Dr. Franklin.—The memory of Mirabeau.—The memory of Dr. Price.—The memory of Mr. Howard."

Copy of the Address to the National Assembly of France.

" It is not from vanity or ostentation that we, the citizens of Belfast, and citizen-soldiers of that town and neighbourhood, take the liberty of addressing the representative majesty of the French people— We address you, with the rational respect due to a title elevated far above all servile and idolatrous adulation, and with that affectionate fraternity of heart which ought to unite man to man, in a mutual and inseparable union of interests, of duties, and of rights; which ought to unite nation with nation, into one great republic of the world.

" On a day, sanctified as this has been by a declaration of human rights, the germ of so much
good to mankind, we meet with joy together, and
wish well to France, to her National Assembly, to
her people, to her armies, and to her King.

" May you, legislators, maintain, by the indefatigable spirit of liberty, that constitution which has
been planned by the wisdom of your predecessors,
and never may you weary in the work you have
undertaken, until you can proclaim with triumphant
security, it is finished! Manifest to an attentive
and progressive world, that it is not the phrenzy of
philosophy, nor the fever of wild and precarious
liberty, which could produce such continued agitation; but that imperishable spirit of freedom alone,
which always exists in the heart of man, which now
animates the heart of Europe, and which, in the
event, will communicate its energy throughout the
world, invincible and immortal!

" We rejoice, in the sincerity of our souls, that
this creative spirit animates the whole mass of mind
in France. We auspicate happiness and glory to
the human race, from every great event which calls
into activity the whole vigour of the whole community, amplifies so largely the field of enterprize
and improvement, and gives free scope to the universal soul of the empire. We trust that you will
never submit the liberties of France to any other
guarantees, than God and the right hands of the
people.

" The power that presumes to modify or to arbi-
trate with respect to a constitution adopted by the

people, is an usurper and a despot, whether it be the
meanest of the mob, or the ruler of empires; and
if you condescend to negociate the alteration of a
comma in your constitutional code, France from that
moment is a slave. Impudent despots of Europe!
Is it not enough to crush human nature beneath
your feet at home, that you thus come abroad to disturb the domestic settlement of the nations around
you, and put in motion your armies, those enormous
masses of human machinery, to beat down every
attempt that man makes for his own happiness?—
It is high time to turn these dreadful engines
against their inventors, and organized as they have
hitherto been, for the misery of mankind, to make
them now the instruments of its glory and its
renovation.

" Success, therefore, attend the ARMIES of France!

" May your soldiers, with whom war is not a trade,
but a duty, remember that they do not fight merely
for themselves, but that they are the advanced guard
of the world: nor let them imagine that the event
of the war is uncertain. A single battle may be
precarious, not so a few campaigns. There is an
omnipotence in a righteous cause, which masters the
pretended mutability of human affairs, and fixes
the supposed inconsistency of fortune. If you will
be free, you MUST; there is not a chance that one
million of resolute men can be enslaved: no power
on earth is able to do it; and will the God of justice
and of mercy? Soldiers! there is something that
fights for you even in the hearts of your enemies.
The native energies of humanity, rise up in volun-

tary array against tyrannical and preposterous prejudice, and all the little cabals of the heart, give way to the feelings of nature, of country, and of kind.

" Freedom and prosperity to the people of France! We think that such revolutions as they have accomplished, are so far from being out of the order of society, that they spring inevitably from the nature of man and the progression of reason ; what is imperfect he has the power to improve ; what he has created he has a right to destroy. It is a rash opposition to the irresistible will of the public, that in some instances has maddened a disposition, otherwise mild and magnanimous, turned energy into ferocity, and the generous and gallant spirit of the French into fury and vengeance. We trust that every effort they now make, every hardship they undergo, every drop of blood they shed, will render their constitution more dear to them.

" Long life and happiness to the King of the French ! Not the Lord of the soil and its servile appendages, but the King of men, who can reserve their rights, while they entrust their powers. In this crisis of his fate, may he withstand every attempt to estrange him from the nation ; to make him an exile in the midst of France, and to prevent him from identifying himself as a magistrate with the constitution, and as a Frenchman with the people.

" We beseech you all as men, as legislators, as citizens, and as soldiers, in this your great conflict for liberty for France, and for the world, to despise all earthly danger, to look up to God, and to connect your councils, your arms, and your empire, to his people, is an usurper and a despot, whether it be the meanest of the mob, or the ruler of empires; and if you condescend to negociate the alteration of a comma in your constitutional code, France from that moment is a slave. Impudent despots of Europe! Is it not enough to crush human nature beneath your feet at home, that you thus come abroad to disturb the domestic settlement of the nations around you, and put in motion your armies, those enormous masses of human machinery, to beat down every attempt that man makes for his own happiness?— It is high time to turn these dreadful engines against their inventors, and organized as they have hitherto been, for the misery of mankind, to make them now the instruments of its glory and its renovation.

" Success, therefore, attend the ARMIES of France!

" May your soldiers with whom war is not a trade, but a duty, remember that they do not fight merely for themselves, but that they are the advanced guard of the world; nor let them imagine that the event of the war is uncertain. A single battle may be precarious, not so a few campaigns. There is an omnipotence in a righteous cause, which masters the pretended mutability of human affairs, the supposed inconsistency of fortune be free, you MUST; there is not million of resolute men can b on earth is able to do; and of mercy? Sol fights for you The native

tary array against tyrannical nd preposterous prejudice, and all the little cabals of the heart, give way
to the feelings of nature, of contry, and of kind.

"Freedom and prosperity to the people of France!
We think that such revolution as they have accomplished, are so far from bein out of the order of
society, that they spring inevably from the nature
of man and the progression o reason; what is imperfect he has the power to nprove; what he has
created he has a right to estroy. It is a rash
opposition to the irresistible ill of the public, that
in some instances has maddend a disposition, otherwise mild and magnanimou turned energy into
ferocity, and the generous an gallant spirit of the
French into fury and vengeace. We trust that
every effort they now make every hardship they
undergo, every drop of bloodhey shed, will render
their constitution more dear t them.

"Long life and happiness to the King of the
French! Not the Lord of the oil and its servile appendages, but the King of en, who can reserve
their rights, while they entrst t powers. In
this crisis of his fate, may he y attempt
estrange him f ke him an
in prevent him
gistrate with the
n with the people.

throne, with a chain of union, fortitude, perseverance, morality, and religion.

" We conclude with this fervent prayer: That as the Almighty is dispersing the political clouds which have hitherto darkened our hemisphere, all nations may use the light of Heaven: that, as in this latter age, the Creator is unfolding in his creatures, powers which had long lain latent, they may exert them in the establishment of universal freedom, harmony and peace: may those who are free, never be slaves: may those who are slaves be speedily free."

REPLY TO THE PRECEDING ADDRESS, AND THAT OF THE SHEFFIELD SOCIETIES.

From the President of the National Assembly of France, Citizen Gregoire.

" Your addresses to the representatives of the French nation, have filled them with pleasing emotions. In imposing on me the honourable duty of a reply, they make me regret that I can but imperfectly express what all with so much energy feel. To have the honour to be a Frenchman or an Englishman, carries with it a title to every degree of mutual affection that can subsist among men.

" The curious in your country are pleased to traverse the globe in order to explore nature; henceforth they can visit Montblanc (Savoy) without quitting France; in other words, without leaving their friends. The day on which free Savoy unites itself with us, and that on which children of high-minded England appear among us, are, in the eye of reason, days of triumph. Nothing is wanting in these affecting scenes, but the presence of all Great Britain, to bear testimony to the enthusiasm with which we are inspired by the name of liberty, and that of the people with whom we are about to form eternal alliance.

" The National Convention has wished to testify its satisfaction to the English, in decreeing that they would conduct in the presence of some of them, the trial of the last of their kings. Sixty ages have elapsed since kings first made war on liberty: the most miserable pretexts have been sufficient for them to spread trouble over the earth. Let us re-collect with horror that under the reign of Ann, the falling of a pair of gloves, and that under Louis XIV., a window opening from one apartment into another, were sufficient causes for deluging Europe in blood.

" Alas! short is the duration prescribed by eter-nal power to our weak existence; and shall then the ferocious ambition of some individuals embitter or abridge our days with inpunity? Yet a little mo-ment, and despots and their cannons shall be silenced; philosophy denounces them at the bar of the universe; and history, sullied with their crimes, has drawn their characters. Shortly, the annals of mankind will be those of virtue; and in records of France, a place will be reserved for our testimonies of fraternity with the British and Irish societies, but especially for the Constitutional Society of London.

" Doubtless the new year, which is now approach-ing, will see all your rights restored. The meeting of your parliament attracts our attention. We hope that then, philosophy will thunder by the mouth of eloquence, and that the English will substitute the great charter of Nature, in place of the great charter of King John.

" The principles upon which our own republic has been founded, have been discovered by the celebrated writers of your nation; we have taken possession of their discoveries in the social art, because truths revealed to the world are the property of all mankind. A people which has brought reason to maturity, will not be content with liberty by halves; it will doubtless refuse to capitulate with despotism.

" Generous Britons! let us associate for the happiness of the human race; let us destroy every prejudice; let us cause useful knowledge to filter through every branch of the social tree; let us inspire our equals with a sense of their dignity; let us teach them, above all, that vices are the inseparable companions of slavery; and let us depend upon it, that our efforts will be favoured by the God of liberty, who weighs the destiny of empires, and holds in his hands the fate of nations."

Extracts from the Belfast Address to the People of Ireland.

" Trained from our infancy in a love of freedom, and an abhorrence of tyranny, we congratulate our brethren of France and ourselves, that the infamous conspiracy of slaves and despots, against the happiness and glory of that admired and respected nation, and against the common rights of man, has hitherto proved abortive.

" Impressed as we are, with a deep sense of the excellence of our constitution as it exists in theory, we rejoice that we are not, like our brethren in France, reduced to the hard necessity of tearing up inveterate abuse by the roots, even where utility was so intermixed as not to admit of separation. Ours is an easier and a less unpleasing task; to remove with a steady and a temperate resolution, the abuses which the lapse of many years' inattention and supineness in the great body of the people, and unremitting vigilance in their rulers to invade and plunder them of their rights, have suffered to overgrow and to deform that beautiful system of government, so admirably suited to our situation, our habits, and our wishes. We have not to innovate, but to restore. The just prerogatives of our Monarch we respect and will maintain. The constitutional power of the Peers of the realm we wish not to invade. We know that in the exercise of both, abuses have grown up; but we also know that those abuses will be at once corrected, so as never again to recur, by restoring to us THE PEOPLE, what we, for ourselves, *demand as our right*, our due weight and influence in that estate, which is our property, the representation of the people in parliament.

" But while we thus state our sentiments on the subject of reform, we feel it incumbent upon us to declare, as we now do, that no reform, were even such attainable, would answer our ideas of utility or justice, which should not equally include all sects and denominations of Irishmen.

" We have now declared our sentiments to the world. In declaring them we spurn with equal disdain, restraint, whether proceeding from a mob or a monarch; from a riot or a proclamation. We look with a mixture of abomination and contempt on the transactions which, on the last anniversary of the French Revolution, degraded the national character of England; when neither the learning, the piety, the public spirit, nor the private virtue of a Priestley, could protect him from the savage fury of the vilest of an ignorant and a bigoted rabble."

BELFAST LIGHT DRAGOONS.

John Burden in the Chair.

" An authentic declaration of the public opinion being now necessary, both for the direction of the legislature and the people; and as the country is not yet, we trust, so far degraded, that its unanimous and persevering demands upon any point of government, can be finally unsuccessful:—We, the members of the Belfast Light Dragoons, have assembled, in order to declare our political sentiments, viz.—

" I. We deem that a government by a King, Lords and Commons, the Commons being freely and frequently chosen by the people, is that best adapted to the genius of this country.

" II. That the object of the people is not to introduce, but to abolish novelties, such as venal

boroughs, octennial parliaments, and pensioned representatives; what we reprobate is *new*—what we
venerate is ANCIENT.

" III. That we are determined to continue our
exertions, until we obtain an impartial representation
of ALL the people—ignorant of any principle by
which a religious denomination should be excluded;
nor could it be the intention of our ancestors to
abridge a man of civil freedom, because he exercised
religious liberty.

" IV. That the only trusty safeguard of a country
is an armed and disciplined people—We will therefore continue embodied, and in the use of arms,
until we shall obtain the objects of our wishes; and
then we will continue in arms that we may defend
them.

Hu. M'ILWAIN, SEC. B.L.D.
16*th Jan.* 1793."

EXTRACTS FROM THE DECLARATION OF THE FRIENDS
OF PARLIAMENTARY REFORM IN BELFAST.—10*th
Jan.* 1793.

Waddell Cunningham in the Chair.

" SEVERAL years have elapsed since many of the
wisest and best men in England, Scotland and
Ireland, stimulated their countrymen to demand a
Parliamentary Reform; under a conviction, that it
would conduce as much to the stability of government, as to the liberty of the people. Had that
demand been unreasonable, or that *reform* unnecessary, both would long since have been forgotten, or
remained neglected. But that demand has gained

strength by age; and *the people,* instead of being lulled into indolence, are in danger of being roused into fury.

" Those honest patriots who first excited the people, and offered their best advice to government, are now called upon to remind and forewarn administration of the consequences of their former supineness, and their present obstinacy. They have also exerted themselves in keeping alive some respect for the *constitution,* and some regard to peace, together with hope of redress. But if their exhortations to government be slighted, they feel that their influence with the people will be equally disregarded. They will then be reduced to a dilemma, which cannot long hold them in suspense. They must take part with government, or they must enlist under the banners of the public. They must either co-operate in establishing a tyranny in their country, or rush into the intemperate measures of an indignant multitude. They may be obliged to renounce an infatuated court, or to meet their dearest relations and friends in arms. Some may seek a remote retreat; and lament in silence the miseries and the crimes by which their native land shall be overwhelmed; but the more numerous and vigorous party will assuredly, after struggling in vain against the torrent, plunge into the flood of civil contest. They may *endeavour* to regulate its course and moderate its rage: but they will give it strength and perseverance. They will not be found among the least formidable enemies, or the least active patriots.

" We wish not to insinuate, that there exists at present any party hostile to *a peaceable settlement.* If there be, we know it not. But this we know, that the public mind is in a ferment; that the public arm is strong; and that the most desperate proposals may speedily become the most grateful.

" We, therefore, who have always sought for reform, within the limits of the constitution, and studied to combine liberty with peace, have determined not to slacken our exertions for the attainment of the one, and the preservation of the other. We have resolved that, whatever may be the result of the present crisis, we shall be blameless; and that neither our rulers nor our fellow-subjects shall have cause to accuse us either of *intemperance* or *remissness.* But we must at the same time solemnly declare, that if the just demands of the people be despised, those who *refuse* and those who *resist* redress will be answerable to posterity, to their country, and to God, for all the crimes and calamities that may follow.

" In order to avert these evils as much as in us lies, by promoting the objects recited above, we have associated under the title of the *Friends of a Parliamentary Reform;* and have drawn up the following fundamental principles, in the hopes that all who approve of their spirit will follow our example, by forming societies of the same kind.

" *Principles.*

" I. A Constitution composed of *the King, Lords and People,* the latter fully and equally represented

K 5

in a House of Commons, *we prefer to every other*—
as admirably suited to the genius, wishes and interests of Ireland.

" II. The present, mode of representation is
absurd, unequal, and inadequate : contrary to the
spirit of our own, and of every free government.

" III. We assert that the basis of election should
be extended to the people of every religious denomination.

" With a constitution so modelled as to restore
the just rights of the collective body, without
infringing on the prerogative of the crown or on
the dignity of the peerage, we think this Nation,
whose loyalty has ever kept pace with its love of
freedom, will be satisfied and rest content."

AT A MEETING OF THE THIRD SOCIETY OF UNITED
IRISHMEN, IN THE TOWN OF BELFAST—*3rd October, 1792*—

Mr. *Clotworthy Birnie in the Chair :*

THE Declaration was agreed to, from which the
following extracts are taken.

" Associated, as we are, for the purpose of producing an union of interest and affection among all
the inhabitants of Ireland, we abhor the idea of
withholding from our Roman Catholic brethren their
civil and religious rights, at the time that we would
wish to enjoy those rights ourselves.

" We are persuaded that the religion of any man,
and his politics, are not necessarily connected: on
the contrary, that the former ought not to have any

connexion with the latter. In a civil view, there, undoubtedly is a communion of interests and rights, and every individual who contributes to the support of the state, ought to have a voice in framing the laws which regulate that state. But religion is personal—the individual alone accountable; we therefore deem it impious to intrude between his conscience and that Almighty Being, who alone knoweth his heart.

" We assert that the right of petitioning in the subject, of whatever denomination, is not only natural, but perfectly agreeable to the spirit of our constitution ; and we confess ourselves ignorant of any mode, by which our Catholic brethren could have so peaceably collected and expressed their sentiments, as by delegation."

If the reader be struck with surprise at the influence of French politics on the minds of the Belfast leaders, in the preceding documents—at the extravagant hopes founded on the revolution in that country—at the extraordinary excitement displayed by its admirers, in their fantastic celebration of its victories, or the anniversary of its outbreak,—he cannot fail likewise to have been struck, even in despite of the extravagance manifested on some occasions, at the exhibition of talent and enthusiasm in the cause of reform, on the part of its first advocates ; and especially, when he examines the discussions and proceedings of these men (an account

of which will be found in the APPENDIX), at their
enlightened views on the subject of civil and religious liberty, which were then so much in advance of
the opinions of their countrymen. The policy was
worthier of the Grand Vizier of Constantinople than
of the British minister, which made rebels of many
of those men who then advocated the questions of
reform and emancipation.

CHAPTER VIII.

By the reports of the Secret Committees, of the Lords in 1793, and of both houses of Parliament in 1797, it appears that the government, at a very early period, had a knowledge of the conspiracy carried on by the United Irish Societies in the provinces of Leinster and Ulster, though not of the persons who formed the directory of the latter province. A regular system of espionage was adopted so early as 1795; and in 1796 there were few secrets of the United Irishmen which were not in the hands of the government. It seems to be one of the necessary results of establishing secret societies, that the more the secrecy of their proceedings is sought to be secured by tests and oaths, the more widely they are published, and the very anxiety for concealment becomes the strongest occasion of treachery.

Mr. Cockayne, in 1794, was the first person who informed the government of the communication between France and Ireland. The agent of the French government, the Rev. W. Jackson, broached his mission to Theobald Wolf Tone and other United Irishmen, at the house of Counsellor Leonard M'Nally,

in Dublin. The treasonable communications were
carried on with his knowledge and concurrence;
the government was apprised of the fact by Cockayne; Jackson was tried and convicted, and Tone
had to quit the country: but M'Nally was not
molested, and being an United Irishmen, and being
generally employed as the professional advocate of
the persons of that society who had been arrested
and arraigned on the charge of treason, his means of
acquiring information were very considerable; and it
was only discovered at his death, that government
had availed themselves of his knowledge, and had
conferred a pension of £300 a-year upon him for his
private services.

I do not here refer to the ordinary gang of spies
and informers domiciled at the Tower, or in the
purlieus of the Castle, under Messrs. Sirr, Swann,
Hanlon, or Brien. These form "the hacks of the
department," of which I shall have to speak hereafter,
and "the battalion of testimony," in general. We
now only have to do with the "half-mounted" and
"squireen" class of them, who appeared in the witness box in the garb of gentlemen, or whispered
yet unsworn informations in the ears of Mr. Cooke,
and drew their bills from time to time on demand;
and several of whom, after all the enormous sums
paid to them during the rebellion, retired from
business on their pensions, provided with the means
of a respectable subsistence.

Mr. Frederick Dutton, who, at an early period was
employed in the north as an informer, and had been
sent especially to Maidstone to ensure the conviction

of O'Connor :—was a regular informer of this class—
a most reckless one in the case of the unfortunate
priest, Quigley, in whose great-coat pocket, by mistake for Arthur O'Connor's, was placed the treasonable
paper on which he was convicted. Mr. M'Gucken,
the solicitor of the United Irishmen, was another of
the private informers, who was intrusted with the
defence of the prisoners charged with treason in
Belfast, and at the same period was in the pay of
government—was largely paid, and ultimately pensioned—and during these frightful times M'Gucken
continued to possess the confidence of the United
Irishmen.

For upwards of twelve months before the breaking
out of the rebellion, several members of the Ulster
United Irish Society were likewise in the pay of
government. John Edward Newell entered on his
duties at the Castle the 13th of April, 1797, and retired
from them, rather abruptly, the 6th of February, 1798.
Nicholas Maguan, of Saintfield in the county of
Down, a member of the provincial and county committees, and also described in the report of 1798, as
a colonel in their military system during the whole
of 1797, and down to June, 1798, regularly attended
the meetings of the county Down United Irish Societies, and communicated to the Earl of Londonderry's chaplain, the Rev. John Cleland, a magistrate
of that county, the treasonable proceedings of those
societies after each meeting.

Mr. John Hughes, a bookseller of Belfast, another
member of the United Irish Society, was apprehended
at Newry, and brought into Belfast the 20th of Octo-

ber, 1797, on a charge of high treason, *and the same
evening was liberated on bail.* Mr. Hughes's character and *past* services, it cannot be doubted, obtained
for him an indulgence so extraordinary in those
times. No date is assigned to the disclosures of
Mr. Hughes, which were subsequently published in
the secret report of 1798 ; but there is reason to
believe that he was known to General Barber as an
informer in the latter part of 1796. On the 7th of
June, 1798, this man again went through the formal
process of an arrest, and was transmitted to Dublin
for special service there. Another member of the
United Irish Society, named Bird, alias Smith, had
from the same period been in the pay of government
—had laid informations against Neilson and several
of his associates, and in the latter part of 1797, like
Newell, abruptly relinquished his employment. Both
refused to come forward as witnesses on the trials of
Messrs. M'Cracken, Flannaghan, Barret, and Burn-
side. Mr. Thomas Reynolds, of Kilkea Castle, at
length supplied whatever evidence was wanting to
enable government to complete its "timely measures."
The Leinster delegates were apprehended on the 12th
of March, 1798, at the house of Oliver Bond, and
the strength of the Union being sufficiently broken
down, there remained no decent pretext for avoiding
"the premature explosion of the rebellion."

The arrest of the Leinster provincial committee,
at Bond's, and the leading members of the Union
the day following, was the death-blow to the plans of
their society. The three members of the directory on
whose talents and resources alone the society could

place any reasonable reliance, in such an emergency, were no longer at the head of its councils—Messrs. Emmett, M'Nevin and O'Connor, were in the hands of government.

The execution of its commands was still intrusted to Lord Edward Fitzgerald, but the confidence he inspired was that of a military leader, and when he likewise was lost to the cause, by his arrest on the 19th of May, the circumstances of the society were as desperate as they could well be.

On the arrest of the old directory, the younger Shears was appointed a member of the new one, and continued to belong to it, concerting with Lord Edward Fitzgerald and others the plan of the insurrection which broke out on the 23rd of May, two days previously to which both brothers were arrested. The outline of the plan was the surprisal of Dublin, the taking of the Castle, the camp at Laughlinstown, the artillery station at Chapelizod on the same night, and simultaneous risings in the counties of Dublin, Wicklow and Kildare.

Had Lord Edward lived to join the insurgents, the government might have had cause to regret the trial of the experiment of their well-timed measures for the explosion of the insurrection.

It is well known that the grand object of the directory of the United Irishmen, was to restrain the impatience of the people, and to prevent a general rising unaided by the French. In the report of the secret committee, it is fully admitted that, " until the middle of March, 1798, the disaffected entertained no serious intention of hazarding a general engage-

ment independently of foreign assistance; indeed,
the opinion of the most cautious of their body was
always adverse to premature exertion." And further
on, the report states—" that it appears, from a variety of evidence laid before your committee, that
the rebellion would not have broken out as soon as
it did, had it not been for the well-timed measures
adopted by government subsequent to the proclamation of the lord lieutenant and council, bearing
date 30th of March, 1798." It is necessary to
ascertain what these well-timed measures were. On
the examination of the state prisoners before this
committee in August, 1798, the lord chancellor put
the following question to Mr. Emmett:—" Pray,
Mr. Emmett, what caused the late insurrection?"
To which Mr. Emmett replied—" The free-quarters,
house-burnings, tortures, and the military executions in the counties of Kildare, Carlow, and Wicklow !!" Messrs. M'Nevin and O'Connor gave
similar replies to the same query.

Such were the well-timed measures adopted by
the Irish government to cause the insurrection, in
Lord Castlereagh's words, "to explode," when the
mischievous designs of the United Irishmen Society
had been long known to that government,—and so
fully, that one of its leading members declared in
parliament, "that the state prisoners had confessed
nothing which had not been known to them before."
Why, then, did they not arrest the leaders of the
Leinster societies long before, and prevent the insurrection which at length broke out?

~ This policy of allowing a people to go into rebel-

lion, when the leaders of it might have been previously seized, and their plans consequently ob-
structed and deranged, is one which, in the recent
commotion in Upper Canada, has been stigmatized in
the British parliament as a proceeding which could
not be defended on any grounds. The policy (worthy
of Machiavelli) had been acted on, however, by Mr.
Pitt so early as 1794, in the case of Jackson, the
emissary of the French government, who had been
denounced to him by his companion, Cockayne.
On Jackson's arrival in England, Mr. Pitt was
informed of his treasonable designs by Cockayne,
and yet he suffered the traitor to proceed to Ireland
on his mischievous enterprize, accompanied by the
informer, to open his mission to the leaders of the
United Irishmen Society in that country, and to
inveigle the imprudent and unwary persons with
whom he was put in communication, into acts of
treason.

The policy which dictated such a proceeding, truly
deserves the worst name that can be given to it.
The duty of an enlightened minister in similar circumstances, in these days, would be considered by
all parties, to prevent, at the onset, the accomplishment of such designs; and where the violence of
political excitement was tending towards sedition,
before the heated partizan had precipitated his followers and himself into the guilt of treason, to check
his course, instead of accelerating his steps. The
process, however, through which the unfortunate
country had to pass before a legislative Union could
be carried, was not to be interrupted. Two years

later, Mr. Harvey M. Morres, a gentleman of rank and a magistrate of the county Tipperary, and then of acknowledged loyalty, wrote to Mr. Secretary Cooke, informing him that the Orange and other factious societies had recently spread into that county, and were productive of mischievous results, which would involve the country in insurrection if they were not suppressed. Mr. Morres expressed his readiness to act in concert with the government in preventing such disorders, and discouraging those societies, which then were exasperating the people. Mr. Secretary Cooke addressed a reply to this gentleman, which could leave no doubt on his mind that the Orange societies were under the especial protection of the government, and the result would be putting the people out of the king's peace : Mr. Morres was thanked for " this proof of his zeal and loyalty," but was informed the government saw no reason for acting on his suggestions, or availing itself, in this matter, of his services.

The person whose disclosures of the designs of the Leinster societies of United Irishmen, government ultimately availed themselves of, was Mr. Thomas Reynolds, a silk manufacturer in the liberty, whose business had been carried on at 9, Park Street, the house in which he was born, on the 12th of March, 1771. On the anniversary of that day, twenty-seven years subsequently, namely, on the 12th of March, 1798, the first striking incident in the drama of his public life took place, at the house of his friend Oliver Bond, in Bridge Street, where the latter and fourteen others of his associates, delegates from various societies of United Irishmen, holding a provincial meeting, were arrested on his information. The following are the names and residences of those persons:—

BOND, OLIVER, 13, Bridge-street, Dublin.
IVERS, PETER, Carlow.
KELLY, LAWRENCE, Queen's county.
ROSE, JAMES, Windyharbour, Dublin.
CUMMINS, GEORGE, Kildare.
HUDSON, EDWARD, 38, Grafton-street, Dublin.
LYNCH, JOHN, 31, Mary's Abbey, Dublin.
GRIFFEN, LAWRENCE, Carlow.
REYNOLDS, THOMAS, Culmuttin, Kilkenny.
M'CANN, JOHN, 159, Church-street, Dublin.
DEVINE, PATRICK, Ballymoney, county of Dublin.
TRAYNOR, THOMAS, Poolbeg-street, Dublin.
BYRNE, WILLIAM MICHAEL, Park-hill, Wicklow.
MARTIN, CHRISTOPHER, Dunboyne, Meath.
BANNAN, PETER, Portarlington.

Bond was a wholesale woollen-draper, who had acquired considerable wealth in his business: Arthur O'Connor speaks of him as " a beloved friend, whom he had himself brought into the undertaking," namely, into the society of United Irishmen. His amiable manners, extensive charities, and generous disposition, had endeared him to his fellow-citizens, of all parties. He was convicted on Reynolds's evidence, and sentenced to be hanged; but was ultimately reprieved, and died shortly after of an apoplectic seizure, in Newgate. The other state prisoners, in the interval between his conviction and the time appointed for execution, had entered into negotiations with government, undertaking to make a full disclosure of their plans, reserving the names of the parties engaged in them, in consideration of Bond's life being spared as the immediate condition, and with a hope of a final stop being put to the executions. This document, signed by seventy-three of the state prisoners, is dated the 29th July, 1798.

While these terms were in process of fulfilment, on the part of the state prisoners—but only the day before the document was formally signed—William Michael Burne was executed on the 28th of July, M'Cann having previously suffered on the 19th of the same month.

The infraction of this compact with respect to the state prisoners themselves, who were parties to it, and who had been given to understand their liberation, and permission to go abroad within a specified period, would have immediately followed their performance of that part of the agreement which belonged to them, and who afterwards were detained in prison for upwards of three years, will be found more particularly detailed in the Appendix.

In one of the most admirable pieces of biography in the English language—"the Life of Curran," by his son—an anecdote is told of Reynolds, which gives some idea of his courage and self-possession. The account is contradicted by the son of this man, in his recent work, in a tone which, to Mr. Reynolds no doubt, seems calculated to persuade the world that truth and fidelity, having been banished from the page of history, had perched on the pen which was destined to write the life of Thomas Reynolds. This modest gentleman says, " there is not a word of truth or probability in the story" related by Mr. Curran.

The particulars of the occurrence, however, have been very recently communicated to me by some of the descendants of Thomas Neilson, whose veracity, I presume, will not materially suffer by a comparison with that of the son of Mr. Thomas Reynolds.

The scene of the struggle alluded to in Mr. Curran's account, was not, properly speaking, in " the liberty," but in the neighbourhood of it; and instead of any personal violence having been used by Neilson in the first instance, on his meeting Reynolds in the street, he stepped before him in a determined manner, and informed him that he must accompany him a little farther, as he had some matters of importance to mention to him.

The friends of Neilson have a vivid recollection of his account of this occurrence, and of his manner, in describing the mode of putting the startling question to Reynolds—" What should I do with a villain who did" so and so?—repeating his acts of treachery to his companions ; and of the latter's cool and deliberate answer—" You should shoot him through the heart." The following is the version of this rencontre given by Mr. Curran.

" Upon one occasion Reynolds saved himself from the vengeance of those whom he had betrayed, in a way that was more creditable to his presence of mind. Before he had yet publicly declared his infidelity to the cause of the United Irishmen, as one of their leaders, Samuel Neilson, was passing at the hour of midnight through the streets of Dublin, he suddenly encountered Reynolds, standing alone and unarmed. Neilson, who was an athletic man, and armed, rushed upon him, and commanded him, upon pain of instant death, to be silent and to accompany him. Reynolds obeyed, and suffered himself to be dragged along, through several dark and narrow lanes, till they arrived at an obscure and retired passage in the liberties of Dublin. Here Neilson presented a pistol to his prisoner's breast : 'What,' said the indignant conspirator, 'should I do to the villain who could insinuate himself into my confidence for the purpose of betraying me?' Reynolds, in a firm tone, replied, 'You should shoot him through the heart.' Neilson was so struck by this reply, that, though his suspicions were not removed, he changed his purpose, and putting up his pistol, allowed the other to retire."

This fact is given as related by an eminent Irish barrister, to whom it was communicated by one of the parties.*

Mr. Reynolds's account of this affair is thus given by his son.

"A short time after the arrests at Bond's, Neilson met my father in the street, and taking his arm, said he had a matter to talk over with him, and began as if to consult about what could be done for those in arrest. They were then near Bond's house, and

* Vide Curran's Life, by his Son, vol. ii. p. 134.

Neilson said Mrs. Bond was anxious to see my father on the subject, and as he himself was sought after by the police, he could not stop longer in the street. Under this pretence he brought my father into the house, and after a few minutes' conversation, requested him to accompany him into a back room to see Mrs. Bond. My father did so without hesitation, and Neilson led the way through the warehouses on the middle floor. The dwelling-house was in Bridge-street; the warehouses went back for at least two hundred yards, and opened by large crane gates into a mews behind. When they had reached the further wareroom, instead of Mrs. Bond they were met by a stout ill-looking man, whom my father had never seen before. Neilson walked up to the man, who stood near the crane gate, which was shut, and after whispering to him, the man went out of the wareroom, and shut the door after him. Neilson then spoke of the general plans of the United Irishmen for a few minutes, when the other man returned with a brace of pistols in his hand, and resumed his former position. Some vague suspicions now flashed across my father's mind, and Neilson abruptly said, 'Reynolds, you have not a minute to live! you are the man who betrayed the delegates!' 'And dare you say that?' said my father, darting at him. At the same time he seized him by the collar with both hands, and thrust him back upon the man with the pistols, with such force that the crane-gate, not being fastened, opened outwards to the mews on being pushed against, and the man fell down backwards into the lane, where Neilson would

have followed had not my father held him up. Neilson directly turned, or attempted to turn the affair
into a joke, saying, " Oh, my dear fellow, how could
you be so violent?   I assure you we only wished to
try you; I fear you have killed him!' My father
replied that he neither understood nor relished such
practical jokes, and walked out of the warehouse,
leaving Neilson to take such care as he pleased of
his companion below.   There were several persons
in the house who had been dining with Mrs. Bond,
but my father passed through the hall without
noticing any one.   It was then between five and six
o'clock in the afternoon, in the month of March." *

The scene of the struggle is, no doubt, correctly
stated in the preceding account, and the result in
the main such as Reynolds describes it; this consummate assurance, and successful assumption of the
tone and manner of an innocent man, injured and
angered by the suspicion of his fidelity, had the
effect of completely astounding his assailant, and in
his momentary confusion, of affording the man he
had believed to be a villain, an opportunity of effecting
his escape.   As to the story of rushing on Neilson,
whom he acknowledges to have been " a very athletic
man"—of his doing this in the presence of a man
with pistols in his hands, not only with impunity,
but with such actual violence even to this person as
to bring him to the ground—these embellishments
to it must be taken, not " cum grano," but " cum
multis granis salis," and an adequate allowance for
the statements of a man like Mr. Reynolds, who was

* See Life of Thomas Reynolds by his Son, vol. 1. p. 201.

desirous of giving treachery a chivalrous aspect of patriotism triumphing over extraordinary perils, and of having every act of his represented as a movement important to the state, and destined to be written in biographical heroics.

It is a very strange circumstance that, notwithstanding Reynolds, long previously to the arrests, had been shunned by several of the more discreet and wary of the United Irishmen, who had some knowledge of his private character and conduct in pecuniary affairs, he was still trusted by the most influential of their leaders; nay, even after the arrests at Bond's, when they were warned against him, he continued to be received by them as a person still faithful to their cause.

Some days subsequently to the arrests at Bond's, there had been a meeting of the provincial committee at the Brazen Head hotel, in a lane off Bridge-street. This meeting was attended, amongst others, by a gentleman then residing in New Row, in the entire confidence of the directory, and from my own knowledge of his character, I should say there was no man more entitled to it, on whose authority the facts are stated which will be found in the following account.

One Michael Reynolds of Naas, who was said to be a distant relative to Mr. T. Reynolds, and who had been particularly active in the society and useful to it, attended this meeting. This young man addressed the meeting at some length; he said, that circumstances had lately transpired in the country, and steps, with regard to individuals, had been taken by

government, which made it evident that a traitor
was in their camp, who must belong to one of the
country committees, and one who held a high rank
in their society: that traitor, he said, was Thomas
Reynolds of Kilkea Castle, and if he were allowed to
proceed in his career, they and their friends would
soon be the victims of his treachery. In a tone and
manner which left an indelible impression on the
minds of his hearers, and which the person I allude
to was wont to speak of as having produced an
extraordinary effect, he asked if the society were
to be permitted to be destroyed, or if Reynolds
were to be allowed to live; in short, he demanded of
the meeting their sanction for his removal, and
undertook that it should be promptly effected.

The proposal was unanimously and very properly
rejected by the meeting. Michael Reynolds was a
young man of great muscular strength and activity,
of a short stature and dark complexion, and somewhat celebrated in the country for his horseman-
ship.

About the middle of April, Reynolds was visited
by a Mr. Kinselah, " who called on him for the
purpose of informing him that one of the brothers
Sheares, who after the arrests of the 12th of March,
had assumed the direction of the conspiracy in Dublin, had arrived at Dr. Esmond's house, near Naas,
and having called a private meeting of some of the
county delegates, had informed them officially in the
name of the directory, that Reynolds was the man
who had caused the arrests of the 12th of March;
upon which they resolved that he should be sum-

moned to attend them the next day at Bell's, (a public
house on the Curragh of Kildare,) and there be put
to death, unless he proved beyond all doubt that he
was innocent of the charge.

On M'Cann's trial, he stated that he had been
informed "the accusation against him, on which
he was to be tried, had been brought down from
Dublin by Michael Reynolds from the provincial
committee.

When the message to attend this meeting was
brought to him, his cousin, Mr. Dunn of Leinster
Lodge, happened to be with him, and on his refusal
to attend, the messengers went away sulky and discontented, and he attributed the preservation of his
life to the presence of Mr. Dunn on this occasion.*

The next morning, Mr. Matthew Kennaa, a respectable farmer of the neighbourhood, called on Reynolds
and urged him to go over to the meeting—Reynolds
again refused, and the consequence was, young Mr.
Reynolds states, that orders were issued to Kennaa
and one Murphy, a butcher, to shoot his father;
and, on the 18th of April, these two men rode up to
the gate. Kennaa alighted and walked up to Reynolds, who was in a field superintending some labourers, leaving Murphy in care of the horses. He
observed that Kennaa seemed much confused, and
was fumbling in his breast as he approached. Reynolds quickly stepped up to him, and said " What
mischief are you after now, Kennaa?" and putting
his hand at the same time on his breast, he felt a
pistol. Mr. Reynolds states, that on his doing this,

* Reynolds's Life by his Son, vol. i. p. 221.

Kennaa trembled exceedingly, and made no resistance to his father's taking the pistol—that he stam-
mered out some expressions of respect for his father,
and acknowledged that he came for the purpose of
shooting him : and yet Mr. Reynolds suffered Mr.
Kennaa to depart unmolested, though there were
twenty work-people in the field at the time this
occurrence took place. There is some truth in this
account, mixed up with the usual embellishments of
Mr. Reynolds's lively imagination ; but that it was
intended to assassinate him, and that specific orders
had been given to this effect, there can be no doubt.

On the 18th of March he attended a meeting of
the United Irishmen, at the house of one Reilly, a
publican, on the Curragh, at which he produced a
letter he had obtained from Lord Edward, recommending the vacancies occasioned by the late arrests
to be filled up ; but a discussion of a very different
kind was immediately introduced, on a proposition
" to change all the officers of the county meetings'
committees, as it was supposed that none others
could have furnished this intelligence on which the
government had acted. *Reynolds seconded this proposition*, he being at the time one of the officers proposed to be changed. Dr. John Esmond was then
appointed to the place of Reynolds, and Michael
Reynolds of Naas in the place of Cummins, who had
been arrested at Bond's. The other delegate for
Kildare, Mr. Daly of Kilcullen, was retained in office.
At this meeting the question of the recent arrests
was loudly and angrily discussed, and insinuations
were dropped which could not leave Mr. Reynolds

particularly at his ease—but not one word on this subject appears in his memoirs. He had spent the night before at Naas, and it appears from the questions put to him on Bond's trial, that, for the purpose of preserving his life, it was necessary for him to take an oath that he was not the person who betrayed the secrets of the society which led to the arrests at Bond's. He was asked about an oath he had taken on that occasion, with reference to his denial of the charges brought against him; he said, " I do not deny it, nor do I say I took it, I was so alarmed— but I would have taken one if desired. When the United Irishmen were designing to kill me, I took an oath before a county member that I had not betrayed the meeting at Bond's."*

On the 3rd of May, Reynolds, on his way to Dublin from Kildare, was met by a Mr. Taylor, and warned if he proceeded on his journey that his life would be taken, as a party at no great distance were waiting for him. Reynolds returned to Naas, and Taylor proceeded to Athy, where being mistaken for Reynolds, whom he resembled, he was attacked and wounded with a pike in the thigh. Reynolds took refuge in the house of an innkeeper of the name of M'Donnell, where he slept that night. Michael Reynolds discovered his place of concealment, and made a proposition to M'Donnell, who was an United Irishman also, to allow him and some of his followers to enter the house at night, and put an end to Reynolds. M'Donnell opposed the project, and gave notice of it to Reynolds, who took all the precautions

* See Bond's Trial; Ridgeway's Report, p. 202.

in his power for his safety, and the following morning he returned to Kilkea Castle.

But there is one circumstance connected with Mr. Reynolds's denial of the charge of betraying the secret of the provincial committee at Bond's, which was not likely, indeed, to be found in his son's memoirs of his life, nor has it hitherto been noticed in any published account of the affairs of those times.

Felix Rourke was the secretary of the society for the barony of Upper Cross, in the county of Kildare, and his friend, Bartholomew Mahon, held the same situation in that of Newcastle. They were appointed to meet the baronial committee at Naas, and subsequently the provincial one, as county delegates. About the period of their latter appointment, I am informed by Mahon, who is still living in the city of Dublin, that Mr. Reynolds, in Kildare, being taxed with being an informer—or one, at least of the county delegates, who must have given the information that led to the arrests at Bond's— vehemently denied the charge; and the names of several of the absent members being mentioned in the course of this discussion, Reynolds fixed on the name of Felix Rourke, then almost a boy, and, from his humble station, of little influence, and plainly intimated that he was the person who was to be suspected. The result of this intimation was, that poor Rourke, a person who subsequently sealed with his blood his devotion to this cause, was placed on his trial by his society—my informant, Mahon, was present on this occasion. Rourke burst into tears

when the charge was repeated : he indignantly re-
pelled it, and was acquitted ; but Mahon states that
his life was in the greatest peril.

The process by which Reynolds was led from his
treason to the state, to his first partial disclosures to
Mr. Cope, and ultimate complete communication of
all the secrets of his society in his sworn informations, it is not difficult to trace. He had extensive
money-dealings with Mr. Cope, and difficulties of an
unpleasant nature arose in the adjustment of those
claims which that gentleman had with him.

These claims had been settled; but the differences
which had arisen between them made it necessary
for Reynolds to keep on good terms with Mr. Cope,
and to evince an increased desire for standing well
in his esteem. Mr. Cope, in the latter part of February, 1798, took occasion to accompany Reynolds to
the country-seat of Sir Duke Gifford, and, in the course
of their journey, contrived to sound his companion on
the subject of the troubled state of the country.

He described the man who could be found to give
information of the designs of the United Irishmen
to government, as one who would be called the sa-
viour of his country—who would have the highest
honours and rewards conferred upon him : a seat in
parliament, and £1,500 or a couple of thousand
pounds a-year from government.

Reynolds was a man both greedy of gain and
ambitious of distinction, and, as his letters and conduct will shew, utterly indifferent to the opinion of
people of his own humble rank, but exceedingly
desirous of being thought well of by the great, and

of being privileged to communicate with public men
in high stations, or to correspond with official persons. He intimated to Mr. Cope, that such a man
might be found, but he would not be known as an
informer; he would not come forward as a witness
against his associates, nor have his name communicated to government; he would accept of no honours or rewards—but, as " he was determined to
quit the country for a time, he would require his
extraordinary expenses to be paid to him, *or other
damages that he might receive;*" and on Mr. Cope's
asking him " what sum would cover the extraordinary expenses or losses?" Mr. Reynolds replied
he did not think they would exceed £500, for which
sum there should be liberty to draw on him. " I
agreed to every thing," says Cope, " and he, Mr.
Reynolds, gave me then such information as he was
possessed of."*

I think it most probable that Mr. Reynolds said no
more than what he meant on this occasion; and that
he really believed he might do a great service to his
friend Mr. Cope, at the expense of the general interests of the society to which he belonged himself,
without involving the lives of his associates in any
extreme peril.

At another interview with Mr. Cope, he was
induced to go on a step farther than he had done at
the last meeting: he was led to make disclosures
about particular societies, and eventually about particular members of them—but he still objected to
come forward as a witness against them; he would,

* Ridgway's Report of Oliver Bond's Trial, p 187.

in fact, only enable the government to lay hold of
these persons, and leave the odium of convicting
them on the evidence of other informers. He was
now ready to sacrifice his friends, but not to be
known as the betrayer of them : he had no objection
to their being taken up on his information, and
convicted, and executed—but he was ashamed of
being seen in the witness-box against them. This,
in all probability, is the customary process through
which the minds of the generality of those persons
who turn approvers are led, before any one of them
stands before the public with the brazen front, the
reckless bearing, and hardened breast of a hacknied
informer. " The respectable" informer has to pass
through these gradations, before he is able or willing
to bear the gaze of the multitude, or the glance of
the prisoner, his former friend or acquaintance, in
the dock : to stand before the crowded court in the
character of an atoning criminal, pardoned for the
purpose of criminating his companions ;—or before he
arrives at the high distinction of interchanging smiles
with the superintendents of police, of hanging about
the public offices at the Castle, of cultivating the
acquaintance of clerks and secretaries—of stipulating
with them for the pieces of silver, or dropping a hint
about the place or pension, which are ultimately
forced on his reluctant acceptance ! These come, of
course, in the progress of events—unbargained for,
unsolicited and unsought. The delicacy of Reynolds's sentiments was hurt, when he was informed
by Mr. Cope that he might expect to be handsomely
rewarded for his information. Reynolds protested

he would accept of none; but he had no objection to be indemnified for his losses : " I told him," says Mr. Reynolds, " that neither honour nor rewards were looked for, nor would be accepted."

These arrests were immediately followed up by those of Thomas Addis Emmett, and Dr. William James M'Nevin; and, on the 19th of May following, of Lord Edward Fitzgerald. Mr. Reynolds, however, had not the merit of having brought his noble friend and benefactor to the scaffold; it was reserved for him, after the death of that friend, in his evidence before parliament, to lay the foundation for an attainder, which was "to visit the cradle of his unprotected offspring with want and misery."

Reynolds's father had married a lady of the name of Fitzgerald, " the eldest daughter of Thomas Fitzgerald, of Kilmead, in the county of Kildare, a descendant of the Earls of Kildare, and consequently a relative of the Leinster family." Young Reynolds was sent abroad and completed his studies at a Jesuit establishment in Flanders. His mother carried on the business in Park-street after his father's death, and on his return to Ireland, he resided with her.

In his life, written by his son, we are informed that, shortly after his return, he had taken his mistress to a masquerade-ball at the Rotunda, and had given her a very valuable diamond ornament, worth £50 or £60, which his mother had placed in his hat, and a sum, moreover, of £24 or £25, which he happened to have in his pocket. His mother, on his return, missed the diamond ornament. He " assured her it should be returned in a day or two : but nothing would pacify her; she called it robbery, and vowed she would send the constables after the girl, when he remarked that, in fact, the pin was his property, and not hers."* The pin, however, it is admitted, had been given to him for this special occasion by his mother, the night before.

It was not only with his mother's ornaments that Mr. Thomas Reynolds made free—but he was accused, his son informs us, by a Mr. Warren, who had the management of his mother's business, " of having stolen silks from his mother's warehouse"—a charge, he states, which was made at the time of the trials of 1798, for the purpose of injuring his father's credit." " The fact was," continues his biographer, " his mother and Mrs. Warren had continually gowns cut from any silks they fancied for their own use, of which no account was taken. My father had, twice or three times, a gown in like manner cut off for this young woman; it was done openly in the wareroom, but Warren and the clerks had particular charge not to tell his mother."†

In 1794, Mr. Reynolds married Miss Harriet Witherington, whose sister was the wife of Theobald Wolfe Tone. With this lady Mr. Reynolds got a fortune of £1,500, and, on his marriage, was taken into partnership by his mother and her then co-partner, Mr. Warren. In 1797, the whole affairs of the house were in his hands. The property was then encumbered with debts, young Reynolds states, to the amount of £9,000, of which £5,000 *was due*

* Vide Life of Thomas Reynolds by his Son. Vol. i. p. 65, 67.
† Ibid.

to Messrs. Cope and Co. There appears, however, to have been sufficient property left to Thomas Reynolds to meet these engagements: he however entered into arrangements with the Messrs. Cope, in consideration of the sum of £1,000 paid down to them, to take a lien on the property of Sir Duke Gifford for the whole of their demand; and a similar arrangement was made with his other largest creditors, Messrs. Jaffray and Co.

On the death of Gifford, when his property became available to Messrs. Cope, Reynolds attempted, unsuccessfully, to set aside the conditions into which he had entered with Cope, and to deduct the £1,000 he had paid to that house, from the claim he had sold on the property of Gifford. On his mother's retirement from the business, an allowance was secured to her of £200 a-year by her son. In the spring of 1797, Mr. Reynolds made an application to the Duke of Leinster for a lease of the lands of Kilkea. Through the interference in his behalf of Lord Edward Fitzgerald with his brother (though this fact is denied in Mr. Reynolds's biography), he was put in possession of Kilkea castle, and about 350 acres of land—" of the first land in the country"— on paying down a fine of £1000, "the reserved rent amounting to no more than £48. 2s. a-year!"*— terms so advantageous, as could only have been obtained by friendly interference, in some quarter, with the owner of the property.

Mr. Reynolds' biographer states that an old servant of the family, named Betty Cahill, some years

* Vide Life of Thomas Reynolds, vol 1. p. 99.

previously to 1798, had placed £175 in the hands of the mother of Thomas Reynolds, and a joint bond was given to the old blind woman, Betty Cahill, by Mrs. Reynolds and her son, for £100. Mr. Reynolds gave another bond for £50, and his note of hand for £25. On one of the occasions of her bringing the bonds to Mr. Reynolds, to receive the interest thereon, and have the amount written on the back, she left the original bonds; and on calling for them subsequently, *she received, by mistake,* a draft-bond, in lieu of one of her own. Mrs. Cahill applied for payment through an attorney, and, on M'Cann's trial, the 5th of July, Mr. Reynolds, on his cross-examination, stated that he had paid both principal and interest. His biographer says—" the last bill fell due on the 1st of July, 1798; on that day my mother went, by my father's directions, to Mrs. Cahill to pay it."

On the 6th of November, 1797, the mother of Mrs. Reynolds died in Dublin, after a short illness : her medical attendant was Dr. M'Nevin. Her son was then from home, and did not arrive in town till the morning after her decease. On the retirement of this lady from the business in Park-street, an annuity of £200 a-year had been settled on her by her son.

The day after her decease, her son arrived in Dublin, and visited the remains of his mother. On the trial of William Michael Byrne, he was asked, on his cross-examination, if he recollected going into his mother's room (on his arrival from the country) and seeing a person taking away a bottle of wine, and running with eagerness, and saying—he would take it himself, as he had sent it? To which question he replied, he could not recollect it, because it never happened. The person, however, who could have sworn that it did happen, was then in Newgate, on a charge of treason : that person was Dr. M‘Nevin, and its occurrence he plainly spoke of as one of which he was cognizant.

The mother-in-law of Mr. Reynolds, Mrs. Witherington, died at a house of his in Ash-street, in April, 1797. On the trial of Oliver Bond, Mr. Reynolds was cross-examined at some length respecting this lady's death. The following are the questions and answers on this subject, as they are given in Ridgway's report of the trial :—

Quest.—She had a complaint in her bowels?

Ans.—She had.

Quest.—You administered medicine?

Ans.—I did ; tartar-emetic.

Quest.—She died shortly after ?

Ans.—She took it on Friday, and died on Sunday.

Quest.—Did you give her any other potion except that ?

Ans.—No, I did not.

Quest.—Do you recollect Mr. Reynolds being charged, in your family, with any thing touching that prescription?

Ans.—Since I have been brought up to Dublin, I have heard that Major Witherington said I poisoned his mother with tartar-emetic.

Quest.—You heard that?

Ans.—And many other ill-natured things too.

Quest.—Very cruel; but the best of men—

Ans.—May err.

Quest.—Did you hear any thing about a pitched sheet for the poor old lady?

Ans.—I did; it was one of the charges of the funeral-bill, which bill I paid. She was a very large corpulent woman; she was kept till her son came to town, and she could not be kept without the sheet.

Quest.—Upon what day?

Ans.—The fourth day after her death: she could not be kept otherwise.

On M'Cann's trial, on a similar cross-examination, Mr. Reynold's stated, that he had paid into her hands a sum of £300, about a fortnight or three weeks before her death. This money it appeared was intended to be applied by her, towards the purchase of a commission for one of her sons, but at her death, the money was not to be found. It is proper to state, that on this trial Mr. Reynolds, in explanation of the circumstance regarding the medicine he had administered to his mother-in-law, said that " a Mr. Fitzgerald, a relation of his family, who had been an apothecary and had quitted business, left him a box of medicines, containing castor oil, cream of tartar, tartar emetic, and such things. He had been subject to a complaint of the stomach, for which Mr. Fitzgerald gave him a quantity of powders in small papers, which he kept for use and found great relief from; they had saved his life, and he had asked Mrs. Reynolds for one of these papers, to give to Mrs. Witherington, and it was given to her."*

* Vide Ridgeway's Report of McCann's Trial, p. 28.

At one or other of the several trials, on which
Mr. Reynolds gave evidence against the prisoners
who had been arrested at Bond's, his testimony was
sought to be impeached, and the following persons
deposed, that they did not believe him to be worthy
of credit on his oath.

Mr. Valentine O'Connor, a merchant of the city of
Dublin.

Mrs. Mary Malloy, his cousin, a nun.

Mrs. Anne Fitzgerald, his mother's sister, a nun.

Major Edward Witherington, his brother-in-law.

Mr. Henry Witherington, ditto

Mr. Warren, his mother's former partner in trade.

Mr. Peter Sullivan, a clerk of Mr. Reynolds.

The following witnesses were produced, in support
of his testimony, and from their knowledge of his
character, declared their belief of his being entitled
to credit in a court of justice.

Mr. Cope, a merchant of Dublin.

Mr. Furlong, an attorney of Mr. Reynolds.

The Rev. Mr. Kingsbury, a clergyman, a friend of
Mr. Kemmis, the crown solicitor.

On Bond's trial, Mr. Reynolds gave a detailed
account of the several oaths he had taken.   He had
sworn to secrecy, on being made a member of the
United Irishmen's Society.   He had taken an oath
of fidelity to his captains on being appointed colonel.
He had taken another, before a county meeting, that
he had not betrayed his associates at Bond's.   He had
likewise taken the oath of allegiance twice, and an
oath before the privy council once, and thrice in the
courts of justice, namely on the trials of Bond,
Byrne and McCann.   Without disparaging the ser-

vices of Mr. Reynolds, it is impossible to look upon him, except as " a kind of man, to whom the law resorts with abhorrence and from necessity, in order to set the criminal against the crime; and who is made use of by the law, for the same reasons that the most noxious poisons are resorted to in desperate disorders."*

It would have been unnecessary to have gone into these details, but for the ill-judged efforts of those who have lately undertaken to represent Mr. Reynolds, rather in the light of a martyr to the purity and disinterestedness of his patriotic principles, than as a reluctant witness, induced to come forward by the persuasions of an influential friend, and in some degree willing to be convinced of his former errors, and to regard the retrieval of his necessitous condition, as one of the casual results of repentant guilt.

His biographer, however, bitterly complains of the treatment he received from the government. Before it was known in the country, that Mr. Reynolds had been converted by Mr. Cope from the evil of his political ways, or had been sufficiently long in the company of Major Sirr, or his domestic chaplain the Rev. Mr. Gubbins, to become a new man and wholly separated from the errors of his popish ancestors, the military took possession of Kilkea Castle, established free quarters there, and spared Mr. Reynolds none of the ravages customary on

* Vide Curran's speech against the Bill of Attainder of Lord Edward Fitzgerald

such occasions. This place of old had been the scene of perfidy and bloodshed.

In 1580, the Earl of Kildare, (Gerald, the eleventh Earl,) Custodian under Elizabeth, of the north border of the English pale, and lord of Kilkea Castle, on his return from England, where he had been imprisoned in the Tower on suspicion of favouring the Irish, to give his royal mistress a proof of his loyalty, courted the acquaintance of his neighbour Fergus O'Kelly, of Leix, who had married the daughter of O'Byrne, of Glenmure, in the county of Wicklow, (now represented by the Byrnes of Cabinteely) and invited him to Kilkea Castle, where he murdered his guest, and then communicated this treacherous murder to the queen, as a satisfactory evidence of his devotion to her interests, in putting to death an Irish rebel. He obtained the O'Kelly lands as the reward of his fidelity, and demised his illgotten possessions to his natural son, Garret Fitzgerald. This Garret left a son named Gerald, long remembered in Kildare for his barbarous cruelties, and finally for his reverse of fortune.*

Previously to the arrests at Bond's, on the 12th of March, Mr. Reynolds returned to Kilkea Castle; but the tables were turned on its modern occupant—he who might reasonably consider himself at this period the supreme arbiter of life and death, was himself treated in his own house as "a mere Irishman." His son tells us, that " his father's steward, William Byrne, was flogged and tortured to make him dis-

* See Hardiman's Bardic Remains, vol. i. p. 187, and the Anthologia Hibernica.

cover the supposed depot of arms. Lieut. Love of the 9th dragoons, being a tall man, tied his silk sash about Byrne's neck, and hung him over his shoulders, while another officer flogged him until he became insensible; and similar acts (he continues) obtained for Mr. Love the soubriquet of the walking gallows."* As this marauding had been duly performed in the king's service, and at the period of its infliction on Kilkea Castle, its owner, unknown to the military, was a white-washed rebel restored to his allegiance, and high in the favour of Cooke and Castlereagh, he sent in a moderate estimate of the property destroyed on this occasion, "conformably to the terms of the act for indemnifying suffering loyalty," amounting only, as his biographer informs us, to the sum of £12,760; a sum which he declares with becoming gravity, "would not have replaced the property lost by one half."*

Now, if this be true, Mr. Reynolds previously to the rebellion must have been worth £25,000. How did it happen that he was obliged so very recently to pass bills and notes for such paltry sums as £10 and £20 to the old servant Mrs. Cahill?—that on giving up business, he had not been able to pay off the debts of the firm, without coming to the arrangements entered into with Mr. Cope and the house of Jaffrey?—that after he had made his disclosures to government, and previously to the trials taking place, when it was so desirable for him to be then clear of the suspicion of having turned informer for the sake of gain, that he was compelled by his neces-

* Life of Thomas Reynolds, vol 1 p 231.

sities to draw on Mr. Cope for the sum of 300 guineas, and again for another sum of 200 ?

On Bond's trial, when asked by the counsel for the prisoner, when he had drawn for the 300 ?—he replied, that it was four or five days before the arrests at Bond's, and the time of drawing for the other 200 was when he was in the county of Kildare, " before he had been injured by the military." " But he had determined to quit the kingdom as soon as Mrs. Reynolds, who was then in her confinement, had recovered, and he wanted to pay some debts before he went away."*

In the second volume of his work, Mr. Reynolds's biographer states, that Kilkea Castle, of which he had a lease for three lives, renewable for ever—estimating the 360 acres of land at twenty-six shillings per acre, at only twenty years' purchase, was worth £8,100. That the property destroyed by the troops, " duly certified," amounted to £12,760, and these two sums, he says, make a total of £19,860 actual bonâ fide loss, not to mention other losses which he has shewn in the body of his work. " Now," he asks, " what has his father received? A sum of £500, paid to him at the time when he expected to be enabled to quit Ireland till the storm had blown over, and an annuity of £1000 Irish, or £920 English, with reversion to my mother, my brother, and myself."†

The statement of the sacrifice of property to the amount of £19,860, some forty years ago, might

* Vide Ridgeway's Report, Bond's Trial, p. 195.

† Vide Reynolds's Life, vol. ii. p. 514.

have been of some avail, but it would be as difficult a matter now to sustain it, as to turn it to any profitable account. Mr. Moore and Dr. Taylor, the able author of the History of the Civil Wars of Ireland, have unhappily fallen under the displeasure of young Mr. Reynolds, for presuming to think that the necessities of his father had no slight share in the proceedings which caused Reynolds to appear to Mr. Cope as "a man who would and ought to be placed higher in his country than any man that ever was in it."

His biographer has put some very serious and important questions on this subject, which deserve to be answered; and though I am fully aware how much more competent to do so, either of the able persons are to whom he alludes, I have taken no small pains to make myself acquainted with the subject, which Mr. Reynolds has, perhaps indiscreetly, made so prominent a topic—and, *perhaps*, a little too triumphantly in his tone has provoked a reply to.

"Perhaps (says Mr. Reynolds) Mr. Taylor could furnish me with the records from which he discovered that my father was distressed for want of money. He may, perhaps, consider Mr. Moore's Life of Lord Edward Fitzgerald as a record, or Mr. Moore himself as a historian, but as I shall notice his work in another place, I shall confine myself for the present to Mr. Taylor. From what source did Mr. Taylor discover that my father had been an active member of the Union; and, above all, from what record did he receive the foul slander that he had sold the secret to government? Could not the same record have supplied him with the price also; and if so, why did he not name it? From what records did he learn that my father had insured to himself by his conduct even the slightest reward? The whole accusation is false as it is malicious." *

Either Mr. Reynolds believes that his questions are unanswerable, or those who could answer them are not willing to do so. Time, however, has unravelled greater mysteries than those connected with the name and exploits of Mr. Reynolds. Documents, whose authenticity cannot be called in question, are in existence, and furnish irrefragable proof of Mr. T. Reynolds having received for his disclosures, not £500 only, but the sum of £5000, in four payments, at the following dates, and in the following amounts :—

" 1798, Sept. 29, Mr. T. Reynolds received . £1000

   ,,   Nov. 16,   Ditto   ditto . . 2000

 1799, Jan. 19,   Ditto   ditto . . 1000

   ,,   March 4,   Ditto   ditto . . 1000"

"—to complete £5000."—And, moreover, on the 14th of June, 1799, Mr. Reynolds received his annuity of £1000, " in full to the 25th of March, 1799 ;" from which period till his death, the 18th of August, 1836, his pension continued to be paid to him.

The amount of that pension was £1000 Irish, or £920 British : he received it for a term of thirty-seven years.

The gross amount for the above period, at

     £920 per annum, is £34,040

Gratuity before the trials of Bond,

     M'Cann, and Byrne   500

* Life of Thomas Reynolds by his Son, vol. 1 p. 103.

Brought forward . . . £34,540

Gratuities between Sept. 1798, and March 4,
1799 5000

Consulship at Lisbon, four years at £1400
per annum 5600

Consulship at Iceland, two years at £300
per annum 600

_____

£45,740

In 1810 he was appointed to the consulate at Lisbon, where he remained nearly four years, the salary and emoluments of which office averaged £1400 per annum.

In 1817 he was appointed to the consulate at Iceland, where he remained about one year, on a salary of £300 per annum; he returned to England, and in 1819 went back to Copenhagen, where he continued a few months, and then, on leave of absence, repaired to France, leaving his son to act in his stead as vice-consul, in which office he continued till 1822; another son obtained a lucrative appointment under the stamp office department at Hull.

This enormous sum of £45,740, the " disinterested friend of his country" received, and as the pension on the Irish civil list reverts to his widow and to his two sons, who are now in the prime of life, it is by no means improbable that one of the parties may survive the person to whom it was originally granted some five-and-twenty or thirty years; and if so, the people of Great Britain will have the further gratification of paying another sum of twenty or five-and-twenty thousand pounds more, for the credit of Lord

Castlereagh's government in Ireland, (nominally of Lord Camden's,) and as a tribute of respect to the memory and worth of Mr. Thomas Reynolds. There are gentlemen in the British parliament, though not forgetful of the services of Mr. Reynolds, and others of his class, who may think this subject deserving of their attention, who may imagine that the children of the starving operatives of Leeds and Manchester, are entitled to as much consideration as those of the gentlemen who made orphans of so many, and who during their lives were amply rewarded for any service they rendered to their employers.

The interference of Lord Edward Fitzgerald, with regard to the lease of Kilkea Castle, in favour of Reynolds, is called, with the usual modesty of his biographer, " a piece of pure invention from be-ginning to end." "Early in 1797, (this gentleman states, his father took from the Duke of Leins-ter the valuable lease of the castle and lands of Kilkea;"—that "he became a United Irishman in February, 1797;—that, "in November, 1797, Lord Edward called on his father, and asked him to take his place as colonel of a regiment of United Irishmen, enrolled in the county Kildare, for a short time. These dates are rather unfortunate for the arduous task of whitewashing the character of Mr. Reynolds's friendship, considering the very advan-tageous terms on which the lease was granted to him, and the confidential communications between Lord Edward and Mr. Reynolds, admitted by the latter, in November, 1797, the very month of his obtain-ing the lease from the Duke of Leinster.

In the information given upon oath by Thomas Reynolds, and afterwards confirmed before the secret committees in 1798, his intimacy with Lord Edward is thus alluded to, " Deponent further saith, that in November, 1797, Lord Edward Fitzgerald, accompanied by Hugh Wilson, met deponent upon the steps of the Four Courts, and told him that he wished to speak to him upon very particular business; that deponent informed Lord Edward Fitzgerald he would be found in Park-street if he called on him there; that deponent and Lord Edward knew each other only personally, and that only from a purchase deponent had been about in the county of Kildare from the Duke of Leinster."*

Here Reynolds himself acknowledges what is positively denied by his son, that in the business relating to the purchase from the Duke of Leinster, Mr. Reynolds had a *personal* knowledge of Lord Edward Fitzgerald.

It would appear from young Mr. Reynolds's work, that his father had a sincere regard for Lord Edward Fitzgerald. It is very probable that he had as much regard for his lordship as it was in his nature to feel for any man—that is to say, he had no personal animosity to this young nobleman; and after the arrests at Bond's, perhaps, had nothing to gain (when he knew the secret of his place of concealment) by betraying him, for the reward of £1000 for his apprehension was not published till the 11th of May, and Reynolds was not then in town. But when it was part of the duty required of him by his em-

* Vide Report of Secret Committee, 1798 ; Appendix XVI. p. 132.

ployers, to deprive the widow and children of his dead friend of the means of subsistence, he was restrained by no compunctious visitings of nature from swearing away the property of his friend, as he had done the lives of his associates.

There are three proofs given by Mr. Reynolds, junior, of the friendship of his father for Lord Edward. Two days after the arrests at Bond's, on his information—(Lord Edward having so far fortunately escaped that peril by the accidental circumstance of seeing Major Swan's party enter the house, when he, Lord Edward, was on his way there, at the corner of Bridge-street,)—Reynolds visited Lord Edward at his place of concealment, at Dr. Kennedy's in Aungier-street, and discussed with his lordship his future plans as to his concealment, &c. Mr. Reynolds discovered " he had no arms of any sort except a small dagger, and he was quite unprovided with cash, which was then scarce, as the banks had stopped all issue of gold. My father called on him again, on the evening of the 15th, and brought him fifty guineas in gold, and a case of good-sized pistols, with ammunition, and a mould for casting bullets."* " He took the pistols, threw a cloak over his shoulders, and left the house accompanied by Mr. Lawless. My father never saw him more." Poor Lord Edward little imagined from what source that money had been derived, or that he and his companions had been betrayed by the very man who had been so recently in his company, and who had already drawn on the agent of government for the first portion of that

* Life of Thomas Reynolds, vol. ii. p. 219.

stipulated sum which was the reward of his disclosures, and placed a part of the price of his friend's
blood in his hands, under the semblance of an act of
kindness.

The present of the pistols, with the powder and
bullet mould, for the protection of a man, whose
peril, he well knew, was the consequence of his own
treachery to him and his associates, was worthy of
Reynolds; villany less accomplished would hardly
have devised so refined an act of specious perfidy.
It was a particular feature of Reynolds's infamy, that
he seems to have felt a gratification in witnessing
the effects of his proceedings on the unfortunate
families of his victims. A few days after the arrests
at Bond's, he paid a visit of condolence to Mrs. Bond,
and even caressed the child she was holding in her
arms. He paid a similar visit of simulated friendship, to the wife of Lord Edward Fitzgerald, on the
16th of March. Mr. Reynolds's son must tell the
particulars of this interview, " She (Lady Fitzgerald)
also complained of a want of gold; my father told
her he had given Lord Edward fifty guineas the
preceding night, and would send her fifty more in
the course of that day, which promise he performed.
Neither of these sums were ever repaid. In the
course of their conversation, my father mentioned
his intention of leaving Ireland for a time; on which
she took a ring from her finger and gave it to him,
saying she hoped to hear from him if he should have
anything of importance to communicate, and that
she would not attend to any letter purporting to
come from him, unless it were sealed with that ring,

which was a small red cornelian, engraved with the figure of a dancing satyr."*

Mr. Reynolds having deprived himself of his pistols, on the 15th of March, the act was considered by him, and at a latter period it would seem, was recognized by government, as one done for *the public service*, for these pistols were replaced by Major Sirr, and the bill for the case purchased on this occasion, by the Major for his friend, was duly presented to Mr. Cooke, and the subsequent payment of it was not forgotten.

" 1798, July 26, Major Sirr, for pistols,
for Mr. Reynolds £9 2 0

So much for the friendship's offerings of Mr. Thomas Reynolds.

The insatiable cupidity of this man, at length disgusted the administration in both countries, and when his importunities were disregarded, in the pathetic language of his son, having settled his accounts " he bade an eternal adieu to his kindred and country, and arrived with his family in London, on the 1st of January, 1800." This melancholy circumstance for the meditation of " his kindred and country," is certainly narrated in very moving terms, but the nature of his faithful attachment to both, could hardly be spoken of in plain and simple terms. " During two years," continues his son, " he did not cease to urge on the English ministers, the promises made to him on leaving Ireland, but to no purpose ; he received much politeness, but the English ministers referred him to the Irish, these again referred

* Vide Life of Reynolds by his Son, vol. ii. p. 219.

him to those in England, until at length disgusted with both, he dropped the pursuit and applied himself exclusively to the care of his family."*

But though it was impossible to satiate Mr. Reynolds's unquenchable thirst for gain, notwithstanding the prodigal liberality with which the public money was lavished on him, it seems to have been still more difficult to appease his appetite for encomiums on his public conduct, and he was constantly addressing letters to distinguished persons, representing himself as a persecuted patriot, whose love for his country had subjected him to the most undeserved animosity. From Lord Limerick, he extorted a communication in 1817, in which he states " that it was from the best and most disinterested motives, he had laid open the conspiracy," &c.

Lord Carleton, formerly chief justice of the king's bench in Ireland, the judge who presided on the trial of the Shearses, addressed another letter to Mr. Reynolds on the subject of his conduct in 1798, and at the trials of that period, and his Lordship gravely informs Mr. Reynolds, that in the whole of his conduct, " he had behaved with consistency, integrity, honour, ability and disinterestedness." With this profound legal gentleman's opinion of the qualities he alludes to, we may form some idea of those qualities that were formerly looked for, in those who were candidates for elevation to the bench.

Sir Jonah Barrington in his Memoirs, speaks of Reynolds, as a man who so far differed from his brother conspirator, Captain Armstrong, " that the

* Life of Thomas Reynolds, by his Son, vol. ii. p. 193.

latter had the honour of an officer and the integrity of a man to sustain, and deliberately sacrificed both!!"

Yet Sir Jonah corresponded with Mr. Reynolds, when the latter was at Lisbon; and in his private letters to him, he addresses him in the most affectionate terms, and begins his epistles with the most endearing expressions. In July, 1812, one of his letters commences with, " My dear Reynolds, I cannot express how obliged I am by your letter." In the same communication, he addresses him " as an old friend."* Considering the person he addressed, Sir Jonah must have entertained notions of the obligation which friendship imposes, different from those of the generality of men, whose principles are fixed, of whatever political shade they may be. Sir Jonah, however, would call a man like Reynolds his dearest friend to-day, and on the following one would .chuckle to hear him described by Curran, as a man " who measured his value by the coffins of his victims, and in the field of evidence appreciated his fame, as the Indian warrior does in fight, by the number of scalps with which he can swell his victory."

Lord Chichester (the Mr. Pelham of Lord Camden's administration) writes to Mr. Reynolds at the same period, informing him that " he can estimate his services more accurately than any other person;" but in referring to some speeches in Parliament, not complimentary to Mr. Reynolds, he tells him that the speeches, in all probability, were never made in the

---

* Life of Thomas Reynolds by his son, vol. ii. p. 352.

terms used in the papers; and concludes with advice somewhat equivocal, in these terms:—" I cannot help, therefore, recommending, in the strongest manner, *your silent submission* to this unprovoked and unmerited censure, conscious of enjoying the continuance of the good opinions of those, who are best qualified to judge of your merits and character."

Lord Camden is dragged forward to the rescue of Reynolds's character: he speaks of his "most disinterested" services, and tells him, that "those who best knew his conduct, have endeavoured to shew their good opinion of him; Lord Chichester, Lord Castlereagh and himself, having each rendered him (Reynolds) services on account of that opinion."

Nothing more flattering could be extorted from Lord Castlereagh than a few vague sentences, in a speech of his on the 11th of July, 1817, in which he stated that "Mr. Reynolds was originally engaged in treason, and by his discovery made the atonement." And, further, " that Mr. Reynolds was also a gentleman in *considerable* respectable circumstances, and therefore by no means likely to prostitute his talents for the public service."*

In 1817 the people of England, who had given themselves very little concern about Mr. Reynolds's doings in Ireland, so long as they were confined to that country, took the alarm rather suddenly, when they found the subject of treason in England, and the system of packing the juries for the trial of the traitors, connected with the ominous name of Mr. Thomas Reynolds. On bills being found by

* Vide T. Reynolds's Life by his Son, pp. 409, 421.

the grand jury of Middlesex against Dr. Watson
and four others, for high treason, the Spa-fields
Rioters), no sooner was Mr. Reynolds's name discovered on the pannel, than the press of England
took the alarm, and the walls of parliament rung
with loud denunciations against the Irish informer.

Lord Castlereagh plainly saw the folly of the
attempt to resort to the old practices, which had
been adopted with so little trouble in the sister kingdom. He left Mr. Reynolds to his fate; and when he
threatened to publish a vindication of his acts, it
was plainly intimated to him, that it was the pleasure of Lord Castlereagh that he should be silent
on these subjects. At length, the coolest sarcasm
on an importunate candidate for public employment
that ever was carried into effect, was put in practice
by Lord Castlereagh in 1818, when he sent that
ardent patriot, Mr. Thomas Reynolds, to freeze in
Iceland. In October, 1818, Reynolds, having sick-
ened of his Iceland consulship, abandoned his post
and returned to London. On his arrival, Mr.
Planta communicated to him " his lordship's extreme surprise, and marked displeasure, at his having quitted his public duties for his private affairs,
without his lordship's previous sanction."*

On the 6th of December, he had an interview with
Mr. Cooke on the subject of his quitting his post.
and, in reference to a letter of Reynolds to Lord
Camden on this matter, his son tells us he said to
him—" You are a madman; you are an imprudent
man : I tell you so to your face—and you were

* Vide Thomas Reynolds's Life by his Son, vol. ii. p. 429.

always an imprudent man, and never will be otherwise. I tell you, you are considered as a passionate
imprudent man." " Mr. Cooke," said my father,
" If I was not so, perhaps Ireland would not at this
day be a part of the British empire : you did not
think me passionate or imprudent in 1798." " I
tell you again," said Mr. Cooke, " you are mad.
Well, what do you intend to do now?" " Really,"
said my father, " I intend to do nothing at all; I
suppose Lord Castlereagh, on his return, will settle
my resignation."* Mr. Reynolds went on to state,
that he had taken the appointment "on the express
condition of living where he pleased ; and his affairs
being urgent, *and Lord Castlereagh being absent*, he
returned as a matter of course." " True," continued Mr. Cooke; " but Lord Castlereagh knows
you to be a very imprudent man, and he would certainly hesitate at allowing you to be in London,
where your imprudence would give advantage to
your enemies, *to bring you into trouble and him too.*
He does not like you to be in London : I tell you
fairly, *that is the feeling.*" †

Mr. Reynolds took his leave, after informing Mr.
Cooke that, " in case he continued to hold this consulship, he expected to be treated with attention
and consideration by the British ambassadors wherever he settled, and that he still held government
bound to provide for his two sons. " I tell you
again," said Mr. Cooke, " I'll see them on it."

This must have been a scene that Gay would have

* Vide Thomas Reynolds's Life by his Son, vol. ii. p. 443.
† Ibid. vol. ii. p. 415.

delighted to have witnessed and to have depicted, for no other hand could have done justice to the little differences of the gentlemen of those golden days of the good old times.

In 1822, the star had set on the prosperity of Mr. Thomas Reynolds. Mr. Canning had come into power, and had been applied to for employment for the former. Young Mr. Reynolds states, that Mr. Planta communicated to his father Mr. Canning's final determination, not to employ any member of our family in his department, as he did not consider himself bound by Lord Londonderry's engagements."*

Mr. Reynolds deemed the time was come to retire from the turmoil of public life: he fixed his abode in Paris, and died in that city the 18th of August, 1836. His remains were brought to England, and were buried in one of the vaults of the village-church of Wilton in Yorkshire. Having spoken much of this man's character, and by no means favourably of it, I freely admit that he did the state some service, and that he was possessed of some qualities, which, had they been under the guidance of sound principles, would have rendered him a man who might be spoken of with respect, and without repugnance: his courage was indomitable; his presence of mind was remarkable; he was cool and collected, on occasions that eminently required calmness and deliberation. His own immediate family appear to have been attached to him; and in his latter days it is said,—and I presume not to call in question the

* Thomas Reynolds's Life by his Son, vol. ii. p. 497.

truth of such a statement,—that his thoughts were turned to futurity, and his deportment, at the close of his career, that of a man who had a lively sense of religion :—that nothing, in short, in life became him so much as the manner of his leaving it.

CHAPTER IX.

THE following narrative of the arrest of Lord Edward Fitzgerald at the house of Mr. Nicholas Murphy, No. 153, Thomas-street, was drawn up by the latter, partly during the period of his long confinement in Newgate; and that portion of it relating to events of a later date, written subsequently to his liberation, at different, and evidently at distant intervals. From the time of his death it remained in the hands of his sister, who is still living in the city of Dublin.

Having come to the knowledge of the existence of this document, and having reason to believe the information it contained might tend to throw much light on a transaction which has hitherto been involved in mystery, I applied to the sister of Mr. Murphy for it, through a mutual friend, and with some difficulty was permitted to take a copy. It may be right to mention the name of that friend as an authority for its authenticity—the name of a man of well-known worth and honesty, Mr. W. Powell.

It is a plain unvarnished tale, told by an honest man in simple language—by one not much indebted indeed to education for any literary attainment; but indebted to nature, at least, for one noble quality, which we have not found many traces of in the subject of the preceding memoir.

I have given Murphy's narrative in his own language, without any other correction than that of the orthography, which this paper certainly stood very much in need of.

An Account of the Arrest of the late Lord Edward Fitzgerald. Written by Nicholas Murphy, in whose house the arrest took place.

" On the night of Friday, the 18th May, 1798, Lord Edward Fitzgerald came to my house, (No. 153, Thomas-street,) in company with a lady,* about the hour of ten or eleven o'clock at night. I did expect him the previous evening; and the reason I state this is, that a friend of his came to me, and requested that I would receive him, as he wished to move from where he was at present.† I was getting the house cleaned down and scoured, and I brought his friend in, and he saw the persons employed as I told him; he mentioned that it was not intended to remove him immediately, but said, ' I think a week or ten days would answer.' I assented; and, indeed, with reluctance :—however, I made no mention of that. In a few days previous to Lord Edward's coming, the government had offered one thousand pounds reward for his apprehension. I certainly felt very uneasy at this circumstance, and I wished very much

---

* That lady was Mrs. Moore, in whose husband's house Lord Edward had been previously concealed.

† The person alluded to was Surgeon Lawless.—R. R. M.

to see Lord Edward's friend; but where to see him I did not know. As a man of honour, I wished to keep my word; and I could not think of refusing him admittance when he came. Unfortunately for him and myself, I did keep my word. I expected him on Thursday, but he did not come till Friday, the 18th of May, 1798.* I perceived he looked very bad and altered from what he appeared *when I saw him before.* The lady that came with him did not stay long; and I made a tender of my services to go home with her, as she lived in the neighbourhood: there was a person that we met on our way who I believe was waiting for her—I had some knowledge of him myself:† I returned to the house with a troubled mind. Lord Edward told me he was very ill with a cold, and it was easy to perceive it. I had procured for him whey, and put some

---

* Lord Edward had been previously concealed in his house for a fortnight on his leaving the residence of the Widow Dillon, "a retired house on the banks of the canal" When Murphy wrote this part of the narrative he was in prison, and evidently did not wish to run the risk of its being discovered that he had previously sheltered Lord Edward.

Mr. James Davock, a respectable silk merchant of the city of Dublin, informed me, a short time previously to his death in 1836, that he and two other persons conducted Lord Edward to Murphy's house the first time he was in concealment there, that about a fortnight before, he met Murphy at the Globe Coffee-house, and told him there was a friend of his who wished to be out of the way for a few days, that he did not mention Lord Edward's name, for Murphy was not an United Irishman: but as a personal favour to him, Davock, Murphy agreed to receive his friend; but, subsequently, he told Murphy who the person was.

† This person was probably Surgeon Lawless —R. R. M.

sherry wine in it. At this time he appeared quite tranquil, and went up to the room intended for him —the back room in the attic story. In the morning he came down to breakfast, and appeared better than the night before. The friend that spoke to me respecting his coming, came, I believe, about eleven o'clock. Then came out, for the first time, an account of the rencontre that took place the night before, between Lord Edward's party and Major Sirr's.* It is perfectly clear, in my humble judgment, that Major Sirr had known of his removal, and the direction he intended to take, for his party and Lord Edward's came in contact in a place called Island-street, at the lower end of Watling-street. They there met, and a skirmish took place, and, in the confusion, Lord Edward got off: however, one of the party was taken, but could not be identified.†

I found my situation now very painful, but nothing to what it was afterwards. In the course of the day (Saturday, 19th) there was a guard of soldiers, and I believe Major Swan, Major Sirr, a Mr. Medlicot, and another, making a search at Mr. Moore's house, the Yellow Lion in Thomas-street.‡ A friend came and mentioned the circumstance to me. I immediately mentioned it to Lord Edward, and had him conveyed out of the house, and concealed in a valley, on the roof of one of the warehouses. While I was

---

* Sirr was accompanied by several persons, amongst whom were Major Ryan and Mr. John Swift Emerson, an attorney.

† William Putnam Macabe.—R. R. M.

‡ Moore had two houses in Thomas-street, nearly opposite to one another.—R. R. M.

doing this, Sam. Neilson came, and enquired of the
girl if I was at home? I believe she said not. ‘Bid
him be cautious,’ I think was what she told me he
said. I considered that conduct of his very ill-
timed; however, I am led to believe it was well
intended. On Saturday morning, the day of the
arrest, there came a single rap at the door; I opened
it myself, and a woman with a bundle appeared, and
enquired if that was Mr. Murphy’s? I said it was.
She informed me that she came from Mrs. Moore,
and was directed to leave that bundle there. I
knew not what it contained; but to my surprise,
when I opened it, I found it to be an uniform, of a
very beautiful green colour, gimpt or braided down
the front, with crimson or rose-colour cuffs and
cape: there were two dresses—one a long-skirted
coat, vest and pantaloons; the other a short jacket,
that came round quite close, and was braided in
front; there was also a pair of overalls, that but-
toned from the hip to the ankle, with, I think, black
Spanish leather on the sides. I suppose they were
intended for riding. The bundle contained a cap
of a very fanciful description, extremely attractive,
formed exactly like a sugar-loaf—that part that went
round the forehead green, the upper part crimson,
with a large tassel, which inclined on one side or
other occasionally when on the head.

“After placing Lord Edward in the valley, on the
roof of the warehouse, I came down in a little time
and stood at the gate, the soldiers still at Mr.
Moore’s. I perceived four persons walking in the
middle of the street, some of them in uniform; I

believe yeomen. I think Major Swan and Captain
Medlicot* was of the party. Towards four o'clock,
Lord Edward came down to dinner; every thing
was supposed to be still. Now at this time, Sam.
Neilson came in to see us. Dinner was nearly
ready, I asked him to stay and dine, which he
accepted.   Nothing particular occurred, except
speaking on a variety of subjects, when Mr. Neilson
as if something struck him, immediately went away
leaving us together; there was very little wine taken.
Lord Edward was very abstemious.   In a short time
I went out; and now the tragedy commenced. I
wished to leave Lord Edward to himself. I was absent I suppose about an hour. I came into the room
where we dined, being the back drawing-room, he
was not there; I went to the sleeping room, he was
in bed. It was at this time about seven o'clock.
I asked him to come down to tea. I was not in the
room three minutes when in came Major Swan, and a
person following him in a soldier's jacket, and a
sword in his hand; he wore a round hat. When I
saw Major Swan I was thunderstruck. I put myself
before him, and asked his business. He looked over
me, and saw Lord Edward in the bed. He pushed by
me quickly, and Lord Edward seeing him, sprung up
instantly like a tiger, and drew a dagger which he
carried about him, and wounded Major Swan slightly
I believe. Major Swan had a pistol in his waistcoat
pocket, which he fired without effect: he immediately turned to me and gave me a severe thrust of
the pistol under the eye, at the same time desiring

* Qy. Lieut. Thomas Medlicot of the City of Dublin Militia?—R.R.M.

the person that came in with him, to take me into custody. I was immediately taken away to the yard, there I saw Major Sirr and about six soldiers of the Dumbarton Fencibles.

"Major Swan had thought proper to run as fast as he could to the street, and I think he never looked behind him till he got out of danger, and he was then parading up and down the flags, exhibiting his linen, which was stained with blood.* Mr. Ryan supplied Major Swan's place; he came in contact with Lord Edward and was wounded seriously. Major Sirr at that time came up stairs, and keeping at a respectful distance, fired a pistol at Lord Edward in a very deliberate manner, and wounded him in the upper part of the shoulder. Reinforcements coming in, Lord Edward surrendered after a very hard struggle. Now the work of destruction commenced. The house was taken possession of by soldiers. An old invalid volunteered to guard me, along with the man who first held me in charge. The old soldier would not let me put my handkerchief to my face, to wipe away the blood. A neighbour came to offer me a glass of wine and water, but the valiant Major Sirr would not allow it. He was going to break the glass, saying, wine was not fit for rebels. There were Invalids at that time in James Street, and they were soon brought down, and took

* This part of the account of the struggle differs from Mr Moore's. There is no mention there of Swan having quitted the room. If he did quit it at all, which I doubt, previously to Lord Edward's being overpowered, it must have been at the commencement of the struggle, and for the purpose of calling Sirr to his assistance.—R. R. M.

possession of the house. I never had such a stock of wine, before or since; I little thought who I bought it for. In some time a carriage came, and I was placed in it, in company with two soldiers of the Dunbarton Regiment, then stationed in Dublin, and brought off to the Castle, and there placed in the Castle guard house. A sad change for me! I was there perhaps an hour or more, when my friend Major Sirr came to me, to bring me into the presence of Mr. Cooke, taking me very friendly under the arm, and telling me to state every thing I knew about the business. I felt no inclination to take his advice on that occasion.

"Well! I had the honour of an introduction to Mr. Cooke. There was a gentlemen lolling on the sofa, who I afterwards learned was Lord Castlereagh. My friend Cooke looked at me very sharply, and now for question and answer. ' How long was Lord Edward in your house?' ' He came there last night.' ' Who came with him?' ' He came with a lady.' ' What was her name?' ' I cannot state the lady's name.'—I declined to answer to that ' in toto.' I mentioned that I was led into the business very innocently, and that would appear on an investigation taking place, and I could procure sufficient bail. Mr. Cooke laughed at that, and no wonder he might, for he immediately wrote out a Castlereagh warrant for me; I was walked back to the guard-house, and a large guard was ordered to prime and load, which was soon complied with. Then I was placed in the centre, and marched off to Newgate— this was about nine o'clock at night. On arriving there, I was left to ruminate on the situation I was unfortunately placed in. The only consolation I had was that there were very respectable men at the time in the same place with me. One friend offered me a part of his bed, which I accepted. I had a heavy heart, and slept but little. In the morning a messenger came to me to let me know I was wanting down stairs. One of the state prisoners in the room bid me to feign illness. I did not take his advice. I went down and was brought ' between hatches' as they called it—and for what purpose? Why to be ironed! The mild Mr. Gregg was waiting for me. I spoke to him to allow me to send home for a pair of boots, as I wore shoes at this time. When I sent home I had neither boots nor shoes to get : however, there was a pound note sent to me. I must state that I was put in the felon side of the prison at that time. The note put Locket and Peachum in good humour, and I was then moved back to my old first lodging.

"I have now to state the treatment I experienced from the soldiers and others that took possession of the house. Alderman Archer, who was one of the sheriffs at that time, but since dead, broke open my secretary and book-case, expecting, I suppose, to get as many papers of a treasonable nature as would convict a hundred, but was disappointed. Next he examined the clothes-press, and then a general search commenced through the rooms ; the office desk was broken open, but no papers to be found that could attach criminality. Plundering the place then commenced. Unfortunately, there was a com-

pany of Invalids stationed in James-street; they
were ordered down; they were known generally by
the name of 'Old Fogies.' Their wives came in great
numbers, and immediately commenced robbing the
place. A large silver gravy-spoon, a plated tea-pot,
and plated goblet were taken—every thing they could
lay their hands on! They were quarrelling, I was
informed, about the plunder; nothing in the house
could escape their Argus eyes. An officer asked the
men 'if they found out the wine cellar?'—it was
soon forced. I never had such a stock of wine,
before or since. They destroyed six dozen of as fine
wine as could be found—claret, port, and sherry.—I
purchased it in the wood. The late Alderman Manders fortunately came in as a magistrate, and I believe did all he could; but it had no avail. I had
a respected sister—a married lady—who came to the
house and conducted herself nobly in the cause of
her unfortunate brother, by doing all that was possible under such circumstances. The soldiers and
'Old Fogies' fell to at the wine. I had some pickled
beef and chickens in a coop; they were soon in
requisition, and my new visitors, regaling themselves,
calling aloud to the servant, 'You old—this and that
—get us some porter,' they wanted it with the beef
and chickens. Fine times with them while it lasted!
They never took the trouble of using a screw, but
struck off the heads of the bottles with the next
thing that came to hand. I have grounds for stating
that when they got tired drinking the wine, they
were selling it in the morning at sixpence per bottle,
and buying whiskey with the money.

"My losses in this unfortunate business amounted to upwards of two thousand pounds, and I never yet received one shilling of compensation from any quarter, and was confined fifty-five weeks a state prisoner, and my house and concerns made a barrack of for ten months and upwards, having ten soldiers—some with wives—besides Invalids, and some of the Rea Fencibles, and the baggage of the regiment in the warehouses. Mr. Brown, the landlord, applied to Mr. Cooke at the Castle, to know if he would pay the rent as he held the place, and he could not apply to Mr. Murphy for it? Mr. Cooke answered, that he would pay no rent; so that when the government thought proper to liberate me, I was obliged to pay the rent and taxes while it remained a barrack—a severe case.

"There is a circumstance I feel I wish to mention. There was an officer, an English gentleman, and he was ordered to my house with his party. He was a very short time in the city, and he mentioned to my next door neighbour, on Sunday morning, the 20th of May, that a large party of men 'of the lowest description, came on Saturday night to destroy the concerns, which he would not assent to,' saying, 'he heard the owner of the place was a man of good character,' and 'that it would make a very good barrack for himself and his men.'

"I have made an estimate of my losses, but not to the full extent.

"I have to mention, that Alderman Archer, then sheriff, came to me the day after my arrest, 20th of May, for my keys, to examine my papers (as he said) after breaking open my drawers the night before,—a fine '*ruse de guerre.*'

" Monday, 21st.—Two state prisoners brought in: Mr. Pat. Byrne, Grafton-street, a bookseller, and Mr. J. G. Kennedy, a brewer.

" Lord Edward Fitzgerald was confined in the most convenient room in the prison. No one was allowed to see him except the medical attendants. There was appointed to take care of him, a Mr. Stone, I believe a lieutenant in the Londonderry Regiment of Militia, as he wore the uniform of that regiment; and great care he took of his charge. I could never get to see him myself, though I often wished it.

" On the 23rd of May, Samuel Neilson was seen hovering in front of the prison. Simpson, the deputy jailer, I am told, beckoned to him with his hand to leave the place; however, Gregg arrested him, and brought him in 'between the hatches,' and ironed him, and then had him placed in the attic story of the felon side of the prison. Nothing could exceed the horror excited in the minds of the prisoners at the appearance of persons connected with the prison, as no person considered himself safe, from the line of conduct that appeared to be in contemplation. I shall give you a description of the discipline of this unfortunate place.

" We should be in our rooms before nine o'clock, and were then locked up till eight o'clock in the morning. None were allowed to see us, only by order of the government. I endeavoured to reconcile myself to this state of things, and the only con-

N

solation I had was that I was in company with gentlemen of respectability and honour. The jailor
furnished us with a 'table d' hote,' for which we paid
twenty shillings English per week. In about two
or three months, the state prisoners sent a memorial
to the government to be put on state allowance, which
was complied with, and we were allowed five shillings
per day, which the jailor received, and gave us breakfast and dinner for it.

" Two surgeons attended daily on Lord Edward
Fitzgerald. It was supposed, the evening of the day
before he died, he was delirious, as we could hear
him with a very strong voice crying out—' Come
on ! come on ! d——n you, come on !' He spoke
so loud, that the people in the street gathered to
listen to it. He died the next day early in the
morning, on the 3rd of June. The surgeons attended and opened the body : then he was seen for
the first time by the prisoners. The bowels were
opened, and whatever was found there was thrown
under the grate, and then the part opened was sewn
up. He had about his neck a gold chain, suspending a locket with hair in it.

" Thus died one of the bravest of men, from a conviction, I believe, that his projects would ameliorate
the condition of his country. I shall endeavour to
describe his person : he was, I believe, about five
feet seven inches in height, and a very interesting
countenance ; beautiful arched eyebrows, fine grey
eyes, handsome nose, and high forehead—thick,
dark-coloured hair, brown, or inclining to black.
I think he was very like the late Lady Louisa

Conolly about the nose and eyes. Any person he addressed must have admired his manner,—it was so candid, so goodnatured, and so impregnated with good feeling; as playful and humble as a child—as mild and timid as a lady—and, when necessary, as brave as a lion. He was altogether a very fine, elegantly formed man. Peace to his name! The lady that came with him to my house lived very near me. Her husband, Mr. Moore, was in some way implicated, and, I heard, a prisoner for some short time. His house was made a barrack as well as my own. I regret to state that, when he was liberated, he made interest to have the soldiers and luggage that were in his house removed to mine, and accompanied them himself. My revered father, since dead, was insulted by some of the party for attempting to remonstrate with them. I felt indignant at Mr. Moore's conduct when I heard it.*

"I procured a copy of my committal, which I have by me as a memento, signed '*Castlereagh*,' also a notice of trial served on me, in consequence of a special commission being issued, bearing date the 11th June, 1798, to be held at the Sessions House, Green-street. The notice is dated 25th day of May, signed 'Thomas Kemmis, crown solicitor.' I have the notice by me. There are upwards of sixty state prisoners embodied in it—the late Lord Edward Fitzgerald's name the first. The most serious part of the business was approaching to a

* Murphy's impressions on this subject were probably erroneous, he then had no means of ascertaining the truth of the stories he heard. —R. R. M.

crisis of the most deplorable description. The court was opened on Monday, the 11th June, 1798; and the first on trial were Messrs. Henry and John Sheares. That great luminary, Counsellor Curran, was their leading advocate; and we·could hear him addressing the jury at five o'clock in the morning, in our beds in Newgate. They were found guilty, and, after conviction, were brought into the prison. A dismal sight it was. They were ordered out at three o'clock the same day to receive sentence, and when that awful ceremony was performed, and they came in (they were ironed at this time), dreadful ideas entered every man's mind in this unfortunate place, to see these gentlemen in such a situation,— the execution to take place next day! I cannot describe the feelings of the state prisoners.

" The fatal day arrived. The Rev. Dr. Dobbin, a Protestant clergyman, attended them. A great number of yeomen and gentlemen came in of course. The prisoners were locked up. I am very sorry I did not procure the trials of these gentlemen, and of the remainder; but it was not that I was thinking of at the time. Next ordered for trial was Mr, John M'Cann—disposed of as the former! and never was a man more resigned; he met death as a brave man, and was quite disposed to meet his fate with firmness. Next trial, Mr. William Michael Byrne's, a very fine young man; I suppose his age about twenty-five years, and married only one year. Mrs. Byrne came to see him—a heart-rending meeting. Then followed Mr. Bond—and his conviction of course. Words cannot now describe the feelings of the state prisoners : no chance of acquittal ! an organized system ! and the miscreant Reynolds the '*avant-garde*' of it ! I will not speak of the juries of 1798 ; I leave that for others to do.

"At this time there was a Mr. Dobbs, a lawyer, and a Mr. Crawford, an attorney—two very good men. There was a proposition, I believe, came to the state prisoners through those gentlemen, I suppose sanctioned by the government, *and that was*—'That the state prisoners would give the government such information as they required, and for the state trials to terminate ; the information not to criminate any person, and the prisoners to emigrate to a country not at war with his majesty.' There was a document to be signed conformable to this agreement. There was not a moment to be lost, as Mr. William M. Byrne was to be executed this day, and Mr. O. Bond on the day following. All the state prisoners in our prison signed the contract, and myself among the rest. The privy council, early on that day, deliberated on the business, and the proposal was unfortunately rejected. In the course of the day, while it was pending, my revered and attached sister hearing what I had done, came to the prison in tears, and asked me if I had done such a thing? I answered, I had, and that I would go to any place to leave that abode of misery. ' The business is now,' I said, ' before the privy council, and if Mr. Byrne is respited, which I hope he will, I will be satisfied to expatriate myself; but, I will promise you, if it is to be done again, I will decline it.' Well, the awful news came ; and the council rejected the proposition, and Mr. Byrne was

executed.   He was an elegant young man, and went
to death with as much composure as if he was going
to dinner.   Well, the next day, the same business
came on for Mr. Bond.   I was now placed in a most
unpleasant situation ; but I was determined to keep
my word.   Mr. Dobbs, a good-hearted man, was
most anxious for the prisoners, and the same business
was again commenced.   When it came to my turn to
sign, I requested to say a few words :—I said, that I
was under great obligations to my family; that one of
them came to me yesterday, in great trouble, in consequence of my signing the paper; and that I then
promised that I would not sign it if it was to do
again : however, I went to Mr. Bond myself, and
stated to him how unhappy my family was at my
signing, and the promise I made; but that if I was
at my liberty, and walking the street, I would sign
for him if it served him.   He very honourably left
me to myself, and requested I would do nothing on
his account, saying, at the same time, ' You know
how you are situated.'   The document went a second
time before the privy council.   The greatest excitement that could be conceived existed at this time in
the prison, to see Mr. Bond, an athletic fine-formed
man, who occupied the first class of respectability in
Dublin, now heavily ironed!—and what made it more
lamentable, was to see Mrs. Bond with him, linked
arm to arm.   The coffin in the yard! the dreadful
apparatus ready!   The sensation it excited could not
be conceived.   I cannot attempt to describe my own
feelings at the time.   Three o'clock came—no news
from the Castle.   Alternate hopes and fears crowded

on the mind. At half-after three, the news came—
'*A respite during pleasure !*' The shout in the street
was the first thing to announce it. There was some
person brought into the prison for shouting in the
street. Joy was now visible in every countenance.
A great change took place in the prison—the place
was now comfortable to what it had been. The state
trials now terminated, and the gentlemen who signed
the agreement expected to go to America; but government decreed otherwise, for reasons best known to
themselves. On the 6th of September, Mr. Bond
died suddenly in Newgate : he was as well as ever he
was on the evening before, and was playing rackets
in the yard, to my knowledge : his apartment was
quite detached from the rooms of the other prisoners,
being convenient to the yard below stairs. Simpson
the under-jailor, Samuel Neilson, and himself, spent
the evening in Mr. Bond's room. It was understood
Samuel Neilson went to bed top-heavy, and left
Simpson and Mr. Bond together. About eleven or
twelve o'clock, Simpson came into the room I was
in. Mr. Pat. Byrne, Mr. J. G. Kennedy and myself,
were in this room. Simpson, I think, brought with
him two bottles of wine, (I was in bed at this time),
they commenced drinking the wine. Mr. G. Kennedy
got powerless, and went to bed as well as he could.
Mr. Byrne being a strong man, kept drinking with
Simpson some time after. I was awake all this time,
and perceived that Simpson wished to provoke a
quarrel with Mr. Byrne; Mr. B. acted with great
command of temper in the business, and with much
ado Simpson went away; I then spoke to Mr. Byrne

and told him I heard all that passed, and that if he had
in future any intercourse with Simpson, I would renounce his friendship, I was so enraged at what I heard.
He agreed with me in what I said. The next morning
about five o'clock, it went through the prison that Mr.
Bond was dead. I immediately arose and went down
stairs, and there to my astonishment saw Mr. Bond,
lying on his back lifeless, with exactly the same dress
he wore the day before. I came and informed Mr.
Byrne and Mr. Kennedy of the fact. Samuel Neilson slept in the room that night, and could give no
account whatever of what happened, or how it happened. S. Neilson appeared very much affected, and
cried like a child. There was a serious alarm in the
prison, and great uneasiness among the prisoners,
fearing there was foul play. Mr. Byrne arose in
the bed, and mentioned with great emphasis, ' Our
lives are not worth an hour's purchase!'—however,
nothing came out that could establish that. As I
was the only person who did not sign the ' Banish-
ment Bill,' the government was endeavouring to
have me brought to trial; and for that purpose, the
trusty Major Swan went to my house, that was a
barrack for three months at that time, with a person
(I suppose one of the ' Batallion of Testimony,') to
look for pikes,—desiring the person to go through
the dormant window of the house, and if he found
one, he would get half a guinea for it. A person
who was in the house, came to my brother with that
word: it was well the fellow did not think of bringing one. However, *nothing was found.* When my
brother heard of this, he went to the Castle and

mentioned the circumstance, I believe to Mr. Cooke, and the answer he got, was—' that there would be no more searching.' Some of my family, endeavouring to procure my liberation, went once, or twice, or thrice, to Lady Louisa Connolly, a very amiable character, to interest herself with Lady Castlereagh, and at one time, she gave my sister a letter to that personage. My sister went to Lady Castlereagh's residence, expecting a favourable answer; and after waiting a considerable time—' Indeed,' Lady Castlereagh said, ' she could not interfere with Lord Castlereagh's affairs !' No hope in that quarter !— well! patience is a virtue, if we could but submit to it.

" On the 18th March, 1799, the state prisoners were ordered to be in readiness to leave. Mr. Arthur O'Connor, while confined in Newgate, was not allowed out of his room ; while there, he appeared dressed in a green coat, vest and pantaloons, and half-boots. Mr. Dowling, Mr. Thomas Russell, Mr. Samuel Neilson, Mr. Dowdall, and Dr. M'Nevin, I heard, came from the Castle. Our friend Major Swan, and his attendants, brought these gentlemen down to the Quay, and they were put on board the ' Anson Smith,' government transport, and there joined the gentlemen sent from Kilmainham and Smithfield prisons. I understand that they were sixteen in number. On the 25th of March, they arrived in Belfast Lough and took in five state prisoners there ; on the 26th they sailed, and on the 30th they landed at Greenock, and on the 9th April, they arrived at Fort George, the place of their destination ; and in

N 5

the year 1801, (in the spring of this year,) peace
being proclaimed, they were shortly after liberated.

" N.B.—I take this from a newspaper, and I believe
it to be perfectly correct.

" I shall now state something respecting myself :—
I was arrested early in the unfortunate business, and
kept prisoner in the yard of my house. First, I
never saw Mr. Ryan, till I saw him coming down
wounded : he was brought on something like a door.
Secondly, my arrest took place before martial law
took place. Thirdly, there was no papers of a treasonable nature found in the house ; it was impossible
there could be any, except they were put there by
themselves. I will mention a circumstance here,
and it is this ;—the rooms were searched with great
care ; one of these feather-bed soldiers brought to
Alderman Manders, a dagger which he said he found
in one of the rooms. My sisters appealed to Alderman Manders, and he honourably said, there was no
dagger there when he searched the room. Another
of these plunderers, wanted to know why my sister
was not put out of the place ? she replied boldly,
' that she would not go ;' that ' it was her brother's house.' I wish I could come in contact with
the ruffian, for he must have a bad mind and de-
praved heart. Fourth, the death of Lord Edward
Fitzgerald taking place, of course there could be no
bill of indictment framed against me, as there was
no overt act to ground it on : I was indebted thus
to providence for my life, and I give God thanks for
it ! Still, there was no prospect of my liberation.
There was a motion made in court, by counsel,

to admit me to bail, but it would not be allowed;
so there I was, incarcerated inside the gloomy walls
of a prison. However, I submitted with patience,
though I found great difficulty in doing so. When I
was first brought to this ' chateau' (the jail), there
was a catholic clergyman attended, and said mass
regularly on every Sunday, and all the prisoners in
the jail, who were catholics, and others, might attend
if they wished it. I understood the gentleman said
mass, the first Sunday I was there; from that Sunday to the time of my liberation, which was upwards
of a year, there was no catholic clergyman allowed
to officiate, but in fact was interdicted from coming
to this abode of misery. The Rev. Mr. Gamble, a
protestant clergyman, a very good man, came sometimes on Sundays, and I feel pleasure in saying he
conducted himself as a gentleman. I had a very
high opinion of him, from his conduct to my fellow
prisoners.

" Mr. Pat. Byrne, bookseller, lent me books to read,
and by that means I passed many a gloomy hour.
There was a circumstance which I would wish to
mention, and which I heard when I was liberated,
and it is this:—The day before the arrest (of Lord
Edward) it rained very hard, and I was told Major
Sirr was seen reconnoitring the rear of the house, in
the gateway. The office had two doors; one of
which was never used, and was fastened only by a
string, and it opened outwards to a small office that
was formerly attached to the house, but was taken
down as having no occasion for it. The entrance
was always by the side-door in the gateway, and that

was locked, generally. I am satisfied in my mind
that the place was reconnoitred before Lord Edward
came. I also heard, in prison, that one of Lord
Edward's body-guard gave some information—and
his name was mentioned to me, and I saw him when
I was liberated;—but he shall be nameless by me,
as this is only a hearsay account given one by a
neighbour. I can state with truth, that though the
intended rising was to take place on the 23rd of May,
I did not know one word about it until I heard it in
Newgate. It is really surprising to me, the system
government pursued on this, as well as in the other
part of this unfortunate business; but, on second
thoughts, it is easily accounted for: in general, man
can be made available in any business, with very few
exceptions.

"I had here, as a companion, a Mr. Denis Taafe,
a man of very strong intellect. When the whipping
and torturing were going on, he wished to go to the
country, and on his way he met some yeomen in
Rathfarnam, or near it: they asked him where he
was going? He said, 'he was going farther,' and
that he 'did not wish to stay in Dublin, it was so
troublesome a place.' He perceived they were getting cross with him, and he wished them a good
morning. He had not gone far when one of them
fired after him; and the ball went in at the elbow
of the left arm, and came out at the wrist. He went
over to a thicket of flaggers, and threw himself on
his face: they fired at him there, and he could hear
them say, 'he is settled,' or something like it. When
he thought they were gone, he arose and tied up the

wound with his neck-handkerchief, and it bled, he
said, very fast. He made what haste he could to a
cabin he saw at a distance, and he saw no one but
an old woman; he asked her 'for God's sake, could
she do any thing for him,' as he was 'getting very
weak from loss of blood?' She bid him go into a
little pig-stye at the end of the cabin; she came to
him shortly after, and stopped the blood with a little
pig's dung—a fortunate circumstance for him! She
treated him with great kindness: the poor woman
was greatly afraid he would be seen—he was fortunate in that circumstance, as no one came while he
was there. In the morning early he took leave of
his kind hostess, and was much obliged to her for
her attention to him. He soon came in view of the
rebels; they were very glad to see him; he wanted for
nothing they could give him. He said, he 'could not
do any thing for them, on account of his wound;'
they said 'they wanted nothing but his advice;' he
said they should have that. They gave him a horse.
At this time there was a regiment called the 'Ancient
Britons,' and they were doing great damage in the
country, and the people were greatly incensed against
them. One day Mr. Taafe was informed by their
videttes, who were on the watch, that 'they perceived the army coming in the direction they were
in.' Mr. Taafe had the command this day, and he
immediately saw there was no time to be lost. There
was a road, and it came a little crooked at the upper
end, which could not be seen at first, and he desired it
to be barricaded at the upper end; there was a thick
hedge on one side, and an olds tone wall on the other,

of this road. He desired the men to post themselves, one part behind the hedge, and the other
behind the wall. The order was quickly complied
with, and shortly after the 'Ancient Britons' came
on in full gallop, as he said, thinking the rebels were
still before them : a barrier stopped them ; then the
firing commenced on both sides of the road, and the
consequence was that great slaughter took place. I
believe only three or four escaped out of the entire troop.

"Some time after, the state prisoners were very
much coerced by those who had the care of the
prison, and it so happened, when any bulletin gave
an account of the success of the rebels (which was
very seldom), the deputy-jailer was apparently civil,
when the king's troops gained any success, incivility
was the order of the day. There was a rumour at
one time, that the rebels were coming in great force,
and it was a false alarm. The jailer told us in the
morning, that the officer on guard wanted him
(Simpson) to give him the keys of the prison, which
he refused. The gentlemen confined were indignant
at this, as they felt inclined to suppose that the place
would be invested by the soldiers on guard, and the
prisoners disposed of in a very summary way ; they
felt inclined, if such a thing should take place, to sell
their lives dear, and intended to prepare for it by
every means in their power. There was another
thing occurred during my stay here : it was said,
government received information that there was
something going on in the three prisons inimical to
them ; the consequence was, that in the dead of night,

our rooms were all opened, and in walked Mr. Gregg. Mr. Carleton (who held a place under government I am satisfied, and who I often saw in town) and a witness, with pen and ink to mark the papers. We were all in the arms of Morpheus, but were desired to get up and open our trunks. We found no difficulty in doing that, as we had no fear on that head. There were two or three letters from Miss Byrne to her father, in French, and our midnight visitors not having got so high in the alphabet, could not make anything of them. I think they took them afterwards to the Castle. We heard that government had received information from some person in Kilmainham prison, which was the cause of the search. I heard that the other two prisoners were examined at the same time we were. We spent our time in this place very unpleasantly, but lived in hopes. My family were doing all in their power to have me liberated—which was their anxious wish. There was a person spoken of, who it was supposed had interest in a certain quarter. There was an interview with this person, and he promised everything, and was to receive a stipulated sum for his trouble, which he got; and I believe he did nothing for it but give fair promises, which I think he never realized. At length, after a severe confinement of fifty-five weeks, I was liberated and never brought to trial. The bail required was two sureties in £500 each, and myself in £1000— the term seven years—all very moderate! Well, I was allowed to leave my (prison) mansion on the 10th June, 1799. When it was known I was at liberty I had many friends coming to see me, of

course, and I felt grateful for the kindness they exhibited towards me. I went to my house and found
it in a deplorable condition :—the kitchen made a
dirt-hole of by the soldiers; the parlour, their kitchen;
the rooms, to answer any purpose they wished. I
got the house and concerns—a mere shell—a house
that I gave £250 fine for, subject to £70 yearly rent,
and on which I expended £1000 in useful improvements. I have now by me an estimate of my losses,
and the amount of what I paid for repairing the concerns, and it amounted to a very serious sum.

" I was determined, on an early day, to have the
pleasure of an introduction to the late Lady Louisa
Connolly, and I went to Castletown for that purpose
with my revered brother, now no more. I was announced by letter and ordered to her presence. She
had a very elegant and commanding figure, with a
very expressive countenance, and with such good
feeling and consideration as exhibited nobility itself.

" Lady Louisa Connolly seemed to feel very much
my situation; but stated very pathetically, ' she
could do nothing for me.' Lady Sarah Napier being
in the place, and hearing of me, sent the Hon. Miss
Napier to me, requesting I would go to see her. I
felt no hesitation in doing so, and complied. Lady
S. Napier was a very nice personage, and we had
some conversation on the unfortunate business, and
she appeared to console me on the privations I was
obliged to submit to. However, I took my leave,
and it was easy to perceive what might be expected
from my reception. I was then advised to address
a letter his Grace the late Duke of Leinster, which I

did; and waited on his Grace at Leinster House.
His Grace allowed me the honour of an interview,
and on seeing me he seemed to feel very much, and
I thought I saw a troubled melancholy on his countenance; however, in our conversation, I clearly understood that his Grace was not inclined in any way
to offer me the smallest pecuniary assistance—although I was spoken to by friends, and recommended
to apply. I then acted agreeably to their advice, and
found it amounted to nothing. My friends were
disappointed in this business as well as myself.

"I endeavoured to raise my trade with very limited
means, and found it very difficult to do so. I felt
now that great men were very easy about the misfortunes of others; and, I am sorry I am obliged to
make the remark—my case was one that was to be
deplored in every point of view.

"There was a large reward offered for the apprehension of Lord Edward, and I fearlessly state that,
if it was ten times the sum, it would be no inducement to me, as I felt myself bound by every sentiment of honourable feeling, when he came to my
house, to admit him and protect him, as far as the
means were in my reach—and what man could do
less for an ill-fated gentleman, endeavouring to
evade the vigilance of his pursuers? I think I would
act on the same principle to my greatest enemy,
under similar circumstances. However, my prospects in business were in a great measure destroyed
by the long confinement I was obliged to submit to,
and the coercive treatment I experienced from my
oppressors. My trade totally disappeared—some of

my friends were afraid to speak to me, from the appearance of the times. Well, I breathed the clear air of my beloved country, and was at liberty; and I felt some satisfaction at the circumstance. I commenced business, and I felt a great want of what is called the 'sinews of war,' and went on as well as the circumstances would admit.

" There took place in the year 1803, unfortunately, an insurrection, encouraged, it was said, by Robert Emmett and others.

" When I left the strong house in 1799, I was determined to preserve a strict neutrality in all cases of a political description—unless such as were allowed by the laws of our glorious constitution in church and state,—the envy of surrounding nations. I can state with truth that I knew nothing of that unfortunate business. The morning of the day it took place, I believe, was on the 23rd July, 1803. There appeared to be a great commotion on the evening of this day, and it was marked with peculiarly unfortunate circumstances: Lord Kilwarden and some of his family, were made victims, as well as others, by an infuriated mob, led astray by popular commotion: however, it was of short duration. I have heard that the government were not prepared, and did not expect such a thing could take place. The officers of justice were very active on the following days, and made several arrests. Alderman Darley came to my house, I believe on the Sunday following, with an officer of the 32nd regiment and two privates, and examined the rooms. No arms of any description were found. The worthy alderman did not forget to let the officer know, 'that was the house the late Lord Edward Fitzgerald was arrested in.'—[I must observe the alderman behaved with great civility.]

" In a few days after the transaction, the government, I understood, issued orders in a very private way for a general search in all directions; and this post of honour was placed in the hands of the yeomen—and I believe with great safety, for their loyalty was not to be doubted. On the morning of the general search, I was of course visited by these military heroes. I had not taken breakfast at the time, when three or four of the party made their appearance, and mentioned that they came for the purpose of searching for arms. I answered I had no arms, and that they might examine the place, which they did with great care. I had a case of pistols, and a very good musket and bayonet, and a small sword, and what is called a ' cut-and-thrust' sword, which were all taken from me in 1798, and never returned to me. In their going through the rooms I opened a clothes-press, in which were a full-dress and an undress uniform of the ' Irish Brigade'—a corps highly respected for the respectability of its members, and to which I had the honour to belong—being then very young. What would you think, gentle reader? these sages in military costume had it immediately—that ' it was the uniform of a rebel general,' and proclaimed it such. There was no use in speaking on the subject—they were judge and jury. The sensations excited by this business in these gentlemen, were truly astounding; they

seemed to be as well pleased as if they had stormed
a fort and took the city by surprise, without firing a
shot or losing a man. I was desired to come down,
and explain the business to their officer. I felt no
hesitation in doing so; the uniform was brought
also for inspection. Their captain, or officer, appeared highly delighted with their conduct in the
matter, and, in a sarcastic and insulting manner,
requested that 'I would oblige him by putting it on !'
This gentleman was quite a Joe Miller in his conduct at
this time, and was quite elated with the difficulty I had
to put on the undress uniform, for it happened that
I outgrew it. These yeomen belonged, I believe,
to the 'Attorneys' Corps,' with a few others with
them. They had a car and horse in the street, and
two or three prisoners they took in their way; there
was also some rod-iron on the car, such as smiths
make nails of. There were packs of wool in the
warehouses, and these assailants cut several of them,
expecting, I suppose, to find arms in them. I was
taken in this manner a prisoner, and marched off
in great triumph. The uniform was exhibited on
the horse. I could not help taking a view of these
military gentry—many of them quite boys, scarcely
able to handle a musket; and their affected knowledge of military tactics, drew from me a smile of
contempt. On our way to the Castle the crowd
increased immensely, every one enquiring—' Who is
that?' Dublin appeared to be in a state of siege.
In Skinners'-row, I saw Sir John White coming up
against us on the other side; I knew his person,
but never spoke to him. He came over to me, and

said to me—'Murphy, you will be hanged to-morrow.' I told him 'I hoped not so soon.' He was fully appointed in military array. I was told he commanded a corps known by the name of the 'Sepulchres,' and was going to meet them at the time. What a melancholy circumstance it is, to be obliged to remark the conduct of respectable characters, wound up to a pitch of phrenzied loyalty, and making use of language degrading to the human species. However, I met this military hero in some time afterwards, and he thought proper to apologize for it, and did appear sorry for his mistaken zeal.

" It is impossible to give a picture of the scene. The crowd was immense, and still increasing. I cannot do justice to these ' sons of Mars,' I mean my body-guard, for they looked tremendous, only that some of them seemed not to be able to carry the musket, it appeared to be rather heavy for them, but they were ' weak and willing !' However, on we marched to the Castle. It would not do to go in at the grand gate ; my guard of honour, took me round the lower gate, and brought me to a temporary guard-house where now stands the Castle chapel; there I was introduced, I suppose, to the general of the staff, who appeared quite pleased, and seemed to enjoy the scene, with the greatest pleasure. In a little time I was removed from this, to the Castle guard-house and there placed in a crib, with several others, a place I could hardly breath in, and there exhibited for public curiosity. A soldier of the 38th, said he wished to have a crack at me. In the course of the day, I was ordered, with others,

to the provost prison, situated in Harbour-hill. I
was brought there under escort. This place appeared to be a new building, and is situated on a
rising ground. I was placed in a room, with five or
six other prisoners; it was intended, I heard, as an
hospital for invalided soldiers : there was not in it,
either table or chair or any thing whatever, except
the walls, and they were thick enough. I sent for a
bed, and I accommodated two of my fellow prisoners
with part of it. If I had not, they would be obliged
to sleep on the floor. The window stools supplied
the place of a table. The wet was running down
the walls in the most copious way. There was in
this place, two hundred prisoners, and from appear-
ances, the principal part of them were of the humblest class of society. It was a horrible place for
any man to be placed in, that was acccustomed to a
respectable situation in society. It required great
fortitude to submit with calmness to this state of
things ; however ' we must bear those ills we cannot
cure.' My house was deserted, my trade destroyed,
my credit injured ! I would prefer being three
months in Newgate, to three weeks in this place.
Sometimes there would come informers, and then
the prisoners would be ordered out for inspection,
two deep, and the informers would view us all round
with the eye of an Argus, trying to recognize any
unfortunate prisoner in the crowd to whom to
attach criminality. I have seen Majors Sirr and
Swan amusing themselves here, laughing at the
misfortunes of others, but at the same time taking
care of themselves. I felt I gave great uneasiness

and trouble to my family, and it caused very unpleasant sensations to myself. I considered this circumstance as a very coercive measure; but I was well
aware, it was to please a certain party, at this time in
power. A friend of mine went to Alderman Manders,
a highly respectable character, and with the greatest
kindness, he went to the Castle, to Mr. Marsden, I
think to enquire what grounds there were for my detention? The answer was, there was no charge exhibited against me; I was well aware of that, for I was
satisfied there could be no charge against me, but
that in a few days, I might expect to be liberated.
I understood I had enemies behind the curtain; one
gentleman said to Mr. Marsden, ' If he let out
persons that way, there was no occasion to take
them up:' very sublime reasoning! If they happened
to be there themselves, they would reason in a very
different way, I think; and they deserved it as much
as I did. My friends were very desirous for my
liberation, and the worthy Alderman went several
times for an answer, and it was still, ' wait a while.'
At length my highly respectable friend, with all
that candour and goodness which dignified the man,
wrote a letter to Mr. Marsden, expressive of his
readiness of being answerable for my person and
conduct at any time the government thought it
necessary for me to be called on, to answer any
alleged charge made against me; and that has not
taken place yet. I was obliged to give bail of two
sureties of five hundred pounds each, and myself for
one thousand pounds, for seven years; very moderate! 'and besides, bail to the same amount was
given in the 1798 business, and for the same term.

"I feel an eternal debt of gratitude to the late Alderman Manders, for his disinterested conduct on this business; for I am confident there could not be a more impartial magistrate or high-minded character to be found in society: he exhibited a kindness of feeling, and felt a pleasure in administering even-handed justice to all. What a melancholy picture presented itself to me, when I came from the provost prison to my house, after three weeks' incarceration in that dismal place—and for what? To please a junto that was lording it over the people; these exclusive loyalists that are living like the bishops— 'on Divine Providence!'

"This business, like the last, injured me very much in my trade. I was recommended at this time to address a letter to His Grace the Duke of Leinster; I did myself that honour when his Grace resided in that spacious mansion formerly occupied by his Grace's ancestors, and himself at this time. In accordance with the wishes of my friends, I went to this mansion, and enquired of the person in care of the front gate, if his Grace was at home? I was answered in the affirmative. There were two approaches to the house: I went the private way, and found in the hall, a servant in waiting. I enquired if his Grace was disengaged? I was told he was. I then gave this person a letter, addressed to his Grace, and said that I respectfully requested an answer; and the messenger shortly returned, and said there was no answer! I immediately withdrew, and came out the same way I went in. On my way back, I was met by a gentleman, who asked 'if I was in the house?' I said I was, and that I had addressed a letter to His Grace the Duke of Leinster on a particular subject, and received no answer. We walked together for some time, and I soon perceived this gentleman to be no other than—the Duke himself! His Grace came out at the front door, unobserved by me, and from the turn the conversation took between us, I looked attentively at him. 'I believe,' I said, 'I am addressing His Grace the Duke of Leinster?'—the answer I received confirmed me in my opinion. I took leave to state that I was obliged to submit to great and rigorous confinement; my house and concerns made a barrack; and my property destroyed by a licentious soldiery and their adherents, and no hope of redress from any quarter. Mr. Cooke of the Castle would not pay half-a-year's rent when applied to by Mr. Browne, the landlord, (although the house had been a barrack for upwards of ten months, and the baggage of the 'Rea Fencibles' in it, and some invalided soldiers of that regiment living in it with their wives.) His Grace appeared to condole with me very much— but it went no farther with his Grace. I understood from his Grace the way he was situated he could do nothing for me, and it was easy to perceive that he was not inclined.* I do think he only made his appearance to see the kind of person I was. I took my leave of his Grace, and found, in nine cases out of ten, there could be placed very little reliance in great men. I do not hesitate to say, I felt very

* I very much doubt the correctness of this opinion, but there is much allowance to be made for poor Murphy's irritated feelings at this period —R. R. M.

much disappointed at th interview with his Grace,
as I was strongly recommended by my friends to
make the application. I saw too late I acted a very
imprudent part, and paid very well for it. If attachment to my beautiful, but ill-fated country be a
crime, I submit to that charge, and I have been
taught ' to bear those ills we cannot cure!'

(Signed,)   N. MURPHY."

There is a note at th end of this statement,
written by Murphy at a later period, and dated **29th
of November, 1831**, relating the circumstances of
Bond's sudden death, th 16th of Septemb
and the embarkation of the state prisoner
of March, 1799, their arival at Fort
9th of April following, ad their detent
the spring of the year 180, when they
on peace being proclaime.

As the note is a mere repetition of
in the preceding narrativ, it is unnece
it here.

In the latter years of h life the af
Murphy were a good eal embar
obliged to mortgage his buse, and
from his sisters and brther. He
end of April, 1833, in his 7th year
stances, but with the chracter of
whose fidelity to one wh trusted
cause of his ruin. He as buried
at Glassnevin: if he had played t
friend, perhaps a monumnt might
to his memory; as it is, here is n
headstone over his grave.

much disappointed at this interview with his Grace, as I was strongly recommended by my friends to make the application. I saw too late I acted a very imprudent part, and paid very well for it. If attachment to my beautiful, but ill-fated country be a crime, I submit to that charge, and I have been taught ' to bear those ills we cannot cure !'

(Signed,)   N. MURPHY."

There is a note at the end of this statement, written by Murphy at a later period, and dated 29th of November, 1831, repeating the circumstance of Bond's sudden death, the 16th of September, 1798, and the embarkation of the state prisoners, the 18th of March, 1799; their arrival at Fort George, the 9th of April following, and their detention there till the spring of the year 1801, when they were liberated on peace being proclaimed.

As the note is a mere repetition of what is stated in the preceding narrative, it is unnecessary to insert it here.

In the latter years of his life the affairs of Nicholas Murphy were a good deal embarrassed. He was obliged to mortgage his house, and to borrow money from his sisters and brother. He died the latter end of April, 1833, in his 77th year—poor in circumstances, but with the character of an honest man—whose fidelity to one who trusted in him, was the cause of his ruin. He was buried in the cemetery at Glassnevin : if he had played the villain with his friend, perhaps a monument might have been erected to his memory; as it is, there is not even a common headstone over his grave.

The Mr. Dennis Taafe, of whom mention is made in Murphy's narrative, was a very remarkable person, whose chequered career furnishes a striking instance of talents of the highest order, neglected and abused. This unfortunate gentleman was a clergyman of the Roman Catholic Church. He was born in the county Louth, of respectable parents, and was educated for the priesthood. He was sent to Prague to complete his clerical studies, where he remained several years; was received into a Franciscan convent, and entered into holy orders as a friar of that rule. He returned to his own country, and proud of his proficiency in classical as well as theological erudition, he used his powers like one conscious of their strength, and only desirous of displaying their superiority. In fact, he was a proud, indolent, slovenly, overbearing scholar, eternally at war with his superiors, and feared and hated by them. At length, his habits furnished a plea for getting rid of the sarcastic retorts and disagreeable pasquinades of the turbulent and satirical young friar. Taafe was suspended on a charge of intemperance, and within a few days of this infliction of ecclesiastical censure, he read his recantation. The promised prize for which poor Taafe "renounced the errors of the Church of Rome," was a Hebrew professorship in the Dublin University, an appointment for which his knowledge of oriental languages well qualified him. He was hardly received into the bosom of his new church, when he quarrelled with his bishop and superior clergy, and after a short interval, " he relapsed into popery ;" but it could hardly be said into his disorderly habits, for he carried

these with him into protestantism, and brought them
back into the old paths of his " Romish religion."

As he advanced in years, he sought a refuge in
study, from these painful reminiscences of his
past life; he gave himself up finally to politics, and
became a public writer.   It was at the period he was
engaged in the turmoil and drudgery of these pursuits, that he took it into his head, at the height of
the rebellion, to see what the United Irishmen were
doing in Wicklow and its vicinity, and accordingly
set out in quest of rebel adventures.   The results of
his expedition are referred to by Murphy; but he has
not stated the place where the occurrences took
place, which Taafe related to him, nor entered into
any particulars, probably from prudential motives,
both he and Taafe being then inmates of Newgate.
This rencontre is what is called the battle of Ballyellis,
and though others, since Taafe's death, have claimed
this victory as their own, the success of the insurgents
on that occasion, was unquestionably mainly due to the
skilful, judicious, and well-concerted plan of ambuscade, devised by Taafe and carried into effect by Holt,
who, to use the words of the latter, " with an advanced
guard met the enemy, keeping all the other people
out of sight, and commenced firing, and then retreated as fast as they could, and everything had the
appearance of a panic."*   It was at this juncture
that Taafe's services came into active requisition, and
that the men in ambuscade, pikemen and mus-
queteers, fell on the military, and in the midst of
the confusion of the latter, that Holt brought a

* Vide Memoirs of Holt, edited by T. Crofton Croker, Esq.
vol i., p 77.

strong reserve of about 1,000 men round upon them, and in a short time they were utterly routed.

Holt makes no mention of Taafe in this affair; but any one who has ever pursued enquiries on the subject of the exploits of the United Irishmen, or the engagements of the military with the former, will not wonder at the eagerness of the leaders of either party to thrust themselves forward in the fore-ground of the picture, and to figure on the scene as the chief, or perhaps the sole actors in it. I have been frequently, in the course of my enquiries on this subject, struck with the jealousy of each other's fame, which seemed to exist between the leaders of a cause, where the nature of their principles, and of their attachment to that cause, might be supposed to leave no room for the selfishness, envy and assumption, which are supposed to be the characteristics of little-minded men of fanatical opinions, rather than of generous enthusiasts, whose errors, even, have generally something of a singleness of purpose and sincerity of feeling, in their mistaken courses.

Men of far higher fame in the struggle of 1798, than Holt, have seemed to me more jealous of one another, less disposed to do justice to each other's merits, and a great deal too much occupied with the interests of their own repute, than was consistent with the good of the sole object that might have been expected to have engrossed their thoughts and affections. When I have noticed this disposition but too frequently, I have not been so much surprised at the failure of their plans, as I might otherwise have been.

There seems to have been a greater bar to "the union between Irishmen of all denominations," than any efforts of their opponents interposed ; and amongst the leaders, too, a great many might have, indeed, denied the charge of being United Irishmen, if, when such charges were made, the merits of them had been literally gone into. It would be very unjust, however, to assert that there were not exceptions, and many exceptions, to such instances. Perhaps, if they had been rarer and less signal ones, the instances of a contrary kind might not appear so remarkable.

Cox, the editor of the Irish Magazine, who was acquainted with Taafe, in speaking of the part he took in the engagement at Ballyellis, says that " his plans were so judiciously directed, that the destruction of the Ancient Britons, which took place on the spot, must be fairly attributed to his courage and judgment, for he fought like a lion, when he had drawn his game into the toils." It was to this conflict he alluded, when he answered a gentleman who was reproving him for his political opinions—" I have taught both ancient and modern Britons I could fight as well as write." It is needless to say, that the person who could make this declaration had sadly mistaken his vocation, when he took on him the duties of a Christian minister. Sir Richard Musgrave gives the following account of the attack at Ballyellis on the Ancient Britons :—

" The rebels being closely pressed, placed their baggage and their cars in the road, and posted a number of pikemen in their front. As soon as our cavalry came in sight of them, at the turn of a road, they charged them with great impetuosity; but when they were within a short distance of them, the pikemen leaped over the hedges at each side: on which the horses in front were entangled in the cars, and those in their rear pressing on them, a shocking scene of confusion ensued—both men and horses were involved, and tumbled over each other. The rebels fired on them from behind the hedges and a park-wall which was near, and, while they were in this state of embarrassment, killed numbers of them with their muskets, and piked such of them as happened to be unhorsed. Colonel Puleston, whose horse they shot or piked, was with difficulty saved by his men. Captain Giffard, of the Ancient Britons, and Mr. Parsons of the Ballaghkeene cavalry, who had served with reputation abroad, and about sixty privates of the military and yeomen, were killed."[*]

Musgrave has underrated the loss of the King's troops on this occasion; but Holt, on the other hand, has in a far greater degree exaggerated the number. He says, " in less than twenty minutes there were 370 of them slain, and our own loss was but four."

George Taylor says, " they piked and shot twenty-five Ancient Britons, eleven of the 5th Dragoons, and eight of the yeomanry, with two loyalists, besides wounding many."

Hay estimates the number of killed at eighty. The probability is, that the loss on the part of the

* Musgrave's History, p. 516.

military, including those who subsequently died of
their wounds, did not fall short of 100.

Dr. Brennan, in his Milesian Magazine, speaking
of Taafe, says, " the success also of this manœuvre
was due to him; and after the engagement, being
severely wounded, he was smuggled back to Dublin
in a load of hay, and put into an hospital, where he
eventually recovered." It must then have been subsequently to his return he was arrested and confined
in Newgate. No informations having been sworn
against him, he was at length liberated. His literary
abilities became known to Mr. John Keogh of Mount
Jerome, and Doctor Macarthy, the late titular
Bishop of Cork. By these gentlemen and others, he
was engaged to devote his talents to some useful
account. He set about writing a history of Ireland,
and he received some pecuniary assistance while he
was employed on it—to a small amount from Mr.
Keogh, and an allowance of £40 a-year from Dr.
Macarthy, which only terminated with the bishop's
death. Poor Taafe went on writing his history—
struggling with poverty, and complaining loudly of
his patrons, till death put an end to his labours and
his sufferings, at the age of sixty, in Thomas-street,
Dublin, in 1813.

He did not live to complete his history. A Dublin
bookseller—to the honour of " the trade" be it told—
Mr. Coyne, did not suffer the frailties of unfortunate
Taafe to deprive him of the sympathy and charitable
assistance he stood so much in need of at the close
of his career. He was likewise indebted to Mr.
Fitzpatrick of Capel-street, for many acts of kind-

ness. Not long before his death, he had a literary quarrel with the editors of the Oxford Review. The old spirit which animated him at Ballyellis displayed itself in the following pasquinade on the editors of the hostile review—who were members of the University, through the sides of which he indulged, on this occasion, in the gratification of piking his opponents with his pen.

" Henceforth, oh, *Oxford*! *Cow*ford be thy name,
  Thou rearest calves, and long hast reared the same."

CHAPTER X.

THERE can be little doubt, but that the person who disclosed the secret of Lord Edward's place of concealment, was one then in his confidence, or in that of the persons about him who were in the habit of visiting him at Moore's, Cormick's, or Murphy's, or forming what was called, his " body guard," when he went abroad. The circumstance of the rencontre in Bridgefoot street, the previous evening; of Sirr and his party being there on the watch for Lord Edward, knowing he was to pass through that street, on the evening in question; is a sufficient proof, that treachery was nearer his person, while he was in concealment, than he or his friends had any idea of.

The persons who occasionally formed his guard, who visited him, or who accompanied him when he went abroad, were the following, Surgeon Lawless, Major Plunkett, Col. Lumm, S. Neilson, J. Hughes, J. Davock, William Cole, Richard Keane, C. Gallagher, Palmer, Rattigan, W. P. M'Cabe and Walter Cox. One of those named herein, was unquestionably the person, through whom the information was derived which led to Lord Edward's apprehension. The night of his rencontre with Major Sirr, he was attended by M'Cabe, Patrick Gallagher, Palmer and Rattigan. Of the three latter, it will be necessary to say a few words, connected as they are with the rencontre between Lord Edward Fitzgerald's party and that of Major Sirr, on the night of the 17th of May. The following account of that affair is given by Mr. Moore:—

"On the 17th, Ascension Thursday, he had been led to expect his noble guest would be with him; but owing most probably to the circumstance I am about to mention, his lordship did not then make his appearance. On the very morning of that day, the active Town-Major Sirr, had received information that a party of persons, supposed to be Lord Edward Fitzgerald's body-guard, would be on their way from Thomas-street to Usher's Island at a certain hour that night. Accordingly, taking with him a sufficient number of assistants for his purpose, and accompanied also by Messrs. O'Brien and Emerson, Major Sirr proceeded at the proper time to the quarter pointed out, and there being two different ways (either Watling-street or Dirty-lane) by which the expected party might come, divided his force so as to intercept them by either road. A similar plan having happened to be adopted by Lord Edward's escort, there took place in each of these two streets a conflict between the parties; and Major Sirr, who had almost alone to bear the brunt in his quarter, was near losing his life. In defending himself with a sword which he had snatched from one of his assailants, he lost his footing and fell, and had not those with whom he was engaged been much more occupied with their noble charge than with him, he could hardly have escaped."

As nothing is said in the preceding account, of the parties engaged in this affair, on Lord Edward's side, the following authentic particulars may be found interesting.

When Lord Edward went abroad, during the time of his concealment, he was usually preceded by one of his guard, thirty or forty yards in advance, and two men on the opposite side of the way, at some distance from one another. On the present occasion, when he was recognized by Sirr, the persons attending him were not seen, and Lord Edward was on the point of being seized, when Sirr found himself in the grasp of two powerful young men; one of them snapped a pistol at Sirr, and the other, Gallagher, struck at his neck with a dagger, and pierced his stock without inflicting any wound. M'Cabe was not present when this scuffle took place. He was at the bottom of Bridgefoot-street, close to Usher's Island at this moment, watching the movements of the other party, by whom he was at length arrested. Major Sirr was in the habit of speaking of this struggle with Gallagher and Palmer, as having been one of life and death, and of Palmer especially, as being the most formidable opponent he ever encountered. Lord Edward, during this struggle having got clear of Sirr and his myrmidons, Palmer and Gallagher thought it prudent to decamp, leaving the major little inclined to pursue them. On the following day, it was determined by

Lord Edward and his friends, that he should remove on the next evening, from Murphy's, to the house of a Mrs. Risk, at Sandy Mount. The appearance of the soldiers, however, in the morning, in Thomas-street, caused him to give up the idea of then removing. His arrest the same evening, however, put an end to all his plans; but his faithful friends, even at this trying moment, did not desert him. The sedan chair in which he was placed, no sooner moved from Murphy's door, than Major Sirr and his party were assailed by a number of persons, and a very desperate attempt was made to rescue their prisoner.

This effort was directed by Edward Rattigan, assisted by Gallagher. Rattigan was a director of the watchhouse of St. Catherine's, and the moment he received an intimation of Lord Edward's danger, he called on the first people he met to accompany him to the watchhouse; then he seized on all the arms that were deposited there, and proceeded with all despatch to Murphy's. Major Sirr acknowledged they must have succeeded, had not the Rainsford-street guard and the picquet-guard of the Castle, chiefly cavalry, for the assistance of which he had previously sent from Murphy's, opportunely arrived.

When M'Cabe was arrested that night, he first said his name was Jameson (a name which Lord Edward went by, when he was at the house of the Widow Dillon at the canal): subsequently he said his name was Brand. M'Cabe was taken to the provost, and examined by Major Sandys. M'Cabe

answered, in broad Scotch, that he was a poor
Scotch pedlar who dealt in muslins, and was going
home peaceably to his lodgings when he was arrested.   A weapon, however, was found upon him,
not very corroborative of his peaceful pursuits:—he
was asked what pedlars had to do with pistols?   He
said the pistol found on him belonged to a friend of
his, who had sent it to be repaired, and had asked
him to call for it that evening.   He was ordered into
confinement, and the following day walked out of his
prison—without the permission of Major Sandys, but
with the knowledge and connivance of a serjeant of
the Dumbarton Fencibles, to whom M'Cabe had
managed to introduce himself, as a townsman whom
he had some recollection of when a boy.

Palmer contrived to make his escape from Dublin;
joined M'Cabe in a few days in the county Wicklow,
and both were in the neighbourhood of Ballinamuck
in the month of August, when the French landed.
They then thought it was time to give up their
cause, and quit the country, which they contrived to
do without detection.   Palmer settled in Holland, and
was drowned by the upsetting of a boat.   M'Cabe
died in France, possessed of considerable means.
The history of this man is so singular, that I purpose giving some more detailed account of his
extraordinary career.

Rattigan and Gallagher, after their ineffectual
attempt to rescue Lord Edward on the 19th of May,
perceived that they had been particularly observed
by a person who happened to be passing by when
they attacked Sirr's party: this person, a Mr. Cu-

sack of the Revenue Corps, they approached, detained him for some time, and threatened him with death, if he did not promise to be silent on the subject of the struggle he had witnessed, and those who were engaged in it.

Cusack, the following day, gave information to Sirr; but Rattigan, in the mean time, had absconded; and on the 21st, the major proceeded to the house of his mother, a widow lady, who kept a timber-yard in Bridgefoot-street, to avenge the injured majesty of his offended person, for Sirr often said "he would teach people to meddle with him or his men;" that the unfortunate offenders were not charged with treason, and their disaffected plate and pictures confiscated to the sideboard or the walls, which represented the state.

The major and his men rushed into the house of the poor Widow Rattigan; searched for pikes, and found the necessary quantity to justify a summary visitation of the major's vengeance. The inmates were thrust forth—all that was valuable in the house was pillaged—the furniture was then thrown into the street, the timber in the yard set on fire, and the house and premises utterly destroyed. This was to teach people how to meddle with the major.

Gallagher, who was shopman to Mrs. Moore of Thomas-street, in whose house Lord Edward had at one time been concealed, was particularly obnoxious to the major.

A plundering expedition on the plea of searching for concealed arms, had a short time before been undertaken, and Messrs. Sirr, Hanlon, and Brien, were baffled on this occasion by Gallagher and his friend Palmer, who happened to be present. They managed to keep the party at bay, till there had been time to remove whatever was in most danger of disappearing, and Palmer concealed himself in a loft in an out-building, where he contemplated taking Sirr's life. He had the loaded pistol in his hand, presented in the direction he momentarily expected to see Sirr approach, when another person accompanying Sirr at that moment to the entrance, threw Palmer off his guard. Major Sirr was told of this circumstance, as related by Palmer, a few years before his death, by a gentleman now living in Dublin, and he acknowledged he had subsequently heard his life was in some danger on that occasion.

Palmer was a remarkably fine young man, of great energy of mind, and strength and activity of body. He was the son of a hosier in Cutpurse-row.

Gallagher, whose dagger had been so near the major's neck on the 19th of May, was arrested, tried by court martial, and sentenced to be hanged. His sister, a young woman of some accomplishments and personal attractions, the following day went with two small children to a gentleman, in whose family she had formerly lived as a governess. This gentleman was a master in chancery, and possessed much influence at the Castle. This poor girl passed herself off as the wife of the prisoner, whose life she besought him to interfere in behalf of, and the children who accompanied her as her own, thinking the application coming from a wife would have more effect than from a sister.

This humane gentleman, whose political opinions were directly opposite to those of Gallagher, went off immediately to the Castle, and succeeded in obtaining the prisoner's pardon. Gallagher was now removed from the provost to a transport that was then lying in the bay, to be sent out of the country.

Some days elapsed before the vessel was prepared for her long voyage. During that time, Gallagher was permitted to see his sister and friends on board, and even to have a parting dance on deck the evening before their intended departure. During the bustle of the party, Gallagher escaped out of the cabin window; the tide was then ebbing, and after swimming some short distance, he was picked up by a boat that was in readiness to receive him, and was taken to Louth. In this boat he was seen by Major Sirr when pulling towards the vessel with some prisoners who were going on board; he suspected all was not right, but was not sufficiently sure of having any grounds for suspicion, and did not chase the boat. Gallagher got to Dublin, and there, disguised as a groom, succeeded in leaving the country. He went to Bourdeaux, entered into business, married respectably, returned some years ago to Ireland, then went back to France, where he died in excellent circumstances and in good repute.

The narrative of Mr. Murphy is a sufficient evidence of his fidelity, to render any vindication of it unnecessary.

The son of Mr. Reynolds has very industriously endeavoured to impress the readers of his book with the opinion that there were a variety of circumstances, so suspicious in their nature, in the conduct of Murphy on the occasion of the arrest of Lord Edward, as to be totally inexplicable. In short, he plainly insinuates, though he does not say it in express terms, that Murphy was privy to the door being left open, by which Sirr and his party gained admission, and as he was standing at the window when they entered, that he must have seen the party in the street on their arrival at the house.

If Mr. Reynolds's father had been living, he could probably have informed him that there was not the slightest ground for these insinuations; though the disclosure of Lord Edward's place of concealment was not made by him, from his subsequent intimacy with the agents of government, he could hardly have been mistaken as to the quarter from which it did come. The person who gave that information was amply rewarded for it—he received £1,000, and the initials of his name were not those of Nicholas Murphy. Nor was Murphy at large when the payment was made. The following date, letters, service, and sum paid for it, show the groundlessness of the suspicions entertained by Mr. Reynolds.

" June 20th, 1798. F. H. Discovery of L. E. F. £1000." These initials may spare the friends of Samuel Neilson the trouble of vindicating his memory—if the recent editions of the Life of Lord Edward Fitzgerald have left any necessity for so doing; and there is one gentleman who, perhaps, will not less rejoice than any of them, that a passage in a work of his (to which a meaning had been affixed he never intended it to convey,) which has been strained into an imputation on Neilson, of being the betrayer of his friend, can no longer be supposed to leave a doubt of the conduct of a man who suffered much in purse and person for that cause in which his dearest friend perished, and for whom he risked his own life in the prosecution of a daring, though ineffectual, plan for his liberation.

In the third edition of Mr. Moore's admirable Life of Lord Edward Fitzgerald, he has inserted an introductory notice respecting the misinterpretation of the passage which had given uneasiness to the friends of Neilson, and its omission in that edition. The considerate manner in which this act of kindness to the living, and of justice to the dead, was done by Mr. Moore, was such as might be expected from him, and such as the friends of Neilson may be amply satisfied with.

The family of Samuel Neilson having placed in in my hands materials for a memoir of his life, from the period of his founding the Society of United Irishmen, in conjunction with Thomas Russell and Henry Joy M'Cracken, and with the subsequent co-operation of T. W. Tone, which will appear in the succeeding series of this work, I will now only refer to those dates which relate to the arrest of Lord Edward, and Neilson's conduct with regard to it.

Lord Edward was arrested at Murphy's on the 19th of May. Neilson had dined there in company with him that day, and after dinner somewhat abruptly left the house. Shortly afterwards, Major Surr's party entered the house, finding the door

open. Whether Neilson shut the door on going out
or not, is unknown. He had been at the house in
the morning, warning the servant to keep "a sharp
look out," as the military were in the neighbourhood
searching Moore's house, as he believed, for Lord
Edward. The probability is, that when he suddenly
left Murphy and Lord Edward in the evening, his
fears of the military being still on the alert, induced
him to go out to see if all was safe in the vicinity,
and most likely with the intention of returning.
Whether he had time to return before Sirr's arrival,
or met with some acquaintance, who drew off his
attention from the object of his going forth, we have
no information. In any case, his imprudence cannot
be denied, but I can safely say that none of those
who were best acquainted with him suspected the
sincerity of his attachment to Lord Edward, however
imprudent his conduct may then have been. At
this period his health was shattered : both mind and
body were broken down by the effects of long sufferings during his protracted confinement—and, finally,
by an indulgence in those baneful habits which
are so easily acquired—at first, embraced for the
sake of the forgetfulness of care and trouble, and
which, at last, confirmed by long indulgence, enslave
the noblest mind. He was arrested in Belfast, the
15th of November, 1796; sent up to Dublin, and kept
in close confinement till the month of February,
1798; he was then liberated on account of severe
illness, from which he was hardly expected to recover.

The 20th of April—in company with Mr. John

Hughes, he visited Lord Edward at Cormick's in Thomas-street, where he was then in concealment. In the report from the Committee of Secrecy of the House of Lords, 1798—on the examination of John Hughes of Belfast—it is stated by the latter, that he went to Dublin on the 20th of April, and remained there about nine days. He called on Samuel Neilson, and went to Cormick's, where he found Lord Edward playing billiards with Lawless, and dined there with them.

"About the 28th of April," he breakfasted with Neilson at the house of Mr. Sweetman, who was then in prison. The former then lived at his house. Neilson and he (the same day) went in Mr. Sweetman's carriage, to Mr. Grattan's, at Tinnahinch. He states that Neilson and Grattan had some private conversation, and after some general conversation about the strength of the United Irishmen in the north, they left Mr. Grattan's, and on their way back, Neilson informed him he had sworn Mr. Grattan. On the 14th or 15th of May, Neilson and Lord Edward, rode out to reconnoitre the approaches to Dublin, on the Kildare side: they were stopped and questioned by the patrol at Palmerstown, and finally allowed to proceed.

Four days after Lord Edward's arrest, Neilson was arrested by Gregg the jailor, in front of Newgate, where he had been reconnoitring the prison, with a view to the liberation of Lord Edward and the other state prisoners; a large number of men being in readiness to attack the jail, and waiting for Neilson's return, at a place called the Barley Fields.

It is then evident, that Hughes was in the full confidence of Neilson, the 28th of April; there is no reason to believe that he ceased to be so, previ ously to the 19th of May; and yet, during this period and long before it, there is very little doubt that Hughes was an informer.

Neilson's frank, open, unsuspecting nature, was well known to the agents of government, and even to Lord Castlereagh, who was personally acquainted with Neilson, and on one occasion had visited him in prison.

Hughes, it is probable, was set upon him with a view to ascertain his haunts, and to enter into com- munication with his friends, for the special purpose of implicating Grattan and of discovering Lord Edward. That his perfidy never was suspected by Neilson, during their intimacy, there are many proofs; and still more, that Neilson's fidelity to the cause he had embarked in, and the friends he was associated with, was never called in question by his companions and fellow prisoners, by Emmett, M'Nevin, O'Connor, &c. or if a doubt unfavourable to his honesty was expressed by John Sheares, in his letter to Neilson, wherein he endeavours to dissuade him from attack- ing the jails, it must be considered, rather in the light of an angry expostulation, than of an opinion seriously entertained and deliberately expressed.

This man John Hughes, previously to the re- bellion, was in comfortable circumstances, and bore a good character, in Belfast. He kept a large bookseller and stationer's shop in that town.*

In his evidence before the Lord's Committee of 1798, he gives the following account of his career as a United Irishman. He became a member of the first Society of United Irishmen, in Belfast, 1793. About July, 1796, he joined the new organization, and was sworn in by Robert Orr, a chandler. There was no oath administered in the former society. He formed a Society of United Irishmen himself in Belfast, shortly after his admission, and that Society consisted of, Mr. Robert Hunter, broker; John Tisdall, notary; J. M'Clean, watchmaker; S. M'Clean, merchant; Thomas M'Donnell, grocer; J. Luke, linen factor; Hugh Crawford, linen merchant; A. M'Clean, woollen merchant; W. Crawford, ironmonger; H. Dunlap, builder; and W. Hogg, linen factor. He was Secretary to the Society, he swore in the members on the Prayer Book,† fur-

* The house where Hughes lived, in Belfast, was lately pointed out to me, No. 20, Bridge Street, within a few paces of a small old-fashioned house, where Thomas M'Cabe, who designated himself, on his sign board, "The Irish Slave," resided, at No. 6, North Street, within two doors of which, lived Robert Orr, a gentleman not very celebrated for his loyalty, while on the opposite side, the site of the house of the chief founder of the United Irish Society, Samuel Neilson, is pointed out, at the bottom of Donegall Street, on which now stands the Commercial Hall. This neighbourhood, in fact, seems to have been a little focus of republicanism.

† It is worthy of notice, that the oath of the United Irishmen, commonly was administered either on a Prayer Book, or the Scriptures, and it mattered not what prayer book was used, the same book serving often for persons of different religions.

nished each with "a constitution," containing the test which was repeated at the table.

In November, 1796, Bartholomew Teeling, of Dundalk, a linen merchant, prevailed on him to go to Dublin to extend the societies there. In Dublin he communicated with Edward John Lewins of Beresford-street. He returned to Belfast in December, 1796. From motives of caution, he did not attend the societies, but in the day time, either in the street or at his own house, exerted himself amongst the young men of his acquaintance. Shortly before the Lent Assizes in 1797, Mr. M'Guckin, the attorney, requested him to go to Dublin to arrange for Mr. Curran's engagement for the prisoners in the several goals on the North-east Circuit, who were United Irishmen. A hundred guineas for each and every town he would have to attend, was agreed on.

The treasurer of the United Irishmen for the county Antrim, was Mr. Francis Jordan of Belfast, and he collected the money for this purpose. Among the subscribers were Mr. Cunningham Gregg, twenty guineas; Charles Rankin, twenty guineas; Robert Thompson, twenty guineas. The subscriptions for the county Antrim, amounted to £700 and upwards, and the county Down, £900. Mr. Alexander Lowry was the treasurer for Down. In the beginning of June, 1797, he was sent for to Dublin, but before going had an oath administered to him by Magennis, that he would not communicate the names of any persons he should be introduced to there. In Dublin, he was informed by Lowry and Teeling, that a national meeting was about being held of delegates from the different provinces, in order to get a general return of the strength of the United Irishmen, to determine whether an insurrection would then be practicable, and he was to report on the strength and readiness of Down and Antrim. He expressed his opinion, that in consequence of the disarming, the generality of the people would not rise. He was afterwards told that this meeting had taken place at Jackson's in Church Street. Teeling shewed him a map of Ireland, at his lodgings in Aungier Street, on which the plan of the insurrection was marked, as he was told, by some Irish officers who had been in the Austrian service, and who had expressed their opinion that the people were not in a state of preparation to succeed, being deficient in arms and ammunition.

The delegates left Dublin to organise their respective counties. They assembled the colonels in each county, to issue their directions for getting their regiments into readiness. The colonels of the county Antrim refused to come forward. Those of the county Down agreed to rise. The other counties of Ulster were disinclined to move, and therefore the intended rising did not take place.

In June, 1797, he breakfasted with Teeling in Dublin, and met Magenniss, of Balcaly, Tony M'Cann, of Dundalk,* Mr. Samuel Turner, Messrs John and Patrick Byrne, of Dundalk, Colonel James Plunkett, A. Lowry, Mr. Cumming of Galway, and

---

* Subsequently a refugee, living in Hamburgh, where Campbell saw him, and on becoming acquainted with his story, wrote that beautiful ballad " The Exile of Erin."

Dr. M'Nevin. The subject of their conference, was the fitness of the country for an immediate rising. Teeling, Lowry, and M'Cann, were in favour of an immediate effort; the others were afraid that the people were not sufficiently prepared for it.

He left Dublin about the 14th of June, 1797, and shortly after attended a meeting at Randal's Town, where there was much difference of opinion— one party being adverse to action without foreign aid, and another party, with whom was the Rev. A. M'Mahon of Hollywood, in favour of rising on their own resources. The meeting broke up in conse- quence of the division among the Antrim colonels. M'Mahon was a member of the Ulster Provincial Committee; he told the meeting he was one of the seven colonels of the county Down who had been ap- pointed leaders, and that he also was a member of the National Executive. Immediately after this meeting, M'Mahon, Rollo Reid, and John Magennis (a bro- ther-in-law of Teeling), fled to Scotland, and M'Mahon went from thence to France. In the latter part of 1797, his (Hughes's) affairs were embarrassed, and he became a bankrupt. "He did not attend any civil or military meeting of United Irishmen from June, 1797, *till the month of March*, 1798, when he sur- rendered himself under the commission in Dublin."

The remainder of this man's evidence is of such a nature, as requires that it should be given without abridgement, as it appears in the report:—

"He went to Dublin on the 20th of April, and remained there about nine days. He called on Samuel Neilson, walked with him to Mr. Cormick, a feather-merchant in Thomas-street. He was introduced by Neilson to Cormick in the office. Cormick asked them to go up stairs; he and Neilson went up stairs, and found Lord Edward Fitzgerald and Mr. Lawless the surgeon, playing billiards. He had been introduced to Lord Edward about a year before by Teeling; he was a stranger to Lawless; so he staid about an hour; no particular conversations; was invited to dine there that day, and did so; the company were Lord Edward, Lawless, Neilson, Cormick and his wife. The conversation turned upon the state of the country, and the violent measures of government in letting the army loose. The company were all of opinion, that there was then no chance of the people resisting by force with any success. He was also introduced by Gordon, who had been in Newgate, and Robert Orr of Belfast, chandler, to Mr. Rattican, the timber-merchant at the corner of Thomas-street. Rattican talked to him on the state of the country and of the city of Dublin, and told him that they would begin the insurrection in Dublin by liberating the prisoners in Kilmainham. Rattican shewed him a plan of the intended attack upon Kilmainham. Whilst he was in Dublin, in April, he dined with Neilson at the Brazen Head. Next day, Neilson called him up at five o'clock, and they went to Sweetman's, near Judge Chamberlaine's, to breakfast; Sweetman was then in prison, but Neilson lived in his house. Neilson took Sweetman's carriage to Mr. Grattan's, and brought him along with him. When they got to Mr. Grattan's, Neilson told him he had some-

thing to say to Mr. Grattan in private, and desired
him to take a walk in the domain. Neilson, however, introduced him to Mr. Grattan first, and Mr.
Grattan ordered a servant to attend him to shew
him the grounds. He returned in about half an
hour. Went into Mr. Grattan's library—Neilson
and Grattan were there together. Grattan asked a
variety of questions touching the state of the country in the north: how many families had been
driven out, and how many houses burned by the
government or the Orangemen? Grattan said he
supposed he was an United Irishman? he said he
was. Grattan asked him how many United Irishmen were in the province? he said he reckoned
126,000. Grattan asked him how many Orangemen there were? he said about 12,000—Grattan
made no particular answer. Neilson and he left
Grattan's about twelve in the day; they walked to
their carriage, which was at Enniskerry; he asked
Neilson what had passed between Grattan and him?
Neilson evaded the question, but said generally that
he had gone down to Grattan to ask him whether
he would come forward, and that he had sworn him.
That Grattan promised to meet him in Dublin
before the next Tuesday. He left Dublin that evening, and returned to Belfast. He has known the
Reverend Steele Dickson, of Portaferry, for two
years intimately.

" On Friday, the 1st of June, Dickson told him
that he was one of the adjutant-generals of the
United Irishmen's forces in the county of Down,
and that he (Dickson) would go to Ballynahinch and

remain there till Wednesday, as it was a central place, from which he could issue his orders to his officers.

" In February last, when the prisoners were trying at the Commission, Priest Quigley introduced him to Citizen Baily, who was an officer in the East India Company's Service, and lived near Canterbury, and also to the younger Binns from England; thinks his name is Benjamin.

" Binns told him he had distributed most of the printed addresses, entitled, ' United Britons to the United Irishmen,' and gave him a copy, and directed him to print an edition of them," &c.

" He heard a Mr. Bonham came with Baily and Binns from London, and was the delegate from England to Ireland mentioned in the paper. He never saw Mr. Bonham; either Binns or Baily told him that the address was written by a Mr. Cosgrave of London," &c.

" *Quest.*—You have said that you were introduced to Mr. Grattan by Samuel Neilson, at his house in Tinnehinch, in April last:—Recollect yourself, and say whether you can speak with certainty as to that fact?

" *Ans.*—I certainly can. About the 28th of April last, I went to Mr. Grattan's at Tinnehinch with Samuel Neilson; on going into the house, we were shewed into the library. Neilson introduced me to Mr. Grattan, and I soon after walked out, and left them alone for full half an hour. I saw a printed constitution of the United Irishmen in the room.

" *Quest.*—Can you say whether Mr. Grattan knew it to be the constitution of United Irishmen?

" *Ans.*—I can, for he asked me some questions about it. He asked me also a variety of questions about the state of the North. When we were going away, I heard Mr. Grattan tell Neilson that he would be in town on or before the Tuesday following; and I understood from Neilson that Mr. Grattan had visited him in prison—and on our return to town, Neilson told me he had sworn Mr. Grattan."

With respect to Hughes's evidence in reference to Mr. Grattan—Neilson, on his examination before the Lord's Committee, being informed " It had been stated to the committee that he had said he swore Mr. Grattan," replied, " I never did swear Mr. Grattan, nor have I ever said that I swore him." Being asked " if he had any interviews with Mr. Grattan since his liberation from confinement?" he answered, " I was twice with Mr. Grattan, at Tinnehinch, in April, 1797. I either shewed Mr. Grattan the last constitution of the Society of United Irishmen, or explained it to him, and pressed him to come forward; I was accompanied at these interviews by John Sweetman and Oliver Bond. But I do not believe Mr. Grattan was ever an United Irishmen."

It seems as if, up to this period, the date of his examination, 9th of August, 1798, Neilson had been still in ignorance of Hughes having made disclosures, and especially of having given information of their visit, about the 28th of April, to Mr. Grattan; otherwise Neilson would hardly have omitted any mention of that interview.

But after his examination, he addressed a letter to the lord chancellor, expressing a wish to correct his evidence, " by stating that he had another interview with Mr. Grattan in company with Mr. John Hughes." *

The evidence of Hughes is the most specious account of the proceedings of the Ulster leaders, that is to be found among the statements of any of the informers given in the secret reports, with the exception, perhaps, of that of Magin of Saintfield.

Even those of the Antrim United Irishmen whose lives were jeopardized by the disclosures of Hughes, who are still surviving in Belfast, admit that his disclosures, in many points, were truthful; free from personal malignity; and, notwithstanding the importance of the information he possessed and gave before the committee, *he never appeared as a witness at the trials of any of those persons he implicated by his disclosures.* They, therefore, speak of him in very different terms from those in which they are accustomed to discuss the exploits of other informers.

This circumstance, on more than one occasion, surprised me a good deal, but the cause of Mr. Hughes being kept back, at a crisis when evidence like his would have ensured the conviction of the Belfast leaders, with few, if indeed with any exceptions, became at once intelligible enough, to leave little doubt that he was reserved for higher functions

* Sir Jonah Barrington, in his Memoirs of the Union, says, when Grattan was denounced in the Privy Council, in 1798, by Lord Clare, " Sir John Blaquiere and Dennis Brown, though adversaries, resisted the obviously vindictive attempt."

than the Reynolds and O'Briens, and more important objects were to be effected by him than he could achieve in the witness box.

This man has carefully suppressed the fact in his evidence, that in the year 1797 he was arrested on a charge of high treason, and immediately after his being brought into Belfast, was liberated on bail. In the "History of Belfast," the fact is stated in these terms: "October 20th.—John Hughes, bookseller and stationer in this town, having been apprehended at Newry on a charge of high treason, was this forenoon brought in here, in a post-chaise, escorted by a party of light dragoons, and lodged in the Artillery Barracks. In the same evening he was liberated on bail."*

Immediately after his liberation, a man who possessed the confidence of Neilson, Russell, and Robert Emmett, one of the most intelligent, active, and trusty agents of these persons, both in 1798 and 1803—the well-known J—— H——, had an interview with Hughes, at his house in Church-street; the particulars of that interview were recently communicated to me by H——, with a great deal of other valuable information, from his own written documents.

After some discourse with H——, respecting his recent liberation, Hughes began inveighing against the inefficiency of the person who was then in the chief command of the Antrim United Irish force— he attributed all the misfortunes which had fallen on individuals of their body, to the unfitness of this man

* History of Belfast, p. 478.

for the post assigned to him, and even intimated that both this person and another were playing fast and loose with the cause, and were only biding their time to abandon or betray it. He plainly said, should he be again arrested, if the authorities threatened him with punishment to extort confession, he would inform them of all he knew of the parties referred to. After some further conversation, he proposed to J—— H—— to get rid of those persons who were represented by him (perhaps not altogether erroneously either) as of doubtful zeal and earnestness in the cause, by at once giving informations against them. H—— replied by pulling a pistol from his breast, and telling him, if ever he repeated such a proposition, he would shoot him.

The use which was made of Hughes, after Lord Edward's arrest, and at the period too at which he had his head-quarters at the Castle in Dublin, is very clearly shewn in the narrative of the confinement and exile of the Rev. William Steele Dickson, presbyterian minister of Pontaferry, in the county Down.

Dr. Dickson was arrested on the 4th of June, 1798, in consequence of the disclosures made by Magin and Hughes.

During his confinement in the house called the Donegal Arms, then the provost-prison of Belfast, the plan was carried into effect which had been very generally adopted, at this frightful period, in other parts of the country, of apprehending some of the least suspected informers, and having it rumoured abroad that such persons had been arrested as ringleaders of the rebels, who were sure to be convicted, and then placing these persons among the unfortunate prisoners, for the purpose of making the latter furnish evidence against themselves and their companions. This proceeding, which would hardly be had recourse to in any uncivilized country, in these times, is thus described by Dr. Dickson, from his own sad experience of it :—

"The first of these persons, of whom I had any knowledge, or by whom I was beset, was the notorious John Hughes, a man some years before of considerable respectability, but with whom I never had any particular connexion, or even intimate acquaintance. However, he was fixed on as most likely to succeed in entrapping me and a few others. With a view to this, opportunity was taken to excite our compassion, either on the day of, or after, his arrest. We were entertained with a fable truly affecting— " that there was no hope of saving his life—that his mind was deranged—that he was treated with great cruelty—and, that he was placed among a crowd of poor wretches, with whom he could neither have conversation nor comfort." This pathetic fiction was immediately followed with an observation, that " if we could possibly make room for him, taking him to us would be an act of the greatest charity." Completely imposed on by the tale, we instantly yielded to the application, and smothering though we were, received him into our *stove*. On his entrance, his looks and manner were wild, unsettled, and strongly marked with melancholy. Afterwards, he talked, in a desponding tone, of the certainty of his conviction, and sometimes of a secret conspiracy against him, in which, as it appeared, he considered some of us as concerned. At other times, he would start, with seeming horror, and exclaim that the sentinel was about to shoot him. On the whole, though he sometimes talked soberly, and generally *listened attentively to our conversation*, he acted his part so well, at intervals, that during two nights, and the intermediate day, I was as fully convinced of his derangement as I was of my own existence; and under this impression, not only prayed with him, and for him, in his seemingly composed moments, but was quite delighted with the *wonderful* comfort which *devotional exercises* seemed to give him. Some of our party, however, suspected him of imposture from the first; and their suspicion was soon confirmed, by his being removed, for some time every day, to a distant apartment, and detained in secret conference. His total removal from us, a few days afterwards, and his *symptoms of insanity* suddenly disappearing, certainty succeeded suspicion, and his name was consigned to infamy, together with those of his employers.

" Besides Hughes, other informers were placed among us, about the same time. One of which was the Mr. Magin mentioned by him, in his deposition, which will appear afterwards. He, like the other, was committed, under the most dreadful denunciations of vengeance, and, as the other had done, expressed the most lively apprehensions of his impending fate, even with lamentations and tears. He made his way to me, frequently, and under various pretexts; sometimes to complain of his melancholy situation, sometimes to borrow trifles, and, at others to affect confidential conversation, or ask advice." *

With respect to Hughes, the circumstances which require consideration, are the following.

In October, 1797, he is arrested and charged with high treason, brought into Belfast, and liberated the same day on bail. He becomes a bankrupt the same year, and in March 1798, he surrenders himself under the commission in Dublin.

In April, between the 20th and 29th of that month, he visited Lord Edward, with Neilson; about the 28th of the same month, accompanied by Neilson, he also visited Mr. Grattan. On the 19th of May, Lord Edward was arrested. Hughes' services are found employed in the north, in the beginning of the next month, worming himself into the confidence of Dr. Steele Dickson, supposed to be the adjutant-general of the county Down, a man of all others of the Ulster leaders, against whom evidence was most desired. For this purpose, we find him apprehended on the 7th of June, at Belfast,† and the immediate object of this colourable arrest, to place him in confinement with the prisoners, recently taken up in Belfast, in order to obtain further and still fuller evidence of their guilt, from some of them. Of this arrest, as well as of the former, Mr. Hughes thought it desirable to make no mention in his evidence.

Quarters in the Castle were assigned to Mr. Hughes shortly after Lord Edward's arrest. The

* Dr. Dickson's Narrative, p. 63.   † Belfast History, p. 484.

following data will afford some clue to the period of his residence there :—

> " *Dec.* 9, 1801.—Campbell, for the use of his rooms in the Castle for Conlan and Hughes, since June, 1798, £22 15s."

Again :—

> " *March* 20*th*, 1802.—Campbell, for lodging of Hughes and Conlan, £22 15s."

It would seem that no expenses of these gentlemen were left undefrayed; even their washing-bills were paid for them.

> " *Feb.* 12*th*, 1801.—Manders, washing for Hughes and Conlan, £11 7s. 6d."

—So that from June, 1798, to the latter end of March, 1802, we find the head-quarters of Mr. Hughes were at the Castle.

The reward for the discovery of Lord Edward Fitzgerald, was offered on the 11th of May; earned on the 19th; and paid, on the 20th of the month following, to F. H. The christian name of Hughes does not correspond with this first initial. The reader has been furnished with sufficient data, to enable him to determine whether those initials were intended to designate this man, or some other individual; whether the similarity of the capital letters I. and F. in the hand-writing in question, may admit, or not, of one letter being mistaken for another; and, lastly, whether the same error (intentional, or only apparently so) had occurred, which caused the name of the Saintfield informer, in the parliamentary report of his evidence, to be set down Nicholas Maguan—and in the written account of the remuneration of his services (and those of his colleagues) to be given as J. Magin. Of the latter person, it may not be foreign to the subject to say a few words.

This Magin (for such was his name), of Saintfield, in the county of Down, was à poor man, holding a few acres of ground in the neighbourhood of Saintfield. In the Commons' report of the Secret Committee, he is made to figure, in the notice of his evidence, as a person of high rank and standing in his society. The Rev. John Cleland, who had been private tutor to Lord Castlereagh, and then was chaplain and agent, both private and political, of the Earl of Londonderry,—in the course of his magisterial duties, which chiefly consisted in hunting after informers for his patron, and arranging with the sheriff for the packing of the juries, who were to try the persons who were informed against by his agents, had succeeded in gaining over an active and intelligent member of the Saintfield society of United Irishmen, of the name of Magin. This man reported to him, after each meeting he attended, what had transpired ; and the first meeting he made a disclosure of the proceedings of, was that of the provincial meeting of Ulster, held on the 14th of April, 1797 ; and he regularly communicated to Cleland the proceedings of each meeting, up to the 31st of May, 1798, which was the last he appears to have attended.

Who can possibly deny that government had been in full possession of the plans of the United Irishmen from the month of April, 1797, through this source at least, not to mention the earlier disclosures made to them by other informers.

If the services rendered by Magin are to be estimated by the amount of their reward, they must have been considerable. The following items, at least, will give some idea of the estimation in which they were held :—

" Aug. 16, 1798—J. Magin . . . £700   0   0
   „   17, „   do. . . . .   56 17 6"

Notwithstanding the immense sum of money lavished on him—from being an industrious honest man previously to his new pursuits as an informer, he became an improvident, indolent, dissipated person, addicted to gambling, and, in the course of a few years, his easily-gotten wealth was gone, and he had to earn his bread in the neighbourhood of Belfast as a common working-gardener, and in this employment he died there, a few years ago.

Of Mr. Hughes, from the month of March, 1802, when his last expenses at the Castle were defrayed, in the preceding month, we find the only payment which appears made to him, in which his name is given at full length ·

" Feb. 6, 1802—John Hughes, of ——, in
   full of all claims. . . . . £200"

This being the only item bearing his name—when the enormous sum of money received by Magin is taken into account, and it is remembered that the evidence of Hughes was of such great importance, it cannot be believed that he received no other recompense.

In fact, the wording of the entry of the 6th of February, " in full of all demands," shews that former sums had been paid, if any judgment may be formed from similar terms in reference to a multitude of other cases of a like description, when the persons at this period were finally paid off, after previous payments. No such items connected with the name of Hughes, are amongst them.

Yet his services were of an earlier date, and of a more important nature, than most of them.

In 1797, M'Gucken had to communicate with the officers of that department of the government, with whom lay the duty of granting licences to king's counsel, to defend prisoners in cases of criminal prosecutions. M'Gucken was then the law-agent of the prisoners of most of the Antrim societies of United Irishmen. The person fixed on for going to Dublin to procure the services of counsel for the unfortunate clients of this gentleman, was Mr. Hughes. Treason upon treason meets our eyes, at every step of the agents, actors, and adversaries too, of this conspiracy. It is painful to trace the revolting progress of such perfidy, but it is needful to unmask and to expose its hideousness, in order to prevent a recurrence to the use or practice of its wickedness.

It will be seen, that M'Gucken's "services," did not go without their reward in this world.

" March 5, 1799. J. Pollock for M'Gucken, sent to him by post to Belfast . . . £60

October 1, 1799. M'Gucken, Belfast, per post, by direction of Mr. Cook · . . 50

January 2, 1800. Mr. Pollock for M'Gucken 100

April 1, 1800. M'Gucken, per Mr. Marsden's
    order. 50
June 11, 1800. M'Gucken, per ditto . . 50
June 21, 1800. Mr. Pollock for M'Gucken 100
January 1, 1801. M'Gucken, per post to
    Belfast. 100
February 20, 1802. J.M'Gucken, to replace
    £100 advanced to him May 16th, 1801,
    but afterwards stopped out of his pension 100
February 12,1803. Mr.Pollock for M'Gucken,
    an extra allowance 50
June 25, 1803. Mr. Pollock for J. M'Gucken 100
September 19, 1803. Mr. Marsden to send
    M'Gucken 100
December 5, 1803. J. M'Gucken, per Mr.
    Marsden's note 100
February 7, 1804. Mr. Pollock for M'Gucken 500"

It may be presumed, for these large sums and his pension, moreover, that Mr. M'Gucken rendered many and important services.

Though the first item which bears his initials is dated the 5th of March, 1799, several other sums of a previous date are set down, with the name of the person only through whom the succeeding payments were chiefly made, and one to the amount of £300.

The earliest proof of Mr. M'Gucken's services that has transpired, was given on the occasion of the disappearance of six brass field-pieces of the Belfast Volunteer Corps, the property of the town of Belfast, which General Nugent issued a proclamation to be given up to him, the 28th May, 1798. Four of the pieces were given up on the 30th; the two others,

Mr. Robert Getty was held responsible for, as the officer of that corps, in whose charge they had been originally placed. The pieces having been carried away clandestinely long before, without the knowledge of Mr. Getty, it was not in his power to produce them: this gentleman was arrested and sent to the provost. This measure excited much surprise in Belfast, even at a period when any outrage on one of the old volunteers, of independent principles, excited little. Mr. Getty was a man of undoubted loyalty; he had been, however, one of the early advocates of Catholic emancipation, but on every political subject, was of very moderate opinions. In those times, few considerations weighed against the secret charges of a recognized informer.

Mr. Getty's life was in imminent peril, and probably, if the crown solicitor, Mr. Pollock, had not visited him in the provost, he would have been hanged. It turned out that some charges, but utterly unfounded ones, had been laid against him. Getty's influence, however, and high character, triumphed over the malignity of the informer, and he was released.

It was only in the year 1809 or 1810, that Mr. Pollock told Getty, that the informer against him was Mr. James M'Gucken, the attorney. He showed Mr. Getty the informations, and I have good authority for saying there was no truth in them. Mr. Getty never could account for this proceeding; he had never given any offence to this man, and from his early advocacy of emancipation, to the last day of his life, was a favourite with his Roman Catholic townsmen, to which body M'Gucken belonged. The late General Coulson, an aide-de-camp at that time to General Barber, subsequently informed a member of his family, that one of M'Gucken's relations had been arrested by him in 1798, of whose guilt there was not the slightest doubt; he was allowed, however, to escape, but why, he did not know.

In the year 1802, there being no longer a field for the services of Mr. Hughes, he was "paid off," and permitted, like Mr. Reynolds, to "bid an eternal farewell to his friends and country." His loss, like that of Mr. Reynolds, no doubt was borne with Christian fortitude.

His acquaintance in Belfast heard no more of him, —where he went to, or what became of him, none of his former friends knew. It was only very recently I obtained any information, that could be relied on, about him. It seems, on quitting this country in 1802, he proceeded to Charlestown, and there embarked in business. About ten years subsequently, he came over from America to Liverpool, with a cargo of merchandize. He called on a merchant of that place, Mr. Francis Jordan, formerly of Belfast, and stated that he wished to consign the cargo he had then for sale, to him. He said he had always a kindly feeling towards his old friends and townsmen, and added, " I know you do not think well of me; but ill as you may think of me, I never appeared against any individual. The information I gave was to save myself, but it injured no one."

After disposing of his cargo, he returned to America, and has not since been heard of in this country.

In concluding the account of this man, I feel bound to say, that having carefully examined his information, and compared it with that which I myself received in Belfast from various persons, and even from some of those persons seriously implicated by his disclosures, that the statement he has given respecting the proceedings of the United Irishmen in the north, are generally to be relied on, and none of his associates speak of him as having been actuated by any malicious or vindictive motives in making these disclosures.

CHAPTER XI.

Of all the barbarities that disgraced this calamitous conflict, whether on the part of ultra-loyalists, a licentious soldiery, or of infuriated rebels, the recurrence to the use of torture for the purpose of inspiring terror, of detecting crime, or of revenging wrongs, was the most atrocious. If this inhuman custom, now happily universally execrated and exploded in all civilized countries, had been only partially practised, and not systematically pursued; if the scene of its infliction had been in distant districts, in wild and lawless places, beyond the reach of the civil and judicial powers, and not in the immediate vicinity of the seat of government itself; if the actors were persons of no distinction, of no rank in society, instead of functionaries exercising authority—whose proceedings, though denied, were never repudiated by it—the proceedings might be considered as the excesses which are usually the unfortunate concomitants of civil warfare. It would now be, not only a painful task, but a culpable act, to rake up the recollection of such enormities, if the denunciation of them were not calculated to prevent the possibility of their repetition.

In concluing the account of this man, I feel bound
to say, tha having carefully examined his information, and compared it with that which I myself
received i Belfast from various persons, and even
from som of those persons seriously implicated by
his discloures, that the statement he has given respecting te proceedings of the United Irishmen in
the northare generally to be relied on, and none of
his associæs speak of him as having been actuated
by any mlicious or vindictive motives in making
these disclsures.

CHAPTE...

...the barbarities that...
c... ...ther on the...
licon... ...ry, or of in...
rence... ...torture...
terror, o... ...rien...
was the n...
now happily...
all civilized co...
tised, and not a...
of its infliction ha...
and lawless places, be...
judicial powers, and no...
the seat of government it...
sons of no distinction, of no...
of functionaries exercising auth...
ings, though denied, were never...
the proceedings might be considered...
which are usually the unfortunate co...
civil warfare. It would now be, not on...
task, but a culpable act, to rake up the...
of such enormities, if the denunciation of...
not calculated to prevent the possibilit...
repetition.

The extraordinary fact, that the employment of torture in the suppression of the Irish Rebellion, in 1798, called forth no general expression of public indignation in England, can only be accounted for by the political circumstances of the time, which made it necessary to keep the people of that country in ignorance of the means, which had been adopted to effect a measure which they were taught to consider so advantageous to their interests as the Union.

It is better that the reckless policy of a minister should be exposed, than that the humanity of a generous and enlightened people, should be left ob- noxious to the charge of inconsistency in the mode and manner of its exhibition. If the same pains had been taken to palliate or conceal the cruelties of exalted individuals in our distant colonies, like those perpetrated in Goree or Trinidad, which have been employed to hoodwink public opinion in England, with regard to the cruelties inflicted on the people of Ireland, the loud voice of public reprobation would never have been raised in condemnation of the scourging to death of the unfortunate soldier, or the tortures inflicted on the poor Mulatto girl.

To ignorance alone of the use of torture in 1798, can be attributed the impunity—so far as the silence on this subject, of public opinion in England, may be so considered—with which these horrid outrages against humanity have been perpetrated in Ireland. For, otherwise, what idea could be formed of the spirit of philanthropy which carries its sympathies to the remotest regions of the globe—which extends its protection to the victims of cruelty and rapacity, of every creed and clime—no matter of what complexion accounted by their oppressors, "incompatible with freedom"—no matter of what tenets derogatory to divine truth, and degrading to man's nature—and could yet withhold its pity and its sympathy from those who are nearest to its influence, and, therefore, especially entitled to its aid? The same mighty spirit that called forth the indignation of the people of England against the oppressors in the West Indies, that caused the echoes of the cries of the Negro slaves to resound in the ears of the English people, while one human being was left subject to the lash, would surely have roused the lion-heart of England to an ebullition of noble resentment, at the first intimation of the outrages on humanity, that were committed on the Irish people in the riding-school of Beresford, the prevost of Sandys, the public buildings of the city, and at the drum-head court-martials in Wicklow, Wexford, and Kildare, if there were not mightier influence at work, that rendered communication between the victim of cruelty and the advocate of mercy, more difficult across the channel than it ever proved to be across the wide waters of the Atlantic. What is there in the fearful pictures that have been drawn of the implements of torture formerly in use in the West Indies; the cart whip, and the collars, and the thumb-screws, of the slave-holders; more horrifying than the representation which every history of this rebellion of 1798, gives of the scourges and the triangles, the pitch-caps and gun-powder conflagrations, the pickettings and half-hang-ings, and other modes and instruments of torture, indicative of an inventive spirit of barbarity that the ingenuity of Spanish cruelty itself has not surpassed.

These cruelties, indeed, were practised on people in rebellion—not unfrequently, on persons only suspected of so being—or whose creed was regarded in too many cases as " prima facie" evidence of disaffection; but the use of torture was abhorrent to the spirit of the laws under which they lived, and even if the enormity of the crime with which they were charged, gave a colourable pretext for the employment of rigorous means, and summary modes of execution, in cases where capital punishments were thought to be required, cruelty in the infliction of them cannot be defended, and should not escape the reprobation of all Christian men.

The infliction of torture on the most abject or unruly colonial slaves, never found an advocacy in English philanthropy, however outrageous the conduct of Negro rebels might have been in any of those periodical rebellions, which constituted epochs in the history of slavery, or marked their suppression with circumstances of signal cruelty. No provocation on the part of the rebellious slave, was ever regarded as an apology for barbarous punishment inflicted on him; " the guilty evidence of a skin not coloured like our own," was never admitted as an excuse for the application of the torture of the cart-whip, to elicit a confession of his guilt, however guilty he might be. The criminality of the suspected rebel nearer home, though his conduct were equally infuriated, can hardly be judged by a less merciful rule of ethics; the guilty evidence of a creed, for which he might not be more accountable than the Negro for his complexion, could hardly justify the laceration of his person for the discovery of the crime imputed to him.

To denounce the application of torture in the case of one pàrt of the human race in one quarter of the globe, at one particular period, and under any peculiar circumstances of society, and not in relation to all mankind, to all times, to all places, to all conditions and to all offences, would be a spurious philanthropy, which would justly deserve to be universally scouted and contemned.

The recent atrocities committed in Damascus, on the unfortunate Jews of that city, no sooner were made known in England, than the outrages perpetrated on these victims of fanaticism and rapacity, called forth the general indignation of the press and people of this country, and the sufferings of these poor strangers, promptly awakened the sympathies of Englishmen of all parties. The victims of oriental cruelty, were indeed few in comparison with those of Irish fanaticism, the whole number of persons subjected to the torture of the " courbash," in Damascus, did not constitute one-thousandth part of the numbers tied up to the triangles and tortured with the scourge, or tormented with the pitch-caps, in the Irish prisons and provosts, in the year 1798. Can it be imagined that humanity admits of one measure of compassion for the sufferings of the Jews of Damascus, and another for those of the Christians of Ireland? It cannot be admitted without injustice to the character of British philanthropy, nor can

Q

the difference in the manifestation of public opinion in both cases, be reconciled, without referring to the fact of the publicity that was given to the one, by the powerful influence of the wealth and station of the leaders of the Jewish people in Great Britain, and the studious concealment in the other, of the enormities committed on the part of an administration, which had broken down the power and the credit of its opponents.

The fact of the employment of torture, as an ordinary mode of proceeding, in the examination of suspected rebels, in 1798, has never been denied, except by Lord Castlereagh, in a qualified form.   It has been openly avowed and defended by members of the Irish government, by the perpetrators of it, and by their advocates in the Irish parliament.   In the debate in the House of Commons, in March 1801, on the Irish Martial Law Bill, in reply to an observation with respect to the use of torture, made by Mr. Taylor, Lord Castlereagh had certainly the boldness to affirm, that "torture never was inflicted in Ireland, with the knowledge, authority, or approbation of government."   Mr. John Claudius Beresford, who was the most competent of all men to speak on that subject, observed, that "it was unmanly to deny torture, as it was notoriously practised;" and in a subsequent debate in the House of Lords on a subsequent occasion, in the imperial parliament, Lord Clare avowed the practice, and defended it on the grounds of its necessity.   But the intemperate zeal of Sir Richard Musgrave, the unscrupulous advocate of Lord Castlereagh's policy (for it was

during his government chiefly, in the months of
May and June, when these tortures were inflicted,)
carried him to the extent, of not only attributing
the suppression of the rebellion to the use of torture,
but even of defending it on the authority of no less
a person than the human and enlightened Marquess
of Beccaria, whose words in reference to punishments, he cites in defence of this practice; and, true
to his ruling passion, perverts the meaning of his
authority to suit his purpose. The following are
the words he quotes, " among a people hardly yet
emerged from barbarity, punishments should be
more severe, as strong impressions are required."
Little did the benevolent Beccaria imagine, that a
line of his admirable book should ever be cited, by
such a man, in support of his sanguinary sentiments!

It did not suit the purpose of this writer, to cite
Beccaria's express condemnation of the use of torture, as an absurd as well as a barbarous mode of
eliciting truth, or of detecting crime. " To discover
truth," says Beccaria, " by this method, is a problem
which may be better solved by a mathematician, than
by a judge, and it may be thus stated, the force of
the muscles and the sensibility of the nerves of an
innocent person being given, it is required to find
the degree of pain necessary to make him confess
himself guilty of a crime."

But Beccaria's condemnation of torture, was not
wanted in these countries, to prohibit its infliction,
in any circumstances and under any form. Blackstone might have informed Lord Clare, when he

acknowledged its employment, or Musgrave when he defended its infliction, that " the trial by rack is utterly unknown to the law of England :" or he might have learned from another legal authority, Lord Ellenborough in the debate in 1801, on the Irish Martial Law Bill," that it cannot but be known to every one, that neither martial law, nor any other law, human or divine, can justify or authorize its infliction."

The reasoning of Sir Richard Musgrave, on the advantages of torture and the beneficial effects of its infliction, will appear to the people of England, more indicative of the wisdom of our ancestors, in the 11th or 12th century, than of the humanization of their posterity in the 18th or 19th age. In a chapter of his History of the Rebellion, entitled, " Observations on Whipping and Free Quarters," we find the following statement :—" To disarm the dis- affected was impossible, because their arms were concealed, and to discover all the traitors was equally so, because they were bound by oaths of secrecy, and the strongest sanction of their religion, not to impeach their fellow-traitors.

" But suppose the fullest information could be obtained of the guilt of every individual, it would have been impracticable to arrest and commit the multitude. Some men of discernment and fortitude, perceived that some new expedient must be adopted to prevent the subversion of government and the destruction of society, and whipping was resorted to." * The men of " discrimination and fortitude,"

* Musgrave's History of the Irish Rebellion, Appendix, p. 178.

included Sir Richard Musgrave himself, Mr. John Claudius Beresford, Sir John Judkin Fitzgerald, the High Sheriff of Tipperary, Hunter Gowan, Hawtrey White, Archibald Jacob Hamilton, and James Boyd, magistrates of the county Wexford, Lord Kingston, Messrs. Hempenstal, Love and Sandys, military gentlemen, and a host of subordinate functionaries, many of whom were liberally rewarded, pensioned, and promoted, for the very services which Lord Castlereagh denied all knowledge of, in the British House of Commons.

The sentiments of Sir Richard Musgrave are, unfortunately, still those of a great portion of his party in Ireland, with whom the doctrine, " salus *factionis* suprema lex," prevails over every other obligation.

" That man," says Musgrave, " who would balance between the slight infractions of the constitution, in inflicting a few stripes on the body of a perjured traitor,* and the loss of many lives and much property, must renounce all pretensions to wisdom and patriotism.

" As to the violation of the forms of the law by this practice, it should be recollected that the law of nature, which suggested the necessity of it, supersedes all positive institutions, as it is imprinted on the heart of man for the preservation of his

---

* During the period of the Whiteboy outrages, when Sir Richard Musgrave was high sheriff of the county Waterford, finding some difficulty in procuring an executioner to inflict the punishment of whipping on a Whiteboy, he performed the office himself, and with all the zeal of an amateur performer.

creatures—as it speaks strongly and instinctively,
and as its end will be baffled by the slowness of deliberation." *

At Castle Otway, in the county of Tipperary,
the champion of torture instances the necessity and
efficacy of this measure :—" Cook Otway, Esq. (says
Sir Richard) a gentleman noted for his loyalty,
was the most active person in the county of Tipperary, next to Colonel Fitzgerald, in putting down
rebellion, for which he was afterwards persecuted.
He raised a yeomanry corps, but was afterwards
obliged to disband the popish members, as they had
taken the United Irishmen's oath. The preservation of the metropolis from carnage, plunder and
conflagration, must in a great measure be imputed
to it, as traitors, on being whipped, revealed the
most important secrets, and confessed where great
quantities of arms were concealed." What other
evidence can be required, to prove the general practice of torture at this period, and the extent of the
evil which imposed the embarrassing necessity on
Lord Castlereagh, of making a solemn denial of all
knowledge of its existence? The fact of its existence,
indeed, could not be denied, for his own colleagues
admitted it. The existence of it, then, even without
his knowledge, left the character of the government
open to the charge of extraordinary remissness, for
it certainly was the duty of the leading member of
that government, to have made himself acquainted
with the measures which were taken for the suppression of that rebellion, and it was his duty to

* Sir Richard Musgrave's History and Appendix, p. 178.

have protected the people against the violation of the laws on the part of the subordinate agents of government.

On the trial of Mr. Finnerty, in 1810, for a libel on Lord Castlereagh, that gentleman submitted a number of affidavits to the court, in proof of the ordinary and systematic employment of torture during the period that Lord Castlereagh filled the office of chief secretary in Ireland. In the address of Mr. Finnerty, in his defence on that occasion, in reference to the observation of Lord Holt—" That a man's omission of his duty should be taken as a presumption of his guilt"—he said, " if it be pretended that Lord Castlereagh did not order torture, that pretence will not avail when you recollect the affidavits that I have read,—when you see that such cruelty was committed in the Royal Exchange, which immediately adjoins the Castle, and from which the cries of the sufferers might have been heard in Lord Castlereagh's office, where his personal interposition—where the mere expression of his will—might have prevented the continuance of the torture.

" Doubts have been sometimes expressed here, as to the actual infliction of torture in Ireland; indeed, I understand that many persons of high rank in this country, have been persuaded to doubt upon the subject—and I am not surprised at it, for I have myself heard Lord Castlereagh, in this country, publicly declare, that it was not practised with the knowledge, approbation or authority of government. The government, indeed, not to know of it! that government which had such a system of espionage established in the country, as threw that of Fouché into the shade, which enabled them to ascertain what was passing in every hamlet and village in the land—to be ignorant of what was notoriously taking place in the most public parts of Dublin, under the direction of the immediate agents and confidential friends of government—in the immediate vicinity of the Castle —in such a situation, that the screams of the sufferers might have been audible in the very offices where the ministers of government met to perform their functions. The pretence of ignorance, therefore, on the part of government, of such notorious transactions, is quite preposterous."

But it is not on the authority of persons who might be supposed to be inimical to the administration of that period, that the charge rests, of connivance at the use of torture, and at the preferment of its perpetrators to places of honour and emolument.

No specific orders, undoubtedly, emanated from the government to Mr. Beresford, to convert the riding-school into a scourging-hall—to Mr. Hempenstal, to make a walking gallows of his person—to Mr. Love, for the half hanging of suspected rebels at Kilkea Castle—to Mr. Hunter Gowen, for burning down the cabins of the Croppies—to the sheriff of Tipperary, for the laceration of the peasant's back, of which Sir John Moore was an eye-witness—to Captain Swaine, for the picketings at Prosperous, or to Sir Richard Musgrave, to write a treatise in defence of torture; and to all the other gentlemen of

" discernment and fortitude," to adopt " the new expedient" for the discovery of crime.

The admitted policy of Lord Castlereagh, was to accelerate the explosion of the insurrection in order to confound the plans of its leaders. For this purpose, it was necessary to drive the people mad with terror; and the subordinate agents of this policy were allowed to take their own ways of accomplishing the minister's designs.

These gentlemen were, therefore, honoured with the confidence of government, and rewarded with its gifts; Mr. Beresford was considered entitled to both; Fitzgerald was created a baronet in 1801; Mr. Gowan was placed on the pension list; Sir Richard Musgrave obtained the office of Receiver of the Customs, with a salary of £1200 a-year, to mark the sense entertained of his humanity; and the subordinate officers who most notoriously evinced the exuberance of their zeal in the discovery of disaffection, and punished the disaffected with a " vigour beyond the law," were promoted in their several departments. With the exception of Sir Richard Musgrave, there is hardly an instance of a cotemporary writer on the subject of this rebellion, who has not ascribed to the administration of that time, a knowledge of the enormities that were committed on the Irish people. Sir Jonah Barrington, whose political tendencies were certainly not on the side of the insurgents, states, in his " Memoirs" of the " Irish Union," that " Mr. Pitt counted on the expertness of the Irish government to effect a premature explosion. Free quarters were now ordered on the Irish population."

He adds in a note, "This measure was resorted to, with all its attendant horrors, throughout some of the best parts of Ireland previous to the insurrection."

" Slow tortures were inflicted under the pretence of extorting confession; the people were driven to madness: General Abercrombie, who succeeded as commander-in-chief, was not permitted to abate these enormities, and, therefore, resigned with disgust. Ireland was reduced to a state of anarchy, and exposed to crime and cruelties to which no nation had ever been subject. The people could no longer bear their miseries. Mr. Pitt's object was now effected. These sanguinary proceedings will, in the opinion of posterity, be placed to the account of those who might have prevented them."[*]

On the same subject, the Rev. James Gordon, rector of Killegny in the diocese of Ferns, a gentleman, to use his own words, "wholly British by descent," and "his natural bias on the side of Protestantism and loyalty,"[†] states that "great numbers of houses were burned with their furniture, where concealed arms were found, or meetings of the United Irishmen had been held, or whose occupants had been guilty of the fabrication of pikes, or of other practices for the promotion of the conspiracy. Many of the common people, and some even in circumstances superior to that class, particularly in the city of Dublin, were scourged, some picketted, or otherwise put to pain to force a confession of concealed arms or plots."

[*] Barrington's Memoirs of the Irish Union, vol. ii. p. 248.
[†] Gordon's History of the Rebellion, pp. 65, 66, 76.

" To authorize the burning of houses and furniture, the wisdom of administration may have seen
as good reason as for other acts of severity, though
to me and many others that reason is not clear."

In speaking of the tortures inflicted on the gentry,
he says, " Mr. Thomas J. Fitzgerald seized in Clonmel, a gentleman of the name of Wright, against
whom no grounds of suspicion could be conjectured
by his neighbours, caused 500 lashes to be inflicted
on him in the severest manner, and confined him
several days without permitting his wounds to be
dressed, so that his recovery from such a state of
laceration could hardly have been expected. In a
trial at law, after the rebellion, on an action of
damages brought by Wright against this magistrate,
the innocence of the plaintiff appeared so manifest,
even at a time when prejudice ran amazingly high
against persons accused of disloyalty, that the defen-
dant was sentenced to pay £500 to his prosecutor.
Many other actions on similar grounds would have
been commenced, if the parliament had not put a
stop to such proceedings, by an act of indemnity for
all errors committed by magistrates from supposed
zeal for the public service. A letter, written in the
French language, found in the pocket of Wright,
was hastily considered as a proof of guilt, though the
letter was of a perfectly innocent nature."

In reference to the barbarities committed on the
bodies of the executed rebels, he says,* " many instances might be given of men, who, at the hazard
of their own lives, concealed and maintained loyalists

* Vide Gordon's History of the Rebellion, p. 212.

until the storm passed away; on the other hand, many might be given of cruelties committed by persons not natives of Ireland; I shall mention only one act, not of what I shall call cruelty, since no pain was inflicted, but ferocity, not calculated to soften the rancour of the insurgents: some soldiers of the Ancient British regiment cut open the dead body of Father Michael Murphy, after the battle of Arklow, took out his heart, roasted his body, and oiled their boots with the grease which dripped from it."

Mr. Edward Hay, in his history of the insurrection of the county of Wexford, states—

"In Enniscorthy, Ross, and Gorey, several persons were not only put to the torture in the usual manner, but a great number of houses were burnt, and measures of the strongest coercion were practised, although the people continued to flock to the different magistrates for protection. Mr. Perry, of Inch, a Protestant gentleman, was seized on and brought a prisoner to Gorey, guarded by the North Cork militia, one of whom (the noted serjeant, nicknamed *Tom the Devil)* gave him woful experience of his ingenuity and adroitness at devising torment. As a specimen of his *sçavoir faire,* he cut off the hair of his head very closely, put the sign of the cross from the front to the back, and transversely from ear to ear closer still; and probably, a pitched cap not being in readiness, gunpowder was mixed through the hair, which was then set on fire, and the shocking process repeated, until every atom of hair that remained, could be easily pulled out by the roots; and still a burning candle was continually applied, until the entire was completely singed away, and the head left totally and miserably blistered."*

" It is said that the North Cork regiment were the inventors—but they certainly were the introducers of pitch-cap torture into the county of Wexford. Any person having his hair cut short, and therefore called a Croppy (by which the soldiery designated an United Irishman), on being pointed out by some loyal neighbour, was immediately seized and brought into a guard-house, where caps, either of coarse linen or strong brown paper, besmeared inside with pitch, were always kept ready for service. The unfortunate victim had one of these, well heated, compressed on his head, and when judged of a proper degree of coolness, so that it could not be easily pulled off, the sufferer was turned out, amidst the horrid acclamations of the merciless torturers." *

" Mr. Hunter Gowan had, for many years, distinguished himself by his activity in apprehending robbers, for which he was rewarded with a pension of £100 per annum; and it is much to be wished, that every one who has obtained a pension had as well deserved it. Now exalted to the rank of magistrate, and promoted to be captain of a corps of yeomen, he was zealous in exertions to inspire the people about Gorey with dutiful submission to the magistracy, and a respectful awe of the yeomanry. On a public day in the week preceding the insurrection, the town of Gorey beheld the triumphal

---

* Vide Hay's Insurrection of the County of Wexford, p. 181.

† Ibid. p. 57.

entry of Mr. Gowan, at the head of his corps, with his sword drawn, and a human finger stuck upon the point of it.

" With this trophy he marched into the town, parading up and down the streets several times, so that there was not a person in Gorey who did not witness this exhibition—while, in the mean time, the triumphant corps displayed all the devices of Orangemen. After the labour and fatigue of the day, Mr. Gowan and his men retired to a public house to refresh themselves, *and like true blades of game,* their punch was stirred about with the finger that had *graced* their ovation, in imitation of keen foxhunters, who *whisk* a bowl of punch with the brush of a fox before their boozing commences. This captain and magistrate afterwards went to the house of Mr. Jones, where his daughters were, and, while taking a snack that was set before him, he bragged of having blooded his corps that day, and that they were as staunch bloodhounds as any in the world. The daughters begged of their father to shew them the Croppy finger, which he deliberately took from his pocket and handed to them. Misses dandled it about with senseless exultation, at which a young lady present hid her face with her hands, to avoid the horrid sight. Mr. Gowan, perceiving this, took the finger from his daughter, and *archly* dropped it into the disgusted lady's bosom. She instantly fainted, and thus the scene ended ! ! ! Mr. Gowan constantly boasted of this and similar heroic actions, which he repeated in the presence of Brigade Major Fitzgerald, on whom he had waited officially; but so far from meeting with his wonted applause, the Major obliged him instantly to leave the company.*

" Enniscorthy and its neighbourhood were similarly protected by the activity of Archibald Hamilton Jacob, aided by the yeomen cavalry, thoroughly equipped for this kind of service. They scoured the country, having in their train a regular executioner, completely appointed with his implements—a hanging-rope and cat-o'-nine-tails. Many detections and consequent prosecutions of United Irishmen soon followed. A law had been recently enacted, that magistrates, upon their own authority, could sentence to transportation persons accused and convicted before them. Great numbers were accordingly taken up, prosecuted and condemned. Some, however, appealed to an adjournment of a quarter-sessions, held in Wexford on the 23rd of May, in the county court-house, at which three-and-twenty magistrates, from different parts of the county, attended.

" In the course of the trials on these appeals, in the public court-house of Wexford, Mr. Archibald Hamilton Jacob appeared as evidence against the prisoners, and publicly avowed the happy discoveries he had made in consequence of inflicting the torture. Many instances of whipping and strangulation he particularly detailed, with a degree of self-approbation and complacency, that clearly demonstrated how highly he was pleased to rate the merit of his own great and loyal services." †

* Vide Hay's Insurrection of the County of Wexford, p. 70.
† Ibid. p. 71.

On the 21st of June, the town of Enniscorthy having been retaken by the king's troops, the house in which the sick and wounded of the rebel party were placed, was set on fire, and above thirty of the unfortunate inmates perished. The Hessian troops distinguished themselves particularly on this occasion. The Rev. James Gordon, a protestant clergyman, in speaking of this atrocious proceeding, says he was "informed by a surgeon that the burning was accidental; the bed clothes being set on fire, by the wadding of the soldiers' guns, who were shooting the patients in their beds."

The son of the late Mr. Thomas Reynolds, in his recent unsuccessful and ill-judged, though probably well-meant effort, to vindicate the memory of his father, in recounting the various atrocities committed by the rebels, is compelled to acknowledge that their barbarities were equalled, and sometimes provoked, by the massacres of their opponents. "At the same time," says this gentleman, "that numerous acts of equal atrocity, and still less justifiable, were, during the same period, and for some time previous to the breaking out of the rebellion, committed by the opposite party. I say, still less justifiable, because they were urged and frequently countenanced by the actual presence of persons of rank and distinction, who indulged their brutality under the assumed mask of loyalty. Such was the murder of Mr. Johnstone, of Narraghmore, as I have already related; the burning of the rebel hospital, in Enniscorthy, with all the rebel sick and wounded it contained, to the number of above thirty persons, (Cloney states the number put to death on the occasion was seventy-six,) the massacre of above fifty unresisting individuals, by a party of the military, under the command of Lieutenant Gordon, of the yeomanry cavalry, which provoked the massacre of Bloody Friday, the slaughter of upwards of two hundred men, after they had surrendered on terms of capitulation to General Dundas, on the Curragh of Kildare; the numerous murders committed in cold blood, in retaliation for those committed by the outlaws, under Holt and Hacket; the flogging of suspected persons and throwing salt into their wounds, to extort confession, and other acts of a similar nature."*

Mr. Gordon says, "The Hessians exceeded the other troops, in the business of depredation, and many loyalists, who escaped from the rebels, were put to death by these foreigners. To send such troops into the country, in such a state of affairs, was in my humble opinion, a wrong step in government, who cannot be supposed indifferent to the lives of loyal subjects. By what influence the plundering was permitted so long to the soldiery, in some parts of the country, after the rebellion was quelled, I shall not at present pretend to state. The publication of some facts, of which I have acquired information, may not perhaps be as yet safe. On the arrival of the Marquis of Huntley, however, with his regiment of Scottish Highlanders, in Gorey, the scene was totally altered. To the immortal honour of this regiment, its behaviour was such, as, if it were universal among soldiers, would render a mili-

* Vide Life of Thomas Reynolds, by his Son, vol. ii. p. 337.

tary government amiable. To the astonishment of the (until then, miserably harassed) peasantry, not the smallest trifle, even a drink of buttermilk, would any of these Highlanders accept, without the payment of at least the full value."

Mr. Charles R. Teeling, in his History of the Rebellion, speaks in similar terms of the tortures and free quarters of 1798.∗ As this gentleman was arrested, on a charge of treason, by Lord Castlereagh himself, his evidence may be considered less impartial than that of Mr. Gordon; but, whoever is acquainted with him, friend or foe to his political sentiments, knows him to be an honest man, and incapable of misrepresenting facts, the knowledge of which few men living had fuller opportunities of obtaining.

In speaking of his arrest, he says, " I was the first victim to the political apostacy of Lord Castlereagh. On the 16th of September, 1796, while yet in my 18th year, I was arrested by him, on a charge of high treason. The manner of my arrest, was as novel as mysterious, and the hand which executed it, the last from which I could have suspected an act of unkindness. Lord Castlereagh was the personal friend of my father, who admired him as the earliest advocate of civil and religious liberty.

" In the year 1790, the representation of Down was contested, and the independence of that great and populous county, threatened through the powerful influence of the Downshire family, and a combination of local interests, hostile to the rights of the people. Lord Castlereagh, then the Honour-

able Robert Stewart, was selected by his countrymen, for his talents and his patriotism; and after
the most obstinate contest ever witnessed in Ireland,
he was triumphantly returned to parliament, not only
by the suffrages, but by the pecuniary assistance of
the friends of civil and religious liberty.

"The penal laws, at this time, operated against
my father's personal exercise'of the elective franchise,
but neither his fortune nor his best personal exertions, were unemployed in the service of his friend."

After describing his having passed the evening preceding his arrest, at a party in the neighbourhood, he
says "Accompanying my father, the following morning, on a short excursion, on horseback, we were met
by Lord Castlereagh, who accosted us with his usual
courtesy and politeness. We had proceeded up the
street together, when, having reached the house of
his noble relative, the Marquis of Headfort, we were
about to take leave of his lordship; 'I regret,' said
he, addressing my father, 'that your son cannot accompany you;' conducting me, at the same time,
through the outer gate, which, to my inexpressible
astonishment, was instantly closed; and I found myself surrounded by a military guard.

"My father entered, and with a firm and determined composure, enquired the cause of the arrest.
'High treason!' replied his lordship. Our interview
was short: my father was not permitted to remain.
My horse was led home by a faithful domestic; but
to that home I never returned."

The young man was sent to Dublin, committed
to Newgate, and kept in confinement there, till the

latter part of 1797, when, broken down in health, he
was indebted to the humanity of Mr. Secretary Cooke
for his release, on condition of surrendering himself,
if called on by the government, but he was left unmolested.   His father's house, in the meantime, had
been assailed by the military, and his entire establishment, in the course of a few hours, had been left
a desolate ruin.*

With regard to the cruelties practised on the
people, Teeling observes : " It was notorious that in
the districts where the (United) system had made the
least progress, the greatest acts of outrage were perpetrated under the sanction of the government; and
in those quarters where the inhabitants were remarkable for a peaceful demeanour, moral disposition, and
obedience to the laws, every principle of justice and
humanity was violated.   Wexford, which was the
scene of the greatest military atrocity, and, consequently, the boldest and most effectual in resistance,
was, at this period, less identified with the organised
system than any county in Ireland.   Of this fact,
government was perfectly aware; and it was only
when the outraged feelings of human nature were no
longer able to bear the torture of the scourge, the
blaze of incendiarism, and the base violation of female
virtue, that Wexford rose as one man.

" From the humble cot to the stately mansion, no
property—no person, was secure."   After detailing
the various atrocities committed in the way of flogging, half-hanging, the pitched-cap practise, &c., he
adds : " The tortures practised in those days of Ire-

* C. Teeling's Narrative, p. 15.

land's misery, has not been equalled in the annals of
the most barbarous nation, and the world has been
astonished at the close of the eighteenth century,
with acts, which the eye views with horror and the
heart sickens to record—not only on the most trivial,
but the most groundless occasions : it was inflicted
without mercy, on every age, and on every condition. In the centre of the city, the heart-rending
exhibition was presented of a human being, rushing
from the infernal depôt of torture and death, his
person besmeared with a burning preparation of tur-
pentine and pitch, plunging, in his distraction, into
the Liffey, and terminating at once, his sufferings
and his life.

" A melancholy transaction occurred in the town
of Drogheda.—The unhappy victim was a young man
of delicate frame; he had been sentenced to five-
hundred lashes, and received a portion with firmness,
but dreading least bodily suffering might subdue the
fortitude of his mind, he requested that the remainder
should be suspended and his information taken.
Being liberated from the triangles, he directed his
executioners to a certain garden, where he informed
them arms were concealed. In their absence, he
deliberately cut his throat. They were not discovered,
for no arms were there.

" About the same period, and in the same populous
town, the unfortunate Bergan was tortured to death.
He was an honest, upright citizen, and a man of un-
impeachable moral character. He was seized on by
those vampires, and in the most public street,
stripped of his clothes, placed in a horizontal posi-

tion on a cart, and torn with the cat-o'-nine-tails, long after the vital spark was extinct. The alleged pretence for the perpetration of this horrid outrage, was that a small gold ring had been discovered on his finger bearing a national device—the shamrock of his unfortunate country."*

The author of a recent publication, under the signature of " A Country Gentleman"—a person, I presume, not unknown to Mr. W. Fletcher, a son of the venerable and just judge of that name—makes the following observation on the subject before us :—

" Thousands were tortured with the connivance of government, and multitudes condemned to death, in defiance of every principle of law and justice." * * * " It has often been asserted, and the writer believes with perfect truth, that the Irish rebellion was fomented and encouraged by government for the purpose of carrying the Union into effect." * * * * " Many were suspected of being rebels who were perfectly innocent; multitudes were falsely accused, and not a few judicially murdered." *

A few brief extracts from Lord Moira's speech in the English House of Lords, on the 22nd of November, 1797, will corroborate the preceding statements. His lordship, on this occasion, brought the subject of the torture, then in full practice in Ireland, before the notice of their lordships. He said, " When I troubled your lordships with my observations upon the state of Ireland, last year, I spoke upon documents certain and incontrovertible; I address you

* Teeling's Narrative, p. 138.
† Lights and Shadows of Whigs and Tories ; 1841.   P. 100.

this day, my lords, upon documents equally sure and staple. Before God and my country, I speak of what I have seen myself. But in what I shall think it necessary to say upon this subject, I feel that I must take grounds of a restrictive nature. * * * * What I have to speak of are not solitary and insulated measures, nor partial abuses, but what is adopted as the system of government; I do not talk of a casual system, but of one deliberately determined upon, and regularly persevered in.

"When we hear of a military government, we must expect excesses which are not all, I acknowledge, attributable to government, but these I lay out of my consideration—I will speak only of the excesses that belong to and proceed from the system pursued by the administration of Ireland. * * * * My lords, I have seen in Ireland the most absurd, as well as the most disgusting tyranny, that any nation ever groaned under. I have been myself a witness of it in many instances; I have seen it practised and unchecked; and the effects that have resulted from it have been such as I have stated to your lordships. I have said, that if such a tyranny be persevered in, the consequence must inevitably be the deepest and most universal discontent, and even hatred, to the English name. I have seen in that country a marked distinction made between the English and Irish. I have seen troops that have been sent full of this prejudice, that every inhabitant in that kingdom is a rebel to the British government. I have seen the most wanton insults practised upon men of all ranks and conditions. I have seen the

most grievous oppressions exercised, in consequence
of a presumption, that the person who was the unfortunate object of such oppression, was his hostility
to the government : and yet that has been done in a
part of the country as quiet and as free from dis-
turbance as the city of London.   Who states these
things, my lords, should, I know, be prepared with
proofs.   I am prepared with them.   Many circumstances I know of my own knowledge, others I have
received from such channels as will not permit me to
hesitate one moment in giving credit to them.

" His lordship then observed, that from education
and early habits, the *Curfew* was ever considered by
Britons as a badge of slavery and oppression.   It
then was practised in Ireland with a brutal rigour.
He had known an instance, where a master of a
house had in vain begged to be allowed the use of a
candle, to enable the mother to administer relief to
her daughter, struggling in convulsive fits.   In former
times, it had been the custom for Englishmen to
hold the infamous proceedings of the Inquisition in
detestation : one of the greatest horrors, with which
it was attended, was that the person, ignorant of the
crime laid to his charge, or of his accuser, was torn
from his family, immured in a prison, and in the
most cruel uncertainty as to the period of his confinement, or the fate which awaited him.   To this
injustice, abhorred by Protestants in the practice of
the Inquisition, were the people of Ireland exposed.
All confidence—all security—were taken away.   In
alluding to the Inquisition, he had omitted to mention one of its characteristic features : if the supposed

culprit refused to acknowledge the crime with which he was charged, he was put to the rack, to extort confession of whatever crime was alleged against him by the pressure of torture. The same proceedings had been introduced in Ireland. When a man was taken up on suspicion, he was put to the torture; nay, if he were merely accused of concealing the guilt of another. The rack, indeed, was not at hand; but the punishment of picketing was in practice, which had been for some years abolished, as too inhuman, even in the dragoon service. He had known a man, in order to extort confession of a supposed crime, or of that of some of his neighbours, picketed until he actually fainted; picketed a second time until he fainted again; as soon as he came to himself, picketed a third time, until he once more fainted: and all upon mere suspicion! Nor was this the only species of torture: many had been taken and hung up until they were half dead, and then threatened with a repetition of the cruel treatment, unless they made confession of the imputed guilt. These were not particular acts of cruelty, exercised by men abusing the power committed to them, but they formed a part of our system. They were notorious, and no person could say who would be the next victim of this oppression and cruelty, which he saw others endure. This, however, was not all; their lordships, no doubt, would recollect the famous proclamation issued by a military commander in Ireland, requiring the people to give up their arms; it never was denied that this proclamation was illegal, though defended on some supposed necessity; but it

R

was not surprising, that any reluctance had been shewn to comply with it, by men who conceived the constitution gave them a right to keep arms in their houses for their own defence; and they could not but feel indignation in being called upon to give up their right. In the execution of the order, the greatest cruelties had been committed: if any one was suspected to have concealed weapons of defence, his house, his furniture, and all his property was burnt: but this was not all; if it were supposed that any district had not surrendered all the arms which it contained, a party was sent out to collect the number at which it was rated; and in the execution of this order, thirty houses were sometimes burnt down in a single night. Officers took upon themselves to decide discretionally the quantity of arms; and upon their opinions these fatal consequences followed. Many such cases might be enumerated; but, from prudential motives, he wished to draw a veil over more aggravated facts, which he could have stated, and which he was willing to attest before the Privy Council, or at their lordships' bar."

The government at this period, it is needless to say, issued no proclamations or precise instructions to their functionaries, to inflict these tortures. It would not have done, in the nineteenth century, to have addressed Lord Camden in the barbarous terms addressed to the Deputy Carew. " Queen Elizabeth, in 1598, in her instructions to Carew, the Deputy of Munster, on his going over to carry 'her gracious pleasure' into effect, authorizes him and her officers, ' To put suspected Irish to the rack, and to torture them, when they should find it convenient.'"* The "laissez faire" mode of accomplishing the same object, answered all the purposes at a smaller expense of official character. Outrages on a larger scale than I have referred to, were perpetrated with like impunity.

Every massacre of the people, at this period, was hailed as a great victory, and received with exultation. The slaughter of the unresisting capitulated people at the Gibbet Rath of Kildare, was regarded as a measure which the emergencies of the time required. The rebels, according to Sir R. Musgrave, amounted to about 3000 in number; they had entered into terms with General Dundas, and were assembled at a place that had been a Danish fort, called the Gibbet Rath. Having offered terms of submission to General Dundas, on the 26th of May, that general despatched General Welford to receive their arms, and grant them protections. Before the arrival of the latter, however, on the 3rd of June, the multitude of unresisting people were suddenly attacked by Sir James Duff, who, having gallopped into the plain, disposed his army in order of battle, and with the assistance of Lord Roden's Fencible Cavalry, fell upon the astonished multitude, as Sir Richard Musgrave states, "pell mell." Three hundred and fifty men under terms of capitulation, admitted into the king's peace and promised his protection, were mowed down in cold blood, at a place known to every peasant in Kildare as "the Place of Slaughter," as well as Mulamast itself, the Gibbet Rath of the Curragh of Kildare.

* Paccata Hiberniæ.

The massacre took place on the 3rd of June; the terms of surrender were made by one Perkins, a rebel leader, on the part of the insurgents, and General Dundas on the part of the government, and with its express sanction and permission for them, on delivering up their arms, to return to their homes. Their leader and his brother were to be likewise pardoned, and set at liberty.

It was when the people were assembled at the appointed place, to comply with these conditions, that Sir James Duff, at the head of 600 men, then on his march from Limerick, proceeded to the place to procure the surrendered weapons. One of the insurgents, before giving up his musket, discharged it in the air, barrel upwards; this simple act was immediately construed into a hostile proceeding, and the troops fell on the astounded multitude, and the latter fled with the utmost precipitation, and were pursued and slaughtered without mercy by a party of Fencible Cavalry, called "Lord Jocelyn's Fox Hunters."* According to the Rev. James Gordon, upwards of 200 fell on this occasion; Sir R. Musgrave states 350.

No part of the infamy of this proceeding attaches to General Dundas. The massacre took place without his knowledge or his sanction. His conduct throughout the rebellion was that of a humane and a brave man.

The scene of the massacre of the peasantry on the hill of Kilcomney, in the county of Carlow, is one that reeks with reminiscences of the deeds of that "beau sabreur" of 1798, Sir Charles Asgill.

* Vide Gordon's Rebellion, p 100.

The Wexford insurgents were encountered by Sir Charles at Gore's Bridge; they fled at his approach, and as they fled, they were still pursued and slaughtered. All this is fair, no doubt, in war—especially in Ireland.

The massacre at Kilcomney, by the yeomanry and militia force, under the command of Sir Charles Asgill, Cloney states, amounted to 140 individuals. The slaughter took place on the 26th of June.*

The band of rebels, who, in their flight from Scollagh Gap, in their attempt to get back to Wexford, had directed their march through Kilcomney, were attacked by the army under Sir Charles Asgill; they fled, and were pursued upwards of six miles, having lost, according to Gordon, two or three hundred.

It was after the disappearance of the rebels, that the unfortunate and peaceful people of Kilcomney were slaughtered in their homes. Asgill's exploits on this occasion are given by one of the rebels, who had the good fortune to escape the sabres of his band—by Thomas Cloney.

" The defenceless inhabitants of an unoffending and most peaceable district—men, women and children—were butchered this day (he says), and neither age, sex, nor infirmity, could obtain exemption from the common fate; they were all slaughtered without mercy." He gives the names of a vast number of the victims, whose only crime was, that a band of rebels, when pursued, had fled through their district. A hundred and forty, he states, were slaughtered in

* Vide Cloney's Rebellion, p. 82.

this way, and, amongst the sufferers, he speaks of a
man of the name of Patrick Fitzpatrick.   When
his cabin was entered by the marauders, his poor
wife, with an infant in her arms, ran to her
husband's side, and, while endeavouring to protect
him, a volley was poured into them, and they fell
dead at the same moment.   The cabin was then set
fire to, as a matter of course, over the heads of the
children of this unfortunate couple—six in number;
and five of them, " poor innocent creatures," ran
into a neighbour's house who had escaped the
massacre, one of them crying out, " My daddy is
killed—my mammy is killed—and the pigs are drinking their blood."   The infant that was left in the
dead mother's arms, Cloney states, a few years ago
was still living, and was called Terence Fitzpatrick.
A poor woman of the name of Kealy, an aunt of
theirs, took them home, and when her scanty means
were exhausted for their support, she became a
beggar to get them bread : the neighbours helped
her—they gave her assistance, and God, in his
mercy to her, enabled her to bring them up.   There
may be no space in the records of the noble deeds of
woman, for the goodness of this poor creature; but
her conduct will not be forgotten, at all events, on
that day, when virtue is destined to receive its own
exceeding great reward—the ample recompence of
all its sufferings and its sacrifices here below; and
where the man of blood will find no act of indemnity
available for his sanguinary and inhuman deeds.

The massacre of the unhappy prisoners at Carnew,
convicted of no crime—imprisoned on mere suspi-

cion—taken out of the jail on the 25th of May, and deliberately shot in the Ball-alley, by the yeomen and a party of the Antrim militia, in the presence of their officers,* is an incident that probably never reached the ears of the people of England. Had it taken place in India or Australia, the perpetrators of it would have been denounced and reprobated; but the victims of this atrocity were Irish, and, at this unhappy period, there was no people in the world whose sufferings and oppression were held entitled to so little Christian sympathy.

A striking instance of the kind of encouragement given to the loyalty of the Catholic members of the yeomanry corps, at this period, is recorded by Sir Richard Musgrave. On the 3rd of May, Captain Ryves, who commanded the yeomanry at Dunlavin, the rebels having made their appearance in his neighbourhood :—" The Captain," says Sir Richard, " marched out of the town with a party of yeomanry cavalry, to encounter the rebels, but they were so numerous and desperate that he was obliged to return, after some of his men had been marked. The officers, having conferred for some time, were of opinion that some of the yeomen, who had been disarmed, and were at that time in prison for being notorious traitors, should be shot. Nineteen, therefore, of the Saunders Grove Corps, and nine of the Narramore, were immediately led out, and suffered death. It may be said in excuse for this act of severe and summary justice, that they would have joined the numerous bodies of rebels who were

* Vide Hay's Insurrection of the County of Wexford, p. 76.

moving round, and at that period threatened the town." *

Thus, the suspected yeomen were deliberately taken out of prison, and put to death—" *pour encourager les autres.*"

The Roman Catholic gentlemen, who had the presumption to join the yeomanry corps, were, in numerous instances, treated as rebels in disguise, and, on some occasions, were even driven into rebellion. In fact, no means were left untried to prevent those of this persuasion from manifesting their zeal in the king's service, and to bring them under the suspicion of countenancing those of their communion who were disaffected.

Throughout the country, the total loss on both sides, in this rebellion, is estimated by Plowden, Moore, Curran and Barrington, at about 70,000; 20,000 on the side of government, and 50,000 on that of the insurgents. It is generally admitted by all, but more especially by the Rev. Mr. Gordon, that very many more were put to death in cold blood, than perished in the field of battle. The number of deaths arising from torture, or massacre, where no resistance was offered, during the year 1798, forms the far greater portion of the total number slain in this contest. The words of Mr. Gordon are, " I have reason to think, more men than fell in battle, were slain in cold blood. No quarter was given to persons taken prisoners as rebels, with or without arms."†

---

* Vide Musgrave's History of the Rebellion, p. 243.

† Vide Gordon's History of the Rebellion, p. 269.

In detailing these enormities, it would be to make one's self the accomplice of ferocity, to attribute all the barbarity of these disastrous times to one party only, and to shut one's eyes against the inhuman acts of its opponents. It is in vain to refer to the barbarities of the Orangemen, to the previous scourgings, the house-burnings, and the various military excesses, for an apology, or even a palliation, of the wicked deeds done at Scullabogue, on the Bridge of Wexford, and at Vinegar-hill. There may be some allowance made for the phrenzy which has driven men to the resistance of tyrannical authority; but there can be none, for the dastardly revenge of armed men, over their defenceless enemies.

I have not gone through the revolting process of enquiring into these loathsome details, without feelings of repugnance, not unfrequently almost insurmountable; but it is not my purpose to take away one iota from the infamy which belongs to the excesses of the insurgents. My object, is to put it out of the power of either party ever to recur to such enormities; to shew the members of a partizan administration, (if ever there should, unfortunately for Ireland, be one in power there, like that of 1798,) that a cruel and remorseless policy, whatever efforts may be made to conceal its wickedness, sooner or later, will be brought to light, and its authors reprobated by all good men. It matters not under what garb of loyalty, they may permit the agents of its policy to lay the mischief which it provoked or aggravated, to the charge of a people infuriated by them: in tolerating, countenancing, or recompensing the excesses

of their subordinate agents, they became responsible
for them.

Of the atrocious massacre committed by the rebels on their prisoners on the 5th of June, Sir
Richard Musgrave states, that " 184 protestants
were burned in the barn of Scullabogue," and that
" 37 were shot in front of it." In all, by his statement, 225; of which number, he subsequently states,
" a few Romanists were put to death in the barn."

" The barn was thirty-four feet long and fifteen
feet wide, and the walls were but twelve feet high."
The number described by Musgrave, in a space like
this, must have perished by suffocation. Gordon
gives the same number as Sir Richard Musgrave.

Cloney states that the total number massacred in
this murderous business, " was about one hundred,
of which number sixteen were catholics."

Mr Hay, on the authority of the most respectable
persons in the neighbourhood in which the nefarious
transaction took place, estimates the number at
eighty. The murders committed by the rebels on
the bridge of Wexford, on the 20th of June, Sir
Richard Musgrave estimates at ninety-seven, after
five hours unceasing slaughter; Cloney at thirty-six,
and Hay about the same number.

The massacre by the rebels, at Vinegar Hill, Sir
Richard Musgrave states, " he was assured, exceeded
500 :" Gordon says, " the number was little short of
400 ;" and Cloney, on the authority of Hay, "eighty-
four.

These are the three signal massacres, in which the
rebels manifested their barbarity. An atrocity on a

smaller scale than the preceding ones, was committed by them, at Enniscorthy, when, according to Hay, they put fourteen unfortunate persons to death, in cold blood. The total number thus slain in all these massacres, Cloney estimates at 257, and the veracious Sir Richard Musgrave, at more than treble that amount.

Independently of the above mentioned massacres, on the part of the rabble of the insurgents, there were many instances of murders of individuals, accompanied by acts of abominable cruelty, and in some cases, but very few indeed, where circumstances shewed religious animosity to have been the motive for the murders. The name of Orangeism, had been made so detestable to the people, by the outrages committed on them by the members of that institution, wherever it gained a footing, that their fury in some cases was directed against protestants and catholics indiscriminately, who were not known to be favourable to their views. The fate of the sixteen victims of their own creed, at Scullagh-bogue, was a proof of this feeling; and throughout the rebellion, there was abundant evidence of their phrenzy being more the impulse of a wild resentment against Orangeism, than any spirit of hostility to the sovereign or the state.

The arrest of the Sheares, on the 23rd of May 1798, was the death-blow to the Society of United Irishmen; from the date of its origin, October, 1791, having existed seven years, whether viewed in its results, the character of its members, or the nature of its proceedings, it may certainly be re-

garded as a confederacy, which no political or revolutionary society, that has gone before it, has surpassed
in importance, boldness of design, and devotion to
its principles, however mistaken they may have
been.

It is unnecessary to refer more at large " to the
well-timed measures pursued," to cause the insurrection to explode ; that partial outbreak, deprived of
its leaders, baffled in its original designs, was sufficiently formidable to require a military force, exceeding 100,000 men, comprising regulars, militia,
yeomanry and volunteering supernumeraries, and the
employment of six general officers, to suppress it.
The yeomanry force alone, according to the report of
the Commons' Secret Committee of 1798, "exceeded
50,000, and might have been increased to a much
greater extent." In 1801, the secretary at war, on
the Irish Militia Bill debate, stated, " the number
of troops then in Ireland, was Regulars 12,000,
Fencibles 20,000, and Militia 28,000, total 60,000 ; a
considerable reduction of the force, must therefore
have taken place in that year. From an army
return, published a few years ago, it appears that the
sum total of the effective force employed in Ireland, including yeomanry, and during the rebellion,
amounted to 114,000 men. The computed expense
of which force, was about four millions per annum.
The quantity of arms of all descriptions, taken from
the rebels, amounted to 120,000, the chief part of
which, consisted of pikes and muskets.

The total number of the rebels who had risen in
the county of Wexford, Sir Jonah Barrington esti-

mates at 35,000. "Wexford," he observes, " is only one of thirty-two counties, by no means the most populous, and far from the most extensive. Had the rising been general, the northern counties might have furnished as many, the southern counties more, and the midland less than Wexford; a rough (but no doubt an uncertain) average, may be drawn from these data, as to what the possible or probable amount of insurgents might have been throughout the entire kingdom, if the struggle had been protracted. Enough at least will be ascertained, to prove that the rebellion never should have been permitted to arrive at that dangerous maturity. It is equally clear, that had the rebels possessed arms, officers and discipline, their numbers would soon have rendered them masters of the kingdom, in which there exists not one fortress capable of resisting a twenty-four hours investment." *

With respect to the actual force of the United Irishmen, we find in the province of Ulster alone, by O'Conner's evidence before the Secret Committee in 1797, 150,000 men were sworn and enrolled in the province of Ulster alone. When Dr. M'Nevin was asked by a member of the Secret Committee of 1798, to what number he thought the United Irishmen amounted all over the kingdom? He replied, " Those who have taken the test, do not, I am convinced, fall short of 500,000, without reckoning women and old men. The number regularly organised is not less than 300,000; and I have no doubt, all these will be ready

* Memoir of Examinations, &c. by Messrs Emmett, O'Connor and M'Neven, p. 74.

to fight for the liberty of Ireland, when they get a fair opportunity."*

I have stated elsewhere, the number which Lord Edward Fitzgerald expected would have flocked to his standard from all parts of the country, on his taking the field, was 100,000 effective men.

The suppression of this rebellion, and the accomplishment of the Union, which was carried into effect by its instrumentality, entailed on Great Britain an enormous expenditure.

The amount of the claims of the suffering loyalists for their losses sustained in 1798, laid before the Commissioners, by Sir Richard Musgrave's statement, was £823,517 sterling; but in 1799, the sum total, according to Gordon, amounted to £1,023,000;" of which, more than the half, or £515,000, was claimed by the county of Wexford; but who, says Mr. Gordon, will pretend to compute the damages of the Croppies, whose houses were burned, or effects pillaged or destroyed, and who barred from compensation, sent no estimate to the Commissioners! Perhaps, if the whole amount of the detriment sustained by this unfortunate island, in consequence of the united conspiracy, were conjectured at £2,000,000, a sum of such magnitude might not exceed, or even equal, the reality."†

The purchase of the Irish Parliament for the accomplishment of the Union, rendered it necessary for Lord Castlereagh to introduce a bill into the House of Commons in the beginning of December,

* Barrington's Memoirs of the Irish Union, vol. ii. p. 256.
† Gordon's History of the Rebellion.

1800, for the purpose of "compensating the proprietors of boroughs." The ugly word for which "compensation" stands, may be well dispensed with—the fact of £1,500,000 having been spent on the last, suicidal Irish Parliament, is a sufficient record of its venality.

It is impossible to estimate the loss occasioned in this rebellion, by the destruction of property consequent on the free quarters' enormities, the pillage of houses, the burning of the cabins of the peasantry, the laying waste of their lands—outrages and injuries which, unlike those committed "on suffering loyalists," admitted of no compensation, but whose perpetrators were indemnified for their atrocities by a special act of parliament. If Mr. Gordon, however, imagined that £2,000,000 would cover the total amount of the value of property destroyed in this rebellion throughout the island, he was exceedingly mistaken. Surely, the injuries inflicted on the property of loyalists, bore no proportion to those which the insurgents and the people who were put out of the king's peace, suffered at their hands, and at those of an army exceeding 100,000 men turned loose upon them? And yet, in 1799, the admitted claims of the suffering loyalists amounted to £1,023,000. The number of Roman Catholic places of worship destroyed during the rebellion, or immediately subsequent to it, may afford some criterion by which we can judge of the number and extent of other outrages on property belonging to persons of that communion. In the Archdiocese of Dublin, by the statement of the Roman Catholic Archbishop of that period, a copy of which I was fortunate enough to procure from the original document, the number of Roman Catholic places of worship utterly destroyed or partly demolished during 1798-9, amounted to thirty-six; and from another document, printed some years ago in America, giving a list of the chapels destroyed or greatly damaged in other parts of the country, the total number will be found to amount to no less than sixty-nine.

If the progress of Sir Charles Asgill in the counties of Carlow and Kilkenny, and the proceedings of Sir Judkin Fitzgerald, in the county Tipperary, Messrs. Hawtrey, White, Hunter, Gowan, and Archibald Hamilton Jacob, had been traced at the time by the tracks of their reckless followers, and the smouldering ashes of the houses and haggards of the suspected gentry; the smoking ruins of the cabins of the peasantry; the demolished doors and windows, and trampled crucifixes of the people's chapels; the exploits of " Burn-chapel Whaley," the brother-in-law of the Lord Chancellor of Ireland; the humbler cabin victories of the Rochforts, Blayneys, Kerrs, Montgomerys, Furlongs, &c. might have furnished records to enable us to form some idea of the value of property of the suffering people, for the loss of which they were not indemnified, but which the gentlemen referred to were indemnified for the destruction of.

As to the expenses the government had to encounter and defray on account of this rebellion, the following calculation may give some idea of the amount :—

From 1797 to 1802, the cost of the large military force that was kept up in Ireland, estimated at £4,000,000 per annum . .	£16,000,000
Purchase of the Irish Parliament .	1,500,000
Payment of claims of suffering loyalists	1,500,000
Secret service money, from 1797 to 1804	53,547
Probable amount of pensions paid for services in suppression of the rebellion and the carrying of the Union, from 1797 to 1842 . . .	1,000,000
Increased expense of legal proceedings and judicial tribunals	500,000
Additional expenditure in public offices consequent on increased duties in 1798, and alterations in establishments attendant on the Union, the removal of parliamentary archives, and compensation of officers, servants, &c.	500,000
	£21,053,547

I am aware that the amount has been estimated at £30,000,000 by some writers, and at nearly double that amount by others. " In three counties," it has been said, " its suppression cost £52,000,000 ; what would it have been, if it had extended to the other twenty-nine counties ? "

I have set down the items which, I believe, constituted the bulk of the expenditure for the excitement, premature explosion, and sanguinary suppres-

sion of the rebellion, and for the corruption, purchase, and abolition of the Irish Parliament; and
that amount, though it falls short of all the calcula-
tions I have seen on the subject, I have given as the
nearest approximation to the actual expenditure my
own enquiries have led to.

CHAPTER XII.

THE preceding details were intended to give some insight into the origin, progress, and "premature explosion," of the conspiracy of 1798.

A full and faithful history of the rebellion yet remains to be written. The object of this work is to place before the public some of the scattered memorials of it, collected from those who were actors in that struggle. The reminiscences of those persons, it seemed to me, were likely to perish with them, had no effort been made, in their latter years, to preserve them. Most of these persons were far advanced in years—some, indeed, on the verge of the grave—and during the last seven years (the period of collecting these materials) many of them have died.

To enter into any lengthened account of the sanguinary struggle—of its successive engagements, from the 20th of May, 1798, when "the rising" of the peasantry commenced in the counties of Kildare and Wicklow, to the 8th of September, when the French, under Humbert, surrendered at Ballinamuck, would be foreign to my purpose. The humbler task remains to be attempted, of illustrating the events referred to in the foregoing pages, by memoirs of those persons who took a prominent part in the rebellion, or of those whose names are associated with it.

The persons who are the subjects of the following memoirs, are those whose histories are most intimately connected with events or proceedings, to which I have particularly endeavoured to direct attention. They do not appear in the order of the influence or eminence of the several leaders of the United Irishmen, but rather in the order of their connexion with the topics I have alluded to. In point of importance to their cause, whether on account of their station in its service, or of their ability in its direction, Emmett, O'Connor, M'Nevin, Lord Edward Fitzgerald, Tone, and Sampson, would take precedence, in my opinion, of all their associates. The arrests, however, of the three first-named leaders, and their confinement during the early part of the rebellion, precluded their connexion with those events which have now to be brought under consideration—namely, the means that were adopted for the suppression of the rebellion, and the administration of justice in the cases of those who were accused of being engaged in it. The lives of the other three leaders have been already written, and it would be needless, as well as presumptuous, to enter anew upon their histories.

In relation to the subject of the compact entered into with the government (when the plans of the United Irishmen had failed), on the part of Emmett,

O'Connor, and M'Nevin, memoirs of these gentle-men will be given in another series of this work, and those, likewise, of the principal northern leaders —Neilson, Russell, and M'Cracken.

BAGENAL BEAUCHAMP HARVEY.

B. B. Harvey, who, in 1798, was compelled to act for a short time as the commander-in-chief of the Wexford rebel forces, was grandson of the Reverend William Harvey, rector of Malrankin, and son of Francis Harvey, Esq. of Bargy Castle, an opulent attorney, who had largely added to the family estate by purchase; and, on his decease, his property de-volved on his eldest son, B. B. Harvey. Mr. Har-vey was educated at Trinity College, Dublin, and was called to the bar in 1782.

Taylor, "the ascendancy" historian of the Wex-ford rebellion (the most accurate of his tribe), speaks of him as "a gentleman who, before the rebellion, was greatly beloved by every description of people." Cloney, a writer no less truthful, but of very oppo-site political sentiments, describes Mr. Harvey as "a most liberal and patriotic Protestant gentleman, a man of high rank and respectable family, distin-guished for his benevolence in every walk of life, and possessing an hereditary estate of about £2000 a-year." Mr. Harvey took an active part in the liberal politics of the period between 1782 and 1794. He was in tolerable practice as a barrister, and was extremely popular with all parties: he was high-spirited, kind-hearted, and good-tempered, fond of

society, given to hospitality, and especially esteemed
for his humane and charitable disposition towards
the poor.

It is necessary to bear in mind, that the early
advocates of reform and emancipation, who had
given umbrage or annoyance to the government by
the agitation of these questions, for some years previously to 1798—men whose loyalty was never called
in question till that disastrous period—were then
marked out as suspected persons; and when the
time came for letting loose the burning zeal and
loyalty of Orangeism on the country, the popular
leaders who had made themselves obnoxious to the
ruling powers in former years, were delivered over
to the tender mercies of the privileged marauders,
and they were ultimately " sacrificed in the confusion of the times." On such occasions, the zeal
for the public service was wonderfully stimulated by
the recollection of old misunderstandings, or of private quarrels of past occurrence. Mr. Harvey had,
unfortunately, distinguished himself by his ren-
contres with several persons, of more or less political
consequence, of his day. He had acquired the character of a man of tried courage, which, in those
times, every judge of any repute on the bench,
or lawyer at the bar, was expected to possess. He
had fought a duel, in 1794, with Mr. Harding Giffard, the son of the well-known John Giffard, then
one of the sheriffs of Dublin.

The cause of this duel was an observation of Mr.
Harvey's, respecting disturbances which had taken
place in the county Cavan. He had said, that " he

lamented any administration could descend to the
mean and wicked policy of fomenting religious animosities among the people, when they were productive of such dreadful consequences." Young Giffard
took charge of the honour of the administration,
challenged Harvey, and had the good fortune to get
slightly wounded in defence of ministers. This duel
took place the 8th of May, 1794.

In 1795, on the proposed recall of Lord Fitzwilliam,
the gentry and freeholders of the county Wexford
held a public meeting on the 23rd of March, at
which a petition to the king was voted, and an address to Lord Fitzwilliam. The meeting was called
by Cornelius Grogan, his brothers Thomas Knox and
John Grogan, Isaac Cornock, and Harvey Hay,
magistrates of the county. The persons appointed
to present the petition to the king, were Cornelius
Grogan, B. B. Harvey, and Edward Hay. The petition to Lord Fitzwilliam was to be presented by Sir
Thomas Esmonde, Sir Frederick Flood, and Bagenal
Harvey. At this meeting B. B. Harvey took an
active part.

The subsequent fate of three of these unfortunate
gentlemen, there is but too much reason to believe,
may be traced to the displeasure and ill-will they
brought on themselves by their proceedings on this
occasion, so far as rendering them "marked men,"
against whom evil reports were likely to be too
readily received.

Harvey was a member of the first society of United
Irishmen of Dublin, so early as 1792. The object
of that society, it has been already shewn, was a

reform in parliament; and Catholic emancipation was the preliminary means by which its leading members expected to effect that measure. Whatever might be the views of individuals belonging to the first society, the great body of its influential leaders, at that period, were reformers—the principles of many of whom did not even go so far as those of Colonel Sharman and the Duke of Richmond.

In 1793, Harvey presided as chairman at some of the meetings of the United Irishmen's Society in Dublin. The 1st of March in that year, he was the chairman of a meeting at which " an address to the people of Ireland" was voted, in favour of reform. The views of the society were plainly set forth in that address. They were denounced by the government press as revolutionary; but it would be difficult to find a single passage in that paper, which would now be considered deserving of that character. The unfortunate Thomas Russell, the friend of Tone and the associate of Robert Emmett, was the secretary at that meeting.

On circuit, the amiable disposition and independent spirit of Mr. Harvey, made him a favourite with his brother barristers. Barrington was well acquainted with his good-nature, and it will be seen by the following anecdote, related in Sir Jonah's Irish Sketches, how far " his old friend and school-fellow" could rely on his good-nature and forbearance, when Sir Jonah had a professional purpose to serve, or a step to gain, by an encroachment on the circle of a legal brother's prospects or practice at the bar.

" At the assizes of Wexford (he states), whilst I

was but young at the bar, I received a brief in the
cause of Sir R. M.,* Bart., against a Mr. H——.
On perusal, I found it was an action by the baronet
against the latter gentleman, respecting his lady, and
that I was retained as advocate for the lady's honour.
It was my first appearance in that town. But, alas!
I had a senior in the business, and therefore was
without opportunity of displaying my abilities. The
ill-fated Bagenal Harvey was that senior counsel,
and he had prepared himself to make an exhibition
in a cause of much importance and such universal
excitement. I felt dispirited, and would willingly
have given up twenty fees in order to possess this
opportunity.

" The cause proceeded before Judge Kelly, the
evidence was finished, and the proper time for the
defence had arrived; every thing as to the lady was
at stake. Bagenal Harvey had gone out to take the
fresh air, and probably to read over some notes, or
con some florid sentences and quotations with which
he intended to interlard his elocution. At the moment the evidence closed, the judge desired me to
proceed; I replied, that Mr. Harvey, my senior,
would return into court directly.

" Judge Kelly, who was my friend, and clearly saw
my wish, said he would not delay public business one
minute for any body; and by a sort of instinct, or
rather impulse, I cannot indeed exactly say what it
was—but certainly it was totally impromptu,—I
began to state her ladyship's case. I always had
words enough at command, the evidence afforded

* The person alluded to was Sir Richard Musgrave.

S

sufficient material for their exercise; and, in fact, being roused by the cause into a sort of knight-errantry, I felt myself completely identified with it. If I should succeed, it would greatly serve me. I forgot poor Bagenal Harvey, and was just getting into the marrow and pathos of my case, when the crier shouted out, 'Clear the way for Counsellor Harvey.' Bagenal came in, puffing and blowing, and struggling through the crowd, scarcely able to command utterance. I instantly stopped, and begged his pardon, adding that the judge had said the public time could wait for nobody. 'So,' continued I, 'let me just show you where I left off, (turning over the leaves of my brief): there, begin there—it will be useless to repeat what I have already said, so begin there.' A loud laugh succeeded, Bagenal became irritated as much as he was susceptible of being, and whispered me, that he considered it as a personal insult: whilst old Judge Kelly gravely said, 'Go on, Mr. Barrington, go on! we can have no speeches by dividends; go on, sir!' So on I went, and I believe, (because every body told me so), that my impromptu speech was entirely successful. I discredited the witness by ridicule, destroyed all sympathy with the husband, and interested every body for the wife. In short, I got the judge and jury into good humour."*

To the utter discomfiture of the baronet, "Sir Jonah" states there was a verdict against him. Subsequent events shewed there were no grounds for the action, but ample reason for the friends of the lady desiring a separate maintenance for her, if Sir

---

* Barrington's " Irish Sketches," p. 98.

Richard was so "insane on all political subjects" as
Barrington represents him to have been, "his imagination being occupied night and day with nothing
but papists, jesuits, and rebels;" and on one
occasion, in the dead of the night, suddenly acting
on the impression that his lady was one of these.
Barrington's conduct on this occasion, on his own
shewing, towards his old friend and schoolfellow
Harvey, was far from being professionally correct or
courteous. But the manner in which he speaks of
Harvey in his subsequent work, evinces no feelings
particularly friendly towards him.

The nature of the intercourse between them it is
difficult to comprehend, till we come to its termination; and then we find its early existence in no
slight degree connected with the last events in the
unfortunate career of B. B. Harvey.

The facts referred to, render it necessary to direct
attention to the peculiarities of one of the parties.—
Sir Jonah's patriotism alternately blew hot and cold.
It accommodated itself to the temperature of the
political atmosphere of whatever place he frequented;
at the Castle, or in the Commons, it usually sunk to
zero. In the company of Grogan, Colclough,
Harvey, and the Sheares, and at the levees of the
lord-lieutenant, or the chancellor, it was seldom
stationary. Its rise and fall was regulated by the
prevailing influence of wit and wine—of patronage
and preferment. Sir Jonah was in the habit of
living on terms of social intercourse, not only with
the aldermen of Skinner's Alley, but with the leading members of his own profession, of the Volunteer

Association, and the society of United Irishmen.
Sir Jonah joined in their convivial revels—he disliked
their politics, but their merrymakings were congenial to his taste; and his presence was no restraint
on any opinions expressed by his good-humoured
associates; when they verged on sedition, he joked
with them about the inconvenience of being hanged;
and when they became "seditious," one day he would
interfere to save "the rebels" from the penalties of
their crimes, and another he would either publicly
denounce their guilt, or revile the administration for
its leniency towards them. For men engaged in a
movement of such vast importance, and especially for
the actors in it, so singularly incautious in their convivial intercourse as many of them were, it would be
a difficulty to conceive a more perilous acquaintance,
than a man of Sir Jonah Barrington's unfixed
opinions and ambiguous principles—one who was
all-in-all with the leading people of every class—who
had no earnestness of purpose to attach him to the
politics of any party; but who was drawn to the
social circles of each, by a love of pleasure or a taste
for company, and who, by his humourous powers in
conversation, and the well-known facetiousness of
his disposition, could make himself a favourite in
every company, and thus acquire opportunities of
rendering the opinions and characters of contending
parties, more familiar to one another than might be
for the advantage of either.

In December, 1793, Sir Jonah was informed by
Mr. Secretary Hobart, "he had managed to secure
for him a very handsome office—the ships-entries of

the port of Dublin," hoping "he would have no objection to a good sinecure,"—the occupant of this office having accepted an annuity from government of £800 per annum, for himself, his son, and his wife, to resign it to Sir Jonah. He was likewise informed, "the lord chancellor (Fitzgibbon) had consented to his being appointed one of the King's Counsel; this, at once, giving him a step over the heads of all his circuit seniors, except Sir Frederick Flood," &c. It is to be presumed, Sir Jonah's past and expected services were held deserving of such signal favour.

The earliest proof that Sir Jonah alludes to, of his ability or desire to realize the expectations that were formed of his merits, was given in the month of April, 1798. The occasion, and the mode of its exhibition, are best described in Sir Jonah's own words :—

" I dined (he says) at the house of Lady Colclough (a near relative of Lady Barrington), in the town of Wexford, in April, 1798. The company so far as I recollect, consisted of about seventeen persons, amongst whom were several other of Lady B.'s relatives, then members of the grand jury : Mr. Cornelius Grogan, of Johnstown, a gentleman of very large fortune who had represented the county ; his two brothers, both wealthy men; Captain Keogh, afterwards rebel governor of Wexford; the husband of Lady B.'s aunt, the unfortunate John Colclough of Tintern, and the still more unfortunate Mr. H. Colclough ; Counsellor John Beauman ; Counsellor

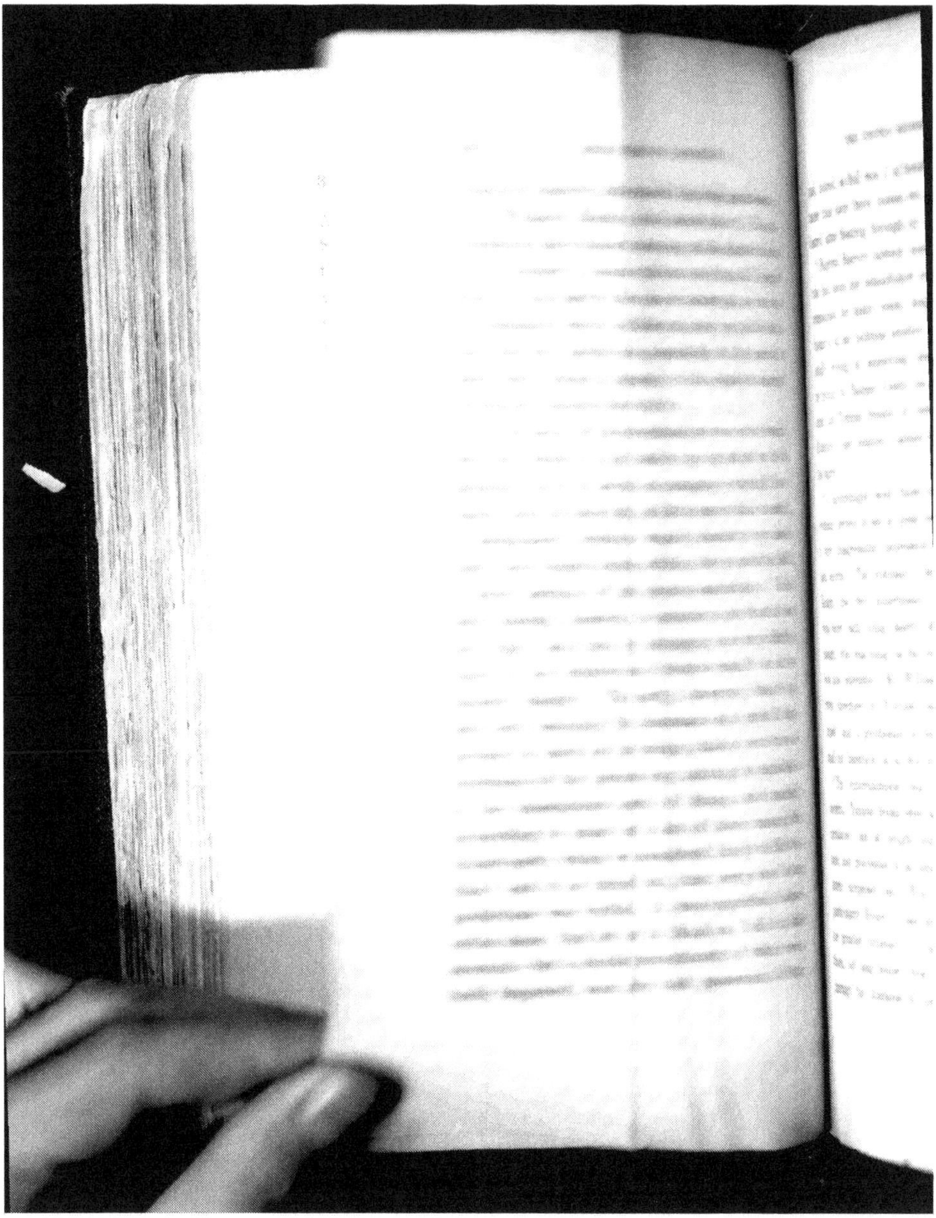

soull was I of forebodings, that I have
...merbeen roused out of my sleep by the
...floing through my mind!

...Hrvey (already mentioned in this work)
...en ...y schoolfellow and constant circuit-
for ...any years, laughed, at Lady Col-
...my political prudery; assured me I was
...ng ...suspecting him, and insisted on
...to Begay Castle, his residence, to meet
...fump friends of ours, on the ensuing
...my ...lative, Captain Keogh, was to be of

...cordingy went there to dinner; but that
...roved ...me of great uneasiness, and made
...isagreeable impression both on my mind
...rs. Tl company I met included Captain
...the tw unfortunate Counsellors Sheares,
...e both ...ung shortly afterwards; Mr. Col-
...ho was..ung on the bridge; Mr. Hay, who
...r execute; Mr. William Hatton, one of the
...irectory ...f Wexford, *who unaccountably es-*
...and a ...tleman of the bar, whose name I
...ot mentio, as he still lives.

...he entertainment was good, and the party
...l. Templereaks were talked over—the bottle
...ated; but ...length Irish politics became the
...and proceed to an extent of disclosure which
...ly surprised me. With the Messrs. Sheares
...icularly Hery) I had always been on terms of
...greatest intimacy: I had extricated both of
...a, not long before, from considerable difficulty,
...ugh the kindness of Lord Kilwarden; and I

Bagenal Harvey, afterwards the rebel generalissimo; Mr. William Hatton, and some others. The conversation after dinner turning on the distracted state of the country, became rather too free, and I begged some of the party to be more moderate, as our ways of thinking were so different, and my public situation did not permit me, *especially at that period*, to hear such strong language: the loyalists amongst us did not exceed four or five.

" The tone of the conversation was soon lowered, but not before I had made up my mind as to the probable fate of several in company—though I certainly had no idea that, in little more than a month, a sanguinary rebellion would desolate my native land, and violent deaths, within *three* months, befall a great portion of that joyous assemblage. I had seen enough, however, to convince me that all was not right, and that, by plunging one step further, most of my relatives and friends would be in imminent danger. The party, however, broke up; and next morning Mr. Beauman and myself, happening to meet on the bridge, talked over the occurrences of the previous day, uniting in opinion as to the inauspicious aspect of things, and actually proceeding to make out a list of those among the dinner-party, whom we considered likely to fall victims! and it so turned out, that *every one* of our predictions was verified. It was superficial observation alone, that led me to think as I did at that moment—but a decided presentiment of what eventually happened, soon after took possession of me;

and, indeed, so full was I of forebodings, that I have more than once been roused out of my sleep by the horrid ideas floating through my mind!

"Bagenal Harvey (already mentioned in this work) who had been my schoolfellow and constant circuit-companion for many years, laughed, at Lady Col-clough's, at my political prudery; assured me I was totally wrong in suspecting him, and insisted on my going to Bargay Castle, his residence, to meet some old Temple friends of ours, on the ensuing Monday:—my relative, Captain Keogh, was to be of the party.

"I accordingly went there to dinner; but that evening proved to me of great uneasiness, and made a very disagreeable impression both on my mind and spirits. The company I met included Captain Keogh, the two unfortunate Counsellors Sheares, who were both hung shortly afterwards; Mr. Col-clough, who was hung on the bridge; Mr. Hay, who was also executed; Mr. William Hatton, one of the rebel directory of Wexford, *who unaccountably escaped;* and a gentleman of the bar, whose name I shall not mention, as he still lives.

"The entertainment was good, and the party cheerful. Temple freaks were talked over—the bottle circulated; but at length Irish politics became the topic, and proceeded to an extent of disclosure which utterly surprised me. With the Messrs. Sheares (particularly Henry) I had always been on terms of the greatest intimacy: I had extricated both of them, not long before, from considerable difficulty, through the kindness ·of Lord Kilwarden; and I

had no idea that matters wherein they were concerned, had proceeded to the lengths developed on
that night. The probability of a speedy revolt was
freely discussed, though in the most artful manner,
not a word of any of the party committing themselves; but they talked it over, as a result which
might be expected from the complexion of the times,
and the irritation excited in consequence of the
severities exercised by the government. The chances
of success, in the event of a rising, were openly de-
bated, as were, also, the circumstances likely to
spring from that success, and the examples which
the insurgents would in that case probably make.
All this was at the same time talked over, without
one word being uttered in favour of rebellion—a
system of caution which, I afterwards learned, was
much practised, for the purpose of gradually making
proselytes without alarming them. I saw through it
clearly, and here my presentiments came strong
upon me. I found myself in the midst of absolute,
though unavowed conspirators. I perceived that the
explosion was much nearer than the government
expected; and I was startled at the decided manner
in which my host and his friend spoke.

"Under these circumstances, my alternative was
evidently to quit the house, or give a turn to the
conversation. I therefore began to laugh at the
subject, and ridicule it as quite visionary, observing
jestingly to Keogh—'Now, my dear Keogh, it is
quite clear that you and I, in this famous rebellion,
shall be on different sides of the question, and, of
course, one or the other of us must necessarily be

hanged, at or before its termination—I upon a lamp-iron in Dublin, or you on the bridge of Wexford. Now, we 'll make a bargain! if we beat you, upon my honour I 'll do all I can to save your neck; and if your folks beat us, you 'll save me from the honour of the lamp-iron!'

" We shook hands on the bargain, which created much merriment, and gave the whole after-talk a cheerful character, and I returned to Wexford, at twelve o'clock at night, with a most decided impression of the danger of the country, and a complete presentiment, that either myself or Captain Keogh, would never see the conclusion of that summer." On his return to Dublin the following day, he continues, " I immediately wrote to Mr. Secretary Cooke, without mentioning names, place, or any particular source of knowledge, but simply to assure him that there was not a doubt that an insurrection would break out, at a much earlier period than the government expected. I desired him to ask me no questions, but said that he might depend upon the fact; adding that a commanding force ought instantly to be sent down, to garrison the town of Wexford. ' If the government,' said I in conclusion, ' does not attend to my warning, it must take the consequences.' My warning was not attended to, but his Majesty's government soon found I was right. They lost Wexford, and might have lost Ireland, by that culpable inattention.'

" The result need scarcely be mentioned, every member of that jovial dinner party, (with the exception of myself, the barrister before alluded to, and

Mr. Hatton,) was executed within three months! and on my next visit to Wexford, I saw the heads of Captain Keogh, Mr. Harvey, *and Mr. Colclough,* on spikes, over the court-house door.

" Previously to the final catastrophe, however, when the insurgents had been beaten, Wexford retaken by our troops, and Keogh made prisoner, I did not forget my promise to him at Bargay Castle. Many certificates had reached Dublin, of his humanity to the royalists, whilst the town of Wexford was under his government, and of attempts made upon his life by Dixon, a chief of his own party, for his endeavouring to resist the rebel butcheries. I had intended to go with these directly to Lord Camden, the Lord Lieutenant; but I first saw Mr. Secretary Cooke, to whom I related the entire story, and showed him several favourable documents. He told me I might save myself the trouble of going to Lord Camden: and at the same time handed me a despatch received that morning from General Lake, who stated that he thought it necessary, on recapturing Wexford, to lose no time in ' making example' of the rebel chiefs; and that accordingly Mr. Grogan, of Johnstown, Mr. Bagenal Harvey, of Bargay Castle, Captain Keogh, Mr. Colclough, and some other gentlemen, had been hanged on the bridge, and beheaded, the previous morning."*

" An unaccountable circumstance was witnessed by me on that tour. Immediately after the retaking of Wexford, General Lake, as I have before mentioned, had ordered the heads of Mr. Grogan,

* Vide Irish Sketches, vol. i. p. 163, 4, 5, 6.

Captain Keogh, Mr. Bagenal Harvey, and Mr. Colclough, to be placed on very low spikes, over the court-house door of Wexford. A faithful servant of Mr. Grogan, had taken away his head, but the other three remained there when I visited the town. The mutilated countenances of friends and relatives, in such a situation, would, it may be imagined, give any man most horrifying sensations! The heads of Mr. Colclough and Harvey appeared black lumps, the features being utterly undistinguishable; that of Keogh was uppermost, but the air had made no impression on it whatever! his comely and respect-inspiring face (except the *pale* hue, scarcely to be called *livid*,) was the same as in life; his eyes were not closed, his hair not much ruffled; in fact, it appeared to me, rather as a head of chiselled marble, with glass eyes, than as the lifeless remains of a human creature:—this circumstance I never could get any medical man to give me the least explanation of. I prevailed on General Hunter, who then commanded in Wexford, to suffer the three heads to be taken down and buried." *

The first circumstance which deserves attention, is the relation in which Sir Jonah stood to the parties he describes. The lady at whose house he dines, was " a near relation of Lady Barrington;" " several of the guests were Lady Barrington's relatives;" Captain Keogh, " the husband of Lady Barrington's aunt;" Bagenal Beauchamp Harvey, Sir Jonah's ' schoolfellow and constant circuit-companion for many years."

* Vide Irish Sketches, vol. i. p. 168.

At another party, on the Monday following, made up for Sir Jonah by his schoolfellow, B. B. Harvey, he meets most of the persons who had been at Lady Colclough's dinner : among others, were the Sheares. " With the Sheares, particularly Henry, he had always been on terms of the greatest intimacy."

At the first party, he states, the conversation turning on the distracted state of the country, became rather too free ; " and I begged some of the party (he says) to be a little more moderate, as our ways of thinking were so different, and my public situation did not permit me, *especially at that period,* to hear such strong language." Then, it would seem, Sir Jonah was conscious that some of his associates must have been aware that there were periods at which such strong language could have been heard by him.

The place where he appears to have been first alarmed at this tendency, was at the table of a lady of high rank : several of the guests " were members of the grand jury." " Mr. Cornelius Grogan, of Johnstown, a gentleman," he states, in another of his works, " of very large fortune, who had represented the county," whom he knew to be an excellent gentleman, no more a rebel than himself."

The company, moreover, he describes to have been " a joyous assemblage." Was this a fitting place for treason to disclose its dark designs? Were the gentlemen of the grand jury—the landed gentry of the county—Colclough of Tintern, or his relative of Ballyteigue, the wealthy Grogan, in his seventieth year—the men who were " fit for treasons, stratagems, and broils?" And if they were so, were they yet such fools as altogether to disregard the presence of a man in the pay and employment of the government; of political principles publicly professed to be opposed to theirs; and to make an open display before him of their disaffection?

How did it happen that a "conversation turning on the distracted state of the country"—than which nothing at that period could be more natural, was no sooner lowered in its tone, than Sir Jonah ventured to express some reluctance "to hear such strong language at that particular period," and that his mind was made up as to the probable fate of several in company?

On what grounds, reconcilable with the common feelings of our nature, did Sir Jonah and Mr. Beauman next morning talk over the occurrences of the previous day, uniting in opinion as to the inauspicious aspect of things, *and actually proceed to make out a list of those amongst the dinner party whom they considered "likely to fall victims, and so it turned out, that every one of their predictions was verified."*

According to Curran, "There are two sorts of prophets: one that derives its source from real or fancied inspiration, yet are sometimes mistaken; the other class, composed of persons who prophecy what they are determined to bring about themselves: of this second, and by far the more authentic class, was Major Sirr; for Heaven, 'tis seen, has no monopoly of prediction."*

* Vide Curran's Speech on Heney's Trial.

Sir Jonah and the Major so far resembled one another in their prophetic character, that they fulfilled their predictions to the letter, though the means by which the same results were produced by one, party were more obvious and less mysterious than by the other.

Sir Jonah states, that immediately on coming to town, he wrote to Mr. Secretary Cooke, informing him of the danger in which Wexford was placed; but giving no names; declining, in fact, to come forward as a public prosecutor. But why did not Sir Jonah give a copy of that letter in his work? There can be only one reply to that question—it did not suit the purpose of the writer to publish it; and there is but too much reason to believe, it would not have served his character to have its contents set before the public. He boasts, indeed, of his having informed his confidential friend, Mr. Cooke, that he would enter into no particulars. Granting that he had done so in his written communication to Mr. Cooke, is it likely, on such an important subject, that no subsequent personal communication would have been sought by the secretary? Mr. Cooke could not, surely, have received a letter disclosing circumstances which involved the peace of the country, without gratefully acknowledging the timely warning, and learning from the writer the quarter from which the danger was to be apprehended. Sir Jonah's punctilios, with respect to withholding names, are but the incipient scruples of all novices, in a line of duty or of business they have newly undertaken. Their feelings at the first, take alarm at the notoriety of their disclosures ; but they are not so much afraid of consigning their associates to death, as they are ashamed of being found out to be instrumental to their ruin.

It was the duty of Sir Jonah Barrington, as a loyal subject, if he suspected his friends and relatives of disaffection, to have determinedly and strenuously remonstrated with them, and if he found his remonstrance of no avail, before he quitted their society, if he really apprehended danger to the state from their designs, as an upright man, faithful to his friends as well as to his country, he should have told these persons frankly and fearlessly, he was no party to their views, he reprobated their designs, and if they persisted in them, he should be compelled to denounce them to government. But Sir Jonah took a very different course, for he had two reputations to keep up, and he could not afford to lose a jot of either. He mixed in society with the ultra liberals of his day; he joked with some of them about treason, at Lady Colclough's table; he shared in the festivities of that "joyous assemblage" he speaks of, under his schoolfellow's roof; enjoyed the society of two gentlemen whom he calls "his most intimate friends," and whom, two years previously, he had known as the editors of a "seditious paper"—the Messrs. Sheares—and whom he designated as rebels, in speaking of his interference on their behalf with the attorney-general; yet not till he meets them at Harvey's table, does he express any alarm at the freedom of their discourse !

He then was convinced they were destined to be

hanged, and he felt himself imperatively called on to disclose his apprehensions to government. Strange to say, in the whole of his conversation, he admits that not one individual " committed himself in the slightest degree, or spoke in terms of approval of the rebellion," which they considered would be the consequence of the outrages that were then committing on the people.

This indeed, is a strange admission, and hardly seems in accordance with the statement of the ground on which he had formed the opinion, that they, and the majority of the company, were destined to be hanged. If he had this impression, it was a cruel act to joke with one of the unfortunate men he knew doomed to such a fate—his own relative, Captain Keogh—on the probability of his approaching end, of his hanging from a lamp-post, without solemnly adjuring him to avoid the evils he apprehended, to retrace his steps, and return to his allegiance.

It was, in the last degree, unfeeling, to sit in the presence of the venerable Grogan, his old acquaint-ance,* whom he knew to be " as loyal as himself," and not to apprise that poor infirm gentleman, of the dangerous company (as he represents most of those present at Lady Colclough's) by whom he was surrounded on that occasion.

It was a foul proceeding, to eat and drink at the same board with two young men of his own profession, his intimate friends, whose private character, he states, was unexceptionable, and to witness such evident

* Sir Jonah Barrington married a Miss Grogan, of Dublin, the daughter of a wealthy silk-mercer.

manifestations of extreme indiscretion on their parts, as left no doubt on his mind of their impending fate, and not to have made one effort to rescue them from ruin. Why did he not reason and remonstrate with them, on the madness of the projects he imputed to them? "A fool-born jest," in reference to his strange presentiments, the next morning, is all that we hear on the subject of his difference of opinion with these unfortunate gentlemen. Sir Jonah proceeded to Dublin, he gave his information, and, however it was given—or subsequently, by what private channel of communication between the secretary and Sir Jonah, the names of the suspected parties were obtained—there can be but little doubt but that every one of the parties mentioned by Sir Jonah, was placed under surveillance previously to the outbreak of the rebellion; and certain it is, that all of them, with three exceptions, perished on the scaffold; that Messrs. Grogan, Colclough,. Harvey, Hay, Keogh, and both the Sheares, met their fate in the fulfilment of Sir Jonah's prophecy.

It has been stated by Hay, Cloncy, and Teeling, and truly stated by them, that there was no systematic concert between the rising of the people in the county Wexford, and the plan of general insurrection formed in Dublin.

" On the arrest of the Leinster delegates at Bond's, on the 12th of March, there was not a delegate, or any return of numbers from the county Wexford."*
" The rising of the people in this county, took place in the direction from Carnew to Oulard, for fear, as

* Hay's Insurrection, County of Wexford, p. 123.

they alleged, of being whipped, burned, or exterminated by the Orangemen, hearing of the number of
people that were put to death, unarmed and unoffending, through the country."*

It would be contrary to truth, however, to assert
that no effort had been made to organize this county;
such an effort had been made by William Putnam
M'Cabe, and was not successful. No history of the
rebellion makes mention of this attempt of M'Cabe.
He spoke of it himself, not unfrequently, as one of
the boldest of his efforts, but one not attended with
much success, though he had sworn in many of the
lower orders, but such was "the apathy" of the
Wexford people in general, and of the gentry in particular, that the organization, as a system, made no
way in that county.

The massacres, especially at Carnew on the 25th
of May, and Dunlavin, had contributed to produce a
general panic in the county Wexford.

On the 27th of May, information reached the town
of Wexford, that the people had risen in great force,
and were then only about twelve miles distant from
the town. A party of the North Cork Militia, under
Lieutenant-Colonel Foote and Major Lombard, were
ordered out, and proceeded to Oulart, where they
encountered the rebels. This party, consisting of
109 men, according to Musgrave, was surrounded
by the rebels, and only Lieut.-Colonel Foote and
three privates escaped. The numbers of the rebels
were estimated by Lieut.-Colonel Foote at four or
five thousand.

* Hay's Insurrection, County of Wexford, p. 87.

They were commanded by Father John Murphy of Boolavogue, whose house and chapel had been previously burned by the yeomen.

Another clergyman of the same name, the Rev. Michael Murphy, we are informed by Hay, "had been so alarmed at hearing of this rising of the people, that he fled into the town of Gorey early on Whitsunday (the 27th of May)." From this place he was returning to Ballicanow, when he learned that his chapel had been attacked, and the altar and windows, demolished by some yeomen. "These depredations," says Hay, "had such weight on him, as to induce him to alter his original intention, and not to fly to such men for protection; and he was led on by the multitude to Kilthomas Hill. The Rev. John Murphy had, from similar unforeseen occurrences, joined the insurgents. These two clergymen had been remarkable for their exhortations and exertions against the system of United Irishmen, until they were thus whirled into this political vortex, which, from all the information I have been able to collect, they undertook under the apprehension of extermination." *

The terrible example of burning houses, and murdering obnoxious or suspected individuals, was followed by the insurgents. Of ten Protestant clergymen of this county, who fell into their hands during the insurrection, five were barbarously put to death. These atrocities, however, were not committed with the sanction or knowledge of the above-named

* Hay's Insurrection, &c. p. 38.

priests. Of those of their communion, who violated their engagements as christian ministers, not one escaped a death of violence. Father Michael Murphy was killed by a cannon-shot at the battle of Arklow, on the 9th of June. Father John Murphy, " the commander of that great column which made an incursion through the county of Carlow into that of Kilkenny, and caused such devastation in that quarter in the rout of Kilcomney, disappeared from his followers (who generally imagine him to be still alive), was apprehended in his flight, and conducted to Tullow, in the county Carlow, where he was executed by martial law." *

He had studied in the University of Seville; and, after a three years' residence there, returned to Ireland in 1785. The Rev. Michael Murphy was ordained in the diocese of Ferns in 1785, and, in the latter part of the same year, went to Bourdeaux, where he entered the Irish college, and remained till the suppression of that institution, at an early period of the French Revolution.

The barbarities practised on the remains of this man are unparalleled, even in the history of Irish rebellions. Mr. George Taylor, in his Historical Account of the Wexfordian Rebellion, says :—" Lord Mountnorris and some of his troop, on viewing the scene of action, found the body of the perfidious priest, Murphy, who so much deceived him and his country. Being exasperated, his lordship ordered the head to be struck off, and his body to be thrown

* Rev. James Gordon's History, &c. p. 225.

into a house that was burning, exclaiming—' Let his body go where his soul is.' " * Other indignities, of a nature no less brutal, had been previously offered to his remains. Mr. Gordon states that he had been told by Captain Holmes, of the Durham regiment, in the presence of several persons, " that he himself had assisted in cutting open the breast with an axe, and pulling out the heart." †

The day after the free-quarters' enormities were commenced on a large scale, in the county of Wexford, Mr. Fitzgerald, of New Park, was arrested on the 26th of May, his house was ransacked, but no treasonable paper or document, that could in the slightest degree commit him, was found. The same night, Mr. Harvey, who at the first intimation of the rising in the neighbourhood of Wexford, that morning had brought into the town the arms of all his tenantry and neighbourhood, was likewise arrested and lodged in jail.

The following day, Mr. John Henry Colclough, of Ballyteigue, about ten miles from Wexford, was also arrested and brought into town. The soldiers of the North Cork Militia, expressed themselves in most violent terms against these three gentlemen, and stated their determination to have the lives of the prisoners. The gaoler found it necessary to put arms in the hands of his prisoners, to defend their lives; and Hay, who was present, states that " had it not been for the indefatigable exertion of the gaoler, the prisoners would have been all massacred.

* Historical Account, &c. by G. Taylor, p. 136.
† History of the Rebellion, by the Rev. J. Gordon, p. 289.

In the meantime, the success of the rebels at Enniscorthy, spread terror in Wexford. On the 29th of
May, several of the magistrates and military officers,
visited Messrs. Harvey, Colclough and Fitzgerald,
and treated with them rather as " governors of the
town, than prisoners." It was arranged, that they
should be liberated on certain conditions, should
give security, in £1,000 each, for their appearance
at the next assizes, but two of them only should be
at large at one time, taking their turns in going
abroad, at their own discretion. Harvey in the first
instance was to remain in prison, and Messrs. Colclough and Fitzgerald to be immediately released,
and to endeavour to prevail on the insurgents to
disperse, and return to their homes.

The arrest of Harvey, Colclough and Fitzgerald,
created the greatest surprize in Wexford. No suspicion had been entertained or expressed there, that
they were in any wise implicated in rebellion.

On the 23rd of May, a meeting of the Wexford
magistrates had been convened by the sheriff, to
take into consideration the disturbed state of the
country. Cornelius Grogan attended this meeting, and
was one of those who signed the resolutions passed
on that occasion, one of which was expressive of the
magistrates' grateful sense of " the manly, spirited,
and efficacious exertions of Mr. Archibald H. Jacob,
for the establishment and preservation of the public
peace."

Here then, was Mr. Grogan manifesting his loyalty
at a meeting of his brother magistrates, on the 23rd
of May, and on the 27th of the following month, the

same gentleman was executed on a charge of treason. Charles Jackson, one of the acknowledged " loyalist" historians of the rebellion, speaking of Mr. Harvey's arrest, says, " nothing occasioned more astonishment among the generality of the inhabitants of Wexford, than when the order came from Dublin to arrest him ; but his future conduct sufficiently proved the accuracy of the information which government had received concerning him."* His previous conduct, there is no reason to believe, proved anything of the kind.

The order from Dublin, included likewise Messrs. Fitzgerald and Colclough. In reference to the state of the adjoining country, on the 30th of May, Jackson says, " there was at this time, in the goal of Wexford, in consequence of an order from Dublin, Mr. B. B. Harvey, Mr. Fitzgerald, and Mr. Colclough, all men of property and of great interest in the country."†

There had been no informations at this period laid against any of these gentlemen in Wexford. The information that was got up there, on a subsequent occasion, was sworn to by Mr. Richard Grandy, on the 23rd of June. This important information was certified by four magistrates of the county, George Ogle, Isaack Cornock, John Henry Lyster, and John Kennedy. The date of this information deserves attention—Harvey and Grogan were tried on the 26th of May, and Colclough on the day following.

* History of the Irish Rebellion, by Charles Jackson, p. 22.
† Ibid. p. 8.

Among the various circumstances deposed to by Mr. Richard Grandy of Ballyshan, in the county of Wexford, in his information, sworn on the 23rd of May, we find the following:—"That he had been one of the persons confined in the barn of Scullabogue; and his life had been spared in consequence of Bagenal Harvey having previously given him a pass. That a mile and a half from Ross he had met B. Harvey, Cornelius Grogan, of Johnstown, in said county, William Devereux, aforesaid, and many others, returning from the battle of Ross." "That he had often heard, whilst in custody, that John Colclough and Thomas Macord were very active in promoting the rebellion." "That deponent heard, and believes it to be a fact, that Cornelius Grogan had the command of the barony of Forth rebel troops, at the battle of Ross."*

It is hardly necessary to say, that the poor gouty old gentleman was not at the battle of Ross, and never had the command of any rebel troops, or was able, from his great infirmities, if he were so inclined during this rebellion, to take any such command. Mr. Grandy, however, gave the formality of a sworn information, to bear out the proceedings of the court-martial, and those of the parliament, by which this unfortunate old man was consigned to death, and an attainder issued against his property. Mr. Grandy of course did not go unrewarded, for his efforts in promoting the ends of justice. His name is found coupled with a few items, which may serve to perpetuate the remembrance of his services:—

* Musgrave's History, Appendix, p. 135.

" 27 April, 1802, Richard Grandy . . . £100
    7 February, 1803, Richard Grandy, per

        Loftus Tottenham 50
  13 February, 1804, ditto, per ditto . . 50"

The perjured evidence of Grandy, with respect to
Grogan's presence at the battle of Ross, and his
command in the rebel army, is sufficiently rebutted,
even by the statements of Musgrave and Duigenan,
as we shall see hereafter in their observations on
Grogan's fate. But that part of it which applies to
Mr. John Colclough, of Tintern, a relative of Mr.
John Henry Colclough, of Ballyteigue, is not ad-
verted to by them; and, indeed, in respect to the
flagitiousness of its falsehood, it exceeds, if possible,
even that displayed in the evidence against Grogan,
because the latter had been in the power of the rebels,
and was compelled to accompany them into Wexford,
and to remain there while they had possession of the
town; but Colclough was not in Ireland when the
rebellion broke out; and there is the clearest evidence to prove that this testimony was resorted to,
for the purpose of criminating a man, who had made
himself obnoxious by getting into a correspondence
with the Duke of Portland, on the subject of the
conduct pursued in Wexford, and the consequences
of this conduct—as the occasion of his absence from
his country at this period.

The result of this correspondence was an order
from the Duke of Portland to the Haverford authorities, directing that Mr. Colclough should suffer
no molestation in that place. In consequence of
this communication, a letter was addressed to his

T

Grace by the high-sheriff of the county Wexford, expressing surprise at the representations that had been made to him, and stating that Mr. Colclough's conduct was not free from suspicion. Mr. Colclough, in consequence of this insinuation, was brought back to Wexford in charge of a king's messenger; and Mr. Grandy's services, thus called into requisition, had made good the suspicion that had been expressed on the spur of the occasion. There were no means of escape or safety left for those, who either fled from the coming evils they apprehended, or were desirous to leave the country when terror had become the order of the day.

Proclamations to the following effect, at this period, were published in the Dublin Journal:—

" For the apprehension of several persons charged with treason, and who are endeavouring to escape justice by departing from this kingdom, and the pre-vention of all persons whomsoever, leaving the kingdom without a passport," &c.; bearing date 26th May, 1798.

Another, of an earlier date, prohibiting all artifi-cers, manufacturers, seamen, and seafaring people, his majesty's subjects, from quitting the kingdom and going beyond the seas.

The entire military force in Wexford, at the time of the approach of the rebels, including militia, sup-plementaries, and armed townsmen, amounted to 1,200 men; " who, as the town-wall was in good condition, might defy as many thousand assailants not supported by a great superiority of ordnance."*

On the 28th, the insurgents encamped on Vinegar-

---

* Vide Hay, p. 99.

hill. They despatched a party to the residence of
Captain Hay, a brother of the historian, a gentleman
who had been in the French service, and in spite of
his remonstrances, they compelled him to accompany
them to their camp. Another party fell in with
Messrs. Colclough and Fitzgerald, near the village of
St. John's, who had been sent out to them by the
Wexford authorities, to induce them to return to their
homes. They detained Fitzgerald, and sent back
Colclough to announce their intention of attacking
Wexford. Colclough, on his return, was permitted
by the authorities to return home, charged with the
preservation of tranquillity in his own neighbourhood,
having previously arranged with Harvey to take his
place in prison the following day. The insurgents
were now approaching the town in large numbers,
but the yeomanry appear to have been more bent on
the destruction of the prisoners than the defence of
the town. The gaoler again had to put the prison
in a state of defence, to barricade the doors, and in
proof of his sincerity for the protection of the prisoners, he offered the keys to Harvey. When word
was brought to the prisoners of the intended surrender of the town, Harvey was found concealed in
the chimney of the room he occupied. He was now
entreated to go out to the insurgents, to stipulate for
the safety of the lives and property of the inhabitants;
but as the insurgents were not from his neighbourhood, and he had no influence over them, he declined to do so : but at the instance of the Lieut.-
colonel of the North Cork Militia, he wrote to the
insurgents, calling on them " If they pretended to

christian charity, not to commit massacre or burn the property of the inhabitants, and to spare the lives of their prisoners."

On the 30th May, the king's troops evacuated the town, and a few hours after their retreat, Wexford was in possession of the insurgents. Hay, an eye witness of the tumult and confusion of the scene which followed, says "The town of Wexford was not only most shamefully abandoned, but was surrendered, to all intents and purposes, when it might have been easily defended." *

The victorious rebels proceeded to the goal, released all the prisoners, and insisted that Mr. Harvey should become their commander-in-chief. Captain Keogh was appointed military commander of the town, Mr. Grogan, of Johnstown, an infirm old man, was brought from his house by actual force, placed on a horse (being then ill of the gout), and conducted by a vast assemblage of armed men to Wexford.

On the 2nd of June, a small vessel was taken on the coast and brought into Wexford, and on board this vessel, Lord Kingsborough and three officers of the North Cork Militia were captured. During his lordship's detention, he was lodged in the house of Captain Keogh, and to his humane, spirited, and indefatigable exertions, and those of Mr. Harvey, his lordship acknowledged that his life was due, on the many occasions that the fury of the multitude broke out against him. There were few men in Ireland, at this period, more unpopular than his lordship;

* Vide Hay, p. 115

his exploits in the way of extorting confessions by scourgings and other tortures, had rendered his name a terror to the people. The difficulty of preserving his life from the vengeance of a lawless multitude, must have been considerable.

During the occupation of Wexford, the rebel force continued to occupy Vinegar Hill. Harvey fixed his head-quarters at Carrigburn, and from thence proceeded to attack the town of Ross, with a force of about 20,000 men; Barrington estimates it at 30,000.

They arrived late in the evening at Corbet Hill, within a mile of Ross, and there Mr. Harvey and his principal officers took up their quarters in the house of a gentleman, where " being regaled (says Hay) with an excellent supper and exquisite wines, they were so well pleased with their cheer, and so far forgot their prudence as commanders, that they had scarcely time to have fallen asleep, when they were roused, according to the orders they had given in their *sober moments,* to commence the attack at the break of day." In plain terms, the general and his staff, the night preceding a battle on the issue of which depended all their hopes, sat up all night drinking and carousing, instead of making their dispositions, and maturing their plan of operations. Their example was followed by their troops the following day: and drunkenness alone was the cause of their defeat on that occasion. Cloney, an eye-witness of these scenes, says, " the leaders found more attraction in Mr. Murphy's good wines, than in the discharge of those arduous duties that appertained to their command."

Harvey had formed a plan of attack on three different parts of the town at once; which Mr. Gordon thinks, "would probably have succeeded if it had been put in execution." "Harvey, (he says) though neither destitute of personal courage, nor, in some respects, of a good understanding, possessed not that calm intrepidity which is necessary in the composition of a military officer, nor those rare talents by which an undisciplined multitude may be directed and controlled."*

Harvey's first act in the morning, was to despatch one of his officers, Mr. Furlong, with a flag of truce, and a summons to the commanding officer in Ross, to surrender the town. Furlong no sooner reached the out-posts, than he was shot in the performance of his mission. Mr. Gordon, a protestant clergyman, in relating this circumstance, says, "To shoot all persons carrying flags of truce from the rebels, appears to have been a maxim with his majesty's forces."

An attack was immediately made on the town, with indiscriminate fury; the plan of the general was totally disregarded. After some hard fighting, they gained possession of the town; but instead of following up their advantage, "they fell to plundering and drinking;" and after being some hours in possession of the town, the great body of the multitude was so inebriated as to be incapable of defending their new conquest. "Such of the insurgents (says Hay) as were not too drunk to escape out of the town, of which they had been by this time some

* Rev. James Gordon's History of the Rebellion, p. 142.

hours in possession, were driven out of the town;" but having recovered a little after their hasty retreat, which in a great measure made them sober, they again returned to the charge, and their intrepidity was more signally displayed than on any former occasion. They again got possession of the town; " but even after this (we are told by Hay) they soon fell into the same misconduct as before, crowning their bravery with drunkenness." They were again driven out of the town; several houses were set on fire, and one in which seventy-five of these unfortunate wretches were shut up, all of whom perished in the flames, with one exception, who, in running away, was fortunate enough to get clear of the fire of the soldiery."*

A Quaker of the name of Cullimore, who had been taken up on the preceding day, when leaving the town on a visit to his family, had the courage and humanity to interfere in behalf of the prisoners who were confined in the market-house; a number of soldiers had rushed in, with the intention of putting the prisoners to death; Cullimore stood boldly forth, and cried out in an authoritative and impressive tone, " You shall not shoot the prisoners, there are some men here as loyal as you are." The manner and the spirit of this single, unarmed, and uninfluential man, awed and overcame the infuriated band; " they retired (we are informed by Hay) without perpetrating the horrid crime they had intended to commit."†

The widow of Mr. Cullimore has recently in-

* Vide Hay, p. 153.   † Ibid.

formed me of the truth of the above-mentioned circumstance.

The insurgents made a third attempt to retake the
town, and on this occasion displayed extraordinary
courage; but the loss of their favourite leader, Kelly
of Killan, threw them into complete disorder, and
they retreated in confusion to Carrickburn. Mr.
Colclough had been at Ross, in the early part of the
engagement, but took no active part in it. He returned
to Wexford, which place he had unwillingly quitted,
in compliance with the orders of the general-in-chief.
The loss of the king's troops, in killed, wounded, and
missing, was admitted to be 230; that of the rebels
has been variously estimated—by some at 500, by
others at 2,000.

The garrison of Ross, when attacked by the rebels,
amounted to 2,000 men, according to Cloney; but
the number of the insurgents by which this force was
opposed, after the first two hours, Cloney states, did
not exceed 3,000; the combat having lasted thirteen
hours, and the great body of the rebel force remaining in the neighbourhood of Corbet Hill. Cloney
speaks of several of "the respectable persons," of
that class called middle men, during the engagement
having a cask of port wine, which they had conveyed
from Corbet Hill to a well-protected spot, under the
shelter of a high ditch, drinking out of wooden
"noggins," and occasionally advancing in warlike
array towards the gate, and then inquiring with
becoming authority, "How goes the day, boys?"
and then returning to the wine-cask while the battle
was going on; which, "if it had succeeded," (says

Cloney), "our way was open to Waterford and Dun-
cannon Fort, both would have been hastily evacuated,
and the province of Munster at once in arms."*

After the battle of Ross, Harvey was deposed from
his command, and Roche named general-in-chief.
Harvey returned to Wexford, and was appointed
President of the Council of Government, "established
for the preservation of life and property." The
battle of Vinegar Hill, and the engagements with
the rebel out-posts in its vicinity, on the 21st of
June, ended in the total discomfiture of the Wexford
insurgents. Their numbers are generally estimated
at 30,000 men, and the force under the command of
General Lake at 20,000. Taylor says the number
that surrounded the hill amounted to 15,000, of
which 3,000 were cavalry. The loss of the former,
on the hill and in their retreat, he states exceeded
500. The different columns of the king's troops
employed on this occasion, at Vinegar Hill, Enniscorthy, and Wexford, were under the command of
the following officers, General Lake, General Dundas, General Needham, General Johnson, General
Sir James Duff, General Loftus, General Moore, and
Major-General Sir Charles Asgill. The necessity
for such an army, and so many general officers, is a
sufficient proof of the formidable nature of the Wexford insurrection. On the 21st of June, Wexford
was taken possession of by the king's troops, after
being in the hands of the insurgents twenty-three
days.

One of General Lake's first acts, was to issue a

* Vide A Personal Narrative, &c., by Thomas Cloney, p. 41.

proclamation for the apprehension of all the rebel leaders. Harvey had gone to his seat at Bargay Castle, when he was informed that the terms which had been agreed upon with Lord Kingsboro for the surrender of the town, would not be ratified. He hastened to the house of his friend Colclough, to communicate this fatal news, and found this gentleman had already fled with his wife and child to one of the Saltee Islands, where he hoped to remain in concealment till the fury of the storm had abated.

Sir Richard Musgrave gives the following account of the apprehension of Harvey and Colclough, on the 23rd of June, in a cave, in one of the largest of the above-named islands, about ten leagues from Wexford :—" Dr. Waddy, *a physician* who served in the yeomanry, having got intelligence of their retreat, had applied to General Lake for a proper party and an armed vessel, to go in quest of them, which he readily obtained.

" On landing, they repaired to the only house on the island, occupied by one Furlong, who rented it from Mr. Colclough.

" They found there an excellent feather-bed, with fine sheets, which were warm, a handsome tea equipage, some genteel wearing apparel, belonging to both sexes, particularly, a pair of pantaloons, which Doctor Waddy had seen on Mr. Colclough, before the rebellion; and near the house some silk shoes and other articles, hid in high ferns. They searched every suspected spot in the island, particularly a place called the Otter's Cave, but in vain, though they had not a doubt of their having been there, as they had found among other things, a chest of plate, concealed in a place belonging to Colclough.

" The doctor resolved to make another effort by going round the island in a boat, for the purpose of reconnoitring the sides of it. In doing so, he perceived on the edge of a high precipice, one rock lighter coloured than the adjoining ones; and as the earth near it seemed to have been recently stirred, he suspected that they had been making preparations there for their concealment. He therefore again ascended the island, and found that the approach to the place which he wished to explore, was steep, serpentine, and through some crags. The light-coloured stone covered the mouth of the cave, and above it, there was an aperture to let in the light. The doctor called out to Colclough, and told him, that if he did not surrender immediately, and without resistance, he should receive no quarter. Colclough asked, ' Is that Doctor Waddy ?' and on his saying ' yes,' he said he would surrender ; and soon after he, at the doctor's desire, gave up his arms through the hole in the cave. The doctor threw down the precipice, the stone which covered the mouth of it, which fell with a monstrous crash, on which Mr. and Mrs. Colclough came forth, dressed in the meanest habits of peasants, for the purpose of disguising themselves. Then B. Harvey came out, saying, ' My God, my God !' and so pale and weak from fatigue and anxiety of mind, that the doctor was obliged to support him. He also had a chest of plate concealed, which he gave in charge to the doctor and his party.

" They arrived in Wexford Harbour, about nine at night; but as the tide was out, the prisoners could not be committed till next morning."*

The news of their arrival, we are told by Hay, " attracted a great number of people to the quay, curious to see them brought in; and amidst this concourse, Mr. Harvey and Mr. Colclough and his lady were landed. These gentlemen were then led through the gazing multitude to the gaol, where they were confined in the condemned cells."

Doctor Waddy, the acquaintance of these unfortunate gentlemen, who so kindly " supported" one of them on coming out of the cave, and beheld poor Colclough torn from his wife and child on the quay, when he was hurried to his prison the day following, must have been highly gratified with his successful practice, in the new branch of his honourable vocation. His claims to notoriety will not be forgotten, even by his professional brethren, though his name may be scrawled on a list of a very different description, from that on which a Hunter's, a Heberden's, or a Bailey's, are recorded.

On the 26th, Harvey and Mr. Cornelius Grogan, who had returned to his seat, at Johnstown, and had been arrested there, were brought to trial before a court martial.

Barrington says, " The semblance of a trial was thought necessary, by General Lake, before he could execute gentlemen of so much importance and fortune;" accordingly, General Craddock was appointed

---

* Sir R. Musgrave's Memoirs of the Different Rebellions. Quarto edition, p. 509.

president of the court martial. The proceedings were summarily and illegally conducted. " It was proved before parliament, when the attorney-general brought forward the bill of attainder, of high treason against these gentlemen, that the members of the court had not been sworn, and even the number of members belonging to it was short of the complement legally required to form a court."

A court thus constituted, had no obligation of a legal kind, " to administer justice according to the evidence." There was the name of a court martial, but the judicial forms were easily dispensed with, in this reign of terror, by one of the sternest advocates of its unmitigated rigour, General Lake. The mockery of a trial lasted for eight hours, evidence was adduced of Harvey having acted as general-in-chief of the rebel army at Ross, and of having summoned the garrison to surrender. He produced witnesses in his defence, to prove that in every instance of any part being taken by him in the affairs of the insurgents, he was constrained by the people to take on him the duties assigned to him. He had no counsel.

He pleaded his own cause, and, in his address to the court, he stated that " he had accepted the command to prevent much greater evils, which would accrue from its falling into other hands, and with the hope of surrendering the command sooner or later, and with greater advantage to the country." *
As to his political principles, he said his only object was to reform the constitution; and, with respect

* Taylor's History of the Rebellion, &c. p. 200.

to the exercise of any influence he possessed over the people, he had no other object or desire than to restrain their violence, and prevent the commission of sanguinary acts." There was abundant evidence of the truth of the most important of these statements; but such testimony was of no avail in the trials of 1798. Harvey was condemned, and executed the following day on the Bridge of Wexford, beside the venerable and innocent man, Cornelius Grogan, whose large estates—valued by Gordon at £8000, and by Cloney at £10,000 a-year—were the dangerous objects which attracted attention, and drew down the vengeance of the reckless men, who were privileged, in those days, to suspect the loyalty of those whose political sentiments were known to be favourable to reform, and especially of those who were independent in property as well as in their principles. The expectation of profiting by the confiscation of the property of those, who were known to be the friends of civil and religious liberty, had no slight influence on these and similar proceedings. It was the custom to pillage the houses of those who were executed, immediately after their execution; and the plunderers, on such occasions, were not the low rabble of military supplementaries, but the half-gentry, and even those of a higher rank. The rapacity of these persons, was not confined to the property of persons suspected of disaffection,—the houses of defenceless royalists were frequently plundered by them, as well as those of persons who were accounted rebels.

Of the indiscriminate ravages practised in the

county Wexford, the Rev. Mr. Gordon has given the following details :—

" The devastation and plundering sustained by the loyalists, was not the work of the rebels alone. Great part of the damage was committed by the soldiery, who commonly completed the ruin of deserted houses in which they had their quarters, and often plundered without distinction of Loyalist and Croppy. [He adds in a note]—I mean not to throw blame on any, who unpremeditatedly, and without neglect of their duty, shared the plunder of houses of reputed rebels, consigned to military depredation. Thus, doubtless, Lord Kingsborough thought his conduct blameless, when he went, the day after his liberation from Wexford, to Mr. Cornelius Grogan's house, and took out of the stable two coach-horses to sell. But if we should find the attention of any general officer so absorbed in a system of plunder, as to leave him no leisure for fighting, perhaps we might not think him so entirely blameless." *

Sir Richard Musgrave, in reference to Harvey's interference on behalf of the prisoners, and of his grief on the occasion of the frightful massacre of Scullabogue, while he reviles his political sentiments, speaks of him as " a man of honour and humanity, filled with the greatest horror on hearing of the massacre at Scullabogue."

" It has been said (continues Sir Richard) that Bagenal Harvey was deposed (after the battle of Ross), because he shewed a want of courage in this action ; but this is scarcely credible, for he displayed

* See Gordon's History, &c. p. 239.

very great firmness in various duels which he had fought in the course of his life." *

His political tendencies, he indeed denounces as of the most pernicious kind, and the grounds for this opinion are stated in the following terms:— " He was a sanguine reformer of our constitution, the various excellencies of which he was as incapable of discerning, as an insect is the grandeur and elegance of a magnificent edifice." †

A letter of Harvey's to Francis Glascott, Esq. while he was president of the rebel council of Wexford, throws much light on his character and position :—

" DEAR SIR,

" I received your letter, but what to do for you I know not; I from my heart wish to protect all property—I can scarce protect myself; and, indeed, my situation is much to be pitied, and distressing to myself. I took my present situation in hopes of doing good, and preventing mischief; my trust is in Providence. I acted always an honest, disinterested part; and had my advice been taken by those in power, the present mischief would never have arisen. If I can retire to a private station again, I will immediately. Mr. Tottenham's refusing to speak to the gentleman I sent to Ross, who was madly shot by the soldiers, was very unfortunate; it has set the people mad with rage, and there is no restraining them. The person I sent in, had

* Vide Sir Richard Musgrave's History and Appendix, p. 432.
† Ibid. p. 509.

private instructions to propose a reconciliation, but God knows where this business will end; but end how it will, the good men of both parties will be inevitably ruined.

"I am, with respect, yours,

"B. B. HARVEY."*

Musgrave acknowledges that Harvey lost his influence over the insurgents, and ultimately was obliged to give up the command, on account of his constant interference on behalf of those who had fallen into their hands. In fact, his whole anxiety appears to have been to preserve the lives and property of those who had fallen into the hands of the insurgents, from violence and spoliation. Evidence to this effect was given on his trial, but such evidence in proof of humanity on the part of a rebel, or one suspected, or feigned to be suspected of being one, was calculated to be injurious rather than beneficial to him. The rector of Killegny, in alluding to this fact, in the case of one Redmond, observes, "The display of humanity by a rebel was, in general, in the trials by court-martial, by no means regarded as a circumstance in favour of the accused; strange as it may seem in times of cool reflection, it was very frequently urged as a proof of guilt. Whoever could be proved to have saved a loyalist from assassination, his house from burning, or his property from plunder, was considered as having influence among the rebels, consequently a commander. This has been, by some, supposed to have arisen from a

* Vide Musgrave's History and Appendix, p. 143.

policy in government to discourage all ideas of
humanity in rebels, that, in case of another insurrection, they might be so completely sanguinary as
to render themselves and their cause as odious as
possible, and, consequently, unsupported. For my
part, I cannot easily believe the members of administration capable of so cruel a policy; and even if
private instructions for this mode of proceeding, had
been given to the officers of the army, I should be a
little surprised that yeoman officers should implicitly
adopt it, if they expected another insurrection, as in
that event their families or friends might be the
victims. In fact, it seems to have arisen from a rage
of prosecution, by which the crime of rebellion was
regarded as too great to admit any circumstances of
extenuation in favour of the person guilty of it, and
by which every mode of conviction against such a
person was deemed justifiable."*

He makes mention of the notoriety of this practice
having drawn the following extraordinary exclama-
tion, from a Roman catholic gentleman who had
been one of the rebels: "I thank my God that no
person can prove me guilty of saving the life or property of any one!"

Harvey was wholly destitute of those stern and
striking qualities, which would have secured him,
for any length of time, the confidence or respect of
a turbulent multitude. At the battle of Ross, Barrington states, he and his aide-de-camp, a protestant
attorney, Mr. Gray, continued inactive spectators of
the struggle, during ten hours incessant fighting.

* Vide Gordon's History of the Irish Rebellion, p. 228.

The morning after the atrocious massacre of the prisoners in the barn of Scullabogue, on the part of a set of miscreants, in their flight from Ross, after the defeat of the insurgents, we are informed by Cloney, that on his return to the camp, " he found Harvey, and several other of the leaders, lamenting over the smoking ruins that covered the ashes of the hapless victims of the infamous atrocity."—" Mr. Harvey, and every one of the leaders who had any influence, used every possible exertion to discover the perpetrators of this horrid deed, which brought such disgrace on the country, but in vain." A proclamation was immediately issued by Harvey, denouncing all similar enormities, robberies, and murders, as crimes that would be punished with death.

Mr. George Taylor, whose views are those of the ascendancy party, states, that Bagenal Harvey, the next morning, was in the greatest anguish of mind when he beheld Scullabogue barn.—" He turned from the scene with horror, and wrung his hands, and said to those about him : ' Innocent people were burned there as ever were born ; your conquests for liberty are at an end.' He said to a friend he fell in with, with respect to his own situation, ' I see now the folly of embarking in this business with these people : if they succeed, I shall be murdered by them ; if they are defeated, I shall be hanged.' "*

Harvey was married about two years before his death, to a Miss Stephens, niece to an innkeeper at Arcklow, who is still living. His estates, after having been confiscated, were restored to his brother, James

* Taylor's History, &c., p. 105.

Harvey, who resided mostly in England. The latter willed the principal part of the lands to a Mr. Harvey, a grandson of the late John Harvey, of Mount Pleasant. James Harvey died without issue. The attainder was reversed, but previously to its reversal he was permitted to farm the lands, and paid a rent to government until they were restored to him. The present possessors of that landed property are the children and grandchildren of the late John Harvey.

B. B. Harvey was about thirty-six years of age; he left no children. A gentleman who was living in Wexford at this frightful period, and to whom I am indebted for much of the preceding information, concludes his account of Bagenal Beauchamp Harvey in these words—" He was much beloved by the people—he was a kind and generous landlord, and very liberal to his workmen, whom he visited in their sickness, and afforded them every kind of relief, for his means were ample, his fortune being about £3,000 per annum, from lands in the county Wexford and county Carlow."

Harvey met his fate with becoming fortitude; even Sir Richard Musgrave acknowledges, " he died in a very decent manner, having been attended by a protestant clergyman, and having prayed most fervently." Hay, in his account of his execution, states that on the 27th, when he was brought out of his cell, " he met Mr. Grogan in the gaol-yard, and accosted him in a feeling and affectionate manner. While shaking hands with him, he said in the presence of an officer and some of the guards, and in the hearing of several prisoners who had crowded to the windows, 'Ah, poor Grogan! you die an innocent man, at all events.' They were then conducted to the bridge, where they were hanged, when the heads of Messrs. Grogan and Harvey were cut off, and placed upon pikes on each side of that of Captain Keogh (who had been some days previously executed), while their bodies were stripped, and treated with the usual brutal indecencies before being cast over the bridge. Mr. Colclough was executed on the day following; but his body, at the intercession of his lady, was given up to her to be interred. Mr. John Kelly, of Killan, whose courage and intrepidity had been so conspicuous at the battle of Ross, now lay ill in Wexford of a wound which he had received in that engagement—he was taken from his bed, tried, and condemned to die. His head was cut off, and his body, after the accustomed indignities, was thrown over the bridge. The head, however, was reserved for another exhibition—it was first kicked along the Custom-house quay, and then brought up into the town, and treated in the same manner opposite the house in which his sister lived," &c.*

The executioner of these unfortunate gentleman was a serjeant of the King's county militia, of the name of Dunn—a monster in the human form, whose brutality and ferocious cruelty has never been exceeded in any country—not even in France, in the worst times of the French Revolution. The clothes of each sufferer, he was accustomed to strip off the moment the body was cut down, in the presence of

* Hay's History of the Insurrection, &c., p. 252.

the victim next in turn for execution, then tied up
the effects in a handkerchief with the greatest
composure ; and proceeded with another victim, and
with a similar disposition of his perquisites. As the
generality of those executed on the Bridge of Wexford were persons of respectability in life, watches
and other valuable effects were not unfrequently
found on their persons, and these Serjeant Dunn was
in the habit of selling to the yeomanry rabble and
supplementaries, as rebel trophies, at the close of each
day's business. The heads of the persons executed,
he used to carry to his own house after the execution,
rolled up in the linen of each, and in the course
of the evening he proceeded to the town-house,
mounted the roof, and fixed the heads on pikes.

For a length of time, the Bridge of Wexford was a
fashionable lounge, for " the bucks and blades" of
the Wexfordian " ascendancy," and Sergeant Dunn
was wont to gather his evening group around him,
and regale his hearers with ludicrous anecdotes of
his official labours.

This brutal man, like one of the ermined jesters
of that day, enlivened the awful scenes in which he
acted a foremost part, by sallies of ribald humour,
and jibes and jokes in reference to the appalling
circumstances by which he was surrounded.   Sir R.
Musgrave gives a list of sixty-five rebel executions on
the Bridge of Wexford, subsequently to the re-occu-
pation of this town by the king's troops, but these
were chiefly men of some rank and station in society,
at least above the class of the common people.   The
executions in Wexford, during the first week of the

re-possession of it, exceeded the number stated by Sir R. Musgrave, as comprising the whole during a period of some months.

CORNELIUS GROGAN.

For the last four years of his life, Mr. Grogan had taken no part in politics. His chief amusement consisted in mechanical experiments.

In 1779, he filled the office of high sheriff for the county. He sat in parliament for the town of Enniscorthy, and on the dissolution of parliament, in 1790, he offered himself for the county of Wexford, and lost it by a small majority. He had two brothers in the yeomanry, the eldest, Captain Thomas Knox Grogan, was killed at the head of his corps, by the rebels, at the battle of Arklow; the other, Captain John Grogan, in 1796, chiefly at his own expense, raised the corps of the Healthfield Cavalry, and had been badly wounded in an action with the rebels. Yet the services of these men to their king and country, could not save their respected and venerable brother, then upwards of seventy years of age, from an ignominious death. Of his innocence of the crime laid to his charge, there could not have been the shadow of a doubt, on the minds of those who conspired against his life.

With respect to the attainder in his case, Sir Jonah Barrington observes, " The only charge the government (to excuse the culpability of General Lake) could prove, was his having been surrounded by the insurgent army, which placed him under surveillance, and who, to give importance to themselves, forced him one day into the town of Wexford, on horseback, a peasant of the name of Savage attending him, with a blunderbuss, with orders to shoot him if he refused to obey their commands. Against his will, they nominated him a commissary, knowing that his numerous tenantry would be more willing in consequence to supply them. He used no weapon of any description—too feeble even to hold one in his hand."

" A lady of the name of Segrave gave evidence, that her family in the town were in want of food, and that she sent to Mr. Grogan, to give her an order for some bread; which request, to save her family from starving, he reluctantly complied with. Through that order, she procured some loaves, and supplied her children; and for that act of benevolence, and on that lady's evidence, Mr. Grogan was sentenced to die as a traitor: and was immediately hanged and beheaded, when unable to walk to the place of execution, and already almost lifeless from age, imprisonment, pain, and brutal treatment. It appeared before parliament, upon interrogating the president of the court, that the members of the court-martial which tried him, had not been sworn—that they were only seven instead of thirteen, the usual number —that his material witness was shot by the military, while on the road between Johnstown Castle and Wexford, to give evidence of Mr. Grogan's entire innocence; and that while General Lake was making merry at dinner (with his staff and some members of the court that condemned him), one of the first gentlemen in the county (in every point far his superior), was hanged and mutilated almost before his windows. The author's intimate knowledge of Mr. Cornelius Grogan for many years, enables him to assert most unequivocally, and it is but justice to his memory to do so, that though a person of independent mind as well as fortune, and an opposition member of the Irish Parliament, he was no more a rebel than his brothers, who had signalized themselves in battle as royalists, and the survivor of whom was rewarded by the same government, by an unprecedented bill of attainder against that unfortunate gentleman, long after he was dead, by which his great estates were confiscated to the crown.

" This attainder bill was one of the most illegal and unconstitutional acts ever promoted by any government ; but, after much more than £10,000 costs to crown officers, and to Lord Norbury, as attorney-general, had been extracted from the property, the estates were restored to the surviving brother." *

When his enemies are compelled to speak in the following terms of his fate, we may fairly conclude that his judicial murder was wholly indefensible. Dr. Patrick Duigenan thus speaks of him in his ' Fair' Representation of the State and of Ireland :

" It is but justice to observe, that it is alleged in behalf of the late Cornelius Grogan, Esq., that his residence was only three miles from the town of Wexford ; that the rebellion broke out very suddenly and unexpectedly ; that his infirmities disabled him

* Vide Barrington's Rise and Fall, p 374.

from retreating from the rebels with that expedition which could give him any reasonable hopes of escape; that the rebels imagined the presumed countenance and support of a gentleman of his rank, would acquire credit to their cause, and when they had him in their power, they conferred on him what title they pleased, in which he was obliged to acquiesce, for the preservation of his life among such a savage banditti; and that he never acted as commissary-general of their army, or in any military capacity among them; and, indeed, it is very certain, that whatever title of general or commander they might have given him, he was utterly incapable of undertaking or performing any active service, being much advanced in years, and a great martyr to the gout." *

Sir Richard Musgrave, in commenting on the charges brought against him, of acting as commissary-general of the rebel army, declares—" It is most certain that this unfortunate gentleman never acted but from compulsion." †

Cornelius Grogan dying without issue—when the attainder was reversed, the property was restored to his nephew, John Grogan, and at his death went to his son, G. Grogan Morgan, the present proprietor of Johnstown Castle.

It now only remains to say a few words of the other companion in misfortune of Bagenal Harvey—

* Vide Duigenan's Fair Representation of the Present Political State of Ireland.

† Vide Sir Richard Musgrave's History, Appendix, p 135

JOHN HENRY COLCLOUGH, OF BALLYTEIGUE.

Taylor truly describes him as a gentleman of respectability, and one who bore a very excellent private character. He was a relative of Sir Vesey Colclough, who had represented Wexford and Enniscorthy in four successive Parliaments. " He was in his stature of a full middle size, had rather a long visage, wore his own hair, which was tied behind. He was about thirty years of age, of a cheerful aspect, and polished manners. Mr. Colclough was also executed on the 28th of June."* When Colclough and his lady, along with Bagenal Harvey, were brought into Wexford after their capture, the latter appeared pale and dejected; but "Mr. Colclough's fortitude (says Taylor) did not apparently forsake him until he approached the jail, where he beheld his friend Keogh's head on a spike. On inquiring whose head it was, and hearing it was Keogh's, he seemed like a man electrified, and sunk into all the anguish of despair *and guilt,* and never recovered any show of spirits." The only charge brought against him was, that he had been seen in the rebel forces at the battle of Ross. He admitted having been compelled to attend the general-in-chief to that place; but he proved that, at an early period of the day, he had taken the first opportunity afforded him of quitting the insurgent force, and returning to Wexford. The defence was of no avail: his death, like that of Grogan and Harvey, had been previously determined.

* Sir Richard Musgrave's History and Appendix, p 135.

John Henry Colclough left a widow and an infant child. His property was not large, and, being chiefly leasehold, no attainder was issued. His widow married a Mr. Young, a magistrate of the county, the present occupier of Ballyteigue. It is stated by Sir Richard Musgrave, that, a short time before his execution, he directed his son to be brought up in the Protestant religion : no such direction was ever given by Mr. Colclough. The circumstance of his being unattended, at the place of execution, by a clergyman of the church to which he belonged, was taken by Sir Richard Musgrave as an evidence of his conviction of " the errors of Romanism," and a probable reason for his desire to have his child brought up in another religion.

The fact is that Colclough, up to the last moment, expected a respite, from his intimacy with some of the officers of the army, then at Wexford, whose interference in his behalf he relied on. This expectation prevented him from calling to his assistance a Roman Catholic clergyman ; he thought, if he had done so, it would operate against him. It is only to be lamented, that any consideration should have so far weighed with one in his awful circumstances, as to deprive him of that spiritual assistance which he stood in need of at his last moments.

Such was the fate of three gentlemen of the highest respectability, of ample fortune, of honourable principles—against whom, at the period of their arrests, not one criminal act could be imputed, and the sole cause of the suspicion of whose loyalty, at the outbreak of the insurrection, and up to the period of Sir Jonah Barrington's prophetic speculations, consisted in their supposed adherence to the opinions of the opposition party, and their presumed attachment to the cause of parliamentary reform. For these "high crimes and misdemeanours," in the eyes of an Irish administration, they were permitted to be "sacrificed in the confusion of the times." Could these things have happened in England?—could they have happened in any other country than Ireland?—can the recurrence of such acts ever again be dreaded in that country? These are questions that must naturally suggest themselves to the people of both countries. With respect to the latter enquiry—so long as Ireland is not governed for a faction, but for the interests of the great body of the people, the question is one, the solution of which can only be inimical to the views of those, who attach more importance to the intolerant and intolerable pretensions of that faction, than to the integrity of the British Empire.

.

INDEX

TO THE FIRST VOLUME.

PAGE

Historical Introduction 1

" English connexion with Ireland . . . ..

" Usages of the Natives adopted by the Anglo-Norman
    settlers . . . .

" Policy of the Tudors to break down the power of the
    Anglo-Irish chiefs 2

" Confiscation of the lands of Leix and O'Fally under
    Mary . . . .

" Failure of efforts to introduce the Reformation . 3

" Claims to the Irish Sovereignty based on a Papal grant 4

" Plan of colonizing Ireland with English Protestants . 5

" Calamitous wars of Elizabeth's reign . . ..

" Colonies planted on forfeited estates of Earl of Des-
    mond . . . .

" Spread of the principles of Puritanism . . 6

" Change from Irish to English tenure of land . ..

" Revolution of landed property . . . ..

" The Commission of Grace, James I. . . ..

" Alleged plot of Tyrone, Tyrconnell, and O'Doherty 7

" Plea for confiscation of Six Northern Counties . ..

" Plans of James for the plantation of Ulster . . 8

" Obligation to erect Bawns or fortified places . ..

" Grants to the City of London; Coleraine and Lon-
    donderry built . . . .

HISTORICAL INTRODUCTION :   PAGE

" New Order of Baronets created . . . 8

" Forfeited estates granted to Scotch settlers, James I. ..

" Do. do. to Mendicant Courtiers, &c. do. . 9

" Origin of the land-jobbing and sub-letting system . ..

" Sanctioned by the City of London . . . ..

" Exhaustion of the stock of forfeited estates . . ..

" Half-a-million of acres previously confiscated . 10

" Another half-million added, on the plea of defective
        titles . . . .

" Subsidy granted to Charles I. on condition of reli-
        gious toleration. . . . . ..

" Money taken, conditions not fulfilled . ..

" Wentworth Earl of Strafford's administration . .

" Attempt to confiscate the entire province of Connaught ..

" Jury opposed to it brought before the Star Chamber . 11

" Puritanism, spread of, conspiracy of natives . . 12

" Veto of Parliament that Popery should be exterminated ..

" Consequent impossibility of conciliating the natives . 13

" Cromwell's arrival, massacres of Drogheda and Wex-
        ford 14

" Puritans masters of Ireland . . . 15

" Cromwell's wholesale confiscations . . . ..

" His Spartan edict, " To Hell or Connaught !" . ..

" Catholics expelled from all walled towns . . ..

" Cromwell's soldiers' representation to Charles II.
        before his accession 16

" Court of Claims to settle disputes about forfeited lands 17

" The Acts of Settlement, legalization of general con-
        fiscations . . . .

" Accession of James II. dismissal of the deputation of
        Irish gentlemen 18

" Tyrconnell's aim to preserve the English interest,
        and destroy Protestant ascendancy . . ..

HISTORICAL INTRODUCTION :—   PAGE

" James II.'s efforts to prevent the Irish gaining the
victory at the Boyne 18

" ———————— to prevent the repeal of the Act
of Settlement . . . .

" Act of Settlement repealed 19

" Flight of James, and new confiscations . . ..

" Nine-tenths of the property of the Country in the
hands of the Settlers . . . . ..

" Penal Laws devised for securing the confiscated lands 20

" Unparalleled barbarity of this code . . . ..

" Spoliation, not fanaticism, the motive for its enactment 21

" Irish Whigs, in Swift's day, inclined to Presbyterianism 22

" A Protestant mob broke into House of Lords, placed
an old woman on the throne . . . ..

" Aspirations for a Protestant republic . . 23

" Checked by the dread of the Irish Catholics . ..

" " The spawn of the Old Covenant " . . ..

" The Calf's-head Anniversary, 30th Jan. in the North 24

" Unvarying picture of Protestant oppression and
Popish insurgency 25

" Whiteboyism, the effect of " misery, oppression,
famine " . . . .

" Origin of Volunteers 26

" Inconsistencies of Volunteers in seeking Reform without Catholic Emancipation . . . ..

" Venality of Irish Parliament . . . 27

" Extermination system in Armagh . . . 28

" United Irishmen, no bond of union between those of
the North and South 31

" Effects of Lord Fitzwilliam's recall . . . 32

" ——— of the barbarities of the French Revolution . ..

" Anomalous position of the Roman Catholic Clergy . ..

" Object and effects of coercion . . . 33

HISTORICAL INTRODUCTION :— PAGE

" New organization of the Society of United Irishmen 33

" Daring project proposed at Belfast . . . 34

" Causes of the failure of the plans of United Irishmen ..

" Calamities attendant on its suppression . . ..

THE UNITED IRISHMEN :—

Eventful period between 1782 and 1798 . . 39

Disabilities of Roman Catholics in the early part of the
    reign of George III. 41

Origin of the Volunteers 44

Objects of ditto . . . .

Conventions of ditto 45

Independence of Irish Parliament . . . 46

Flood's objections to the mode of adjustment . . ..

Pitt's sentiments in reference to this measure . . ..

Grattan's conduct ditto 47

Debate on ditto 48

Sir Simon Bradstreet and Mr. Walsh on ditto . . 50

Illusory nature of the Parliamentary Independence . 51

Necessity felt for Reform and Catholic Emancipation . ..

Mistaken views of Volunteers with regard to the latter . 52

Proceedings of the Volunteers of as questionable a nature
    as those of the United Irishmen . . . ..

Lord Charlemont's opinion of these measures . . 53

Flood's plan of Reform 54

Bishop of Derry in favour of immediate emancipation . ..

Mr. Fitzgibbon's violent denunciations . . . 55

——————, his early declarations in favour of Par-
    liamentary Independence . . . ..

——————, his subsequent advocacy of Union . ..

Hon. Robert Stewart a member of the Convention . 56

Hostility of Government to the Institution . . 57

The services of the Volunteers over-rated . . 58

PAGE

Their proceedings with regard to Catholic Emancipation. 60

Messrs. Fitzgerald, Burrowes, Ogle, Sir Boyle Roche, on
    Catholic Emancipation, in Convention .   . ..

Lord Kenmare and Sir P. Bellew, correspondence with . 61

Dr. Lucas and Lord Charlemont opposed to Emancipation 62

The Society of United Irishmen sprung from the ashes
    of the Volunteer Association .   .   . 63

— First Society of United Irishmen advocates of Reform
    and Emancipation 65

The incongruous association of persons in the Volunteer
    Association 66

Address of Col. Sharman, Col. Rowley, &c. to Volunteers 67

Hon. Robert Stewart a Reformer in 1783 .   . 67

Theobald Wolfe Tone, ditto in 1791 .   . 68

Volunteer plan of Reform in 1783 .   .   . 70

Grattan, sentiments respecting office, in 1785 .   . 74

Mr. Pitt's propositions in 1785 .   .   . ..

Grattan's speech on ditto 76

The " Incipient Creeping Union," discovered in the pro-
    positions 79

Messrs. Grattan, Ponsonby, Daly, &c. invited to London
    in 1795 82

Consultations with Lord Fitzwilliam and the Duke of
    Portland .   .   .   .

The terms of the Irish Members .   .   . ..

Dissolution of the Volunteers in 1793. .   . 83

Lord Fitzwilliam and the Beresfords .   .   . 84

Lord Fitzwilliam's letters, on his recall, to the Earl of
    Carlisle 85

The Eleven Propositions' debate in England .   . 94

——————————————— Ireland .   . 97

De Lolme, in 1787, recommended a Union .   . 98

Mr. Williams, in 1787, wrote a pamphlet also in its favour ..

PAGE

The Annual Register, in 1790, plainly announced the
    necessity of it 99
Mr. Pitt and the Reform Clubs in England . . 100
Mr. Reeves' Association ' 101
Democratic doctrines, those expressed by Duke of Norfolk ..
———————————, by Mr. Pitt, the Duke of Richmond 102
———————————, by Mr. Erskine, Mr. Grey, Major
    Cartwright 104
Reform Meeting in 1782 at the Thatched House . ..
Mr. Pitt and John Horne Tooke . . . 106
The English Political Clubs, from 1778 to 1795 . 107
Society for Constitutional Information, origin and pro-
    ceedings 108
Friends of the People, ditto 109
Revolution Society, ditto 110
Friends of Universal Peace, &c., ditto . . . ..
Westminster Committee of Reform, ditto . . ..
Society of United Englishmen, ditto . . . 111
London Corresponding Society, ditto . . . ..
National Convention . . . .
Origin of Trades' Unions traced to a suggestion of Sir
    W. Jones 112
Manchester Constitutional Society . . . 113
Whig Club 114
Irish Political Clubs and Societies . . . 115
The Whig Club . . . .
The Northern Whig Club . . . . ..
Friends of Parliamentary Reform . . . 116
——— of the Constitution, Liberty, and Peace . ..
The various Volunteer Clubs . . . . ..

PAGE

THE ILLEGAL SOCIETIES IN IRELAND FROM 1784.

Peep-of-day Boys, or Protestant Boys, or Wreckers, or
    Orangemen   119
Orange Society, origin and acts of   .   .   . 121
Rules submitted to Grand Lodge in 1798; T. Verner,
    President, J. C. Beresford, Secretary .   . 123
Lord Gosford's address to Armagh magistrates   . ..
Oath of Orangemen 125
Purple Test .   .   .   .
Government declared the Parent and Protector of these
    Societies, by A. O'Connor   .   . 126
———————— introduce Bills of Indemnity to protect
    their members.   127
Orange Societies the cause of the terror which drove the
    people into rebellion .   .   .   . ..
The Skinners' Alley Aldermen   .   .   . 128
Orangeism a matter of land and money, rather than
    religion   130
The conversion of the soil of the old inhabitants to the
    use of the new settlers .   .   .   . ..
The conversion of souls a secondary consideration   . ..
Agrarian outrages   131
The White Boys   132
The Defenders   .   .   .   .
The Right Boys   133
———————— merging into United Irishmen   . 134
————————, James Napper Tandy, interview with 135
United Irishmen's Society, Tone's account of .   . ..
First Members of ditto   .   .   .   . ..
A Secret Committee so early as 1791 .   .   . ..
Declaration and Test of United Irishmen, Belfast   . 136
A. H. Rowan and Dr. Drennan leaders in Dublin   . 138
Butler and Bond committed to Newgate, 1793 .   . ..

PAGE

Address to the Volunteers in 1792 . . . 139

A. H. Rowan committed to Newgate, 1794 . . ..

Sheriffs Giffard and Jenkins 141

The Tailors' Hall, in Back Lane, the place of meeting
 of United Irishmen 143

The Tholsel, place of meeting of Volunteers, &c. . ..

The civil organization of the United Irish Society . 144

——————————— calculated to excite suspicion 146

Imprudence of the press of the United Irishmen . ..

The employment of Spies and Informers on the part of
 Government 147

Government, at an early period, informed of their proceedings . . . .

Carnot's knowledge of the meditated Union . . 148

Emmett's examination respecting Government's knowledge of their proceedings . . . 149

Treachery on the parts of the agents of both parties . ..

Mr. W. Cox, editor of the Union Star . . 150

The United Irishmen had friends in the highest quarters 151

Col. L. the friend of Lord Edward Fitzgerald . . 152

The new organization of the United Irishmen . . 153

Letter from a Catholic leader to Tone . . 154

Conference between Tone and Emmett . . ..

Tone's departure from Ireland . . . 155

Correspondence with France . . . . ..

Early views of Tone and Russell respecting independence ..

Tone attributes his opinions on this subject to Sir L.
 Parsons 156

Sir Laurence Parsons' Poem 157

Determination of Directory to seek foreign assistance,
 1796 158

Arrival of a French Agent in 1796 . . . ..

Bantry Bay expedition . . . . ..

PAGE

Lewins sent to France as Agent of the Directory, in
    March, 1797 (printed 1799, at) . . 158
Dr. M'Nevin sent to France in June, 1797 . . ..
Amount of succours demanded . . . 159
French Armament in the Texel . . . ..
Last application for French succour, in Jan. 1798 . ..
Expedition under Hoche 160
Number of Troops, destination, and result of ditto . 163
Military organization of the Society of United Irishmen
    in 1796 166
Total effective force . . . .
Duties of Military Committee 169
Period of Emmett, O'Connor, and M'Nevin becoming
    United Irishmen . . . . ..
Plan of Insurrection, March, 1798 . . . 170
Effective Force estimated by Lord E. Fitzgerald . ..
Views of Lord E. Fitzgerald with respect to "the Rising" 171
First objects of the United Irishmen . . . 179
Those of the Belfast leaders 180
Belfast Politics, Henry Joy, 1794 . . . 181
First efforts in the North in favour of Catholic emanci-
    pation 182
Declaration of views with respect to Reform . . ..
Names of the Belfast Reformers in 1792 . . 184
Change of sentiments, dinner to Lord Castlereagh in 1816 ..
Belfast celebration of the French Revolution, 1792 . ..
Belfast address to the National Assembly . . 190
Reply of the National Assembly . . . 194
Belfast address, on the subject of Reform, to the people
    of Ireland 196
Declarations of Reform Societies of Belfast . . 198
Early knowledge of the Government of the plans of the
    United Irishmen 205

PAGE

Rev. W. Jackson's Mission to Ireland discovered . 205

Employment of Spies and Informers .   .   . 206

Cockayne, Dutton, M'Gucken, Newell, Magin, Hughes . .

Arrest of the Leinster Provincial Committee at Bond's. 208

Time of the intended rising 209

" The premature explosion" occasioned by free quarters 210

Policy of allowing a people to go into rebellion which

    might have been suppressed .   .   . . .

Mr. H. M. Morres communication to Government . 211

Mr. Thomas Reynolds, the Informer .   .   . 212

Persons arrested at Bond's 213

Bond's trial, conviction, reprieve, and death .   . 214

Reynolds, rencontre with S. Neilson .   .   . 215

———————, proposed assassination of .   .   . 219

——— ———, his insinuation against Felix Rourke, on the

    subject of the information given to Government 224

———————, his first disclosures to Mr. Cope, and subse-

    quent stipulations 225

Process through which Informers usually pass before

    their appearance in the witness box .   . 227

Arrests of Emmett, M'Nevin, and Lord E. Fitzgerald . 228

Reynolds connected with the Fitzgerald family—his

    early history, marriage, &c. .   .   . 229

———————, difference with Mr. Cope—difficulties in

    meeting his engagements—retirement from busi-

    ness—obtaining possession of Kilkea Castle . 230

———————, his money matters with the old blind servant,

    B. Cahill—mistake about her bond—his mother's

    death, &c. 231

———————, his mother-in-law's death—his administra-

    tion of medicine to her, &c. .   .   . 232

———————, impeachment of his evidence .   . 234

———————, number of oaths he had taken .   . . .

PAGE

Reynolds, Kilkea Castle 236

————, free quarters and half-hangings there . ..

————, his estimated losses . . . 237

————, the amount of public money received by him 238

————, his intimacy with Lord E. Fitzgerald . 243

Lord E. Fitzgerald's interference respecting the lease of
Kilkea Castle 242

Reynolds's presents to Lord E. Fitzgerald . . 244

————, his visits to Lord Edward, and subsequently
to his lady 245

————, his visit of condolence to Mrs. Bond . ..

———— reimbursed for his presents to Lord Edward . 246

————, certificates of his disinterested conduct, &c. 247

————, his name on the Westminster Grand Jury
List in 1817 249

————, The press of London, and the walls of Parliament, ring with denunciations on this occasion 251

————, Lord Castlereagh appoints him Consul at
Iceland 250

————, his squabble with Mr. Cooke . . 251

————, Mr. Canning's refusal to employ him . 252

————, his retirement from public service, and death 253

Nicholas Murphy's narrative of the arrest of Lord E.
Fitzgerald 255

Bond's death 269

Rev. Denis Taafe, his exploits at Ballyellis . . 277

————————————, a brief memoir of his life and death . 290

The discovery of Lord E. Fitzgerald . . . 299

His rencontre with Major Sirr's party, in Watling-street ..

M'Cabe, Palmer, Ralligan, and Gallagher . . 301

The initials of the man who betrayed Lord E. Fitzgerald,
and the reward received by that person . 306

Exculpation of Samuel Neilson and Nicholas Murphy . 307

PAGE

J. Hughes, some account of his career . . 308

———, his visits to Neilson, to Lord E. Fitzgerald,
and Mr. Grattan 310

———, his evidence before the Secret Committee . 311

Conference on the subject of an immediate rising, with
the following persons— . . . 313

Anthony M'Cann, the hero of Campbell's " Exile of Erin" ..

Mr. Samuel Turner . . . .

Col. James Plunkett . . . .

Mr. Cumming, of Galway . . . . ..

Dr. M'Nevin 314

Rev. A. M'Mahon, of Hollywood . . . ..

Mr. Magenniss of Balcaly . . . . ..

Mr. A. Lowry . . . . . .

Messrs. Byrne, of Dundalk . . . . ..

Division between the County Down and Antrim Colonels ..

Flight of M'Mahon, Rollo Reid, and Magennis . .

Hughes's evidence respecting Neilson and Grattan . 315

———, his allegation of Neilson swearing in Grattan . 316

——— employed as a Spy and Informer . . 320

———, rencontre with J. H. . . . 321

———, confined with Dr. Steele Dixon . . ..

———, employed conjointly with Magin as Spies . 322

———, his visit to Lord E. Fitzgerald, and object of it 324

———, his pay and quarters at the Castle . . ..

Discovery of Lord E. Fitzgerald . . . 325

J. Magin, the informer of Saintfield . . . 326

The Rev. John Cleland, Lord Castlereagh's tutor, &c. ..

Magin's services, and their reward . . . 327

J. M'Gucken, Attorney, ditto . . . 328

Mr. Getty's arrest and imprisonment . . . 330

Hughes's subsequent fate 331

The use of Torture in Ireland in 1798. . . 333

PAGE

The use of Torture, in Wicklow, Wexford, and Kildare   335

——————————, taws, pickets, triangles, pitch-caps, &c.   ..

—————————— deprecated by Englishmen .   . 336

——————————, Lord Castlereagh's denial of   . 336

——————————, Beccaria's and Blackstone's opinion of   337

——————————, Sir R. Musgrave's defence .   . ..

——————————, persons who had recourse to   . ..

——————————, Finnerty's trial, in 1810 .   . ..

——————————, Sir John Moore an eye-witness of .   ..

Case of Mr. Wright 347

Burning of houses .   .   .   .

Case of Mr. Perry .   .   .   .

Inventor of the Pitch-cap .   .   . 349

Mr. Hunter Gowan's trophy .   .   . 350

Burning of the rebel hospital at Enniscorthy .   . 352

Conduct of the Hessians .   .   .   . ..

Arrests by Lord Castlereagh, executed by his lordship . ..

Case of Bergan 357

Lord Moira's speech on coercion .   .   . 358

Massacre at the Gibbet Rath of Kildare .   . 363

Lord Roden's Fencibles .   .   .   . ..

Massacre at Kilcomney 364

Case of Patrick Fitzpatrick's family .   .   . 366

Total loss during the Rebellion on both sides .   . 368

The Massacre at Scullabogue .   .   . 369

—————— on the Bridge of Wexford .   . 371

—————— at Vinegar-hill .   .   . 372

King's troops employed during the rebellion .   . ..

Force of the Rebels throughout the Country .   . 373

Compensation to suffering loyalists .   .   . 374

Total expenditure of suppressing rebellion and carrying
    the Union 377

Memoir of Harvey, Grogan and Colclough .   . 381

PAGE

Case of John Colclough, of Tintern Abbey　　.　　.　408

Mr. Grandy's informations　　.　　　.　　　.　　　.　..

———————— services　　.　　　.　　　.　　.　409

John Colclough, of Tintern, attempt to implicate　　.　409

Proclamation to prevent persons leaving Ireland with-

　　out passport .　　.　　　.　　　.　　.　410

—————————————— artificers, tradesmen, &c. &c.　..

Military force at Wexford　　.　　.　　　.　　　.　..

Vinegar Hill, camp at　　.　　.　　　.　　　.　..

Wexford abandoned .　　.　　.　　　'　　.　412

Rebel force under B. B. Harvey　　.　　.　　.　413

Carousing of the leaders at Ross　　.　　.　　.　..

Drunkenness of the rebels　　.　　.　　　.　　.　..

Furlong, with a flag of truce, shot　　.　　.　　.　414

Cullimore, a Quaker, preventing a massacre of prisoners　415

Battle of Ross　　.　　.　　　.　　　.　　.　..

———— Vinegar-hill .　　.　　　.　　　.　　.　..

Apprehension of Harvey and Colclough　　.　　.　418

Trials of Harvey, Colclough and Grogan　　.　　.　420

Harvey's conduct at Scullabogue　　.　　.　　.　426

Execution of Harvey, Grogan and Colclough .　　.　429

Memoir of Cornelius Grogan .　　.　　.　　.　431

———— John Henry Colclough　　.　　.　　.　433

END.

D

Printed by E BREWSTER, Hand Court, Dowgate

J. MADDEN & Co.'s

LIST OF RECENT PUBLICATIONS.

In 8 vols. 8vo. cloth, £5 12s.,

HISTORY of BRITISH INDIA. By the late JAMES MILL, Esq.

Fourth Edition, with Notes and Illustrations, and a continuation of the History, by H. H. WILSON, Esq., M.A, F R S., Boden Professor of Sanscrit in the University of Oxford Vols. I to VI already published. Vols. VII. and VIII. preparing for immediate publication.

" With all its merits, therefore, something was wanting before ' Mill's History of British India' could take rank as a standard national work. The deficiencies have now been amply supplied ; indeed, no living man could be found better able to correct Mr Mill's errors, and modify his too sweeping conclusions, than Professor H. H Wilson, a distinguished Oriental scholar, long a resident in India, and familiar with the habits and manners of its diversified inhabitants."*Athenæum.*

" There is scarcely, perhaps, another man in England so well qualified to undertake a new edition of this great work as the Boden Professor of Sanscrit at Oxford. Mr. Wilson brings to the labour an intimate knowledge of the literature and history of the East, and has already rendered important services to his country by his labours In editing a new edition of ' Mill's History of India,' there is much to be done, which Mr. Wilson is well able to do, and which, as far as these volumes enable us to judge, he will do with the best effect, in correcting the numerous errors of opinion as well as fact which are scattered through that great work. Mr. Wilson's notes are full and well to the purpose ; and, upon the whole, this work, thus edited, is likely to form an era in the historical literature of the age."--*Atlas.*

In One Volume, post 8vo , price 5s

THE EAST-INDIA VOYAGER ; or Ten Minutes Advice to the Outward-bound. By EMMA ROBERTS.

"The manner of the ' East India Voyager' is as agreeable as its matter is curiously instructive. To the general reader many of the facts will seem minute, but looking at the persons for whom the volume is primarily designed, this is a necessity and a merit."—*Spectator.*

" This work is of a very superior class to Williamson's, or even the celebrated Dr. Gilchrist's ' Vade Mecum ' It gives excellent instruction to the ' Outward-bound Griffin,' and we recommend the book to their especial notice. Whether Cadet or Civilian, the reader will find a vast quantity of useful information on those very points on which he most needs it ; because they are points which every one is supposed to know something about, and yet in fact knows nothing, till too late to profit by knowledge The directions in the ' East India Voyager ' are excellent. With Miss Roberts's book in hand, we cannot fancy a more agreeable mode of passing the tedious voyage out."—*Naval and Military Gazette.*

In 2 vols. post 8vo., Maps.

NOTES of a HALF-PAY in SEARCH of HEALTH;

or, Russia, Circassia, and the Crimea, in 1839-40. By Captain W. Jesse, Unattached.

" Nothing extenuate, nor set down aught in malice."

" We have rarely met with a pleasanter brace of volumes, nor is their liveliness by any means their only recommendation They comprise a great body of novel and interesting information, and touch upon many important features of the countries to which they refer. Captain Jesse has given us a better insigh into the habits, and manners, and institutions of Russia than any modern author."—*United Service Gazette.*

" His style is pleasant and gossiping, as well as descriptive and easy; and he takes his reader along with him in that pleasant seductive style which forms the charm of such works."—*Globe.*

"Whatever may have been the degree of ennui of which he may have cured himself, we are quite satisfied that the most inveterate dyspeptic cannot peruse his notes without deriving more benefit from them than from the prescriptions of a dozen doctors Let all, therefore, who may labour under the disease ' throw physic to the dogs,' and gird up their loins through two volumes of Russia, Circassia, and the Crimea, with our friend the *Demi-Solde*, and we will guarantee them against a recurrence of this complaint "—*Naval and Military Gazette.*

" Captain Jesse's volumes are never tedious. The style is gay, removed from flippancy on the one hand and seriousness on the other. In his tours he has collected a large amount of information, and placed it before us in an agreeable form. Those who can be content to enjoy plain sense in plain language, who love truth more than metaphor, and who think facts preferable to fine writing, we advise to consult ' Captain Jesse's Notes;' certain that they will not fail to derive considerable pleasure from their perusal."—*Britannia.*

In one closely-printed Volume, post 8vo , nearly 600 p   s.

WHAT TO OBSERVE ; or, the Traveller's Remem-

brancer By Colonel J. R. Jackson, Secretary to the Royal Geographical Society. In this portable volume are propounded questions on almost every subject of human investigation. The ignorant in such matters are taught, the well-informed are reminded, What they Should Observe. in order to derive all possible information and benefit from their travels; and the least scientific will find that they may, by the simple observation and collection of facts, as pointed out in the present work, confer immense benefits on science, and greatly promote the spread of useful and interesting knowledge

" This volume may be declared to be a library in itself It contains so much information in the shape of instruction to travellers, ' *What to Observe*,' that it makes travelling for the sake of acquiring knowledge almost superfluous. We may learn what we wish so fully from its pages. that our reading room may answer most of the purposes of a fatiguing journey over distant lands. It is, indeed, an excellent work, systematic, comprehensive, intelligent, and so full of useful matter, that it seems as if nothing had been forgotten."—*Lit. Gaz. June 26th.*

In 2 vols. 8vo., cloth, price 1*l.* 1*s.*

MAJOR SIR WILLIAM LLOYD'S NARRATIVE

of a JOURNEY from CAUNPOOR to the Borendo Pass, in the Himalaya Mountains, viâ Gwalior, Agra, Delhi, and Sirhind : with Captain ALEXANDER GERARD's Account of an Attempt to penetrate by Bekhur to Garoo, and the Lake Mansarovara, &c. &c. &c. With Maps. Edited by GEORGE LLOYD.

" Pioneers through a region daily acquiring a greater degree of national importance, the accounts of these various and toilsome journeys among the lofty Himalaya mountains must excite a strong feeling of interest, not only in the minds of those connected with our Indian Empire, but of every reader for whom the grandest scenery of nature possesses attractions, and the daring spirit of human enterprise furnishes a theme of curiosity and admiration."—*Literary Gazette.*

" A more valuable and engaging work we would strive in vain at this moment to name among the recent mass of new books. * * * The Major writes not only as a Christian should do, but like a frank soldier. We are pleased to find his sentiments as healthy as they are elegant and elevated."—*Monthly Review.*

" Sir William Lloyd is by no means a dull writer, and his journal cannot fail to be interesting. The portions of the work contributed by the two Gerards are valuable. Geographical science is highly indebted to these two indefatigable gentlemen, who may indeed be said to have sacrificed their lives in its service."—*Asiatic Journal.*

" Of the three tours, the two by the enterprising brothers Gerard, were purely scientific in their objects. * * * Major Sir W. Lloyd's contribution is in the form of a journal ; and is the most popular portion of the work, not merely for the subjects he handles, but for the character of the man."—*Spectator.*

" These are two volumes of exceeding value and interest "—*Britannia.*

In One Volume, 8vo. cloth, large Original Map, price 14*s.*

CAPTAIN ALEXANDER GERARD'S ACCOUNT

of KOONAWUR in the HIMALAYA, &c. &c. Edited by GEORGE LLOYD.

What has already been published (MAJOR SIR W. LLOYD AND CAPT. GERARD'S TOURS IN THE HIMALAYA, 2 VOLS. 8vo. 21s.) together with what is contained in this, completes all Captain A. Gerard's Observations and Journeys in the Himalaya.

" It is a *multum in parvo.* Unquestionably it will be regarded as a precious contribution to science and geographical knowledge. Every page of it exhibits enthusiasm, manly earnestness and philosophical simplicity of character. There is an exactitude and good faith, together with a generous appreciation in all that is said of the tribes and races spoken of, that must endear the narrative to readers of every description. True, the contents are very frequently of a scientific nature, but even then the descriptions are so plain and straightforward, and the things described so wonderful and striking, that the feelings and imagination are carried irresistibly along."—*Monthly Review.*

" Intelligence of much interest will be found in every part of this Volume, which we cordially recommend, in connexion with Mr. and Sir W. Lloyd's former publication."—*Literary Gazette.*

In one volume 8vo. price 7s 6d.

MEMOIR on the COUNTRIES about the CASPIAN

and ARAL SEAS, illustrative of the late Russian Expedition against Khiva. Translated from the German. By Captain MORIER, R.N. With a Map by John Arrowsmith.

" This is purely a scientific work, treated in a scientific manner, and as unlike the flashy, unsatisfactory, and ephemeral tours that are abundantly published, as light is to darkness. This book contains facts valuable to all ages, and is a sort of landmark by which to note that silent progress of alternation which is slowly changing the face of the crust of this globe. This book, though a small one, is eminently deserving of a conspicuous station in all well-provided libraries, and we recommend it also to the attention of the general reader."—*Metropolitan, March.*

" This is an invaluable work to the geographer, the statist, the student of military strategy, who extends his speculations to Asia; and indeed, to all who are interested in positive facts Lieutenant Zimmermann, assisted by Von Humboldt, and other scientific men of eminence, has brought together all that is known of Khiva, and the districts adjacent to the Caspian and Aral Seas, and classified and digested the facts he has collected. The positions of places, the height of mountains, the character of the country, the number and names of its productions, both animal and vegetable, and a tabular view of the tribes which inhabit it, will all be found in this small volume. There is also some general information; the most interesting part consisting of observations on the former and present state of Western Central Asia, ' ascribed to the Graf Von Cancrin.' A Map by Arrowsmith, after the original, accompanies the volume "—*Spectator.*

Edited by MAJOR SABINE, F.R.S.

REAR-ADMIRAL VON WRANGELL's NARRATIVE

of his EXPEDITION to SIBERIA and the POLAR SEA Undertaken by order of the Russian Government, with a view to the Discovery of a supposed Polar Continent. In 1 thick 8vo vol with a Map, engraved from the Original Survey, by J. and C. WALKER.

" There are three principal points in which the interest and importance combined in this volume are eminently deserving of consideration, and which render it altogether one of the most valuable contributions to the great inquiry respecting the Arctic Regions, which at any time issued from the press. In the first place, it opens a new hope that this sea may be safely and successfully navigated. In the second place, it affords us a connected chain of history, which unfolds the circumstances of preceding explorations; and in the third place, it gives us a narrative of personal adventure, and an account of native life and manners, which is at once very affecting and extremely curious. With these advantages, Von Wrangell's ' Narrative' must meet with a cordial reception."—*Literary Gazette, June*

" There is scarcely a page which does not contain something interesting in the description of nature or man, or some particulars of hardship or anxious adventure."—*Spectator.*

" The volume before us is almost the first work of the kind published under the authority of a Russian discoverer; and the value of its details is considerably increased by a sketch of former voyages of a similar nature, of which no account has ever appeared before "—*Atlas.*

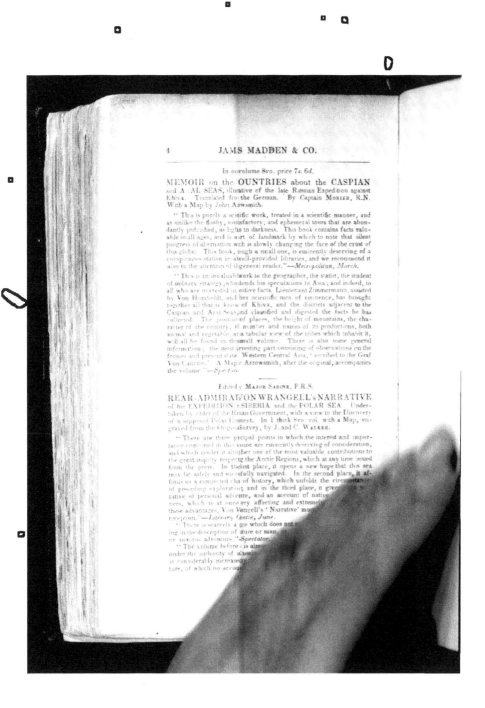

4 JAMS MADDEN & CO.

In one volume 8vo. price 7s. 6d.

MEMOIR on the OUNTRIES about the CASPIAN and A AL SEAS, illustrative of the late Russian Expedition against Khiva. Translated from the German. By Captain MORIER, R.N. With a Map by John Arrowsmith.

" This is purely a scientific work, treated in a scientific manner, and as unlike the flashy, unsatisfactory, and ephemeral tours that are abundantly published, as light to darkness. This book contains facts valuable to all ages, and is a sort of landmark by which to note that silent progress of alternation wch is slowly changing the face of the crust of this globe. This book, ough a small one, is eminently deserving of a conspicuous station in a well-provided libraries, and we recommend it also to the attention of the general reader."—*Metropolitan, March.*

" This is an invaluable work to the geographer, the statist, the student of military strategy, who tends his speculations to Asia; and indeed, to all who are interested in native facts. Lieutenant Zimmermann, assisted by Von Humboldt, and her scientific men of eminence, has brought together all that is know of Khiva, and the districts adjacent to the Caspian and Aral Seas, and classified and digested the facts he has collected. The position of places, the height of mountains, the character of the country, the number and names of its productions, both animal and vegetable, an a tabular view of the tribes which inhabit it, will all be found in this small volume. There is also some general information; the most interesting part consisting of observations on the former and present state 'Western Central Asia,' ascribed to the Graf Von Cancrin.' A Map by Arrowsmith, after the original, accompanies the volume."—*Spectator.*

Edited y MAJOR SABINE, F.R.S.

REAR-ADMIRAL VON WRANGELL's NARRATIVE of his EXPEDITION SIBERIA and the POLAR SEA. Undertaken by order of the Russian Government, with a view to the Discovery of a supposed Polar Continent. In 1 thick 8vo. vol. with a Map, engraved from the Original survey, by J. and C. WALKER.

" There are three principal points in which the interest and importance combined in this volume are eminently deserving of consideration, and which render it altogether one of the most valuable contributions to the great inquiry respecting the Arctic Regions, which at any time issued from the press. In the first place, it opens a new hope that this sea may be safely and successfully navigated. In the second place, it affords us a connected chain of history, which unfolds the circumstances of preceding exploration; and in the third place, it gives a narrative of personal adventure, and an account of native ters, which is at once very affecting and extremely these advantages, Von Wrangell's 'Narrative' mu reception."—*Literary Gazette, June.*

" There is scarcely a ge which does not ing in the description of ture or man, er anxious adventure."—*Spectator.*

" The volume before is alm under the authority of a is considerably increased ture, of which no accoun

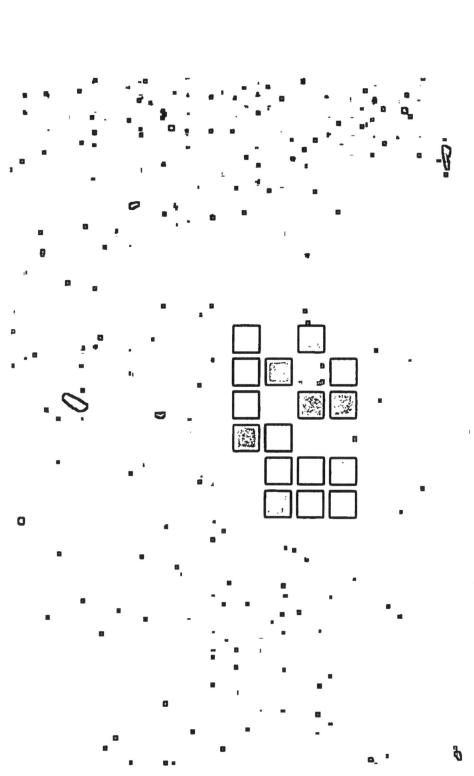

Ingram Content Group UK Ltd.
Milton Keynes UK
UKHW020801080323
418175UK00008B/600